Livio Maitan

London: NLB

Atlantic Highlands: Humanities Press

Party, Army and Masses in China

A Marxist Interpretation of the Cultural Revolution and its Aftermath

Translated by Gregor Benton and Marie Collitti

Acknowledgment

This book is a revised and updated version of the original Italian edition published in 1969. I would like to thank Gregor Benton of the Department of Chinese Studies at the University of Leeds for anglicizing references and suggesting further materials. I would also like to thank Quintin Hoare and Robin Blackburn of NLB for their assistance in editing this edition.
LM

Partito, Esercito e Masse nella Crisi Cinese was first published by Samonà e Savelli, Rome 1969

This edition first published 1976

© NLB

NLB, 7 Carlisle Street, London W1

Filmset by Servis Filmsetting Ltd, Manchester
Printed by Lowe & Brydone, Thetford, Norfolk
Designed by Ruth Prentice

ISBN No. 902308 815

Contents

Contents

Introduction

The triumph of a socialist revolution in China was undoubtedly one of the decisive events of human history. It was a definitive defeat for the imperialist powers. These had invaded and pillaged China for over a century, undermining the fabric of the traditional social order and seeking to divide up the spoils of conquest and subjugation between themselves, with the collusion of the local possessing classes – landlords, corrupt and oppressive Government officials, cynical military officers, commercial intermediaries and dependent indigenous capitalists. Such a mighty victory over such a varied and powerful array of enemies could only have been encompassed by a genuine and deep-rooted social revolution, liberating the fundamental productive forces of Chinese society. In a country comprising a quarter of the world's population capitalism was to be suppressed, along with the traditional forms of exploitation and oppression upon which it battened, especially in the countryside. The landlord, the money-lender, the corrupt tax-collector, the vicious warlord and the comprador businessman were all swept away by a mighty torrent of popular revolt. Though there have been many popular uprisings in China's long history, none of them had ever produced the fundamental changes which were involved in the revolution which led to the proclamation of the People's Republic of China in 1949. By their victory over old and new oppressors, the peasant and worker masses were able to achieve for themselves a quite new position in society.

Such a mammoth upheaval could only have the most far-reaching consequences for the whole world. It immediately broke the capitalist encirclement of the Soviet Union, doing so at a time when the forces of imperialism, orchestrated by the United States, were undertaking the massive anti-Communist mobilization known as the Cold War. Moreover, the liberation of China could only give a powerful impetus to the movement of national emancipation elsewhere in Asia, Africa and Latin America. Indeed, following the triumph of the Chinese revolution there was a multiplication of anti-imperialist struggles in every continent in the Third World. Although the capitalist countries were to enjoy an unprecedented boom in the period after the second world war, capitalism had already suffered this decisive and irreparable blow, even if its real significance was far from being fully appreciated at the time. One quarter of the world had been lost to capitalism, imposing upon it a more constricted field in which to work out its internal contradictions.

The society and the politics which emerged from this momentous transformation are clearly of the utmost interest. However, the real dynamic of the Chinese revolution has often eluded or baffled the outside world. The leaders of the Chinese Communist Party are themselves partly to blame for this. Whereas the Russian Bolsheviks proclaimed in ringing tones the historical and global significance of their revolution, the Chinese Communists have frequently found it convenient to camouflage the nature of the revolutionary process. In the period leading up to the proclamation of the People's Republic of China in 1949 they were often regarded as mere agrarian reformers and they themselves declared that their goal was 'New Democracy' and not a socialist revolution. It was, of course, true that the contingents of the People's Liberation Army which swept the Nationalist forces of Chiang Kai-shek from the whole of mainland China were predominantly peasant in social composition. However, an understanding of the contending social and economic forces in China requires a knowledge of the earlier history of Chinese Communism. In the first instance Communism developed in China in the 1920s among Marxist intellectuals and among the militant mass of urban workers. Most of the key cadres of the Communist Party and the People's Liberation Army were formed during this period. Although Chinese Communism was to be deeply influenced by its peasant base, it could never be wholly defined or explained by it. This is why it was able to follow very moderate agrarian policies, favourable to the rich peasants and 'patriotic' landlords during the period of the second united front with Chiang Kai-shek after 1937. It is also the reason why the new Government was able to collectivize peasant land holdings in the 1950s.

Once it was accepted that the Chinese revolution did have a socialist character, there was a tendency to view the new China as simply a puppet of the Soviet Union and to see Chinese Communism as a faithful imitation of Soviet Stalinism. Again the pronouncements of the Chinese leaders themselves were to give some credence to this view. To this day they insist that Stalin is one of the progenitors of Chinese Communism. And despite the fact that Stalin had given disastrous advice to the Chinese Communists in the twenties and had urged them to do a deal with Chiang Kai-shek in the forties, there is some truth in this. The Chinese leaders consistently gave lip-service to Stalin's political line and went some way in following his advice even in the 1940s. However, at this fateful turning point the intransigence of Chiang Kai-shek and the elemental upsurge of the peasants of North China helped to impel Chinese Communism along a revolutionary path. Faced with the acid test the Chinese Communists, despite their obeisance to the Stalinist formulas, were forced to identify themselves with a revolutionary impulse from below which inescapably challenged the capitalist and imperialist order in China. This contrasts with Stalin who could only sponsor revolution 'from above', as in Eastern Europe. Whereas Stalin had liquidated all the elements of proletarian democracy developed by the October revolution and murdered millions of Russian workers and Communists in the process, the leaders of the Chinese Communist party had been the agency of a triumphant socialist revolution that was to bring immense and immediate benefits to the vast mass of the oppressed and exploited in China. However this is not to say that Chinese Communism was not profoundly affected by the Stalinist model. At no point did the Chinese Communist leaders seek to develop the sort of revolutionary democracy that had made possible the October Revolution in Russia. Inside the Party there were none of those open and wide-ranging debates that characterized the Bolsheviks up to the time of Stalin's ascendancy. Though there may have been disputes at the top of the Party they never involved the mass of Party members. The decisive instrument of the revolution in Russia were the Soviets of workers, soldiers and peasants, in which the Bolsheviks won a majority. In China the decisive instrument embodying the new power was the People's Liberation Army, a military structure that was close to the masses but which was not under their control. In fact the political structures of the People's Republic shared one crucial feature with those of the Soviet Union after the rise of Stalin – all decisions, and indeed all real political discussion, were reserved for a tiny group of top Party leaders. Ordinary Party members, peasants and workers, were left with the task of implementing policies which they had not participated in formulating. This book will seek to explore all the contradictions which flow from this crucial aspect of China's political system. As we shall see, it systematically comes into collision with the underlying momentum of the socialist revolution itself.

It will be the contention of this book that the immense possibilities opened up by the revolution of 1949 are partially frustrated and denied by a bureaucratic political system. In the first part of the book a brief account is given of the economic and social tensions which the bureaucratic system tended to foster even in the midst of the great advances which the destruction of imperialism and capitalism had made possible. It is argued that the leaders of Chinese Communism themselves recognized the necessity of overcoming the many negative features of the bureaucratic system but without ever being prepared to sacrifice their own political monopoly. In Part II the most far-reaching crisis of the political system of the People's Republic is examined in detail – the Cultural Revolution of 1965–9. We argue that this crisis was resolved decisively in favour of a new bureaucratic restabilization – involving an even greater concentration of power among even fewer leaders at the top. Because of the revolutionary origins of the Chinese Party and State such a crisis did, however, involve the emergence of radical political currents who worked for the elimination of the bureaucratic system as a whole. These currents were to be defeated, but not before they had elaborated many of the elements necessary for a genuine radicalization and renewal of the Chinese revolution. In Part III the continuing crisis in the top levels of the Party and State that involved the ousting of Lin Piao in September 1971 is surveyed and analysed.

The literature on contemporary China has been dominated by two schools of writing. Firstly there are the many works inspired by anti-communism and the Cold War whose aim is to attack and discredit the Chinese revolution. Although some works of this sort are designed to impart objective information in the interests of 'knowing the enemy', they are necessarily devoid of any real appreciation of the basic dynamic of the revolutionary process. For them the masses are always manipulated by the Communist leadership and never act in response to their own class interests. Conflicts within the leadership are reduced to simple power struggles and are not seen as the reflection of underlying political and social forces. The other school of writing is that which simply echoes with naïve enthusiasm the particular official ideology of the moment. These works are often written by those who have spent a month or two travelling in China and are understandably impressed by what they have seen. Very rarely is any attempt made at an independent political assessment of the achievements and contradictions of the revolutionary process. Since, as we shall see, the leaders of Chinese Communism indulge in exceptionally virulent and mendacious attacks on defeated opponents this leads to a complete inability to grasp the nature of political struggles in China. The present work seeks to avoid all these pitfalls by attempting a Marxist assessment of developments since 1949, based wherever possible on official sources and first-hand accounts, but not subordinate to the official mythology.

For many observers of both varieties referred to above, the sharp move to the right in Chinese foreign policy in 1971 and the re-emergence of many officials who had been removed in the Cultural Revolution was a baffling epilogue to the supposedly triumphant movement against rightism and bureaucracy. The critical account of the Cultural Revolution given in Part II is directly brought to bear on the subsequent course of Chinese policy analysed in Part III, and hopefully makes it possible both to understand and explain these developments. In addition to writings of the sort indicated above there are also a significant number of scholarly works and of first-hand reports which are of undeniable value – a number of them will be drawn upon in this book – but such writing does not seek to measure Chinese Communism against its own proclaimed commitment to Marxism and Leninism. Such a critical assessment is attempted in this book both in the hope that it will contribute to the understanding of the Chinese revolution and as an act of solidarity with the masses of Chinese workers and peasants who have always been the force propelling the revolution forward.

Livio Maitan

Part 1
The Context: 1949–65

The Period of 'Rehabilitation and Transformation' 1949–52

On 1 October 1949 the revolutionary government in Peking formally proclaimed the foundation of the People's Republic of China. For decades the country had been a prey to civil war and foreign invasion, and these left the new administration facing a whole range of vast and pressing problems which had to be tackled before it could get the economy moving or set about further transforming social relations.

Its first task was to restore some measure of unity to China, which had been dismembered during the war with Japan (1937–45) and the subsequent civil war (1946–49). In the liberated areas alone, where the economy had been organized on a regional basis, the revolutionary authorities had issued at least eight different currencies. In May 1949, after Shanghai had fallen to the revolution, a single unified currency was established.

In order to create the minimum conditions for a resuscitation of the economy it was above all necessary to halt inflation, which continued to devastate business life even after the proclamation of the new Republic. The index of prices in Peking for 1949 shows the rate of this inflation: June 1949, 100; October 1949, 407; November 1949, 1,107; December 1949, 1,454. Between December and March a further increase of 100% took place. In March 1950 the government took a series of measures, at once firm and flexible, to deal with this problem. One such measure was the introduction of a commodity unit system whereby the purchasing power of bank deposits, salaries and wages was guaranteed in terms of specified quantities of four or five commodities.[1]

The new administration also reorganized the state budget, which had a huge deficit. To bring about a reduction in this deficit it took three main steps: it centralized taxes, thus equalizing the fiscal burden of

[1] S. Adler, *The Chinese Economy*, London 1957, pp. 18–20.

town and country, it issued a forced loan and it drew large profits from state-owned industry and trade.

Lastly, the national market was substantially unified, thanks to the stabilizing influence of the state. One particular measure the government took towards this end – and to fight inflation – was the flooding of the market with agricultural products gathered under the reorganized tax system, payments for which were chiefly in kind. In overcoming the dispersion of the national market the government succeeded in eliminating one of the main breeding-grounds for inflation. The necessary foundations for this new-born unity were completed with the reorganization of transport and in particular of the railway network, which was badly hit during the war.

Generally speaking, China's efforts to revive production during the period of rehabilitation were highly successful. By 1953 the net domestic product was up by about 20% – 6% per capita – on 1933, which is generally taken as the year of reference. From 1949 to 1952 national income went up by 69.7% according to China's State Statistical Bureau.[2] (Note that some of the increase can be accounted for by an improvement in statistical coverage.) In the same period industrial production went up by 151%, with an average annual rise of about 36%. In general, production outstripped the best years in the period before the revolution.[3] The main agricultural yields also exceeded pre-war records.[4] The most important social consequences of these trends were a sharp drop in unemployment, a remarkable rise of 97.5% in the total number of industrial workers and other employees and a 50–120% rise in average wages and in the income of peasant families. The purchasing power of the rural population rose by 25% in both 1951 and 1952.[5] The most appreciable advantages the working class obtained were a sliding scale in wages (with purchasing power expressed in goods) and the implementation of social legislation.

The new administration could have achieved none of these results if it had not first introduced revolutionary changes into Chinese society. These changes included the nationalization of key sectors of the economy, land reform and the establishment of a state monopoly in foreign trade – an instrument essential to defend the economy against imperialism and to prevent the latter linking up with the remnants of the national bour-

---

[2] *Ten Great Years*, Peking 1960, pp. 16 and 20. (Hereafter *Ten Great Years*.)
[3] *The Socialist Transformation of the National Economy in China*, Peking 1960, pp. 68–69 (hereafter *The Socialist Transformation*); UNO *World Economic Report, 1951–52*.
[4] Adler, op. cit., p. 128.
[5] Adler, op. cit., pp. 30–31.

geoisie. The leadership was always careful in pursuing this policy to keep to a moderate course: to cooperate with other classes, avoid drastic reversals of former policies and observe certain basic economic principles.

A major step in the reorganization of the economy was the expropriation, without indemnity, of 'bureaucratic' capital, i.e. capital belonging to that section of the bourgeoisie directly linked with the defeated Kuomintang. By the end of 1952 the state owned the railways, almost all the banks, 60% of coastal shipping lines, roughly 80% of heavy industry and 50% of modern light industry. State enterprises produced one-third of the industrial product in 1949 and one-half in 1952.[6] But it is important to remember that industrial production only accounted for 10% of the national income.

These measures, together with its financial and commercial levers, gave the new regime firm control over the country's economy. The government not only nationalized the banks but also set up a vast network of state stores and cooperatives. In March 1950 it created six state companies to control the trade in foods, textiles, salt, coal, building materials, products destined for agriculture and various other goods.

But that part of industry belonging to the 'national bourgeoisie' – generally smaller businessmen not directly associated with the Kuomintang – remained in private hands. ('National' capital comprised a large part of light industry and even some sectors of heavy industry.) The regime did not hesitate to make concessions to private capitalists. It retreated immediately if its policies threatened to place too great a burden on this class, as was the case with certain anti-inflationary measures in the first half of 1950. In June 1950 the Central Committee of the Communist Party, on the initiative of Mao Tse-tung himself, adopted new policies giving private industry large state orders and generous credit terms. It also took steps to restrict the state monopoly in foreign trade. The Common Programme, adopted in September 1949, declared among other things that the People's Republic 'must protect the public property of the State and of the cooperatives, and must protect the economic interests and private property of workers, peasants, the petty bourgeoisie and the national bourgeoisie' (Art. 3) and that the State 'shall coordinate and regulate State-owned economy, cooperative economy, the individual economy of peasants and handicraftsmen, private capitalist economy and state capitalist economy in their spheres of operations'. (Art. 26.) Even the Five Antis campaign (*wu-fan*) of 1952.

[6] For further information see *The Socialist Transformation*, pp. 27–28.

was aimed not at eliminating but at remoulding those merchants and industrialists still operating their businesses.[7] Liu Shao-ch'i's reports and speeches, even in the years immediately following the period of rehabilitation, clearly approve of the role of the national bourgeoisie (see for example his presentation of the new Constitution). Mao Tse-tung himself ordered a plaque to be set up in memory of Fan Hsu-tung, founder of the Yungli Chemical Company, describing him as 'an eminent leader of industry, a meritorious contributor to the nation'.[8]

Land reform was inevitably a very complex operation. This was due above all to the disparities which had arisen between areas liberated earlier on and areas (particularly in South China) liberated in the final stages of the civil war. The different areas fall into four main categories:

(1) In those areas in which the Communist leadership first consolidated its power (North China, Manchuria and parts of Central China) the new land laws were promulgated in October 1947 and carried out in 1947–48. In the greater part of these areas the incursion of the Japanese armies, the collapse of the KMT and the developing resistance to Japanese rule all combined to undermine traditional social relations and to destroy the Chinese bourgeois-landlord state which defended them. The defeat of Japan and the withdrawal of its military forces had helped to unleash a powerful peasant uprising. In 1946 there was a limited reform which only applied to landlords considered pro-Japanese. But this did not satisfy the peasant masses. The later laws decreed the complete expropriation of rich peasants and landlords in favour of the landless peasants. They affected about 36% of the rural population.

(2) In other areas (containing about 41% of the rural population) the land was distributed in 1950–51 in accordance with the law of June 1950. This law was more moderate than that of 1947. It did not apply to personal property or land belonging to rich peasants: it was intended to be gradual.

(3) In other areas still – containing about 22% of the rural population – the reform was carried out later on the same lines as above.

(4) In regions inhabited by national minorities, land reform was not even started.

According to official sources land reform gave 700 million *mou* (more than 46 million hectares) of land to about 300 million peasants, who were thus freed from the crushing burden of rent. This rent had usually

---

[7] *The Socialist Transformation*, p. 52.
[8] Adler, op. cit., p. 48, note 20.

amounted to 50% and often reached as much as 75% of the harvest. After the reform the state took about 17% in tax.[9]

The aim of land reform was to organize the countryside on the basis of innumerable peasant farms, thereby eliminating or drastically reducing the old exploiting classes. No society has ever experienced such a colossal and widespread upheaval. But whereas we must recognize the immense historical significance of these events, we should still remember that differentiation among the peasantry not only persisted but even sprang up again under the new conditions. At the same time causes of friction between peasants and state emerged in spite of the revolutionary government's great prestige and even though the state itself, by acting as a buyer of agricultural goods and a seller of industrial goods, did a great deal to check capitalist penetration of the countryside and prevented a growing together of the urban capitalist sector and the spontaneous tendencies towards capitalism which continually resurfaced in the countryside itself.

Social differentiation in the countryside was evident in such things as the right of rich peasants to employ wage-labourers and purchase or rent out land. 'The farms of rich peasants are under the protection of the laws of the People's Government', wrote the *People's Daily*, 10 July 1950. The general causes of friction between government and peasants concerned issues such as the supply of industrial goods, the price of agricultural goods, the level of agricultural taxation and interest rates on loans.[10]

The toppling of the old Kuomintang ruling class and the expropriation of the bureaucratic bourgeoisie and the dominant classes in the country-side were in themselves a great democratic revolution. They wrought a profound change in the political structure of China. In the countryside the peasants' associations had emerged as the true driving force behind the land revolution and the democratization that came after it, even though they did not appear everywhere and were not always democratic-ally elected.[11] In the towns the political changes were less radical. Policies such as collaboration with the so-called 'national bourgeoisie' tended to take the edge off the movement and diminish its power to

[9] For further information on land reform see the articles by the Chinese Trotskyist Kim in *Quatrième Internationale*, October 1952 and January 1953, and Adler, op. cit., pp. 29–31. For a vivid account of the peasant upsurge which preceded and accompanied it see Jack Belden, *China Shakes the World*, London 1973.

[10] See *The Socialist Transformation*, pp. 38–39, 57–58, for a description of actions taken by the state against capitalist penetration of the countryside.

[11] See the above-mentioned articles by Kim.

reconstitute the state apparatus and the administrative machinery. Inevitably the old traditions and the corrupt and dishonest practices lingered on. Recognizing this, the government later launched the *san-fan* (Three Antis) and *wu-fan* (Five Antis) campaigns – the first of these in 1951 against corruption, waste and red tape among Party cadres in official positions and the second in 1952 against bribery, tax evasion, fraud, theft of government property and theft of economic secrets by merchants and industrialists. However even complete success in such campaigns would create an efficient and honest bureaucracy rather than a revolutionary administration based on the direct participation of the workers and peasants. The immense tasks confronting the new Government impelled it to rely heavily on the administrative structures and personnel inherited from the old order. These operated on the lines laid down by the Party leadership and the various military administrations set up in the wake of the People's Liberation Army (PLA) but this supervision from above was not complemented by supervision from below embodied in organs of revolutionary democracy.

The most negative aspect of the system established by liberation was the absence of real Soviets – a network of democratic and revolutionary councils through which workers and peasants could actually wield power. Such institutions had made possible the Russian revolution, the first successful socialist revolution. Initially the Bolshevik Party asserted itself in and through the Soviets of workers, peasants and soldiers which it converted into the ruling state institutions. The role of the Soviets was subsequently weakened as the ravages of civil war, imperialist intervention, famine and pestilence took their toll on the Russian working class and undermined mass support for the revolution, especially in the countryside. The ascendancy of Stalin converted the Soviets into purely formal, rubber-stamp bodies subordinate to the political monopoly exercised by the Party leadership – and the Party itself was also thoroughly bureaucratized. In China the broad popular support for the revolution and the fact that it was able to bring immediate benefits to both the urban and rural masses created favourable conditions for establishing and sustaining genuinely democratic institutions of revolutionary power. Yet when the PLA swept the KMT forces out of entire provinces and regions, including the major cities, no attempt was made to begin the work of setting up institutions of popular power. The Party asserted its leadership through the military administrations and through various mass organizations, but the latter were not given independent powers. Revolutionary democracy based on Soviets of workers, peasants and soldiers would have provided the best guarantee for the future course of the revolution. In the event, the transformation of social relations in the countryside and the mobilization of the rural masses was to be much more thoroughgoing than in the towns. As we have seen, the countryside witnessed a veritable *fan-shen* (turning upside down) of the whole social order within a relatively short period of time. In the towns such a *fan-shen* was precluded by the formula of 'New Democracy' with its whole-sale concessions to 'national' capital. The new administrations were formed from the top downwards; they were based on the PLA, some civilian Party cadres and on the wholesale integration of the former government departments. When the first cities were liberated, there were a number of instances of lower level cadres seeking to stimulate class struggle and to develop forms of popular control of the administration. The Party leadership attacked this for 'bringing rural methods into the city'. A directive entitled 'Correctly Carry Out the Policy of Benefit to Both Labour and Capital' criticized 'agricultural socialism' (*nung-yeh she-hui-chu-i*) and 'the mistake of too strongly advocating the one-sided, temporary interests of the workers'.[12] In Tientsin street-level committees had been set up by rank and file cadres in the aftermath of liberation with district-level governments based on them; in June 1949 the street-level committees were abolished and the district governments reduced to district offices of the municipal government set up by the Military Control Committee.[13]

No doubt it was necessary at this time to restrain the purely economic demands of the workers in the liberated areas but that did not necessitate dampening down their political aspirations. In general the greatly stimulated class consciousness of the workers was prevented from developing into directly political forms but was channelled into the expansion of trade unions. These were agencies of labour discipline rather than of workers' power. Factory Affairs Committees were also established and they compare favourably with the industrial structures prevailing at this time in Eastern Europe and the Soviet Union. But they had no political functions and were charged mainly with increasing production: the manager of the enterprise was chairman of the Committee and could

---

[12] Mao Tse-tung *et al.*, *New Democratic Industrial and Commercial Policy* (*Hsin min-chu-chu-i kung-shang cheng-ts'e*), Hong Kong, New Democratic Publishing Company, January 1949.

[13] Kenneth Lieberthal 'Mao versus Liu? Policy towards Industry and Commerce: 1946–49', *China Quarterly*, July–September 1971, no. 47, pp. 494–521, p. 516. On the general neglect of the cities in the strategy of the CCP after the twenties see Isaac Deutscher, 'Maoism: its organs and outlook', *Socialist Register 1964*.

veto any of its decisions. In the nationalized sector the manager was appointed by the Military Affairs Commission and every effort was made to persuade former managers to stay on in the nationalized companies. In the private sector wages were to be frozen, a system of individual incentives devised and the employer to be allowed to take all necessary steps to raise efficiency, including the dismissal of workers.

The decisive institutions in the new China were the Communist Party and the People's Liberation Army. In the battle against the former ruling classes they were clear embodiments of the social forces on which the revolution was based but neither of them expressed the new class character of the state in a democratic manner. The PLA, even though quite different in organization from a bourgeois army, was still essentially a military command structure. The Chinese Communist Party was heavily influenced by the Russian model, with all discussions and decisions reserved for a tiny group of leaders at the top. As just one indicator of this, we may note that there was to be only one Party Congress between 1945 and 1969. Even the Central Committee of the Party had relatively little power, meeting on average less than once a year. In the account which follows of the course of events after 1949, it should be borne in mind that the Chinese leadership is not forced to submit its plans and policies to any systematic popular ratification. In consequence there is no immediate feedback from the masses built into the system; this helps to explain both the growth of bureaucracy and the often erratic course of policy, with periodic, voluntarist campaigns used as a corrective to bureaucratic inertia. Many of the initiatives taken by the leadership were, in fact, more or less ingenious attempts to discover *a substitute* for the dialectic that could exist between democratic institutions of revolutionary power and the leading role of a Leninist party.[14] In their different ways all the crucial slogans and campaigns of Chinese Communism – 'mass line', 'hundred flowers', 'cultural revolution' – were attempts to produce all the benefits of real proletarian democracy without ever abandoning the ultimate political monopoly exercised by the leading group.

[14] On the necessary complementarity between soviet-type bodies and revolutionary parties, see Ernest Mandel, *The Leninist Theory of Organization*, London 1971.

2

The First Five-year Plan and the New Structural Changes

The period of reconstruction saw great structural changes and steady economic advance. However, a considerable part of industry remained in the hands of the national bourgeoisie. Because of this there were less opportunities for the state to accumulate capital, it was difficult to plan effectively and there arose a number of economic, social and political tensions. Even though industrial production had risen above its pre-revolutionary ceilings, it was still far too low to meet increased needs, let alone to get industrialization off the ground. In the countryside the redistribution of the land had a shattering social effect, but it was not enough to break through the natural limitations of small-scale farming in the decisive area of labour productivity. On the other hand, the differentiation between the upper strata of rich peasants and the mass of poor peasants became progressively more pronounced. According to official figures, each peasant had on average three *mou* of land – in many cases only one *mou* or even less – and the poor peasants had no draught animals or adequate tools.[1] Suggestions that the land reform created a majority of middle peasants should be treated sceptically. A large part of the peasants were actually middle peasants of the lower strata, and as such very close to the poor peasants. Together these two groups made up 60–70% of the rural population.

An effort to overcome these weaknesses, tensions and contradictions became all the more urgent when China, freshly emerged from decades of revolutionary war, was drawn into a war with American imperialism in Korea. The menacing world situation called for higher production targets and the weeding out of those social classes which in the event of a crisis might join forces against the new regime with international

---

[1] See *The Socialist Transformation*, pp. 91–92, 101; Liu Shao-ch'i's report in *Eighth National Congress of the Communist Party of China*, Peking 1956, vol I, pp. 24–25 (hereafter *Eighth Congress*).

capitalism: the national bourgeoisie and the rich peasants.

These were the main factors underlying the decision to launch the first five-year plan and undertake new structural changes during the years 1953–56.

The first five-year plan set itself the following general objectives:

(a) A rapid and substantial rise in production in the base industries (steel, coal, electricity, oil, cement, etc.), giving priority to industrial investment and promoting heavy rather than light industry – a programme generally inspired by the example of the Soviet Union. (According to Li Fu-ch'un this programme mainly involved 694 projects, the nucleus of which were 156 projects of Russian origin.)

(b) Rises in agricultural production to meet the needs of an ever-growing population with greater purchasing power and greater requirements, to furnish industry with the necessary raw materials and to increase exports to pay for foreign industrial equipment and industrial raw materials.

In order to furnish the necessary materials and finances the first frail steps were taken to tap the country's resources; the state engaged in primitive accumulation by transferring to itself profits previously flowing into the hands of the privileged classes and foreign capitalists, appropriating any unconsumed surplus (by regulating taxes, prices and wages) and exporting certain products, chiefly agricultural. In 1954, for example, China exported $1\frac{3}{4}$ million tons of grain, compared with an average 1.55 million in 1950–53 and 1.15 million in 1927–30. According to Yen Ch'i-chuang, Minister of Foreign Trade, 10% of the eggs, 20% of the tea and 6% of the pork produced in 1954 were exported.

Contrary to what many people think, investment did not claim an excessive share of total income. According to Po I-po, the rate was 15.7% in 1952, 18.3% in 1953, 21.6% in 1954, 20.5% in 1955 and 22.8% in 1956. Economists in the West estimate the rate of gross investment as one-fifth of the total product in 1952 and during the whole of the first five-year plan, rising to one-third at the time of the Great Leap Forward.[2] Other sources confirm this estimate.

The first five-year plan certainly achieved spectacular successes, as even writers unsympathetic to the revolution have had to recognize. The gross national product grew each year by between 8% and 9%. Bourgeois specialists maintain that at the very worst the average annual rate of increase was 6%,[3] whereas official Chinese estimates put it at 9%.

[2] *An Economic Profile of Mainland China*, Washington 1967, pp. 125–126.
[3] Ibid., p. 56.

In 1957, the last year of the plan, steel was up 296% on 1952, coal 96%, electricity 166% and cement 140%.[4] In 1956 the government announced that the targets for 1957 had already been met in major products.[5] Key branches of industry were modernized and their productivity substantially raised. Structural changes in industry were complemented by the enthusiastic efforts of the masses and the full use of industrial capacity. Li Fu-ch'un stated in his report on the plan that 70% of the increase in 1952–57 came from firms already in existence before 1952. Hundreds of thousands of skilled and semi-skilled workers were trained; in 1957 there were 8,700,000 more workers than in 1952, unemployment had dropped considerably and wages were about 30% higher.[6] The foundations were laid for a Soviet-style planning system.

The process of modernization and structural change was reinforced by substantial Soviet aid. The volume of this aid, however, was not as massive as the Russians liked to make out. During the years 1950–57 only 16.2% – i.e. 336 million dollars – of Soviet credit to China was in the form of economic loans; the remainder of the credits comprised debts from the Korean war (34.3%), the cost of buying back Russian shares in four joint Sino–Soviet companies transferred to China (23.8%) and 'unidentified' (presumably military) aid.[7] But aid was not only in the form of loans. Over ten thousand Soviet technicians also gave valuable technical assistance in the installation and running of plants. In 1951–57, 6,500 Chinese students were educated and 7,100 workers trained in the Soviet Union.[8] Soviet technical and material assistance was crucial in the early stages of the mining of Sinkiang's mineral wealth. All aid, technicians and blueprints were to be abruptly withdrawn in 1960, at the height of a severe crisis in China's economy. Li Che-jen, a senior trade official, announced later that all credit had been repaid in full by the beginning of 1965. Soviet credit and aid, then, was an important reinforcing factor in the growth of the Chinese economy and in some fields a decisive one.

Basic agricultural production grew by about 20% during the first five-year plan, thus keeping ahead of the growth in population, which was 11%. This is equivalent to a growth over five years of 9% per head of population, or roughly 1.5% a year.[9] Cereal crops in 1957 were 20% and

[4] *The Socialist Transformation*, p. 83.
[5] *Eighth Congress*, p. 37.
[6] *The Socialist Transformation*, p. 85.
[7] Quoted in Jean-Pierre Brulé, *China Comes of Age*, Penguin 1971, p. 70.
[8] Choh-ming Li, *Communist China*, Penguin 1968, p. 165.
[9] *An Economic Profile*, p. 257.

cotton 26% higher than in 1952.[10] Peasants' incomes grew by about 30% and the exchange ratio between industry and agriculture was adjusted in favour of the peasants.[11]

The achievements of the first five-year plan must not blind us, however, to the shortcomings and bottlenecks in the economy. Firstly, the targets achieved were still modest in absolute terms. Steel output, for example, was about one-tenth of that in the Soviet Union and one-twentieth of that in the United States. Per capita production of cereal crops was 286 kg. in China, compared with 655 kg. in the Soviet Union and 928 kg. in the United States. Chinese agriculture still employed 80% of the population and accounted for half the national income.

Per capita consumption had still not been restored to its 1933 level, which meant that the living conditions of the working masses continued to be very poor.[12]

Secondly, the rhythm of growth in industrial production was uneven. Already in 1954 it was increasing at a slower rate than in 1953 (16.7% compared with 31.7%). 1955 accentuated this downward trend with a mere 7.8% increase. In 1956 there was a reassuring increase of 31%, only to be followed by another sharp drop in the rate of growth in 1957 (+ 10.9%). The two years 1956–57 also saw a fall in the combined rate of increase for agriculture and industry, which was 16.5% and 7.8% respectively.[13] There are other indications from Chinese sources that the gross increase in industrial production for 1957 was only 6.9%.[14]

While the plan was being carried out new and pressing problems began to arise. Foremost among these was the neglect of quality in favour of quantity – a problem long familiar to Stalinist planners in the USSR and later Eastern Europe.[15] During the Great Leap Forward problems such as these became rampant in certain areas of production – an official report in 1960 claimed, for example, that only 35% of the coal mined was of good quality.[16]

1953 and 1954 were bad years for agriculture, and this in turn had

[10] *The Socialist Transformation*, p. 83.

[11] Ibid., pp. 85–86.

[12] Ibid., p. 240; *An Economic Profile*, pp. ix, 252.

[13] *The Socialist Transformation*, pp. 89–90; *Selections from China Mainland Magazines*, no. 633, p. 5 (from now on quoted as SCMM).

[14] Adler, op. cit., p. 225 of the Italian edition, *Dal Kuomintang alle Comuni del Popolo*: the English edition does not contain this chapter.

[15] See Adler, op. cit., p. 89; M. Pablo, *L'industrialisation et la collectivisation en Chine* in *Quatrième Internationale*, December 1955, p. 16.

[16] *Le Monde*, 27 September 1962.

negative repercussions on industrial production. The sluggish pace of growth was partly due to natural disasters but mainly to the proliferation of small-scale farms, which acted as a brake on production. Cattle production also experienced difficulties and according to Ch'en Yun, a high-ranking official concerned with trade, it even decreased in 1955. The overall rate of growth in agricultural production in the five-year period was fairly restricted: roughly 20% compared with the 23.3% forecast.

Finally, in certain fields – a number of large industrial projects, for example – China became economically dependent on the Soviet Union. At the Eighth Congress Chou En-lai explicitly rejected the theory of self-sufficiency when he declared: 'Another view, that we can close our doors and carry on construction on our own, is wrong too. Needless to say, the establishment of a comprehensive industrial system in our country requires assistance from the Soviet Union and the People's Democracies for a long time to come. At the same time it is also possible for us to develop and expand economic, technical and cultural exchanges with other countries.'[17]

In the period covered by the first five-year plan the structural transformation of the Chinese economy was completed. Already in 1953 resolutions were adopted announcing these changes. In September 1954 the First National People's Congress proclaimed the new Constitution. In 1956 the revolution entered a new phase both in trade and industry and in agriculture and state ideologists declared that 'the socialist revolution was fundamentally complete as regards the means of production'.[18]

This is not the place to describe even briefly the methods the regime adopted or the stages through which it passed – it is enough to say that the new leadership did not hesitate to use all the powers at the command of the state, profiting not least by skilfully manipulating what Lenin called the state capitalist sector.[19] But we are more concerned here with the tempo of the transformation of the economy. Mao Tse-tung himself had forecast that new democracy, which meant the continuance of capitalism, would last for 'several decades'. Why, then, did the leadership move much more rapidly in the direction of a total transformation of the economy than had been foreseen in their original theories?

In the first place, as the government began to introduce planning into

---

[17] *Eighth Congress*, vol. I, p. 282.
[18] *The Socialist Transformation*, p. 238.
[19] See *The Socialist Transformation*, Chapter 3; Adler, op. cit., pp. 33–36.

the economy it clashed more and more with the irrepressible anarchy of capitalism. Accumulation of capital by the state was restricted to the extent that private capitalists took their own share of profits. The countryside itself was invaded by private industrialists and traders, who thereby strengthened the rich at the expense of the poor peasants and placed even more obstacles in the path of large-scale cooperation. Finally, private capitalism directly exploited sections of the working class, imposing anti-democratic management methods which in the long run would have created serious conflict between government and masses. It was also necessary to look at all these problems in the light of certain long-term dangers: if the government had not rapidly taken steps to transform the economy, private capitalism would hardly have remained satisfied with the *status quo* and would sooner or later have gone over to the offensive in order to extend its domain.[20] Moreover the necessity to mobilize against capitalism within was very much underlined by the necessity to mobilize against imperialist intervention from without: the Korean war and the building up of a new Nationalist army on Taiwan with lavish US assistance both made this a very tangible threat. The situation was in many ways similar to that before the decision in 1946–47 to launch the stormy movement that ended up in the seizure of power. It called for a decisive choice, and the Communist leadership took that choice. In doing so it once more confirmed the class nature of the Party and proved all those people wrong who had rushed to make analogies between China and those backward capitalist countries where the private sector coexists with a strong state sector.

The general strategy of the Communist leadership was the total elimination of the old dominant classes, but within this framework it preferred to adopt 'moderate' methods and aimed at 'peacefully' liquidating the national bourgeoisie. It is important to understand this fact if we are to explain certain later developments. The first step was to restrict profits. This later gave way to a policy of expropriation with indemnity. These indemnities were to be paid for an indeterminate period and official propaganda took pains to point out that this would help private capitalists overcome any difficulties created by the upheaval in their lives. They were also promised permanent managerial posts where they could put their experience and training to good use. Many of them stayed on to help manage enterprises they had formerly owned.[21]

[20] *The Socialist Transformation*, p. 215, records the resistance on the part of private capitalism.

[21] See *The Socialist Transformation*, pp. 184–185.

The interest accruing to former capitalists after January 1956 ran to some 120 million *yuan* a year. This compares with state profits of 56,000 million *yuan* in the years 1953–57. There were 1,140,000 beneficiaries: of these, 810,000 continued to work in management. In 1962 the National Assembly decided to extend payment of indemnity for another three years, and then reconsider the question.[22]

It is clear that the government was anxious to avoid sudden breaks and the economic disruption that these would certainly have provoked. It was also anxious not to alienate those whose skills and training were rare in such a backward country. In this situation it would have been totally wrong to insist on abstract and irrelevant principles, all the more so since Marx and Lenin never made a hard and fast rule on this issue. However, many of the generalizations concocted in China in these years were decidedly suspect. A crop of theories were invented which in effect mystified class relationships: the bourgeoisie, it was announced, could be utilized for building socialism and the conflict between it and the toiling classes was non-antagonistic in form during the transitional period; according to propaganda the bourgeoisie did not only acquiesce in the expropriation of its property but positively welcomed it. Ironically, this period in China therefore witnessed one of the first surfacings in the Communist movement of the theory of a peaceful transition to socialism.[23]

Contrary to claims made during the Cultural Revolution, Liu Shao-Ch'i was not the only one to propound views such as these. Mao Tse-tung himself wrote in one well-known essay: 'In our country the contradiction between the working class and the national bourgeoisie belongs to the category of contradictions among the people.'[24] Elsewhere he comes out explicitly in favour of a 'peaceful' transition.[25] In November 1955 he invited a group of representatives of the capitalists to a discussion and what he said 'gave great encouragement to the capitalists of China, largely eliminating their sense of insecurity'.[26]

At the start of the plan, innumerable peasant farms covered most of the cultivable surface of the land. A few cooperatives had begun to appear, together with some pilot projects for state farms in Manchuria. During 1952 'mutual aid teams' were set up in the countryside, as a sort of transitional stage towards collectivization.

[22] *Hsinhua New Agency*, 17 April 1962 (from now on quoted as HNA).
[23] See Liu Shao-ch'i's report in *Eighth Congress*.
[24] Mao Tse-tung, *On the correct handling of contradictions among the people*, Peking 1966, p. 3.
[25] See the *Draft Programme for Agricultural Development*, Peking 1956, p. 4.
[26] *The Socialist Transformation*, p. 219.

A mutual aid team would generally comprise about ten households, which cooperated in farming each other's land – an idea already used in liberated areas during the civil war and before. The second stage in the reorganization of agriculture was the 'semi-socialist' agricultural producers' cooperatives. In this lower form of cooperative, income was distributed among members not only according to the amount of work they had done but also according to the amount of land and capital they had initially pooled. Before the end of the five-year plan, socialist co-operatives were already the predominant form, including 88% of all peasant households.[27] In these higher cooperatives, land, tools, cattle and labour were pooled and income distributed solely according to work done.[28] One higher cooperative embraced several lower cooperatives and generally covered the area of a whole village.

One of the reasons for the launching of the collectivization campaign was the slow rate of growth of production in 1953–54 and, more generally, the level of production in cereals and industrial raw materials, which was nowhere near high enough to meet the state's growing requirements. In 1953, grain speculators and rich peasants had already intensified their efforts to exploit the gap between supply and demand. Some even hoarded grain in expectation of a rise in prices. Mao himself spoke of the 'new rich peasants springing up everywhere and many well-to-do middle peasants striving to become rich peasants' and of 'many poor peasants still living in poverty for lack of sufficient means of production, with some in debt and others selling or renting their land'.[29] Furthermore, differentiation was continuing in the countryside: the poor peasants and many middle peasants were still living in wretched conditions, while the rich peasants were consolidating their position and even beginning to rent out land and hire manpower.[30]

The government was therefore faced with a number of tasks: it had to step up production, reconcile agriculture with planning and prevent classes basically hostile to it from growing stronger and weakening its links with the poor peasants. To these ends it began to encourage the spread of cooperatives. In the summer of 1955 collectivization was speeded up. By June 1956, 110 million families out of a total of 120

[27] *Ten Great Years*, p. 28.
[28] See Adler, op. cit., p. 107, for further information.
[29] See *The Socialist Transformation*, pp. 56–60 and Mao Tse-tung, *On the question of agricultural cooperation in China*, Peking 1966, pp. 18–19.
[30] See *The Socialist Transformation*, p. 101 and Mao, op. cit., p. 26.

million had joined cooperatives – 75 million in the higher 'socialist' cooperatives, 35 million in the 'semi-socialist' ones. At the end of 1956 cooperatives embraced 96% of the peasant families; 88% were in higher cooperatives.[31]

There was some resistance to collectivization among the peasants and this resistance found echoes inside the Party itself. In 1955 there were even movements away from the cooperatives. The resistance mainly came from the higher strata of peasantry. In the Party, criticism centred around the difficulties that would arise in consolidating the cooperatives, the obstacle constituted by the poverty of the poor peasants and the danger that if production were rationalized there might arise a surplus of manpower. There are official reports that many cooperatives were broken up during the course of collectivization.[32] Although there was no large movement in this direction on a national scale, things were different in some provinces. Mao says that 15,000 cooperatives out of 53,000 were dissolved in Chekiang. An article published in 1968 said that 200,000 cooperatives were broken up.[33]

In general, however, collectivization was carried through without any serious conflicts and at a quicker pace than the leading group had originally thought possible. Mao himself had estimated that by the spring of 1958 not more than 55 million peasant farms would have joined the lower-level cooperatives and that the other 50% would only be collectivized (again on the lower level) in 1960.[34] This is further proof of the empirical and flexible attitudes of the leading group, which continued to put the accent on gradual change and voluntary cooperation and preferred to use economic incentives and persuasion through propaganda rather than force. A resolution of the Central Committee of October 1955 insisted that peasants should not be forced to join cooperatives. Mao made the same point on 31 July of the same year, when he also said that in certain cases cooperatives might be dissolved. The private rights and interests of the peasants (for example, the right to farm an individual plot) were generally upheld.[35] It is also worth noting that official publications frequently quote a well-known passage from Engels which opposes the use of compulsion and which in its time was criticized by Stalin.[36]

[31] See *The Socialist Transformation*, p. 132.
[32] See *The Socialist Transformation*, p. 130.
[33] *Peking Review*, no. 12, 1968, p. 25.
[34] See Adler, op. cit., pp. 104ff., for further details.
[35] See Mao, op. cit., p. 14.
[36] E.g. *The Socialist Transformation*, pp. 94–95.

At a certain point, however, the pace of collectivization was forced or it would not have been completed. The price the government had to pay for this was an exodus from the land by many peasants and an unsatisfactory harvest in 1957.[37]

However, if China's agriculture was less productive than that of advanced countries with widespread rural mechanization it was in other terms rather highly developed. It would be quite erroneous simply to assimilate China to some anonymous model of a Third World country populated by impoverished and primitive peasants. Traditionally Chinese agriculture has been considerably more productive than that of any area outside the advanced capitalist countries. China's ancient civilization, its sophisticated political and social system, not to speak of its gigantic population were only possible on the basis of a highly productive system of cultivation. It should be remembered that China's population growth consistently outstripped that of Europe. During the relative peace of the Ming and early and mid-Ch'ing dynasties China's population rose six-fold; from about sixty-five million persons in 1400 to some four hundred million by 1800.[38] A population growth of this magnitude could only be sustained by a simultaneous expansion of the cultivated area and an increase in agricultural yields. The crisis of the Ch'ing dynasty in the mid and late nineteenth century – exacerbated by foreign incursion and domestic rebellion – restrained the rise in population and probably led to some decline in agricultural yields. In the twentieth century up to the revolution of 1949 population rose at a rate of about 1% per year with agricultural production only just keeping pace. However, despite more than a century of successive disruption of Chinese agriculture by dynastic decline, imperialism and civil war, the productivity of Chinese agriculture was still impressive. Tables 1 and 2 give comparative data for rice yields and *per capita* grain output for China, India and Japan at various periods, together with similar information for certain other Asian countries.

It will be seen from these figures that China's *per capita* output of grains in 1953 was higher than that in Japan for the whole period 1934–59 and that it was much higher than the figure for India. This in turn

[37] See Edgar Snow, *The Other Side of the River*, New York 1962, p. 424, for a further opinion on this. In his speech of July 1955, Mao affirmed the temporal priority of collectivization over mechanization. This is why he insisted on the exemplary value of the Russian experience of the 1930s, which in fact was very different in important respects from the Chinese experience of the 1950s.

[38] Dwight H. Perkins, *Agricultural Development in China, 1368–1968*, Edinburgh 1969, p. 24.

Table 1
Rice Yields (catties per *mou*)

Country	Year	Yield per sown mou	per cultivated mou
China	1957	359	457
Japan	1878–82	337	
	1953–62	631	
Taiwan	1953–62	391	
India	1953–62	181	
Thailand	1953–62	184	
Indonesia	1953–62	232	

Table 2
Per Capita Grain Output

Country	Year	Per capita output	(kilos unhusked grain) supply
China	1953	269	267
China	1957	286	285
Japan	1934–38	246	286
Japan	1947–48	213	230
Japan	1957–59	246	289
India–Pakistan	1934–38	202	208
India	1957–59	183	191
Pakistan	1957–59	215	230

Source: Perkins, op. cit., pp. 34–35.

reflected the high rice yields obtained by Chinese agriculture – a yield which seems to have been about twice as high as that obtained in India or Thailand and significantly higher than that in Indonesia. These yields were obtained by an intricate combination of traditional techniques and notably a highly developed irrigation system ensuring a constant supply of water. And even in imperial China there had been a steady diffusion of knowledge about improved seeds and great attention paid to the question of adequate supplies of fertilizer. Good supplies of water made possible the planting of two rice crops a year in many areas; hence the discrepancy between yield per sown *mou* and yield per cultivated *mou* in Table I which boosted China's total rice crop by nearly a third. China's irrigation system encompassed immense water-works covering entire regions of the country like the elaborate flood control mechanisms of the Yellow River or the extended man-made water-way of the Grand Canal. But most important were the much smaller scale systems of dikes and canals which served the majority of villages. Such a system would typically comprise several miles of dikes and would irrigate several thousand acres of land – its upkeep would be largely a matter for the local authorities. Although the depredations of the war and civil war were terrible enough, they did not fundamentally destroy the local irrigation systems on which the high yields of Chinese agriculture depended; they did however expose the Chinese peasantry to the ravages of natural catastrophes which led to great loss of life in some regions in the thirties as a consequence of flood or drought. The period of rehabilitation allowed for a widespread overhaul of the entire traditional system of irrigation, while extensions of the transport system linked the rice surplus regions to the rice deficit regions – notably the opening of the railroad from Shensi to Chengtu in 1956.

The successes of the rehabilitation period in agriculture mostly related to the restoration of the traditional system of cultivation with its relatively high yields. However by the mid-fifties the scope for further enhancing productivity and growing enough food to feed the rapidly expanding towns had come to an end. The very stability of government which had helped to make possible the restoration of traditional agricultural techniques also led to a more rapidly expanding population. The annual average increase in population rose from about 1% before the revolution to about 2% after it. At the same time there was not a great deal more land which could easily be brought into cultivation. And the traditional irrigation system was sufficiently developed to have reached the limits of which it was capable. As Perkins writes: '. . . there were no ways within the "traditional" system for the pace of discovery and the adoption of new seeds to be raised to meet the accelerated growth of population.'[39]

Indirectly the achievement of China's traditional agriculture helped prepare the ground for the socialist development on which China was embarking. These achievements had been possible only because of the

[39] Perkins, op. cit., p. 189.

high degree of productive cooperation on the village level. Every peasant was aware that his own capacity to produce was dependent on the maintenance of the irrigation system and a certain amount of collaborative labour during the sowing, transplanting and harvesting periods. The Chinese peasant was thus unlike the individualist European peasant whose cultivation process was largely self-sufficient. Marx always contrasted the 'collective worker' produced by modern capitalism to the small-holding peasant. Whereas the modern proletariat was to be the protagonist of socialism, the peasantry was condemned to a subordinate role by its very conditions of existence. In a famous passage Marx wrote: 'The small-holding peasants form a vast mass, the members of which live in similar conditions but without entering into manifold relations with one another. Their mode of production isolates them from one another instead of bringing them into mutual intercourse. The isolation is increased by France's bad means of communication and by the poverty of the peasants. Their field of production, the small-holding, admits of no division of labour in its cultivation, no application of science and, therefore, no diversity of development, no variety of talent, no wealth of social relationships. Each individual peasant family is almost self-sufficient; it, itself, directly produces the major part of its consumption and thus acquires its means of life more through exchange with nature than in intercourse with society. A small-holding, a peasant and his family: alongside them another small-holding, another peasant and another family. A few score of these make up a village, and a few score villages make up a department. In this way, the great mass of the French nation is formed by the simple addition of homologous magnitudes, much as potatoes in a sack form a sack of potatoes. In so far as millions of families live under economic conditions of existence that separate their mode of life, their interests and their culture from those of other classes, and put them in hostile opposition to the latter, they form a class. In so far as there is merely a local interconnection among these small-holding peasants, and the identity of their interests begets no community, no national bond and no political organization among them, they do not form a class. They are consequently incapable of enforcing their class interests in their own name, whether through a parliament or through a convention. They cannot represent themselves, they must be represented. Their representatives must at the same time appear as their master, as an authority over them, as an unlimited governmental power that protects them against the other classes and sends them rain and sunshine from above. The political influence of the small-holding peasantry, therefore, finds its final expression in the executive power subordinating society to itself.'[40]

Any comparison of the nineteenth century French peasantry at the time of Louis Napoleon and the twentieth century Chinese peasantry in the context of a socialist revolution would have to be made with all due caution. But it is worth drawing attention to the fact that on a local level the Chinese peasant was involved in more cooperative and collectively undertaken activity than the French peasants described by Marx, and this may well have made them more amenable to collective solutions in the organization of production. The Communist Party first developed in China's cities among urban intellectuals and workers. However, it had later been able to defend peasant interests against the landlords and government officials more effectively than any organization the peasants had themselves developed. After liberation the Communist Party and the PLA, enjoying tremendous support among the rural masses as a consequence of their support for peasant interests, were in a very strong position when it came to transforming Chinese agriculture. It is this historical context which helps to explain the paradox of a revolution based mainly on peasant support leading within a few years to the collective ownership of the land. It also helps to explain the large measure of autonomy possessed by the leaders of the Chinese Communist Party in developing their economic strategy.

Although on a local level the Chinese peasantry was accustomed to a measure of collective work (upkeep of the local irrigation system and, perhaps even more important, transplanting of rice seedlings), this certainly did not achieve anything like the scope of even a primitive industrial division of labour. China's poor communications and the poverty of the peasantry encouraged strong localistic limitations in peasant consciousness and organization. Whereas a modern working class naturally produces trade-union organization on a national level, the Chinese peasants were only able to sustain peasant associations with the assistance of the Communist Party. In nineteenth century France the Bonapartist bourgeois state, sustained by the support of a small-holding peasantry, could raise the executive 'above society', sending rain and sunshine from above. In twentieth century China the destitute peasants and landless labourers sustained a socialist revolution which could, in a different way and for different ends, also raise itself 'above society' and impose upon them advanced forms of collective ownership.

[40] Karl Marx, 'The Eighteenth Brumaire of Louis Bonaparte' in *Selected Works in One Volume*, London 1968, pp. 171–172.

3
The Eighth Congress and the Rectification Campaign

On 5 April 1956 an important editorial entitled *On the historical experience of the dictatorship of the proletariat*, reputedly written by Mao Tse-tung himself, appeared in the *People's Daily*. In December of the same year there followed a second article, *Once more on the experience of the dictatorship of the proletariat*. These articles mark the first intervention of the Chinese Communist Party in the polemics of the world communist movement after the Twentieth Congress. In general they express approval of the criticisms levelled at Stalin, while making chronological distinctions and insisting that Stalin's 'achievements' outweighed his 'mistakes'. These reservations aside, the articles warmly welcome the Soviet Congress and criticize Stalin's theory of the intensification of the class struggle. They also criticize the great-power chauvinism of the Soviet Union, in particular its attitude towards Yugoslavia, and advance the idea that contradictions among the people are different from antagonistic contradictions and should be resolved in a different way. The Chinese leadership continued to express its approval of the Twentieth Congress even after the events in Hungary of 1956.

In July a volume was published in Peking containing articles on the Twentieth Congress and on Stalin written by the leaders of various Communist Parties, together with resolutions from the different Parties. The July session of the National People's Congress freely criticized the government's political and economic policies. Chou En-lai acknowledged these criticisms and promised to lose no time in dealing with them. Li Wei-han, the Central Committee member responsible for applying the united front line, stressed the role of the other parties in the internal dialectics of revolutionary society while Li Fu-ch'un, after denouncing excesses and abuses during the drive for collectivization, came out in favour of a better balance between heavy industry, light industry and agriculture.

In September 1956 the Eighth Party Congress convened in Peking. Although the leaders tended to stress the continuity of their policies, the Congress in fact provided a more solemn setting in which to take up and deepen the themes of rectification and self-criticism. At the same time there was a drift towards a certain 'liberalization' and a number of calls were made for more attention to the needs and aspirations of the masses. Criticisms were voiced of arbitrary methods used in industrialization and the collectivization campaign and of overall economic policies. Such criticisms were intended to warn against the dangers of forcing the pace, violations of the principle of voluntary cooperation, paying too little attention to good economic management and paralysing the administration with bureaucratic elephantiasis. On the more strictly political plane, the Congress stressed cooperation with the other parties and rejected the resort to force or violence, condemning abuses by the police.[1]

The revision of the Party Rules seems to have been aimed at an appearance of greater internal democracy; the cult of the leader was formally condemned.[2]

Many critics denounced bureaucratization in the unions and, more importantly, reaffirmed the positive role of the unions in the fight against bureaucracy. Lai Jo-yu, Chairman of the All-China Federation of Trade Unions, developed this point in his speech: 'Some people seem to think that because the working class wields state power, the state as a whole will safeguard the interests of the working class, and the trade unions have lost their function as protector of the workers' interests. This view is wrong. The reason is that classes have not yet been completely eliminated in our country, while various bureaucratic tendencies will inevitably continue to manifest themselves among us and it will take us a long time to overcome them. Under these circumstances, the material interests and political rights of the mass of workers and employees are not safe from damage by bureaucracy.'[3]

On the cultural plane, the Congress articulated the 'hundred flowers' theme in its most liberal interpretation. This campaign was anticipated by Chou En-lai as early as January 1956 (i.e. before the Twentieth Congress) and launched by Lu Ting-yi in a speech on 26 May.

But the rectification campaign only really got into full swing in the first months of the following year. In February Mao made his famous speech 'On the correct handling of contradictions among the people', in

[1] *Eighth Congress*, vol. II, pp. 113–114, pp. 121–122.
[2] *Eighth Congress*, vol. I, pp. 200–201.
[3] *Eighth Congress*, vol. II, p. 238.

which he enlarged upon ideas set out in the two articles on the experience of the dictatorship of the proletariat and certain themes raised at the Eighth Congress. He admitted among other things the possibility of mass unrest provoked by bureaucratism. On 7 April the *People's Daily* published an important article on the relations between leadership and masses, denouncing bureaucratism and arguing the need for cadres to take part in manual labour. Contradictions between leadership and masses, the article pointed out, were the result of bureaucratic methods: hence the need for a thoroughly democratic style of work. On 2 May the same paper published a similar article calling for the right of the people to freely express differences of opinion.

On 7 May Chou Yang raised the temperature even further in a sensational interview in which he recognized the legitimacy of strikes and protest demonstrations, declared that it was wrong forcibly to suppress such dissent and called for a redistribution of the national income so as to avoid marked inequalities. During the same period an embryonic form of workers' management grew up in the Peking Tram Company, where a workers' conference won the right to control management, set up plans for production and finance, elect the directors and his associates and decide on wage problems, social welfare, etc. The press devoted much space to this experiment. (It should not be forgotten the above-mentioned article of December 1956 looked fairly favourably upon the 'experiments in democratic administration' taking place in Yugoslavia.[4])

In the columns of the press, debates started up in which daring criticisms and heretical opinions were voiced, often in the most forthright language. Student groups with names like 'Hegel and Engels Tendency', 'The Frank Speech Association' and 'The Bitter Medicine Association' began to spring up and publish newspapers such as *The Flame, Voice of the Rank-and-file* and *Open Door*. Lin Hsi-ling, who having joined the Liberation Army at the age of thirteen was now a twenty-year-old student at a college for Communist Party cadres, wrote: 'The upper strata of Chinese society today do not coincide with the socially-owned economic base, because the party and the State have become a bureaucratic apparatus which governs the people without democracy.' She also quoted Engels to show that socialism could not be built in one country and declared she was in favour not 'of reformism, but of a fundamental change'. A rectification campaign would not achieve such a change: an 'action of the people' was necessary. During the polemics of 1966, Lin

---

[4] *Once More on the Experience of the Dictatorship of the Proletariat*, Peking 1957.

Hsi-ling was to be attacked in *Red Flag* and other places as a friend of Teng T'o.[5]

The reader should not lose sight of the particular conjuncture of the Chinese revolution into which the so-called movement for destalinization became inserted. Destalinization in the Soviet Union was provoked by a set of circumstances many of which had not yet arisen in China. In the same way China was not threatened by the same ground-swell of discord which had hastened on the events in Poland and Hungary. China at that time was more closely linked than ever to the Soviet Union and she neither could nor would oppose the new leadership or the line it was taking. But, as we have seen, prevailing trends in economic policy and the principles underlying the structural transformation of China had combined with a growing bureaucratization of state and administration to produce dangerous tensions of which the leadership was beginning to take note. In particular, during the first five-year plan the development of the economy, the elaboration of the state and the growth of the Party resulted in the secretion of large and complex bodies of officials which gradually grew stronger, detaching themselves from the masses and acquiring the habits and mentality of a privileged caste. Chou En-lai, for instance, talked at the Eighth Congress of a 'mammoth' apparatus of ministries and State Council departments. Because the leading role in any field of work always rested with the Party, it was inevitable that the Party apparatus grew and the Eighth Congress repeatedly drew attention to examples of bureaucratism. Paradoxically, the influence of the working class in the management of the economy – which was practically nil anyway – declined even further when management passed from private into state hands. For their part the trade unions (as Lai Jo-yu made clear in his speech to Congress quoted above) were developing in the same way and neglecting to defend the living standards and elementary rights of the masses. There were also too many paid officials in the unions.[6]

The result was a separation between the masses on the one side and the leadership and leading cadres at various levels on the other. Sometimes this separation widened into real conflicts of the sort Mao mentioned in his talk on contradictions. The new directions apparent in the Eighth Congress, the self-criticisms, the denunciations, the promises, the campaign for rectification – all these were an attempt to remedy this

---

[5] See Mei Lei-tar's report in *SWP Discussion Bulletin*, vol. 21, no. 3, New York 1960, pp. 11–12. See also: Snow, op. cit., pp. 393–398; T. Mende, *China and her shadow*, London 1961, p. 81; *The Socialist Transformation*, p. 234.

[6] These reports are available in *Eighth Congress*.

situation by eliminating the worst imbalances and tensions, improve relations with the masses by meeting some of their demands and restore the prestige of the cadres by rectifying their style of work and their attitude towards the people. At a certain point this policy was being so widely implemented that the Chinese Communists found themselves in the van of the movement for reform blazed at the Twentieth Congress.

But the campaign for self-criticism and rectification was short-lived, at least in its above sense. Already on 8 June 1957 the *People's Daily* published an editorial marking the turning-point in the campaign, which was now transformed into a violent attack on 'rightist' tendencies. This attack was aimed principally at groups of intellectual critics, who were accused point-blank of wanting to organize a movement against socialism.

Chou Yang made a speech on 16 September which draws together the various arguments put forward by the state. In it he accuses intellectuals like Ting Ling, Hu Feng and Feng Hsueh-feng of wanting to set up a Chinese Petöfi Club (the Petöfi Club intellectuals were an important force in the Hungarian uprising of 1956) under cover of the New May Fourth Movement and calling for freedom of artistic expression with the aim of using that freedom to attack the socialist order.[7] A number of the intellectuals singled out for attack had already been denounced in previous years and forced to undergo self-criticism. We should remember, however, despite all the accusations made in the course of the polemics, that almost all these men and women were Communist intellectuals with a history of struggle. (Ting Ling, the authoress, had received the Stalin prize in 1951.)

Leaders of the minor parties – in particular Lo Lung-chi and Chang Po-chun, leaders of the Democratic League – were also vehemently attacked and forced to make humiliating self-criticisms. It is typical of the approach of the Chinese Communists that many of the 'rightists' were afterwards 'rehabilitated'.

Some people have interpreted the unexpected turn taken by the rectification campaign as a Machiavellian manoeuvre, in which Mao invited the free expression of criticism the more easily to weed out his enemies. The truth is that on a number of occasions during 1956 and 1957 the Chinese leadership swung first this way and then that, at times giving the impression that it was pursuing a zigzag course between the extremes of anti-bureaucratic reformism and repression. (One indication of this wavering to and fro is the fact that Mao's speech was not published

[7] See *A Great Debate on the Literary Front*, Peking 1958.

until months later and with a number of changes. As for the repression, there are claims that some students were executed.[8]) It is very likely that the intensity of some of the attacks, the appearance of reactionary points of view and the conflicts that broke out among the masses (in particular certain struggles waged among students) highly alarmed the leadership, which feared that centrifugal forces would spring up everywhere and sever its links with important sections of the people. To continue on the road of reformist concessions would have entailed serious risks, all the more so because the margins, at least on certain levels, were fairly narrow. For this reason the Chinese Communist leaders chose to brake sharply, and it was probably from that moment on that they started to reflect critically on the events of 1956 and their implications for the unity of the so-called socialist camp. At the 1957 Moscow Conference, by way of contrast, Mao Tse-tung was the most resolute upholder of this unity – an attitude determined above all by China's international needs and the Sino–Soviet nuclear sharing agreement of 15 October 1957.

[8] Snow, op. cit., pp. 403–404.

The Great Leap Forward, the People's Communes and the Readjustment

4

At the end of the first five-year plan China – notwithstanding considerable achievements – was confronted with several crucial problems. She had not only to maintain but to increase the rhythm of industrial growth, on the one hand guaranteeing the flow of capital into the modern sector and on the other promoting secondary (traditional or local) industries. She had to expand agricultural production considerably – the uncertain rhythm of growth in agriculture was the underlying cause of fluctuations in industrial production itself – with the aim firstly of satisfying the growth of internal demand for basic foodstuffs and industrial raw materials and secondly of increasing exports: the more China exported, the more foreign currency she had for vital imports. Economic growth at an accelerated rate was essential for many reasons: to fulfil the ambitious social objectives set by the revolution, to safeguard it against the continuing menace of imperialism and to enable the People's Republic to play a role in the world arena. General MacArthur's attempt to cross the Yalu river and thrust into China during the Korean war, the US government's vigorous support for Chiang Kai-shek's pretensions and its efforts to stem the tide of socialist revolution in Indo-China all emphasized the reality of the threat from that quarter – and in the long run the swift economic recovery of Japanese capitalism was scarcely less disturbing.

Po I-po declared in a speech in 1957 that agriculture was lagging behind the requirements of industrial development and consumption, especially considering the accelerated rate of growth of the population. Another persistent obstacle to growth in the countryside was the bottleneck of under-employment, which could best be eliminated by the rational reorganization of agriculture. Collectivization was an important step along this path: the average number of days worked in a year jumped from 125 in 1955 to 200 in 1957.[1] (In a 1955 speech on collectivization

[1] See R. Dumont, *Révolution dans les campagnes chinoises*, Paris 1957, p. 337; Adler, op. cit., Italian edition, p. 229, note 11.

43

Mao had fixed the target for 1957 at 250 days.) Finally, China had to exploit to the full the new relations of production which were being consolidated in the face of continuing resistance and attempts to repel the movement for collectivization. We have already recorded instances of resistance above. These continued during the 1957 rectification campaign. Wu Chih-p'u, secretary of the Honan provincial party, mentions for example that some members of the party committee tried to split up all the large cooperatives.[2]

Ignoring the particular ideas and circumstances upon which it is still difficult to shed light, the Great Leap Forward and the people's communes were an attempt – bolder and more decisive than the draft for the second five-year plan or the collectivization campaign – to tackle these problems. In the very first year of the second plan (1958) a call went out for enormous increases in industrial production, announcements were made of startling achievements in agriculture and – especially after the Central Committee's intervention at the end of August – there was an upsurge in the ambitious commune movement.

The results announced in the second half of 1958 and at the beginning of 1959 created a sensation, nourished by the victory hymns of official propaganda. Normally sceptical economists succumbed to the propaganda onslaught, indulging in their turn in every kind of hyperbole and even joining in the exultation of the back-yard steel furnaces which seemed to warrant at the very least an attitude of caution. René Dumont wrote in *Le Monde*: 'What is taking place in China is the most impressive advance ever made in agriculture in the history of the world.'[3] Solomon Adler said of industrial development: 'The size of this increase has no parallel in economic history. . . . As for manpower, bottlenecks have been brilliantly avoided by making iron and steel technology a national pastime as well as an employment.'[4] The infatuations of the *bien pensant* clearly existed even before the cultural revolution.

Given the unreliability of official statistics, it is not easy even today to translate into figures the results of the Great Leap. It is worth recording, however, that according to official sources steel production doubled in 1958, coal more than doubled and total industrial production went up by 66% over the previous year. There were also announcements of record harvests, reaching about 375 million tons in grain – more than double the 185 million harvested in 1957. (According to official figures for 1958 –

[2] Snow, op. cit., p. 429.
[3] 12 October 1958.
[4] Op. cit., Italian edition, pp. 236 and 238.

after the statistical revisions – the global increase in agriculture and industry was 48% and in national income 34%.[5]) Next year steel production reached 13,350,000 tons (an increase of 67% excluding backyard production) and coal production increased by 29%. Grain was up by 8% and cotton by 14.76% in spite of natural disasters, while gross agricultural and industrial production combined was up by 31.1% (with increases of 16.7% and 39.3% respectively). Total national income was up by 21.6%. This meant that the main objectives of the second five-year plan were reached in 1959, i.e. three years ahead of time. Official commentators afterwards claimed that the plan was basically fulfilled in 1960.[6] Bourgeois economists later assessed the increase in national income between 1957 and 1958 at 13%, with a sharp decline in agriculture starting in 1958.[7]

But it was not long before the unthinking optimism of slogans like 'produce more, more quickly, better and more economically' became apparent. Already in the summer of 1959 water was thrown on the fire with the disclosure that important statistical errors had been made. The State Statistical Bureau revised the 1958 grain harvest downwards from 375 to 250 million tons and cotton production from 3.35 to 2.1 million tons. It revealed that the 3 million tons of steel produced in the backyard furnaces – more than a quarter of the declared total – was generally of such poor quality that it was of little or no use.[8] It was also in 1959 that agriculture entered its crisis period. 1960, in Edgar Snow's words, 'was not a great leap in the economy as a whole, but a mere hop, made largely on one leg, industry, with the lame leg of agriculture dragged behind it'.[9] Some Western sources put growth in industrial output for 1960 at 4%.[10]

It is true that during the Great Leap, when the productive capacity accumulated during the first five-year plan was exploited, production reached levels which were unattained during the next ten years. But a serious decline quickly set in and the situation began to assume crisis proportions. Bourgeois economists estimate that in 1961 the national product was 15% down on 1958. This figure represents a per capita drop of 19% and a return to the 1955 level.[11] The estimated net value

[5] See *The Socialist Transformation*, p. 265 and *An Economic Profile*, p. 30.
[6] *HNA*, 1 January 1966.
[7] *An Economic Profile*, p. 10.
[8] *People's Daily*, 27 August 1959.
[9] Op. cit., p. 188.
[10] *An Economic Profile*, p. 275.
[11] Ibid., p. 53.

added in 1961 was 42.6 billion *yuan* as against 61 billion in 1960 and 23.4 billion in 1962.[12] Snow, while speaking of 'agricultural bankruptcy' tells us that 'in all probability China's combined output value for 1960 was less – and possibly considerably less – than in 1957'.[13] According to Field's calculations,[14] the level of industrial production changed in the following way:

1956....100	1960....188.5
1957....109.4	1961....124.5
1958....143.8	1962....109.6
1959....181.6	

The same source gives 1959 as the peak year for the net national product.[15] This was because agricultural production – which reached its peak in 1958[16] – fell between 1958 and 1960. It must be pointed out, however, that there are no really reliable figures for this period since official sources stopped providing sufficient information.

A number of reasons can be given to explain the onset of this crisis. In July 1960 Russian aid and experts were withdrawn abruptly, causing havoc in whole sections of the economy and bringing major projects to a standstill. The withdrawal did not take place, however, until after the difficulties had set in and despite its grave consequences for China it cannot be seen as the main cause of the crisis.[17] The three years 1959–61 also saw an almost unprecedented wave of natural disasters: in 1959 one-third of China's crop-lands suffered from drought or floods and in 1960 the turbulent lower course of the Yellow River almost ran dry for a month in the maritime Shantung province.[18] Catastrophes on such a scale would have caused severe disruption in the economy even under normal circumstances, and combined with other factors the damage they wrought was colossal. The main causes of the crisis, however, should be looked for in the desire to impose an excessive pace of work – a pace which in any case could not be kept up for long – and in the ignorance or neglect of economic and technical factors which could not be brushed aside by what was essentially a pure effort of will. This was especially true for agriculture, where work was organized almost on military lines:

[12] Ibid., p. 69.
[13] Snow, op. cit., p. 188.
[14] *An Economic Profile*, p. 273.
[15] Ibid., p. 50.
[16] Ibid., p. 70.
[17] For the Chinese assessment see e.g. *HNA*, 1 January 1966, p. 7.
[18] Anna Louise Strong, *The Rise of the Chinese People's Communes – and Six Years After*, Peking 1964, pp. 120 and 124.

the working day was prolonged beyond endurance and essential rest-periods were done away with. The result was that increases in production – inasmuch as there were any – were not sustained. Very soon agriculture, with its insufficient rate of growth, once more became the main bottleneck on the road to industrialization: a bottleneck broken through only in the economic imagination of the apologists.

At this point we must briefly discuss the commune experiment.

The commune movement was launched at the end of August 1958 along the lines of a pilot experiment begun in April of the same year. It spread at an even faster rate than the collectivization campaign had in its crucial phase. In the short space of time between April and November the passage was made from the very first experimental projects to the communization of 99% of the rural population: 26,000 communes (later reduced to 24,000) took the place of 740,000 advanced agricultural cooperatives. The communes were meant substantially to extend the area of collective property, reducing to a minimum – if not totally abolishing – the peasants' private property; to replace the work-points system in force in the cooperatives with a system which combined the 'communist' principle of the satisfaction of needs in kind with the 'socialist' principle of a wage-payment according to the amount of work done; and to set up canteens and dormitories to enable women to take part more completely in production and revolutionize family life. At the same time the commune was to become the basic political and administrative unit, involving itself not only in agriculture but also in trade and industry and fulfilling the tasks (transport, upkeep of roads, education, etc.) of local administration.

In its first flush of elation, official propaganda blazoned the communes as embryos of communist society, as bridgeheads into the communist future. The *People's Daily* argued that communization would ease the transition 'from collective property to property of the whole people', which was seen as taking from three to four or from five to six years; the transition to communism proper would take place a few years later.[19] Not long before, the same paper had written that the commune 'will not only be the primary unit of our society in the present phase, but will grow and become the primary unit of the future socialist society'.

But it was not long before the first readjustment. The plenary session of the Wuhan Central Committee (28 November–10 December 1958) prudently extended certain deadlines (it estimated that transition to the 'property of the whole people' would take fifteen to twenty years and perhaps longer) and declared that China was not on the brink of Com-

[19] 3 October 1958.

munist society; remuneration was to be on the basis of work done and payment in kind was to be considered as a part of wages; any personal property which had been collectivized was to be given back, use of canteens and dormitories was to be optional, at least eight hours were to be allotted for sleep and four for meals and recreation. Finally, the plenary session declared that the commune experiment should not be prematurely extended to the cities. (In fact, the urban counterpart of the commune was only tested on a limited scale and to perform for the most part very elementary tasks.)

In August 1959 a new resolution from the Central Committee revived a number of criticisms, levelling its aim in particular at certain forms of hypercentralism and egalitarianism. The resolution reaffirmed that effective economic control was to be vested in the brigade – the same level of production as the old cooperative.[20]

The communes probably achieved some of their objectives, although the serious lack of information makes it difficult to form an opinion. In the first place they enabled the government to deal more successfully with the crucial problem of rural underemployment and made it possible to mobilize manpower more rationally and concentrate it where most needed: on infrastructural works aimed at taming the elements and irrigating the fields, on soil preservation and on basic political and administrative communication networks, cutting down on the inflated administrative machinery and setting up truly democratic forms at the lower levels.[21] Some writers have stressed the greater feasibility of large-scale production under the commune system, but this is difficult to prove. It would be possible to argue, for instance, as does the Chinese Trotskyist Makhi,[22] that given the levels of mechanization in China even the cooperatives might have produced similar results. The total irrigated area increased even before the advent of the communes from 21.5 million hectares in 1949 to 26.7 million in 1955–56 and 28 million (56% of all cultivated land) in June 1958.[23]

It is clear, however, that the manner in which the campaign was launched provoked opposition. The pace of reorganization was feverish and not only precluded any real reference to the wishes of the peasantry

[20] See the *Eighth Plenary Session of the Eighth Central Committee of the Communist Party of China*, Peking 1959, p. 10.

[21] See Jan Myrdal, *Report from a Chinese Village*, Penguin 1967, pp. 441–455.

[22] *SWP Discussion Bulletin*, vol. 21, January 1960, p. 21.

[23] For a more extensive appraisal of the positive aspects of the communes (written in the author's usual apologist vein) see Enrica Pischel, *La Cina rivoluzionaria*, Turin 1965, pp. 66–67.

but also made the use of force – naked or veiled – inevitable. 'Everything was simply decided by decree in a hastily organized movement', wrote Makhi in the article cited.[24] Some of the negative features of the campaign sprang from what can be seen as an attempt universally to introduce production and property relations for which the necessary basis hardly existed: hence the forced pace of work, the adoption of measures which could not objectively be justified and the brusque lack of regard for the aspirations of the peasantry.[25] Such methods inevitably gave rise to resistance on the part of the peasants, who in some areas consumed excessive amounts of their produce, squandered and neglected resources and set about precipitately slaughtering livestock.[26] There were failures of production. Very soon tendencies towards differentiation began to spring up again amongst the peasantry. Property forms began to reappear which the leadership thought it had once and for all superseded, and this gave rise to tensions which were analogous – although not identical in either form or context – to those which were originally to be weeded out or given new dimensions.[27]

At the beginning of 1961 the Chinese leadership adopted a policy of 'readjustment'. It radically changed direction in its economic policies and noticeably revised many of its ideas and methods. It more or less admitted that the Great Leap Forward had failed and for the time being gave up long-term planning and set annual targets instead. It gave priority to agriculture and put the accent on foodstuffs and industrial consumer goods rather than on the further development of heavy industry. This retreat took place above all at the expense of the communes: first the 'production brigade' (analogous to the old cooperative) and then the 'production team' (analogous to the level of the old mutual-aid team) became the basic unit; economic incentives regained their former importance, and both the private plot and the free market were once more given official blessing. The commune survived mainly as an administrative unit, as a centre for organizing large-scale public works and as the motor force of mechanization. During the cultural revolution all these changes were the object of constant attacks; critics revealed that industry had also observed more rigid economic principles.

It is difficult because of the lack of official statistics to draw up an

[24] Makhi, op. cit., p. 6.

[25] See the Canton revolutionary rebels' reference to violence exercised against the peasantry in *Survey of China Mainland Press*, Hong Kong, no. 4123, p. 1 (hereafter *SCMP*).

[26] See *People's Daily*, 24 September 1958; *Political Studies*, Peking, no. 10, 1958; *Ta Kung Pao*, 8 December 1958; *SWP*, op. cit., pp. 17–18.

[27] See Snow, op. cit., p. 421, for the 'great initial loss' sustained by the communes.

exhaustive balance sheet for this period. However, after the three years of hunger and even starvation (the result of harvest failures which before 1949 would undoubtedly have caused much more widespread devastation[28]) the economy began to recover, above all between 1963 and 1965. About two years after the onset of the crisis industry was once more beginning to exploit unused productive capacity and regain the levels reached before the Great Leap Forward; in some sectors like oil and chemical fertilizers it even considerably surpassed these levels. This industrial growth, made possible in part by the purchase of basic industrial plant from countries like Japan, Britain and France,[29] is recorded in the following index of the net national product, as reconstructed from Chinese data:

(Figures are in billions of yuan.)

1959.... 176.8   1963.... 107.4
1960.... 155.9   1964.... 117.3
1961.... 127.5   1965.... 126.2[30]
1962.... 99.5

Agriculture also began to recover, although without regaining its previous highest levels and in particular the harvest of 200 million tons of grain. Chou En-lai nevertheless claimed that 'after the successive increases in output in 1962 and 1963 and the still better harvests this year [i.e. 1964], agricultural production has reached the level of the high-yielding years of the past'[31] and other Chinese sources declared that the 200 million ton grain harvest was almost achieved in 1965.[32] The 1965 cotton yield, however, was lower than that for 1957,[33] while official sources said that cotton climbed at a faster rate than grain crops.[34] The China Association (a body made up of British firms working with China) said that industrial production rose by 20% in 1965 (19.9% in 1964) and although there were difficulties in grain there was an overall 5% growth in agriculture. The Association also said that China was experiencing difficulties in the production of tractors, while Chou En-lai claimed that in 1964 there were four times as many tractors in the fields as in 1957.[35] From 1961 China had to import from five to six million

[28] See Pischel, op. cit., p. 78.
[29] *An Economic Profile*, pp. 36–37.
[30] Ibid., p. 50.
[31] *Peking Review* (hereafter *PR*), no. 1, 1965, p. 8.
[32] *An Economic Profile*, p. 68.
[33] Ibid., p. 71.
[34] *PR*, no. 12, 1966, p. 11.
[35] *PR*, no. 1, 1965, p. 8. For the readjustment phase in general, see *PR*, no. 11, 1964, pp. 6–9.

tons of grain from the capitalist countries at an annual cost of three to four million dollars.

It is worth emphasizing here that it was precisely during this period, apart from a brief interlude after the fall of Krushchev,[36] that the Sino–Soviet conflict became most virulent. The conflict erupted in 1958, as a result both of the tension provoked by the incidents in the Taiwan Strait and of the reserved if not openly critical attitude of the Russian leaders towards the Great Leap Forward and the communes. It grew sharper when Krushchev unilaterally broke the nuclear sharing agreement and then withdrew all Soviet aid together with thousands of Soviet technicians. In spite of the compromise reached at the second world conference of Communist Parties in November 1960, the conflict became more and more open and intense in the years 1961 to 1963. Krushchev's despicable resort to economic sabotage must certainly have done much to poison relations in a lasting way. It was understandable that the Chinese leaders reacted firmly against a policy which added dramatically to their difficulties during a particularly harsh period. There was little chance of any short-term improvement on the domestic front and the imperialist threat loomed large on the world front. They began to see things in terms more and more at variance with those of the Soviet Union and the majority of communist parties. Contrary to some interpretations this option was not pushed through by Mao Tse-tung in the face of opposition from the alleged 'Kruschchevites' in the Chinese Party. It was later to be claimed that during the whole period 1959 to 1963 Mao's power of decision was greatly restricted and men like Liu Shao-ch'i and P'eng Chen carried most weight, but in point of fact some of the most eloquent Chinese criticisms of the positions of the Soviet Communist Party, and of the parties which followed its leadership, were written by these men. While they vigorously attacked Soviet conceptions of 'peaceful coexistence', the theories of a peaceful transition from capitalism to socialism and other manifestations of 'Soviet modern revisionism', they did not indulge in the wild and unscientific excesses of later Chinese polemics. In particular they never sought to describe the Soviet Union as a capitalist or an imperialist power. However, there is some evidence that Mao was already pressing for declarations of this sort in the early sixties – the Report adopted by the Ninth Congress in 1969 attributes to Mao a 1964 statement that the Soviet Union was capitalist. That these differences were not purely semantic will be considered at a later stage of our analysis.

[36] See *HNA*, 14 June 1965, for the Chinese explanation of this episode.

5
The First Fifteen Years:
a Balance Sheet

Economic objectives unfulfilled

Because of the lack of official statistics – in itself significant – it is difficult to draw up an overall balance sheet for the period up to 1965. It is clear that a recovery began in 1963, but this recovery was not nearly enough to satisfy the enormous needs of the country. All in all it would seem reasonable to agree with those observers who maintain that China regained her 1958 levels (or from the point of view of per capita production her 1957 levels) in 1965.[1]

It is interesting to look back at the long-term forecasts made before the heady days of the Great Leap Forward. According to the above-mentioned twelve-year programme for agriculture, grain yields should have been up by 150% and cotton by 200% between 1956 and 1967 (the August 1959 plenum of the Central Committee even predicted that this plan would be fulfilled ahead of time). Clearly these objectives were not achieved and growth in the economy only just kept ahead of growth in the population.[2] Mao Tse-tung himself had predicted increases of 100–200% over the best pre-1949 harvests, but his predictions were not borne out.[3] On the occasion of the launching of the second plan predictions were made of a 35% rise in production by 1962, but these were also not fulfilled.[4] As for industry, Mao had forecast in 1957 that China would achieve her target of 20 million tons of steel by 1967 or soon after, but the actual quantity produced in 1967 has been put at a mere 11 million tons.[5] (This must be set against the estimated 12 million tons produced,

---

[1] See also R. Guillain's articles in *Le Monde*, 18–20 September 1964, for a general discussion of China's persistent backwardness.

[2] See S. Adler, op. cit., p. 147; *Eighth Plenary Session*, edition cited, p. 12; *An Economic Profile*, p. 70.

[3] See *The Socialist Transformation*, p. 69.

[4] *Eighth Congress*, vol. I, p. 284.

[5] See J. P. Brulé, op. cit., p. 60.

according to sympathetic observers, in 1965.[6]) The Eighth Congress was also proved wrong in its projection for 1962 of $10\frac{1}{2}$–12 million tons of steel and a doubling of overall industrial output. All in all the leadership did not succeed in its aim of a 'comprehensive industrial system' as envisaged by Chou En-lai in his report on the second plan.[7]

In his 1955 speech on cooperation Mao had said: 'If we cannot fundamentally resolve the problem of agricultural cooperation in a period of roughly three five-year plans, that is to say, if our agriculture cannot make a leap from small-scale farming with animal-drawn farm implements to large-scale mechanized farming, including extensive state-organized land reclamation by settlers using machinery (the plan being to bring 400–500 million *mou* of waste land under cultivation in the course of three five-year plans), then we shall fail to resolve the contradiction between the ever-increasing need for marketable grain and industrial raw materials and the present generally low yield of staple crops, we shall run into formidable difficulties in our socialist industrialization and shall be unable to complete it (p. 19).' Mao's fears have largely come true and industrialization – notwithstanding advances in certain fields, e.g. nuclear weapons – continues to run into a whole series of problems.

Social tensions and contradictions
The restricted rate of industrial growth gave rise to a growing disproportion between the drift to the towns and the ability of the urban economy to absorb new manpower. The town population, swelled by newcomers in search of jobs, higher wages and generally more comfortable conditions, reached 130 million at the beginning of the sixties, whereas the administrators had spoken of a ceiling of 110 million.[8] If we consider that the population of China rose every year by between 14 and 16 million and that every year about 10 million young people reached working age, we can gain some idea of the dimensions of the problem. In some periods there have been large-scale returns to the countryside, and one outcome of the cultural revolution was a massive *hsia-fang* or rustication campaign which saw the dispatch of millions of youth from the cities to the communes.

It is hard to say how much real unemployment still existed (even though there is no doubt that under-employment was a serious problem).

[6] *Far Eastern Economic Review* (hereafter *FEER*), 31 March 1966.
[7] *Eighth Congress*, vol. I, p. 281.
[8] See Anna Louise Strong's interview with Po I-po, January 1964.

It is clear, however, that towards the end of the fifties it was fairly severe.[9] In his speech on cooperation Mao had said that the problem of unemployment would be resolved in the five or seven years from 1956. Considering the failure of the mass mobilizations of the Great Leap Forward and the grave crisis of 1960 to 1962, it seems very unlikely that this objective was achieved. Official sources had maintained that unemployment was eliminated 'in the main' in 1957.[10] In 1958 there was a 43% rise in non-agricultural employment, compared with an annual average of 1.5% between 1953 and 1957, but later this trend was reversed and in 1964 non-agricultural employment was 25% lower than in 1958.[11]

Another contradiction was that whereas illiteracy was rapidly being conquered and the general cultural standards of the young raised, there was a shortage of jobs in which educational qualifications could be used. In the ten years up to 1960, 3.3 million students graduated from secondary and senior high schools, while in the next six years this figure rose to some 23 million. Even then the authorities were unable to give higher education to all who wanted it.[12] Japanese observers reported that there was fierce competition for places at certain levels: only one student in ten was accepted into senior middle school and one in thirty into university,[13] despite the fact that the demand for high-level specialists exceeded the supply.[14]

Agriculture continued in the main to dominate the economy and backward conditions persisted at every level: 80% of basic foodstuffs was consumed by the producer, mechanization was confined to a few sectors (according to Edgar Snow[15] 94% of the country's surface was cultivated without mechanized equipment) and electrification was only in its first stages.[16] The aim of the commune experiment was to bring about a big increase in production and at the same time remove those social tensions which had persisted despite collectivization. On both counts it largely failed, and the readjustment policy and the reorganization of the communes were an implicit recognition of this failure. Therefore the course of the Chinese economy continued to fluctuate between collectivism on

[9] According to Guillain, Le Monde, 28 September 1962, about 20 million people were sent to the countryside in 1961.

[10] The Socialist Transformation, p. 85.

[11] An Economic Profile, p. xiv.

[12] See An Economic Profile, p. 682, and Snow, op. cit., pp. 231-232.

[13] Quoted in Victor Nee, The Cultural Revolution at Peking University, New York 1971, p. 37.

[14] Ibid., p. 15; An Economic Profile, p. 529; Adler, op. cit., pp. 77-79.

[15] Op. cit., p. 211.

[16] See Bettelheim, La Construction du Socialisme en Chine, Paris 1965, p. 87.

the one hand and private accumulation, private plots and the free market on the other even after the communes and especially, as the subsequent flood of criticism revealed, during the years 1961 and 1962. In short, China resolved neither of the two main problems she faced: the contradiction between the need to finance economic and industrial growth by more effectively expropriating the agricultural surplus and the need to avoid conflict with the peasantry; and the contradiction between the need for material incentives to stimulate middle and poor peasants to produce more and the inevitable growth of private fortunes and inequalities that material incentives give rise to.

Differentiation and stratification

There was not the same degree of stratification in China between 1949 and 1965 as there was in the USSR in the thirties, and this is even reflected in certain aspects of official ideology. All the same, tensions and differentiations did arise.

Above all there was a disparity between living conditions in the towns and those in the countryside: it is significant that when the peasants were mobilized at the beginning of 1967 their main demand was that this gap should be narrowed.[17]

Secondly, as a result of varying opportunities for accumulation and varying wage-rates, inequalities at village level not only persisted but even tended to deepen. Reports published by the Chinese themselves spoke of differentials as high as 1:4.[18] Edgar Snow mentions peasants with bank accounts living in privileged conditions compared with the masses and refers in passing to the use of outside seasonal labour on one commune.[19] Moreover, forms of contract-labour existed in the co-operatives.[20] At the one extreme there were peasants living exclusively from what they earned and at the other rich peasants able to accumulate considerable savings.

Clearly this was partly the result of the retreat after the Great Leap Forward. Not only did the peasants once again begin to spend more time on their private plots and other individual pursuits, but more generally collective property was regrouped into smaller units: first into brigades, as originally projected, and then into production-teams. This meant that ownership, generally speaking, was now at a lower level than during the

---

[17] See also Mao, *On the correct handling of contradictions among the people*, pp. 25–26.
[18] *HNA*, 6 April 1967, p. 14.
[19] Op. cit., pp. 446–448.
[20] *SWP Discussion Bulletin*, no. 20, 16, 1959, p. 21.

cooperative phase,[21] even though the pattern was not completely uniform across the whole country.[22] Within these production-teams an average of something like 60% of the product, after deductions for costs, taxes, social security contributions and basic capital accumulation, was distributed in money or in kind among the members. Bettelheim says that private plots (which occupied only 5% of the cultivated surface) produced between 15% and 30% of the peasants' income.[23]

The peasants naturally attached considerable importance to the level of taxes and to the prices paid by the state for produce delivered to it. Official sources have always insisted that taxes were never a real burden,[24] even though they seem to have increased in the first stage of the communes when they possibly reached as high as 30% or more of total income.[25] After 1961 the basis of calculation was said to be 10% of annual production[26] and from then onwards this figure remained unchanged despite bigger harvests.

Prices are much more difficult to estimate, but there is no doubt that during the period of rehabilitation the system of state-regulated prices was a boon to the peasants and kept them out of the hands of the speculators. Later on, however, problems began to arise. There is evidence that the administration attempted, in particular during the first phase of the communes, to price certain products too low and thereby favour the state.[27] A further cause for rural discontent were the occasions on which the state made excessive compulsory purchases of grain, etc. In general, however, the quota of compulsory purchases was fixed in absolute figures on the basis of the previous year's harvest and in negotiations between the commune and the state planning services. The production-team is said to have had the last word. On average the quota was fixed at 20% of basic food produce with no increase when the harvest was good and a reduction when it was bad. The price was kept stable.[28] All in all a system was eventually adopted which avoided the harshness typical of Russia in Stalin's days and ensured the peasantry a measure of stability.[29]

[21] See *HNA*, 1 January 1966, p. 25.
[22] Snow, op. cit., pp. 453–454.
[23] See also Snow, op. cit., pp. 436–437.
[24] See Mao, *On the correct handling of contradictions*, pp. 25–26.
[25] See *SWP Discussion Bulletin*, 21 January 1960, p. 24.
[26] See *HNA*, 19 February 1966, p. 12, and Bettelheim, op. cit., p. 88.
[27] *SWP Discussion Bulletin*, 21 January 1960, p. 25.
[28] See Bettelheim, op. cit., pp. 87–88. On her return from China Joan Robinson, the economist, in a private conversation at which the author was present, supported the view that prices paid by the state are remunerative.
[29] The Socialist Transformation, p. 61.

Dissatisfaction among the working class sprang mainly from a fairly rigid wages policy. During the fifties increases were made, but they were nowhere near as high as rises in productivity. According to some sources wages rose by 52% between 1949 and 1959, whereas the total value of production practically quadrupled. Other sources maintain that in 1956 wages had risen by 33.5% and productivity by 70.4% over 1952.[30] In 1956 Li Fu-ch'un told the National People's Congress that during the first three years of the plan industrial productivity had climbed by 41.8% and wages by only 14.7% (or 6.9% according to a more credible estimate). In the whole five-year period the workers' real income reportedly increased by 30%.[31] Industrial growth on such a scale required immense efforts on the part of the workers. The pace was especially feverish during 1949 and 1951, when workers in Tientsin, for example, worked as much as thirteen and in some cases seventeen hours a day.[32] After the Great Leap there were no real wage rises, even after the recovery – the 'increases' of 1963 were mainly connected with changes in category.[33]

A further source of tensions was the wage-differential among workers of approximately 1:3.[34] These tensions were aggravated by the use of piece-work, the introduction of bonuses, the concession of extra rations and holidays, the presence of temporary workers and, in some sectors, insecurity of employment and delays in the payment of wages.[35] The wages and conditions of temporary and contract workers were especially bad, as many reports made clear at the beginning of 1967.[36] Earlier, in 1962, there were reports of Anshan workers demonstrating against harsh living conditions and against the transfer of workers who insisted on their right to criticize.[37] Resistance also built up against the practice of enforcing excessive and sometimes unpaid overtime: the press was forced to intervene, affirming that only well-paid bureaucrats could ignore the demands of the workers.[38]

Over against the workers and the overwhelming majority of the peasants were the wealthy and privileged strata. The remnants of the

[30] Snow, op. cit., p. 187.

[31] *The Socialist Transformation*, p. 85.

[32] *HNA*, 9 November 1967, p. 3.

[33] E. Germain, *Essai d'interprétation de la révolution culturelle* in *Quatrième Internationale*, June 1967, p. 35 and *An Economic Profile*, p. 494.

[34] *An Economic Profile*, p. 495, and Snow, op. cit., pp. 203–205.

[35] See *An Economic Profile*, p. 682.

[36] E.g. a Central Committee resolution 17 February 1967, quoted in *Current Background* (hereafter known as *CB*), American Consulate General, Hong Kong, no. 852, p. 83.

[37] *Le Monde*, 27 September 1962.

[38] *People's Daily*, 18 June 1965.

old ruling classes were anything but negligible and despite expropriations the former capitalists were enjoying conditions far better than those of the mass of the people. The *New York Herald Tribune* estimated in 1965 that compensation (5% a year of the value of confiscated property) was fairly substantial and was paid to something like 90,000 families.[39] A former capitalist interviewed by Guillain[40] claimed that there were 90,000 recipients of interest in Shanghai alone and that the figure for the whole of China was $2\frac{1}{2}$ million, 100,000 of whom were big capitalists. Barry Richman, a Canadian economist, visited eleven Chinese cities in the period April to June 1966 and afterwards wrote that some capitalists were receiving colossal amounts of interest – from 32,000 to 40,000 dollars a year and in one exceptional case 320,000 dollars – besides monthly salaries which were well above average.[41] The Chinese themselves revealed that more than 170 former capitalists were employed as managers in Shanghai's commercial sector. A pamphlet circulated during the cultural revolution said that former capitalists were paid high salaries and enjoyed privileged conditions: some of them received in two days what it would take a commercial employee two weeks to earn.[42]

But differentiation did not only exist as a remnant of the past. It also sprang up in different forms within post-revolutionary society itself. Technicians and managers were paid practically twice as much as the highest-paid workers, and salaries in the very top grades were exceptionally high.[43] Differentiation was practised not only in straightforward salaries and wages. According to a 1967 wall-newspaper, bonuses in an electrical factory were 15–20% of basic pay in the case of workers and 45–50% of a much larger salary in the case of managers. In practice the managers' bonuses alone were higher than the average monthly wages of a senior skilled worker.[44]

In the state machine and in the administration in general there were as many as twenty-six grades and party officials could be sure of very substantial salaries.[45] Among the highest salaries were those paid to generals.[46] Edgar Snow talks of 'different levels in wages and rations' and

---

[39] 16 September 1966.

[40] *Le Monde*, 22 September 1964.

[41] *Harvard Business Review*, January 1967, quoted in *World Outlook*, 3 February 1967, p. 119. See too the same author's *Industrial Society in Communist China*, New York 1969, pp. 897–898.

[42] *SCMM*, no. 619, passim.

[43] See Mao, *On the correct handling of contradictions*, p. 26; Richman, op. cit., p. 121.

[44] *HNA*, 3 December 1967, p. 5.

[45] See Germain's above-mentioned article for a decision taken by the Council of State on 18 July 1955.

[46] Snow, op. cit., p. 289.

'extra allowances',[47] and maintains that 95% of party officials (in 1955 there were 300,000 and the number undoubtedly grew) were paid considerably more than the workers. The Chinese themselves have published evidence showing that the wage-differential taken as a whole was 1:8.[48]

But it was above all at the highest echelons of party and state that the practice of giving lavish perks and privileges became most firmly established. This has long been obvious, but after 1966 it was confirmed by Red Guards and Revolutionary Rebels who denounced officials for living in luxury and not sharing the conditions of the masses, for squandering resources and for embezzling public funds for their own use. Denunciations of this sort were only aimed at Mao's (presumed) opponents, as was all official propaganda during the cultural revolution. There was no rational reason, however, for such a distinction. The luxurious quarters that became the targets of the Red Guards in Autumn 1966 were frequented not only by former capitalists but also by members of the bureaucracy and their foreign guests, as some of the latter have testified.

There are countless examples of the luxurious conditions enjoyed by high officials. The Red Rebels of Canton published a document on 15 January 1967 in which T'ao Chu, for a long time one of the chief protagonists of the cultural revolution, was accused of using public funds to build for himself and people of his rank 'a large number of high-class guest-houses', of owning various 'villa-type guest-houses not only in Canton but also at some scenic spots within the province' and a 'country house' near some thermal springs, of spending four million *yuan* on the construction of a ballroom and of arranging banquets which cost more per head than the monthly wage of a top-grade worker.[49] P'eng Teh-huai is supposed to have said in a speech on 7 August 1959 that 'many provinces have built villas for Chairman Mao. This is obviously not done with Chairman Mao's permission.'[50] Whether Chairman Mao gave his permission or not, episodes of this sort are indicative of a certain social and political climate. Teng Hsiao-p'ing, general secretary to the Party's Central Committee, and Ho Lung, a marshal in the People's Liberation Army (PLA) and member of the Politbureau, were the objects of particularly vehement attacks in which they were accused of living in luxury and squandering public funds.[51] In March 1967 Teng Hsiao-

---

[47] Ibid., p. 416 and note.
[48] See *HNA*, 6 April 1967, p. 15.
[49] See also *CB*, no. 825, p. 20.
[50] *CB*, no. 851, p. 25.
[51] *SCMP*, no. 3903, pp. 1ff.; *CB*, no. 859.

p'ing was further accused, together with P'eng Chen, former mayor of Peking, of frequenting luxurious clubs.[52] Similar information had also emerged during the 1957 rectification campaign. Liu Shao-ch'i told a delegation of Sinhalese Trotskyists that 'there is a serious bureaucracy.... Mass criticism is spreading to every corner of China, including the factories, the agricultural enterprises, the schools and other organizations. The target of criticism is the leadership'.[53]

This social stratification was also reflected in the composition of the student body, especially at the higher levels. The percentage of working class students at university was reportedly as follows:

1952....20.46%   1962....42.34%
1958....36.42%   1966....49.65%[54]

At Peking University, between 1960 and 1962, there is said to have been a sharp reduction, from 66.8% to 37.7%, in the number of students from worker or peasant families enrolled.[55] Between 1959 and 1962 only 5% of the new students came from worker and peasant families, compared with 30% from the families of top intellectuals.[56] During the cultural revolution there was a flood of articles denouncing the various ways in which this social selection operated and calling for an end to the special boarding schools which gave a privileged education to the children of cadres and managers.[57] It must be emphasized that the growth of bureaucratic privilege could only inhibit economic mobilization as well as violate the egalitarian sentiments which any socialist revolution tends to arouse in the masses. Both official cynicism and mass apathy would be deadly enemies to rapid economic growth if allowed to grow unchecked.

Intellectuals too occupied a special position in Chinese society, although they never enjoyed the same mandarin-like status as orthodox intellectuals in the USSR. The fact that they shared the same life-style as top officials meant that they were part of a privileged layer of society, whatever their class background. Like the bureaucrats, they were a frequent target for attacks during the cultural revolution.[58] Despite these privileged conditions, however, relations between intellectuals and

---

[52] *SCMM*, no. 576, pp. 4–7.

[53] *People's Daily*, 19 May 1957. See also Chow Ching-wen's *Ten Years of Storm* in which the author, a former member of the Central Committee of the Democratic League, an ally of the Communist Party, describes the privileges of the ruling group.

[54] K. S. Karol, *La Chine de Mao*, Paris 1966, p. 395.

[55] Victor Nee, op. cit., p. 41.

[56] *HNA*, 1 March 1968, p. 4.

[57] *HNA*, 20 June 1966; Nee, op. cit., pp. 75–84.

[58] E.g. *CB*, no. 825, pp. 9–10.

political leadership were not at all good. There were two main sources of friction: firstly, the inevitable difficulties posed by intellectuals who still bore the stamp of the old society; and secondly, the tensions that grew up between on the one hand that section of intellectuals (in particular those belonging to the political and cultural élite) who demanded freedom of speech and research and saw their role as that of critics of the new society and on the other the authorities, who wanted to use the intellectuals to organize and smooth out the state's administrative, cultural and propagandistic activities under the strict control of top party organs.[59] As long as the intellectuals kept to their places and put forward 'corporative' claims, they were normally treated with benevolent paternalism or even, in some periods, a measure of liberalism. But as soon as their discussions and criticisms took on a more political character and the intellectuals started, even unconsciously, to become the spokesmen of more generalized needs, they were denounced with the vehemence of a Zhdanov and accused point-blank of wanting to organize anti-socialist political movements. The same thing happened, as we have seen, when the intellectuals were attacked during the rectification campaign and again in the first stages of the cultural revolution when the Wu Han and Teng T'o group was to be accused of presenting opposition groupings in a favourable light and preparing an alternative leadership of the Petöfi Club type.[60]

As well as conflicts of this sort, which tended to arise at critical junctures, cultural polemics continued practically non-stop with occasional interventions (as in June 1964, for instance) from Mao Tse-tung himself. We recall, among other things, the discussions between the supporters of the official line and those of the philosopher Yang Hsien-chen, the discussions on 'writing about middle characters', 'human interest' and 'love of mankind' and the transformation of Peking Opera.[61]

Political apparatus and centres of decision
It should by now be clear that on the eve of the cultural revolution China was rent by wide-ranging and fairly clear-cut social divisions and dominated by an increasingly distinct and ramified bureaucratic stratum. To round off this analysis we shall now try to answer one fundamental

[59] See *People's Daily*, 11 April 1955, and Chou En-lai quoted in *HNA*, 29 January 1956, also reported in Snow, op. cit., p. 382.

[60] See in particular *HNA*, 5 June 1966, pp. 17 and 19.

[61] See e.g. Kuangming Jihpao, 29 May 1964, and *Summary of the forum on the work in literature and art in the armed forces with which Cde. Lin Piao entrusted Cde. Chiang Ch'ing*, Peking 1968.

question: who took the big economic and political decisions?

The first point to make is that most people generally overestimate the actual degree of economic centralization that existed in 1965 or, for that matter, that exists today. Central planning has always left a margin of considerable freedom especially, for obvious reasons, in agriculture.[62] Secondly, there were real possibilities for people at lower levels to make democratic choices. This was true above all of the countryside, where the overwhelming mass of the population lived and where the peasants directly participated in tackling a whole range of problems. This sort of direct democracy, however, was essentially restricted to production-team or brigade level, while at commune level, where no substantial changes were made after the administrative reorganization, actual power remained in the hands of party leaders and party officials.[63] It should be remembered that most communes are very large, grouping together tens of thousands of people. The 29 August 1959 resolution on communes ruled that administrative bodies on a local level, i.e. in the townships, should become the administrative bodies of the communes. This resolution, which also applied to administrators, party officials and councils, meant that primacy was vested in the party apparatus and in particular in the party secretaries.

As for the role played by workers in the running of factories, we have already mentioned the accusations made at the Eighth Congress and experiments like the one carried out in the Peking Tram Company. We should also remember the 'movement of the two participations', which envisaged the participation of cadres in production and of workers in management and in whose wake there sprang up embryonic workers' councils.[64] But nothing came of these beginnings and participation from below was reduced to a minimum. For a whole period actual management was ultimately in the hands of the party committee, which represented the party at factory level rather than the workers themselves. Even official sources record that later, at least in some sectors, the principle of one-man management was introduced; at the same time profit was taken as the base indicator and the administrative apparatus enlarged. The result was, as the Chinese leaders themselves have admitted, that apart from the occasional development here and there the workers in most branches of industry were totally subordinate to their superiors. There is evidence

---

[62] See Bettelheim, op. cit., chapters 1–3, and Richman, quoted in *World Outlook*, 3 February 1967, p. 120.

[63] Snow, op. cit., pp. 444ff.

[64] *SWP*, vol. 20, no. 16, p. 18.

to show that many factory elections were only a formality, despite the fact that workers were frequently expected to take part in factory discussions. One observer claims that in most of the factories he visited there were no workers at all on the party committee, while in others the number of workers never exceeded 10%.[65] The Chinese press has carried a great many articles denouncing cadres who only go through the motions of participating in production, who try to silence critical workers with threats and reprisals and who are not interested in securing real workers' participation in management.[66]

But the decisive factor, as even observers sympathetic to Maoism readily admit, is the immense power of decision vested in the top party and state organs. Such organs, which in China overlap even more than in other collectivist regimes, are responsible for all those major economic and political decisions which in the last analysis condition what goes on at local level and in the different sectors of industry. It is well known that the Constitution of 1954 provided for the setting up of various bodies, the most important of which was the National People's Congress, supposedly the seat of popular sovereignty. The Congress turned out to be a fairly ineffective body whose members were selected rather than democratically elected. It did not normally hold its sessions, which lasted from one to two weeks, more than once a year and only rarely debated issues of any real relevance.[67] Neither the Standing Committee of the National People's Congress nor the earlier Chinese People's Political Consultative Conference – an unelected body which was supposed to play the role of a sort of united front – had any real powers.[68] The important decisions had traditionally been taken by senior bodies such as the Politbureau and its all-powerful Standing Committee. The Politbureau itself was elected by the full Central Committee, but this body met fairly infrequently – it was not convened between September 1962 and August 1966.

The state and party machines, whose tendency to harden into a layer separate and apart from the masses had already been the object of self-criticism at the Eighth Congress, are said to have subsequently become even further detached from the workers and peasants: they were accused of being a more and more conservative tool in the hands of privileged groups which were inclined to favour the status quo and shun radical

[65] Richman, quoted in *World Outlook*, 3 February 1967, p. 121.

[66] *HNA*, 6 April 1967, p. 14. For more general information see Bettelheim, op. cit., pp. 30 and 46–48.

[67] In 1963 Congress was doubled in size and its principles of representation restated. See *HNA*, 15 December 1963.

[68] See, for example, Snow, op. cit., p. 321.

change. Mao is reported to have said in 1968: 'In the seventeen years since liberation we have alienated ourselves from the masses to a rather serious extent.'[69] It is true that there were no democratic channels within the party – which wielded total power – through which the rank and file could express its will or translate that will into reality. The partial reforms introduced at the Eighth Congress, such as the statute fixing a maximum five-year deadline for convoking the congress and an annual plenary session of the previous congress, very soon became a dead letter. In so far as there was an internal dialectic, it was limited to the top Party personnel and took the form of clashes between rival groups in the party machine or between rival potentates, each of whom was strongly entrenched within the positions he had conquered and within his sphere of influence (this became clear, among other things, from the denunciations of 'independent kingdoms' and 'bourgeois dictatorships' set up in this or that sector). Even though there were no incidents comparable to those which took place in the USSR in Stalin's days, groups or individuals considered critical of the leadership were subjected to harsh repression, and the police network was so far-flung that there were even reports of microphones in the homes and offices of Mao and Lin Piao.[70]

Paradoxically it seems that the strengthening of the bureaucracy was accompanied by a certain 'democratization' of decision-making within it. The setbacks produced by the voluntarist policies of the Great Leap Forward period by diminishing Mao's power led to a growing involvement of top Party and State functionaries in the making of decisions. Although the formal leading bodies of the Party met very infrequently, there were a relatively large number of meetings known by the name of Central Work Conferences, or Central Committee Work Conferences. Attendance at these conferences was by no means coextensive with membership of the Central Committee but would usually include members of the Political Bureau, Vice-Premiers of the State Council, Secretaries of the Central Committee Secretariat, First Secretaries of the six Central Committee Bureaux, Directors and selected Deputy Directors of the Central Committee departments, First Secretaries of the Provincial Party Committees and selected officials from the People's Liberation Army General Staff and regional military commands. A gathering of these categories would exclude the decorative and retired members of the Central Committee and would include operative functionaries of the Party and State, especially in the provinces, who were not members of

[69] *SCMP*, no. 4201, p. 4.
[70] *SCMP*, no. 4146, p. 9; no. 4182, p. 4; no. 4230, p. 1.

the CC. Presumably those responsible for issuing invitations to these meetings wielded considerable power. Between 1960 and 1966 there were nineteen meetings of this sort according to evidence made available during the cultural revolution.[71] The Central Work Conferences would last as long as two months and tended to be associated with the more important policy shifts. It may be imagined that this partial 'democratization' of the bureaucracy itself displaced some power from the very top and was a development that did much to nourish Mao's distaste for bureaucracy since it drained power from his own hands.

The international setting

These tensions must be seen in a world setting if we are to gain an overall view of the situation in which the crisis of 1965–69 broke out. The break with the USSR was by now almost complete and the world communist movement was deeply split into a number of shifting alliances. The evolution of the Soviet Union under Krushchev and Brezhnev posed serious questions to the Chinese leadership. It searched for a way out of the crisis which had overtaken the Stalinist system on a world scale since the early fifties. It was now that the tendency to see Soviet developments as part of a restoration of capitalism took hold though the significance of this was not immediately apparent. A number of defeats suffered by the colonial and ex-colonial peoples and above all the Indonesian débâcle, in which the strongest of the pro-Peking parties was tragically routed, doubtless strained the situation even more. Lastly, the growing international implications of the Vietnam war meant that China could not help but feel threatened by the danger of direct imperialist aggression; the New Year message for 1965 spoke of 'the eventuality of a war which American imperialism might soon be able to unleash on a large scale'.

Crisis in the leadership?

In spite of appearances, the inner life of the Chinese Communist Party during the ten years up to the cultural revolution was fairly tempestuous. In the mid-fifties a serious crisis broke out and Kao Kang was accused of wanting to set up an 'independent kingdom' in the vital industrial region of Manchuria. In 1956 and 1957 fierce struggles were waged against 'rightists' and groups of intellectuals; even sections of the masses came into conflict with the administration. In 1958 and 1959 the Great

---

[71] R. M. Field, 'Research Notes on Changing Loci of Decision in the CCP', *China Quarterly*, no. 44, October–December 1970. See also *Mao Tse-tung Unrehearsed*, edited by Stuart Schram, London 1974, pp. 158–188.

Leap and the communes gave rise to disagreements which were much more serious than was believed at the time, and Mao's decision not to stand as a candidate for the Chairmanship of the Republic and his acceptance of a sort of separation of powers was the outcome of a struggle in which he had to make concessions. Later the press admitted that Mao's thought had been 'undermined' in this period.[72]

1959 saw further power-struggles in which P'eng Teh-huai, Minister of Defence and protagonist of the right wing, was disgraced and dismissed from his position. P'eng Teh-huai listed his views in a letter addressed to Mao Tse-tung and later circulated (probably by the Soviet Union) among the leaders of the different communist parties. The letter, which was put out in China during the cultural revolution, acknowledged the successes of 1958 but criticized the excessive pace and the inflated propaganda claims. It argued strongly that such methods had damaged the relations between workers and peasants and between the rural and urban populations in general, and that leftist errors had alienated the support of the masses. 'Putting politics in command', the letter continued, 'is no substitute for economic principles, still less for concrete measures in economic work'.[73] P'eng had already criticized many of these policies even before he sent the letter, which is dated 14 July 1959. In particular he had criticized the leadership for making the transition to communes before the results of the advanced stage of collectivization had been properly evaluated. The situation in the Party leadership was undoubtedly grave and there were even reports that Mao had said he would have been forced to take up guerrilla war if the army had followed P'eng.[74]

The September 1962 session of the Central Committee marked the opening of a new phase of struggle between the more obdurate critics of the Great Leap Forward and those who wanted to modify the retreat. The struggle ended with a small reshuffle in the senior organs of the party: T'an Chen-lin and Huang K'o-ch'eng were removed from the secretariat and K'ang Sheng, Lu Ting-i and Lo Jui-ch'ing took their places. Later polemics talked of fierce conflicts and manoeuvres during the 1962 plenum.[75] The National People's Congress sat in April, before the plenum, and is said to have held quite stormy sessions behind closed doors in

[72] E.g. *HNA*, 4 November 1957, p. 10.

[73] *CB*, no. 851, p. 22.

[74] The documents and information quoted in this paragraph can be found in an anti-P'eng pamphlet compiled by a group at Tsinghua University and translated in *CB*, no. 851.

[75] E.g. *HNA*, 24 November 1967, pp. 9–10.

which provincial delegates reported on the gravity of the economic situation; the Congress made concessions to the national bourgeoisie.[76] Some sources maintain that in September the supporters of the Great Leap Forward were defeated by the supporters of readjustment. However, there is much confusion as to who supported what. Many observers place Liu Shao-ch'i, Teng Hsiao-p'ing and Li Fu-ch'un among the former, Chou En-lai, Ch'en Yi and Ch'en Yun among the latter and Mao Tse-tung himself wavering in between.[77] Liu Shao-ch'i later declared, in his self-criticism of October 1966, that the resolutions of the 1962 plenum had begun to correct his mistakes and bring about a radical change in the situation. More generally, the prevailing line seems to have been one of greater tolerance towards critics, a greater opening towards the intellectuals and a recognition of the need for individual incentives for a fairly long period.[78]

A number of the future themes of the cultural revolution appeared in 1962–63 with the launching of the socialist education movement[79] and in 1964 with Mao's calls to 'learn from the army' and his speeches on cultural problems. Especially in 1961–62, groups of intellectuals like Teng T'o and Wu Han carried on a veiled political campaign in allegorical form in certain newspapers and were beginning to find a response in some quarters. On 27 June 1964 Mao sent an 'instruction' in which he declared that 'in the last fifteen years these [literary and cultural] associations, most of their publications (it is said that a few are good) and *by and large* the people in them (that is not everybody) have not carried out the policies of the Party'.[80] There is no need to underline the importance of a statement of this kind or its inevitable implications.

It is still hard to say what were the exact differences among the leadership before November 1965. The information furnished by later polemics is too one-sided and too obviously distorted by political bias to be of real use. Probably the different positions were not always so drastically clear-cut, but overlapped and intermingled, and perhaps occasionally coincided. However that may be, the leading group was already moving towards a deep split which was to demolish the broad group which during a long period of struggle and crisis had formed the backbone of the party. To quote Edgar Snow, division was by now breaking up 'the 800'.

---

[76] *HNA*, 17 April 1966, p. 6.
[77] E.g. Robert Guillain, *Le Monde*, 29 September 1962.
[78] *People's Daily*, 6 March 1962.
[79] See e.g. *HNA*, 24 November 1967, pp. 9–10.
[80] *Peking Review*, no. 23, 1967, p. 8.

We repeat that it is still not possible to say in precisely what form the split came about. However, the basic questions which arose were: What should the government do to move beyond the phase of readjustment and boost production? Where could it best concentrate its efforts in order to achieve maximum linkage effects in the rest of the economy? What should it do to tackle the persistent difficulties and recurring differentiation in the countryside? How could it mobilize the working masses and commit them once more to an intense effort in production? How should the Communist Party deal with the problems of the younger generations and resolve the problem of its relations with the intellectuals? How could it stop China degenerating like the USSR and the other collectivist countries? How could the trend towards bureaucracy be reversed? What should it do about the crisis in the world communist movement: step up the attack or negotiate? What position should it take up in the face of the Vietnam war? With what sort of army and what sort of political and military strategy should it prepare against possible aggression? And with which allies? What general orientations should it adopt towards the struggle in the colonial and neo-colonial countries?

These are some of the questions which inevitably gave rise to fierce clashes and deep differences of opinion.

Part 2
The Three Years of the Cultural Revolution

6

Preliminary Skirmishes

The first broad phase of the cultural revolution, which is how the Chinese officially designated this great political and social upheaval, runs from November 1965 to the end of July 1966, that is up to the Eleventh Plenary Session of the Central Committee. It opens with the emergence of a serious split at top levels and closes with the first stages of a general mobilization of the students. Its outstanding features are the dispute in the army, which resulted in an initial victory for Mao and Lin Piao, and the 'cultural' controversy, which culminated in the overthrow of the Peking group and its leader P'eng Chen. The events of June and July, on the other hand, were a sort of tormented interlude, of considerable importance for later developments.

The dispute in the army
One of the first battles in the great crisis was fought out in the army. Quite apart from the intrinsic importance of strategic and military questions, Mao could not afford to underestimate the importance of winning the army over to his way of thinking and thus gaining control of it. We need only think forward to the decisive role of the army in 1967–68 in order to grasp the importance of the outcome of this opening battle.

Even before the 'official' opening of the cultural revolution, the whole of 1965 was characterized by military and political-military polemics, conducted for the most part in an indirect and implied way. Apart from domestic preoccupations, world developments and especially the American escalation in Vietnam clearly influenced this controversy considerably.

At this point we would like to draw out one factor that was common to all the struggles that broke out during the cultural revolution. The controversy in the army during 1965, as in all other fields, was in no sense a new development. On the contrary, disputes over military policy had arisen regularly at crucial junctures, often following hard on formal decisions that were intended to banish them for ever (in 1958, for instance, the Enlarged Session of the Military Affairs Commission of the Central Committee 'finally' settled the question by coming down firmly on the side of the Mao group, only to witness a renewed outbreak of factional disputes in 1959). At the heart of these conflicts is frequently to be found the contradiction between China's military needs and her inability to produce the full range of modern weapons. Even the most politically conscious guerrilla commander appreciates access to modern weaponry when confronted by imperialist fire-power and air-power. And for China the Soviet Union has often seemed the only conceivable source of such weapons.

The Chinese themselves say that the first clash came about immediately after the end of the Korean war, the conduct of which had already given rise to bitter polemics and serious tensions between China and Korea, to the partial advantage of the USSR. At the centre of this clash was Marshal P'eng Teh-huai, commander-in-chief of the Chinese forces in North Korea during the war. P'eng was accused several times of having ignored Mao Tse-tung's suggestions and general principles during military operations, with very grave consequences. He was particularly reproached for not concentrating his main attack during the first phase on South Korean troops, choosing instead to attack the British and the Americans. He was also accused of taking up chauvinistic attitudes and thereby causing serious difficulties with Kim Il Sung, the North Korean leader.[1]

Another area of controversy was what sort of army China should adopt, now that she was emerging from the phase of rehabilitation. The group closest to Mao wanted to continue in the traditions and according to the experiences of the revolutionary army, keeping to the basic principles developed during the war against Japan and the civil war, while P'eng's group is said to have favoured a regular army along modern lines, like that of the Soviet Union. Various documents[2] went so far as to accuse P'eng specifically of collusion with the Soviet Union and in particular with Krushchev.[3] Though these later allegations probably projected themes of the Sino-Soviet conflict back into the past, it does

[1] *CB*, no. 851, pp. 8–9.
[2] Ibid., for some of these.
[3] For the official position as restated during the cultural revolution, see *HNA*, 2 August 1966, pp. 4–5, and 21 August 1966, p. 4; also *PR*, no. 32, 1967, pp. 40–41 and 46.

seem that P'eng's experiences during the Korean war led him to stress the importance of China acquiring modern weaponry.

The second clash came about in 1959, when the dispute with the USSR had already begun to take shape. Once again the main protagonist was P'eng Teh-huai, who at that time was doing his utmost to gain support for his ideas. As we have already seen, P'eng's disagreements were not restricted to the military field, and the documents of the Lushan Plenum and even those published much later during the cultural revolution do not even mention military disagreements.[4] The formal reason for this may have been that accounts were settled on the military question at the Enlarged Military Affairs Commission of the Central Committee, which was called immediately after the Plenum and ended with P'eng's removal. On the domestic front, as we have seen, P'eng had called for a critical balance sheet of the Great Leap Forward. Production had been increased, the problem of unemployment tackled and the masses had acquired some valuable technical experience with the backyard furnaces. But by mid-1959 the continued pursuit of the methods of the Great Leap Forward was entailing a heavy price: there was widespread economic chaos and waste, covered up by falsified reports and encouraged by 'petty bourgeois exaltation' and an 'authoritarianism divorced from the masses'. P'eng had already on an earlier occasion spoken against the 'superstitious cult of personality', so his opposition to Mao was fairly comprehensive and could be represented as echoing certain Soviet themes. However there is no evidence that P'eng supported the Soviet interpretation of 'peaceful coexistence'. In fact there seems to have been a political bond between him and P'eng Chen, the mayor of Peking and scourge of 'Soviet revisionism'. Writers such as Wu Han and Teng T'o, who occupied positions in the Peking cultural apparatus protected by P'eng Chen, were to wage a campaign for the rehabilitation of P'eng Teh-huai in the early sixties.[5] The military disagreements themselves were more or less the same as before, but Maoist sources talk of a more open tendency to remove the army from the direct control of the Party and to shelve political duties: in other words military groups – like their counterparts in certain periods in the USSR – were pressing for more autonomy and professionalism in their specific field of action. P'eng himself is supposed to have poured scorn on the tendency to concentrate all efforts on political

[4] *HNA*, 18 August 1967, pp. 3ff.
[5] The relevant documents on P'eng Teh-huai's position are collected together as appendices to Simon Leys, *Les Habits Neufs du Président Mao*, Paris 1971, pp. 257–258. See also the references given in footnotes 73 and 74 of the previous chapter.

work, saying: 'The results in training our units and the results in the study of military science of our cadres at all levels should constitute the fundamental criteria in the future for judging the fighting power of our army.'[6] He is said to have been in favour of leadership based on personal responsibility as opposed to the collective leadership of the party committee and was accused of jeopardizing the mass line and the democratic system in the army. Further reports allege that he neglected military preparation, claiming that the outbreak of a war was 'unlikely'. Serious disagreements are said to have arisen over the reintroduction of the militia or *minping* system and over the question of how much weight should be attached to the political education of militia members. There are also reports of a dispute over naval policy, involving Liu Shao-ch'i and Lo Jui-ch'ing, but the episode is obscure and Liu's role has clearly been distorted.[7] Even the value of Mao's thought is said to have been called into question: P'eng Teh-huai allegedly went so far as to say that it was 'out of date and not applicable'.[8]

In 1965 the argument flared up again on all fronts: the primacy of politics, the structure and role of the army, the relations between party and army, and so on; at the same time the international situation gave a dramatic colouring to the issues involved and linked them more closely with questions of general political strategy. The bombing of North Vietnam by the United States and the arrival of ever larger US reinforcements in the South posed with great sharpness the question of united action by the Soviet Union and China.

From an examination of various statements put out between 9 May and 11 November it is possible to reconstruct fairly precisely the different positions held by some of the main figures involved. On 9 May the *People's Daily* published an article entitled 'The historical experience of the war against fascism'. Besides paying a warm tribute to Stalin, this article maintains among other things that '. . . the history of the anti-fascist war shows that a people's war is sure of victory, that it is entirely possible to defeat the imperialist aggressors, that imperialism is a paper tiger, which is outwardly strong but actually weak, and that the atom bomb is also a paper tiger and that it is people and not weapons, of whatever kind, that decide the outcome of war.' It goes on to underline the importance of popular risings, refuting the 'revisionist' view that the

[6] *HNA*, 31 August 1967, p. 7.

[7] *HNA*, 27 December 1967, pp. 3ff.

[8] For these various points see *HNA*, 21 August 1967, p. 4; 7 August 1967, p. 7; 22 August 1967, p. 28; 13 September 1967, p. 9.

USSR was 'the only force smashing the German Fascist machine' and noting that 'whereas there was then only one socialist state, the Soviet Union, there is now a socialist camp consisting of a number of socialist countries'.[9]

The next day *Red Flag* published an article by Lo Jui-ch'ing, chief of staff of the PLA, in which, after a tribute to Stalin, he declared that the socialist countries were the base areas of the world revolution and the main force in the fight against aggression. He continued: 'Countries which have won victory should support and help the revolutionary struggles of those countries and people that have not yet won victory. The socialist countries should serve as base areas for the world revolution and as the main force in combating imperialist aggression.'[10] However, the two articles differed in several ways: (1) Lo Jui-ch'ing uses the expression 'active defence', which does not appear in the other article; (2) Lo seems to underestimate the contribution of the European resistance when he writes that the United States in their war of aggression in Asia, Africa and Latin America 'unlike Hitler . . . is confronted by the solid resistance of unprecedentedly broad national liberation movements';[11] (3) the *People's Daily* polemicizes against the proposal for 'unity against the enemy' and 'concerted action' put forward by Krushchev's successors, whereas Lo makes no reference to this at all – on the contrary, although he does not mention the USSR explicitly, he suggests the broadest possible united front against US imperialism and ends up with an expression of his esteem for the Soviet people and the Soviet army and of his conviction that 'we will be united on the basis of Marxism–Leninism and proletarian internationalism, (and) will fight shoulder to shoulder against our common enemy'.[12]

On 1 June a decision taken by the Council of State on 24 May was made public: ranks and insignia were abolished in the army. This was a clear sign that the leadership intended to put the accent on the democratic and egalitarian ideas that had frequently come to the fore during the dispute with the Soviet Union. This theme was taken up again on the occasion of the anniversary of the foundation of the army in an article by Ho Lung, Vice-president of the National Defence Council and one of China's leading military exponents. (Ho was soon to be subjected to violent attacks when Red Guard pamphlets described in lurid detail his ostenta-

[9] *The historical experience of the war against facism*, Peking 1965.
[10] *CB*, no. 469, p. 17.
[11] Ibid., p. 19.
[12] Ibid., p. 22.

tious style of living.) The article was considered important enough to
warrant simultaneous publication in several newspapers, including the
People's Daily and *Red Flag*. It draws on the experience of the civil war
and the anti-Japanese war, and is both a concise statement of the democratic and egalitarian principles of army organization and a firm attack on
the opponents of those principles. Ho inveighs particularly against those
who wanted to question the collective leadership of the party committee
and change the very nature of the army; he also tackles the problem of
democratic control of a highly technological army and ends up by
suggesting that democracy in the army is a model valid for society as a
whole.[13] The limits of this democracy, however, are revealed in Ho's
confirmation of the need for 'the absolute leadership of the Party over the
army' – we have already touched on the structure of the Party up to
1965 and we will return to this problem further on. The day this article
was published, *People's Daily* attacked the Soviet leaders and denounced
their appeal for unity and for setting aside differences as a manoeuvre
aimed at imposing a capitulationist line.[14] On 21 August a well-known
article written by Mao in 1938, *Strategic problems in the anti-Japanese
guerrilla war*, was reprinted. As usual there was a precise political reason
behind the decision to republish it. This is clear from the preface, which
denounces a certain deviation for undervaluing the importance of
partisan warfare in favour of regular warfare and underlines the crucial
importance of the idea of a people's war.[15]

At the beginning of September Lin Piao's well-known article *Long
live the victory of people's war* appeared.[16] Apart from a number of fundamental ideas that we will examine elsewhere, this article contains a
criticism of opportunist policies towards the united front, insists on the
role of the party, gives prominence to the contribution of the people to
the victory in the war against the Nazis and the anti-Japanese war,
refutes Krushchev's idea that nuclear weapons are necessary to achieve
victory and declares that no aggressor could ever hope to win a large-
scale ground war against China. On 3 September, on the occasion of the
twentieth anniversary of victory, Lo Jui-Ch'ing made a speech at Peking
in the presence of all the senior party leaders except for Mao and Lin
Piao. Lo quoted Lin Piao's article, repeatedly praised Mao's thought,
criticized the Soviets, said that China had won the war against Japan

[13] *PR*, no. 32, 1965.
[14] *HNA*, 1 August 1966, p. 10.
[15] *PR*, no. 35, 1966.
[16] Peking 1965.

'without any outside help' and in general did not touch again on any of the matters dealt with in his May article. However, he spoke of the socialist countries as a 'powerful camp' with a population that had grown from 200 million to over a thousand million and hinted at a *de facto* united front ('The present united front against American imperialism is much broader than that set up at the time of fascism'[17]). It is perhaps no accident that Lo, unlike Ch'en Yi at a later date, did not challenge the Soviet revisionists to 'come over land and sea', as he did the imperialists.[18] Everything once more suggested that an argument was going on behind the scenes.

This argument continued during the following weeks, while the Mao group stepped up its offensive. A week before Lin Piao's directive to the army reaffirming Mao's ideas, the *People's Daily* of 10 November published an all-out attack on the proposal for unity of action, representing it as a fraud aimed at covering up the policies of compromise promoted by Krushchev's successors and avoiding public controversy. The logic of the discussion propelled the authors of the article into a position where they were forced to take up a stand on the class nature of the Soviet Union. United action was impossible, they argued, because of the antagonism between the social systems of China and the USSR – an antagonism stemming from the restoration of capitalism after Stalin's death. Everything indicates that within the leadership the daggers were drawn.

The conference on political work in the army, convened by the general political department of the PLA, drew its conclusions. For three weeks or so, up to 18 January, it discussed instructions from the Central Committee and from Mao in the presence of several top party leaders, including the aged Chu Teh. Chou En-lai, Teng Hsiao-p'ing and P'eng Chen all spoke, but the main contribution came from Hsiao Hua, chairman of the department. There are no reports of the presence of Lo Jui-ch'ing, who might have already been ousted: his deputy, Yang Ch'eng-wu, attacked him forcefully. The official communiqué said, among other things: 'The general view taken at the conference was that the principle of keeping politics in the fore formulated by comrade Lin Piao complies with the consistent teachings of Chairman Mao Tse-tung; it was put forward in accordance with the historical experience of the Chinese people's armed forces and the present situation, in accordance with the laws of development and the economic basis of socialist society, and with the fact that classes and class struggle still exist in socialist society. This principle is the foundation on which to strengthen the revolutionization

[17] *PR*, no. 36, 1965.
[18] *PR*, no. 41, 1965.

or modernization of the army . . .'[19] Hsiao Hua expressed himself as plainly as possible when he said: 'Some people say military affairs are politics, military affairs and politics are of equal importance, and military affairs and politics should be given first place in turn. Such views are absolutely wrong, they are most harmful and run counter to what Chairman Mao has always taught. . . . Carry through the principle that military affairs must be run by the whole Party, and strengthen the Party's absolute leadership over the army. . . . The system of dual leadership by the military command and the local Party committees, under the unified leadership of the Party's central committee, must be resolutely enforced.'[20]

Hsiao Hua's 'some people' were later revealed to be P'eng Teh-huai and Lo Jui-ch'ing. This means that the debate that had broken out immediately after the Korean war was still raging, while the question of relations with the USSR – also from the angle of military needs – had been pushed into the forefront by the imperialist aggression in Asia. Lo Jui-ch'ing and his followers would have liked to have seen greater attention paid to technical needs and apparently stressed above all the crucial importance of nuclear weapons in the event of a general conflict, hence concluding that Soviet support was indispensable. They were later reproached for having said 'We can rely on the Soviet Union for long-range guided missiles', for having suggested purchasing arms in the West and for declaring that 'military training is the regular central task for our army in ordinary times'.[21] A particularly virulent attack was launched by Yang Ch'eng-wu, who accused Lo of promoting the study of Marx, Engels and Stalin in order to obstruct the study of Mao.[2]

The military conference had, therefore, notably strengthened the position of Mao and Lin Piao, guaranteeing them control of a valuable instrument. The Central Committee communicated Lo Jui-ch'ing's suspension to Party organizations in a circular dated 16 May, in which reference was made to a report by a work-team set up by the Central Committee itself. One symptom of the volatile situation within the army is the rumour that went round in July of an attempted military coup d'état in February. (Teng Hsiao-p'ing denied the rumour in a speech on 2 August, but Maoist publications speak of a sort of plot masterminded by Liu Shao-ch'i, Ho Lung, P'eng Chen, Lo Jui-ch'ing, Lu Ting-i and

[19] *HNA*, 19 January 1966, pp. 9–10.
[20] *HNA*, 25 January 1966, pp. 25ff.
[21] *HNA*, 29 August 1967, p. 6, and 31 August 1967, p. 7.
[22] *HNA*, 4 November 1967, pp. 6ff.

Yang Shang-k'un.[23]) Even now, however, despite the outcome of the military conference, the situation was not fully stabilized: differences of opinion arose once more in the army in the following months and years, particularly over the use of the armed forces during the most critical phases of the cultural revolution.

Apart from polemics of this sort, which often verged on quibbling, the problem as restated in 1965 and at the beginning of 1966 clearly transcended questions of military technique and involved orientations and perspectives of a political and a strategic nature. It was not so much a question of assessing in the abstract the efficacy of this or that weapon, as of foreseeing what form a possible conflict might take. The prospect of a limited war fought out by indigenous protagonists lent support to those who harked back to the experiences of the civil war, the military traditions of that era, the importance of partisan and people's warfare and the need for the army to carry out economic and political duties. However, if the prospect were one of conflict involving massive and direct imperialist intervention, then inevitably such an attachment to the past would be largely symbolic and propagandistic and China would be forced to confront the question of her relations with the USSR. It should be stressed that our arguments are based on the view that China and the Soviet Union are similar in having a non-capitalist social structure, and we know of no serious analysis produced by Mao or his followers to confute this view. This implies that there is an objective antagonism between imperialism on the one hand and both the Soviet Union and China on the other – though, of course, Soviet or Chinese leaders may seek to deny or minimize the fact. Indeed it would be a disaster for either power if the other was reconquered by capitalism and imperialism. In 1965, with Krushchev just recently replaced by a new leadership, the Soviet Union had been making cautious overtures to China. Labelling the Soviet Union a capitalist country at this time no doubt seemed a convenient way of accentuating the polemics against the new Soviet leaders. But in the long run such a characterization could not but have very far-reaching consequences, since it implied a wholly new relationship of forces in the world. Once the Soviet Union was labelled a 'social imperialist' as well as a 'capitalist' power, then the way would be open to regarding it as an enemy as dangerous as, or perhaps even more dangerous than, the United States itself. If such a conclusion was reached then even the conflict in Vietnam would take on a new significance and China would have to weigh up its policy towards the imperialist rivalry in Indo-China between the Soviet Union and the United States. Of course such ideological formulas should not be taken just at face value and they can be dropped with as little ceremony as they were first adopted (e.g. the Soviet leaders managed without any difficulty to resume relations with the Yugoslav Communists despite the fact that they had earlier been solemnly denounced as fascists after Stalin's break with Tito). At the same time it reminds us that, though to begin with on many issues the Chinese leadership were criticizing the Soviet Union from the left, this could still lead them in certain circumstances to 'rightist' conclusions. It is certainly the case that from 1965 onwards the Chinese position was very different in emphasis when compared with the early days of the Sino–Soviet dispute. Thus a typical issue of *Peking Review* in the early sixties would publish a strong attack on the Soviet concept of peaceful coexistence or the policies of the Italian Communist Party, but would also contain a challenge to the leaders of the Soviet Party to unite with China in the face of imperialist assault. Thus *Peking Review*, no. 29, 1963, carried a lead editorial from the *People's Daily* entitled 'We Want Unity, Not a Split' followed by a Commentary entitled 'No Meddling in Sino–Soviet Differences by US Imperialism'. After 1965 there were many fewer political critiques of Soviet policy and after a while they were to be entirely displaced by abusive attacks on the 'new Tsars' in the Kremlin and other fanciful substitutes for scientific political analysis. At the same time there were no calls for any sort of unity with the Soviet Union and there were even reports that China was impeding the flow of Soviet supplies to Vietnam. It seems that no vehicle manned by Soviet personnel was permitted to cross Chinese territory, though after a while arrangements were devised for a clumsy trans-shipment process at the border. Justifying their actions the Chinese leadership declared: 'Having carefully observed the actions of the new leaders of the CPSU on the question of Vietnam over the past year, we can only reach the following conclusion: in calling so vehemently for "united action" on the Vietnam question and trying by every means to bring about a summit conference of the Soviet Union, Vietnam and China and an international meeting of the socialist countries and the fraternal Parties, the new leaders of the CPSU have no other purpose in mind than to deceive the world, to tie the fraternal countries to the chariot of Soviet–US collaboration for world domination, to use the question of Vietnam as an important counter in their bargaining with the United States, and to isolate and attack the Chinese Communist Party and all other fraternal Parties which uphold Marxism–Leninism.'[24]

There is little doubt that the new Soviet leaders were anything but principled defenders of the revolutionary struggle of the Vietnamese people. But that does not mean that they were not disturbed at the precedent established by US imperialism in launching a sustained bombing campaign against the territory of a 'socialist country'. At this time US imperialism showed every sign of imagining it could impose a military solution on Vietnam and was in no mood to do a deal with the Soviet Union. Ironically enough when the heroic resistance of the Vietnamese eventually forced US imperialism to seek a negotiated settlement of the Indo–Chinese question it was to be Peking as much as Moscow which was to 'use the question of Vietnam as an important counter in their bargaining with the United States'. Having rejected 'united action' with the Soviet Union at the beginning of the cultural revolution the Chinese leadership was to act in unison with the Soviet leaders in 1972 by the time the cultural revolution had run its course – but this was to be the unity of opportunism, not that of solidarity.

Even if the Chinese description of the USSR were correct, it is difficult to see how the Soviet leaders could permit imperialism to unleash a war of destruction against China, for an American victory would decisively alter the world balance of power and pose a serious threat to the Soviet Union from an American-dominated Asia.

As for the political and social aspects of the military dispute, in so far as distinctions of this nature are possible in the case of China, there were clearly conflicts between the more strictly political bureaucracy and large groups of the military bureaucracy. Apart from their common background, the army bureaucrats have particular interests and aims and are inevitably inclined to think how they can best defend these interests and carry out their duties, while enjoying some independence and autonomy.

The military debate was important, therefore, for a whole number of reasons, and when we consider its various aspects it is at once clear why it flared up again and again during these fifteen years.

The 'cultural' controversy

The military controversy, because of the very form in which it was conducted, had already drawn to an end by January 1966 without attracting too much attention. The 'cultural' debate was an entirely different affair. Its direct political implications were transparent from the very

[24] 'Refutation of the New Leaders of the CPSU on "United Action"', by the Editorial Departments of *People's Daily* and *Red Flag*, Peking 1965, pp. 21–22.

first; it lurched noisily from one episode to another and was a prime detonator of the cultural revolution.

The roots of the controversy stretch back to the launching of the socialist education movement in 1963 and some of Mao's utterances on cultural problems made the following year. The Maoists claim that some people in the leadership tried to confine Mao's attempt at rectification within certain limits and used propaganda and organizational tricks to back up their manoeuvres. It is clear that after mid-1965, when the 'Group of Five in charge of the cultural revolution' appointed by the Central Committee was already at work, different groups were moving in directions which appeared parallel but were in reality opposed, even if not yet explicitly so. In July, for example, Hsiao Wang-tung, head of the Ministry of Culture, made a report to the Group of Five which was approved by the majority and repudiated by K'ang Sheng – the only member of the Group to retain his positions until the end of the cultural revolution. In August the same Hsiao Wang-tung convened a conference for political work and prolonged the closing session so that there would be room for contributions from P'eng Chen and Lu Ting-i in the final report. In September, at the same time as a Central Committee working conference, a national conference of cultural bureau heads took place, once again under the auspices of Hsiao Wang-tung and after consultation with Liu Shao-ch'i.[25]

It was at this working conference that Mao asked for Wu Han's play *Hai Jui Dismissed from Office* to be condemned for its political content. (This play, on the surface, was a tribute to a functionary of the Ming dynasty – he lived from 1515–57 – who showed exemplary intransigence in his opposition to oppression and did not fear to criticize the emperor himself. In reality, it was a scarcely veiled allusion to the criticisms of the Great Leap Forward made by P'eng Teh-huai and to his subsequent disgrace.) P'eng Chen's reaction, according to the Maoists, was not to oppose Mao's call openly but to blunt the attack by concentrating on the academic aspects of Wu Han's play.

The cultural controversy was nothing new. It had been going on almost non-stop in previous years and had been given widespread coverage in the press. We need only think of the discussion around the idea of 'one divides into two' upheld by supporters of the official line and the idea of 'two combine into one' upheld by the philosopher Yang Hsien-chen's group; the debates on the transformation of traditional opera and the

[25] *HNA*, 4 September 1967, pp. 5–6, and *CB*, no. 842, pp. 28 and 30, which contains a *Bulletin of the Cultural Revolution* with a chronology for the period 1961–65.

literary debates on 'middle characters'.[26] The form these debates took was often thoroughly academic, but the political meanings which Mao's supporters in particular wanted to attach to them gradually became clear. By September 1965 these political aspects were given even greater prominence: after all, why was there so much fuss about a work published four years earlier if the question was purely a literary and academic one?

Later developments, however, made it clear why Mao had decided to go into battle on what appeared to be such a minor matter. It was not only because he considered that the principles upheld by Wu Han and his group were counterposed to his own or because he feared that certain new ideological standpoints would prove to be the Trojan horse of capitalism: it was above all because he wanted to prevent a political trend from taking definite shape and growing in strength under cover of a cultural debate. Wu Han, remember, was P'eng Chen's second-in-command.

After the September meetings the struggle continued along factional lines, bypassing the bodies which in theory should have taken the decisions. Whether because he found the Group of Five reluctant to tackle the problem boldly or because it had taken a decision of which he did not approve, Mao now suggested the move which was later to be seen as the official opening of hostilities in the cultural revolution. On 10 November Yao Wen-yuan's now famous article attacking Wu Han was published in Shanghai. Publication was decided upon by the Shanghai Party Committee; the content of the article was inspired by Mao himself and by Chiang Ch'ing, his wife.[27] According to reports, P'eng Chen protested against the decision of the Shanghai Committee and delayed publishing the article in Peking until 30 November, even then relegating it to a literary corner.[28] The controversy was carried on for several months in newspapers all over China, some articles supporting Wu Han and others opposing him. People like Teng T'o wrote under pseudonyms and Wu Han entered the fray with a partial self-criticism. The main point of controversy was whether to look at Wu Han's play from the point of view of its historical and literary value or for its political implications, as an attempt to defend and rehabilitate certain Party leaders now removed from power. The number of articles favourable to Wu Han and the attempts to keep the debate on academic lines eventually convinced Mao that his line was being challenged: hence his second

[26] *Kuangming jihpao*, 29 May 1964; *PR*, no. 38, 1964.
[27] *HNA*, 4 July 1966, p. 6.
[28] *HNA*, 21 April 1967, p. 10.

intervention on 21 December, made public only later, in which he insisted that the play was political and that an analogy was intended between Hai Jui and P'eng Teh-huai.[29]

In February, after the military conference, the tensions and conflicts within the leadership gave rise to a sensational clash. While P'eng Chen was actually drawing up the document of the Group of Five, Mao and Lin convened a kind of forum at Shanghai which was led by Chiang Ch'ing and was to deal with work in literature and art in the armed forces[30] (2–20 February). P'eng's document and the transcript of the forum, which were circulated at various levels in the Party, expressed two quite distinct positions (at least in so far as P'eng Chen's text can be judged on the basis of quotes furnished by his opponents). P'eng's document – drawn up 'behind the backs of K'ang Sheng . . . and other comrades' according to the Central Committee's Circular of 16 May 1966[31] – put·the accent on the academic value of the debate and on the need to examine the questions on their merits and for their intrinsic meaning, to avoid despotic methods typical of bourgeois technicians and scientists and to follow the axiom 'without construction there can be no real and thorough destruction'. The forum report, on the other hand, anticipating the Central Committee circular of 16 May, spotlighted in a rather crude fashion the class significance even of cultural disputes, drew up a negative balance sheet of cultural developments during the sixteen years of people's power, criticized even Stalin for his 'liberal' attitude towards classical Russian literature and Soviet literature in general, inveighed against the literature and art of the thirties and affirmed the need to select revolutionary themes.[32] Lin Piao sent the minutes of this forum to members of the Standing Committee of the Military Affairs Commission after Mao had personally checked through them three times.[33] P'eng's document, by contrast, was sent to Party organizations, which began to put it into practice as early as 12 February. At the end of the Shanghai forum Lin Piao in effect entrusted Chiang Ch'ing with responsibility for controlling cultural work in the army, thus confirming the view that opposed tendencies were by that time openly manoeuvring

[29] *HNA*, 30 May 1967, p. 8.
[30] Published as *Summary of the Forum on the Work in Literature and Art in the Armed Forces with which Comrade Lin Piao entrusted Comrade Chiang Ch'ing*, Peking 1968.
[31] Printed in Joan Robinson, *The Cultural Revolution in China*, Penguin 1970, pp. 70–80; *PR*, no. 21, 1967, pp. 6–9.
[32] *HNA*, 30 May 1967, passim.
[33] *PR*, no. 23, 1967, p. 9.

for positions. There is also evidence in the Circular of 16 May that Mao was losing confidence in normal Party channels ('most Party committees concerned have a very poor understanding of the task of leadership in this great struggle and their leadership is far from conscientious and effective').[34]

Counterposing these two documents, which each reflected a distinct position in the conflict, inevitably hastened a more direct clash. The various factions set about defending themselves. Mao managed to get the Central Committee first to condemn the Group of Five's document and appoint a new group to run the cultural revolution, and later to dismiss the entire Peking group – the dismissal was made public on 3 June. Lin Piao and the army played a leading role in the affair, and this was reflected in the stand taken by the army press. On 7 May Mao himself had sent an instruction to the army calling on it to participate actively in the cultural revolution.[35] On 8 May the *Liberation Army Daily* published Kao Chu's article *Open Fire against the Anti-Party Anti-Socialist Black Line*,[36] which was afterwards acclaimed as a milestone in the cultural revolution. On 18 April the PLA's newspaper had developed the themes contained in the transcript of the February forum.

What, then, were the criticisms levelled during this phase at the Peking group and its allies and expressed in various polemical articles between May and July?

The principal targets for the time being were not P'eng Chen or Lu Ting-i, who were only later attacked publicly, but Wu Han, Teng T'o and Liao Mo-sha, the so-called 'revisionist trio', as well as other members of the editorial staff of the *Peking Daily*, the *Peking Evening News* and the magazine *Frontline*. They were accused among other things of making insincere and inadequate self-criticisms of their past activities and backing Wu Han in the debate of some months earlier (this accusation was mainly directed at Fan Chin, a woman member of the editorial staff of the first two above-mentioned newspapers who was dismissed along with the others). According to Mao's and Lin Piao's supporters the class struggle was still going on in China and their opponents were, in the last analysis, the expression of a tendency whose aim was the restoration of capitalism. These enemies of the workers and peasants, who were willing to support anyone – even counterrevolutionaries – if they opposed Mao, had transformed their citadels (e.g. Peking or Nanking

[34] Joan Robinson, op. cit., p. 77.
[35] *HNA*, 4 September 1967, pp. 6–7; *HNA*, 8 May 1967, p. 6.
[36] Translated in *Communist China*, Penguin 1968, pp. 603–606.

University) into actual bourgeois dictatorships directed against the proletariat.

On the organizational level they were accused of adopting factionalist methods, resisting the application of the party line and exploiting important resources, among which the control of newspapers, magazines, publishing houses and even the great majority of literary and artistic organizations (one particularly effective instrument for exerting a wide influence was the unscrupulous use of special columns in certain newspapers). They were also accused of acting in accordance with an overall plan. Their tactics were said to be flexible, and they were not afraid to carry out clandestine operations under cover of formal professions of loyalty to Mao's thought; they were preparing a 'time-bomb'. The most frequent accusation was that they had tried to present in a favourable light, with artful analogies taken from history, the idea of an opposition party and had aimed at setting up alternative leading groups (and Petöfi Clubs).

On the cultural level, the 'revisionists' were said to have criticized the crude and simplistic imposition of the study of Mao's thought and to have favoured a more flexible line, a more liberal interpretation of the hundred flowers policy, 'equality before the truth', a more detached and 'academic' attitude to certain problems, a literature based on a less narrow interpretation of realism, the adoption of Soviet-style teaching methods, a relaxation of party control and more autonomy for intellectuals. They were said to have criticized those who lost all sight of any objective criteria and automatically appealed to censorship and to have upheld certain 'historicist' ideas, counterposing 'historical facts' to the 'revolution in the science of history' inaugurated by the Party in 1958. Among the targets of this wave of criticism was the well-known historian Chien Po-tsan.[37]

They are said to have expressed views on problems of an economic nature, criticizing both the Great Leap and the People's Communes, the forced pace and the irrational use of manpower; favouring a 'smooth development', a drive towards individual economy and material incentives; adopting the ideas of the economist Sun Yeh-fang, who called for the application of the law of value to the economy and propounded Libermanist ideas; criticizing the policy of self-reliance; and coming out in favour of collaboration with the USSR, from which China, as they saw it, had much to learn.

[37] See *Red Flag*, no. 15, 1966, in *SCMM*, no. 556, pp. 1ff., and *HNA*, 10, 11 and 13 February 1967.

Finally, they were said to have accused the leadership of incompetence; to have promoted the idea of a 'democracy for capitalists'; to have exalted the 'royal road' as against the 'tyrant's road'; to have criticized the cult of Mao; to have taken up a whole range of Krushchevite ideas; to have used revisionist terminology, such as 'rehabilitation'; and to have even gone so far as to prophesy a 'thaw' for China (the expression 'thaw' was used by Teng T'o in an article of 4 February 1962, but omitted from a collection of articles published later).[38]

At this stage we will not discuss the real positions of the groups and individuals who were criticized. The official 'reconstruction', however, clearly reveals many of the main themes upon which Mao and Lin Piao based their subsequent attacks. The cultural 'revisionists' could be represented as a threat to the ideological monopoly exercised by the leading group: they and their powerful protector, P'eng Chen, were thus the most vulnerable element in the bloc which had frustrated Mao since the late fifties.

Significant standpoints

In April, when the crisis was already in full swing, two conferences were called, one on work in industry and transport, the other on political work in the departments of industry and in transport. They were organized jointly by the State Economic Commission and the competent department of the Central Committee and heralded in the *People's Daily* with the sonorous title 'Run enterprises in line with Mao Tse-tung's thinking'.[39] After stressing the need firmly to take up a prole-tarian class-standpoint, the report speaks of the need for the three-sided cooperation of managers, technicians and the masses and draws the following conclusion: 'To run enterprises in line with Mao Tse-tung's thinking, it is necessary to ensure absolute leadership by the Communist Party. . . . Ensuring absolute leadership by the Party over the enterprise calls for unified leadership by the Party. That is to say, on the one hand, all the tasks from the higher administrative, technical and other organiza-tions should, without exception, be under the unified control of the Party Committee of the enterprise and be carried out according to actual conditions in the enterprise. On the other hand, all work in various spheres, such as that of the enterprise's Communist Youth League branch, trade union branch, women's association branch, and the

---

[38] For the various positions criticized, see *HNA*, 2, 3, 4, 5, 6, 7, 12 and 17 June 1966 and 4, 19 and 21 July 1966.
[39] *HNA*, 4 April 1966.

militia, should be done under the unified leadership of the Party Committee of the enterprise.' Similar ideas were taken up in a *Liberation
Army Daily* editorial, which exalts the experience of one industry in the
military sector where the principles propounded by Lin Piao and the
Central Committee were put into practice: 'Some people say that the
job of factories is production and that they should turn out products.
Their foremost task should be the turning out of products. . . . Our
factories must persist in the socialist direction, take the socialist road
and serve socialist construction and the broad masses of the working
people. How are they different from capitalist factories if their sole
purpose is to turn out products?'[40]

The offensive launched under the slogan 'Politics in command' – a
slogan which constantly recurs, like a sort of *leitmotiv*, throughout the
cultural revolution – was generally aimed at those who over-emphasized
the importance of the work of specialists: 'Some of our comrades who
have come under the influence of bourgeois thinking have consciously or
unconsciously developed the tendency to pay attention to technical
matters only. They immerse themselves in their job and pay scant attention to politics, and so lose sight of the correct direction for their work. . . .
If, on the question of building socialism, [a socialist country] considers
that "cadres decide everything" or "technique decides everything", then
in practice the tendency will arise to get immersed in the job while
neglecting politics, and there will grow up the style of work of commandism and isolation from the masses, and, as a result, bourgeois
elements and political degenerates will find their way into various branches
of work in the guise of "specialists" and "scholars" and will seize the
leadership in some places and some institutions.'[41] The primacy of
politics, the absolute leadership of the Party, and Mao's thought were
also the main topics of an enlarged meeting of the Party Committee of
the Academy of Sciences in May. This meeting warned particularly
against the use of material incentives to weaken the revolutionary morale
of the masses and the tendency of people with specialized knowledge to
adopt the manners of an aristocratic élite.[42]

Throughout this whole period there were no signs of an abatement in
the bitter quarrel with the Soviet Union. On 24 March *Red Flag* carried
an article commemorating the anniversary of the Paris Commune which
listed the main positions from which the Chinese assailed Krushchevite

[40] *HNA*, 23 June 1966, p. 2.
[41] *HNA*, 15 April 1966, pp. 4–6.
[42] *HNA*, 3 June 1966, p. 4.

'revisionism'. These were: the need for the revolutionary conquest of power and the violent smashing of the bourgeois state machine; the idea of the Commune as a new-style organ of power in which legislative and executive functions were combined; and the democratic and egalitarian value of this historical experience.

Thus the recurring themes of the cultural revolution were almost all stated during the very early stages of the crisis. The same can be said of the difficulties and obstacles that Mao came up against at the various levels of the Party as he fought for his policies. These difficulties were simply a reflection of the deep-seated differences of opinion that existed at the top, even though it is possible – even probable – that the alignments had not yet acquired a fixed form. Mao almost certainly had a majority in the Standing Committee of the Politbureau for the dismissal of P'eng Chen and, given the make-up of this Committee, the motion to dismiss P'eng could hardly have been carried if Liu Shao-ch'i and Teng Hsiao-p'ing had opposed it.

Up to the fall of the Peking group at the beginning of June, Mao did not resort to any mobilization of the masses. His tactic, as we have seen, was to give his backing to moves which were only just within the norms of Party organization and leadership and to continue to manoeuvre on the level of the Party apparatus, setting the Shanghai Committee against the Peking Committee and the PLA apparatus against P'eng's Group of Five. The next stage, however, was to witness the first change in course: the students at the universities began to mobilize.

The struggles in the universities: a tormented interlude

The objective Mao and Lin Piao seemed to set themselves in the tormented and yet decisive interlude between P'eng Chen's dismissal and the calling of the Plenary Session of the Central Committee at the beginning of August was the launching of an all-out offensive against the groups of intellectuals which they saw as posing a major political threat. It is above all from this point on that the theme of the cultural revolution (only glimpsed in fleeting outline up to now) came more and more into the open.

The first targets for attack were the academic circles in the universities, which were accused both of perpetuating the conservative traditions of the past and spreading ideas similar to those of the Krushchevite revisionists. Mao intended to make the most of his victory over the Peking group and to eradicate all traces of its influence. He started his campaign with the universities in the capital, which for obvious reasons were of key importance.[43] At the same time, in tones reminiscent of earlier campaigns, he launched an offensive against the system of higher education as a whole. This move was bound to be welcomed by the student body, or at least broad sections of it. The students were quite aware of the unjust social selection that governed entrance to higher education. What is more, they probably disliked the cramming, the authoritarian teaching methods and the system of entrance examinations – all factors which played a large part in sparking off the world-wide student revolt. One important measure taken by the Central Committee and the State Council on 13 June[44] was the abolition of the system of entrance to higher education by examination. The new system, which was still not properly defined, was to combine 'recommendation and selection' so as to ensure that proletarian politics were kept to the fore and the mass line was applied. At the same time it was decided to postpone admissions for the new year by six months. Various articles[45] criticized the system in force as an instrument for defending the old ruling classes, while many people asked for a shortening of the course of studies (this may have been because of the shortage of specialized cadres in certain sectors). We should also bear in mind that one of the chief criticisms levelled at the old system was that it did not allow enough time for politics and above all for studying the thought of Mao (which in the opinion of the critics should be compulsory). One illustration of such criticisms was the case of the students of a school in the capital city of Hunan province, who denounced their teachers for not setting aside more than ten days a month for the campaign in course. (Chou En-lai seemed to have been inspired by totally different principles in 1956, when he demanded that intellectuals devote at least five-sixths of their working week – i.e. forty hours – to their work.)

Issues such as these were used to mobilize the students, to a limited extent at first, especially in some of the larger university centres. There are indications that this mobilization took place against a background of already-existing tension, albeit sporadic and uneven, among Chinese students as a whole. For example, Peking University had experienced conflicts as early as October 1964, during the socialist education movement, and Victor Nee claims that tense relations between young leftists and university bureaucrats 'persisted throughout the period between the

---

[43] See 'Sweep out all monsters and ghosts', *People's Daily*, 1 June 1966, and the front-page editorial of 3 June attacking 'bourgeois authorities in the field of historical studies'.

[44] Commented upon extensively in the *People's Daily*, 18 June 1966.

[45] E.g. *HNA*, 20 June 1966, passim; 14 June 1966, passim.

Great Leap and the Cultural Revolution'.[46] In 1965 groups of students who had criticized the administration of Lu P'ing, president of the university, were 'recklessly' attacked and discredited and forced to take part in a 'rectification' session held at Peking's International Hotel, where they are said to have stayed for no less than seven months.[47] On 25 May there appeared the first *tatzupao* or big character poster, which openly and violently criticized Lu P'ing and P'eng P'ei-yun, vice-secretary of the Peking University Party Committee, for their failure to respond to the political campaign going on in the country and for taking the wrong line in the controversy over Wu Han's play. The document was signed by seven 'philosophy instructors',[48] foremost among whom was Nieh Yuan-tzu, a forty-five year old lecturer who had been secretary of her department's Party Committee in 1961–62 and a member of the International Hotel group in 1965.[49] The authors of the *tatzupao* were clearly aware of the 16 May Circular of the Central Committee – Nieh says in her interview that it was the Circular that encouraged them to draw up their list of criticisms. The Communist youth organization at once sprang to the president's defence and heated discussions broke out among the students. The issue was then settled for the time being by the sensational intervention of Mao himself, who not only defended Nieh Yuan-tzu's *tatzupao* but even had its contents broadcast and subsequently published in the press. (It seems from K'ang Sheng's speech[50] of 28 July that the Central Committee approved of the stand Mao had taken.) Nieh and her group had given the signal for a general 'uprising' throughout China's universities. As the ferment among the students grew, the press began to talk more and more of the need to trust in the masses and for the masses themselves to intervene. The aim of the movement, however, still appeared to be no more than to eliminate certain political groups on the staffs of the universities and to reorganize the system of studying. It seems, however, that even those in charge of the cultural revolution had no clear ideas on this question.

Lu P'ing and P'eng P'ei-yun were finally dismissed from their posts in the small hours of 3 June, as part of the general collapse of the Peking group. On 15 June the collapse spread to the local leaders of the youth organization. Lu P'ing was accused of having abandoned the methods of

[46] Op. cit., p. 41.
[47] *HNA*, 6 June 1966, p. 7; *SCMP*, no. 3960, p. 2; Nee, op. cit., pp. 42–43.
[48] Ibid., p. 54.
[49] Text and signatures are in *PR*, no. 37, 1966. *SCMP*, no. 3960, p. 2, contains the translation of an interview with Nieh Yuan-tzu.
[50] *CB*, no. 819, p. 1.

the 'revolution in education' after 1961, favouring instead experiments with new systems of education; of cutting down on the amount of time given over to manual work and political activity; and of saying that China should learn from the USSR.[51] It is clear from speeches made by Chiang Ch'ing, Ch'en Po-ta, K'ang Sheng and T'ao Chu in July and early August[52] that there was a great deal of uncertainty and confusion about the situation in the universities and what solutions to propose.

Although the veiled struggle of the last few months was by no means over, decisions during this phase were as a rule taken through the normal channels, which means that compromise agreements were probably reached (the disagreements that broke out during the latter half of July and the conflict at the August Plenum may well have been brought on partly by differing interpretations of agreements of this kind). The group around Mao constantly reaffirmed that the power of decision rested with the Party's top bodies and that the leadership of the cultural revolution was in the hands of the Party. The result was to reassure those who were wavering and encourage those in the leadership who had little enthusiasm for the campaign to join in, galvanize the Party machine and in some cases even press for criticisms and extreme measures; the guarantee was supposed to lie in the fact that it was still the Party leadership that was managing the operation.[53] (Even in late July K'ang Sheng was using the same tactic to justify the withdrawal of the work teams.)

A few restrictions were in fact brought into force, and an attempt was made to tone down the attacks on organizations singled out for criticism.[54] Other such measures specified that in certain cases individuals should not be criticized without the approval of the Central Committee. (Although this rule was included in the August documents, there are reports[55] that it was formulated as early as March 1965 in accordance with the wishes of Liu Shao-ch'i and Teng Hsiao-p'ing.) The principal method adopted, however, was for senior party bodies at various levels to send out work teams – often led by very important figures – to take control of more difficult situations. Work teams were dispatched not only to the universities, but also to ministries, institutes and departments of various kinds, including for example the Ministry of Culture, where

[51] See the interview with Chen Pi-lan, who joined the Party in 1922 and was later expelled for Trotskyism, in *World Outlook*, 14 July 1967.

[52] *CB*, no. 830.

[53] See the *People's Daily* editorial, 24 June 1966, for the leadership role of the party.

[54] See e.g. T'ao Chu's 1 July speech printed in *CB*, no. 830, p. 1.

[55] See *CB*, no. 842, p. 26.

they are said to have been wrongly used by Hsiao Wang-tung, one of T'ao Chu's collaborators.[56]

The work teams were nothing new, of course. They were widely used during the socialist education movement and the 'Four Clean-Ups' in 1964 (one team was even sent to Peking University) and as late as 25 January 1967 the Central Committee still thought it had been right to send them in, even if they had made mistakes.[57] There is considerable argument, however – the importance of which there is no need to underline – about who decided to send them in this time.

At the same time as the Peking group was toppled the new Municipal Committee announced that it had decided to send a work team, headed by Chang Ch'eng-hsien, to take the 'leadership over the great proletarian revolution in Peking University'.[58] There is no doubt, therefore, of its formal competence, and it is probable that the Central Committee itself either took or approved of the actual decision – it is hardly likely that the Municipal Committee, which had only just been appointed, would dare to step out of line with the instructions of the Central Committee, or that the latter would allow a decision that it opposed to be announced in a joint communiqué. Teng Hsiao-p'ing confirmed in a speech of 2 August that the work team had been sent 'by the new Municipal Committee of Peking according to the instruction of the Central Committee', adding significantly, however, that the responsibility 'must be borne principally by us comrades of the Central Committee in Peking'. This would appear to suggest that voting on the measure was disputed and that Central Committee members resident in Peking had tipped the balance. (The Central Committee often took decisions without convening a pleanry session, and even though this practice was acceptable under normal conditions it naturally called forth protests during a period of crisis.) Chiang Ch'ing gave her version of what had happened in a speech of 28 November 1966, when the attacks had already started up against Liu and Teng: 'She touched on the question of sending cultural revolution work teams to various organizations and said this was an error in the great proletarian cultural revolution, and what these work teams had done in the course of their work was still more erroneous. . . . On the other hand some work teams followed correct principles and policy and did not make mistakes. . . . As early as June this year our Chairman Mao made the point that work teams should not

[56] *HNA*, 5 September 1967, pp. 6–7.
[57] See *CB*, no. 852, p. 52.
[58] *HNA*, 8 June 1966.

be sent out hastily, but a few comrades sent out work teams hastily without asking Chairman Mao's permission.'[59] A third version came from K'ang Sheng, who in a speech on 25 July 1966 said that it was untrue that the work teams were sent out by the Central Committee or by Mao.[60] K'ang also said that many work teams had been sent out in great haste and confusion, without proper instructions and in response to requests from schools whose Party Committees had been smashed.[61] At a later stage in the cultural revolution the blame for the work teams came to be apportioned directly to Liu Shao-ch'i and Teng Hsiao-p'ing. (Remember that Mao absented himself from the capital throughout most of the 'Fifty Days of white terror', as the period of the work teams came to be called, and that in theory control of affairs therefore fell to Liu, chairman of the government, and Teng, general secretary to the Central Committee. There were even rumours that Mao forced the convening of the subsequent August Plenum by drawing up units of the army around Peking.[62]) The criticism levelled at Liu and Teng was that the work teams under their influence had carried out wholesale and over-hasty purges of cadres. Naturally these charges encouraged the distortion and bias which have tended to cloud the circumstances under which the original decision was taken, and it is even more difficult to sort out the truth because most of the criticisms brought against the work teams were made during the bitter polemics of 1967.[63] It is possible – if we do not reject Chiang Ch'ing's version of the facts as simply an attempt to set up an alibi after the event – that Mao wanted to proceed more cautiously in order to avoid a clash with the students; but he was by no means opposed in principle to the work groups or to the idea of the Party apparatus intervening in this way. These had been established at a time when Mao's group were supporting Liu against the cultural revisionists; they began to be disavowed as the work teams ran into difficulties which could be turned against Liu himself.

Things did not go according to plan for the sponsors of the work teams, who wanted a 'controlled' campaign. The campaign came up against resistance from two diametrically opposed quarters. On the one hand some academic authorities were against it, declaring that there was no need for it in their institutes, hindering every move from below, stopping

[59] *HNA*, 4 December 1966.
[60] *CB*, no. 830, p. 5.
[61] Ibid.
[62] See Neale Hunter, *Shanghai Journal*, New York 1969, p. 64.
[63] E.g. *HNA*, 21 April 1967, p. 11; 3 July 1967, p. 5; 22 July 1967, p. 8.

students putting up *tatzupao* and even resorting to repression. The events at Nanking University are one of the clearest examples of this sort of attitude. Nanking's Vice-Chancellor K'uang Ya-ming, who was dismissed during June, opposed the wall-newspapers put up by his students, described their authors as 'reactionaries' and took repressive measures against more than sixty students and some lecturers and workers, including various members of the Party and youth organization.[64] One traveller reportedly found a similar attitude in the capital of Inner Mongolia, where the University's Vice-Chancellor declared in early June that there were no revisionists in his institute and that therefore the campaign was unnecessary.[65]

On the other hand, the work teams often clashed headlong with groups of students who were interested in seriously mobilizing and who disliked the actions and the authoritarianism of the work teams' members. Peking University and Tsinghua University were typical in this respect.

The events at Tsinghua University were subsequently to become notorious mainly because the work team was led by Liu Shao-ch'i's wife, Wang Kuang-mei. Wang's team is said to have adopted the method of 'hitting at a great many in order to protect a handful' between 9 and 23 June and later until 15 July, singling out for attack the student K'uai Ta-fu who was accused of opposing the established line and was even arrested at one point. The struggle continued until the beginning of August, when the work team withdrew. Chou En-lai himself reportedly intervened to have K'uai Ta-fu released.[66] According to Wang Kuang-mei's own version 'K'uai Ta-fu himself asked that his freedom be restricted in order to ensure his personal safety'.[67] She added that although errors may have been committed the work team did not take the line of 'suspecting everything'; the same held for Liu Shao-ch'i, who she said would never have 'branded' K'uai Ta-fu as a counterrevolutionary. However, there are many indications that the situation on Tsinghua campus became extremely tense: K'uai himself went on hunger strike, a young lecturer committed suicide and one student wounded himself in a suicide attempt.[68]

The Peking University work team also found itself in serious difficulty. K'ang Sheng reported that the team's leader angered the students by

[64] *HNA*, 17 June 1966, p. 28, and 5 April 1967, p. 3.

[65] Quoted in G. Blumer, *La rivoluzione culturale cinese*, Milan 1969 (*Die chinesische Kulturrevolution*), who unfortunately omits precise references.

[66] *PR*, no. 15, 1967.

[67] *CB*, no. 848, p. 13.

[68] See Wang's 'trial' in *CB*, no. 848.

speaking for four hours on end in an attempt to overwhelm them.[69] A serious incident took place on 18 June, when some students dragged a party leader out of bed to 'struggle' against him and were branded as hooligans and counterrevolutionaries by the work team (this incident was frequently referred to in the speeches at Peking University quoted above: one symptom of the confusion was Chiang Ch'ing's confession that she had at first shared the work team's view of the incident of 18 June).[70] On 12 July, however, events took a new turn: five students in the geophysics department signed and put up the first *tatzupao* attacking the work team.[71]

At the same time, the rather vague way in which even the chief protagonists of the cultural revolution stated their objectives, the violent disputes, the increasingly frequent proclamations of radical democracy and the calls for mobilization combined to produce a climate in which different groups clashed and conflicts of various kinds became more acute. The situation in the party leadership was also very confused. Teng Hsiao-p'ing, referring to what was going on at Peking University, said that 'we of the Central Committee can do nothing'.[72]

All this could not help but swell the ranks of the waverers who, judging from the number of words spent on attacking them, must have been fairly numerous. Waverers were particularly accused in the press of fearing the masses.[73] K'ang Sheng said in his speech at Peking University that some *tatzupao* openly voiced the fear of chaos.[74] The situation also had repercussions in the leadership itself, which became even more deeply divided. However, after various interventions by the leaders of the Peking University institutes and in advance of the August Plenum, the work teams were withdrawn and suppressed. The group in charge of the cultural revolution had already decided to dissolve them on 26 July,[75] and the Central Committee shortly afterwards gave instructions to this effect (the Peking Municipal Committee took its decision on 28 July, but on the same day K'ang Sheng said in a speech[76] that the decision was so far limited to only three institutes). At the same time as the work teams were being withdrawn renewed appeals were made to the students

[69] *CB*, no. 830, p. 5.
[70] Ibid., p. 9.
[71] *HNA*, 3 June 1967, p. 5.
[72] *CB*, no. 819, p. 5.
[73] See e.g. *HNA*, 21 July 1966, p. 28; 25 June 1966, p. 4; July 1966, pp. 8 and 9.
[74] *CB*, no. 819, p. 2.
[75] See Ch'en Po-ta's speech published in *CB*, no. 830, p. 5.
[76] *CB*, no. 819, p. 1.

to elect committees and hold democratic debates which respected the opinions and rights of the minorities. T'ao Chu, for instance, took his solicitude for the minority so far that in a speech at Peking University he even suggested that minority speakers should be given a round of encouraging applause.

This was the situation on the eve of the August Plenum of the Central Committee. While the split in the top leadership and the apparatus was widening, student pressure was mounting. It is still difficult to say exactly what happened during the last ten days of July. Many different versions were put about and as we mentioned above there were even rumours that Lin Piao intervened with the army to back up Mao.[77] (Blumer suggests that the PLA intervened directly as early as 1 June, when Mao allegedly had the editorial offices of the *People's Daily*, the radio station and the most important printing works put under the control of a small detachment not subject to the Peking garrison.[78]) Official sources repeatedly claimed that Mao's return to Peking came at a 'crucial moment'[79] and accused Liu Shao-ch'i of having profited from Mao's absence during the first days of the cultural revolution.[80] Many sources speak of various manoeuvres to convene Politbureau and Central Committee meetings and of a request from Mao, who was out of the capital, to postpone these meetings, but there are no concrete or verifiable references to back up these reports. There is no doubt, however, that the struggle was fought with no holds barred and that the Plenum was to be a first settling of accounts.

In July, before any of the top party leaders had been openly criticized, the attack on Chou Yang was noticeably stepped up. Chou had been a militant writer and critic since the thirties. He was the first vice-president of the Writers' Association, Minister of Culture between 1949 and 1954, a delegate to the National Congress since 1964, an alternate member of the Central Committee since the 1956 Congress and vice-director of the Department of Culture and Propaganda. For many years he was considered one of Mao's most loyal supporters. He could always be relied upon to discover real or imaginary deviations among the intellectuals and he was one of the most powerful men in his field.

He was now accused of being one of the chief exponents – even *the* chief exponent – of the bourgeois line in art and literature since the

---

[77] A version particularly favoured by Yugoslav correspondents.
[78] Op. cit., p. 189.
[79] *HNA*, 21 April 1967, p. 11, and 3 June 1967, p. 5.
[80] *HNA*, 22 February 1968, p. 7.

thirties, of treading the same path as Wang Ming, who was denounced alternately as a right-wing capitulationist and a left-wing opportunist, and of having refused for twenty-four years to apply the line laid down by Mao in his Yenan talks. Among the more recent charges were that he had falsely interpreted the hundred flowers campaign as a liberalizing measure, denied the fact that art has a political content, supported the idea that destruction is relatively easier than construction and opposed the idea that the Party must lead in the cultural field. He is also said to have criticized the exaggerated praise of Mao, not to have taken a definite stand in the controversy over Wu Han's play[81] and to have claimed special payments for writers and artists over and above their regular pay.[82] Some of the charges brought against Chou were similar to those brought against P'eng·Chen – he was accused, for instance, of saying that 'everyone is equal before the truth'.[83]

The fall of Chou Yang was an eloquent episode. Mao and his allies had decided to carry through an all-out attack against the cultural groups who had taken critical stands on crucial political issues and above all had failed to commit themselves in the sense indicated by the clashes of 1964–65. The re-publication of Mao's article of 1942 was a clear sign of the path ahead: China was witnessing an attempt to demonstrate the unerring continuity and total infallibility of a master-line which transcended the countless twists and turns in the long history of the Party.

[81] See the chronology in *CB*, no. 842, passim.

[82] *HNA*, 21 July 1966, p. 5.

[83] For the attacks on Chou Yang see in particular *HNA*, 2, 6, 7, 19, 20, 21 and 30 July 1966.

7

Conflicts at the Top and the Red Guards Movement

The August Plenum of the Central Committee

In the period preceding the August Plenum the leadership came up against serious obstacles and provoked dangerous conflicts in its attempts to channel the movement onto the usual lines of a campaign of mobilization and rectification.[1] Although Mao was not opposed to work teams in principle and had probably not yet begun his all-out struggle in the Politbureau, his absence from Peking meant that he in fact stood aside from the decision-making bodies and was already thinking of using and furthering the movement that was taking shape among the students. (As for Mao's absence from Peking, Liu Shao-ch'i is alleged to have said in his self-criticism of October 1966: 'During a certain period prior to 18 July, when Chairman Mao was absent from Peking, the Central Committee's daily work was pivoted around me.'[2]) Mao must have been well aware that if the majority that probably existed at that time in the Politbureau and its Standing Committee were to become cemented, the result would have been a set of policies which, while making a gesture or two in his direction, would actually carry on along the path blazed in the readjustment phase. It must also have been clear to him that on the organizational level such a majority would have eaten into his decision-making powers. We should not forget, on the other hand, that Mao's relatively weak position in the apparatus was partly compensated for by Lin Piao's successes in the army, the most obvious results of which were the military conference and the dismissal of Lo Jui-ch'ing. The reason we insist on this point, the importance of which was to become glaringly obvious during the more dramatic turns of the following year, is because it was only the existence of this stabilizing element or 'guarantee' that

---

[1] See Point 7 of the 16 Points in Robinson, op. cit., pp. 90–91 and *PR*, no. 34, 1966.
[2] *Collected Works 1958–1967*, Hong Kong 1968, p. 357.

permitted Mao to risk a profound upheaval in the Party apparatus and the political apparatus in general with his calls for a mass movement.

Although there were many different shades of opinion at the Plenum, it is possible to talk of three main positions or tendencies. The first tendency, headed by Mao and Lin Piao, thought the Party needed a thorough shake-up involving a change in the leadership and a return to the policies first applied during 1958–59 and echoed, on a lesser scale, in the socialist education movement of 1963–64. To this end it intended mobilizing the student youth. A second tendency, to which Liu Shao-ch'i and Teng Hsiao-p'ing probably belonged, defended the work teams and warned against the dangers that such a movement might entail at all levels. Finally a centrist and conciliationist tendency was doing all it could to prevent what already looked like the most serious split the Party had ever known, at least since Mao and his group had been leading it.[3]

The Central Committee sat from 1 to 12 August and was enlarged, apart from the cadres and officials admitted to previous sessions, to admit representatives of 'revolutionary teachers and students' from institutions of higher learning in Peking.[4] Mao made a strong attack, symbolically adopting the *tatzupao* method. His *tatzupao* of 5 August was an open declaration of war against 'some leading comrades from the central down to the local levels' and more precisely against those who had made use of work teams and who were explicitly accused of 'adopting the reactionary stand of the bourgeoisie' and having 'enforced a bourgeois dictatorship and struck down the surging movement of the Great Cultural Revolution of the proletariat'.[5] The fact that Mao's *tatzupao* is dated 5 August suggests that he decided to take the step, the significance of which he cannot fail to have realized, after things had not gone his way during the first stage of the Plenum.[6] While Mao was putting up his *tatzupao*, preparations were going on for the Red Guard demonstrations, which were seen as a way of putting pressure on the Central Committee itself. The first of these demonstrations happened on 10 August while the Plenum was still sitting. Mao himself attended the demonstration and urged those present to take part in state affairs and carry through the cultural revolution to its end.[7]

[3] See e.g. *PR*, no. 34, 1966.

[4] *PR*, no. 34, 1966.

[5] Robinson, op. cit., pp. 80–81.

[6] Blumer, op. cit., p. 202, says, without giving any sources, that Mao's *tatzupao* had already been written on 1 or 2 June. This is absurd, however, for Mao criticizes the 'fifty days' which lasted from 10 June to the end of July.

The best known of the Plenum documents are the Sixteen Points, adopted 8 August, but the final communiqué of four days later is also very informative. It not only develops certain ideas at greater length than in the Sixteen Points but also contains a ratification of the international policy followed during the last few years. It explicitly relates the cultural revolution to the socialist education movement, formally ratifying a number of earlier documents and approving a series of positions enunciated by Mao in the past four years. The documents ratified were a decision of 20 May 1963 concerning work in the countryside and the report of a national work conference convened by the Politbureau on 14 January 1965. (Incidentally, this procedure confirms the oligarchical structure of the Party: vital decisions were taken in the name of the Central Committee outside the plenary session and by special bodies under the control of the Politbureau, while the Plenum was called upon to ratify them years later.) The reason we are insisting on these elements of continuity is because they bear out one of the conclusions of the present study, that is, that from the political and theoretical point of view the cultural revolution, far from introducing anything really new, was in fact relaunching with greater impetus ideas formulated at an earlier date. What was new – or relatively new, if we bear in mind the events of 1946–47 and 1950–51, mentioned above – was above all the method of resorting to a mobilization of the masses outside the normal channels of the Party.

The Sixteen Points revolve around this decision to mobilize from below against the tendency which prevailed during June and July. The document acknowledges that 'shortcomings' of one sort or another were bound to arise, but states categorically that 'the general revolutionary orientation' of the young people 'has been correct from the beginning', and that they represent 'the main current in the Great Proletarian Cultural Revolution' (Point 2). It repeatedly proclaims that it is necessary to 'trust the masses, rely on them and respect their initiative' (especially Point 4). In order to meet the demands that were gaining ground among young people and to win a real basis of support for the mobilization which would ensure them an advantage over their opponents, Mao and his supporters developed a series of revolutionary-democratic themes. The Sixteen Points call, for instance, for the setting up of 'cultural revolutionary groups, committees and congresses' which 'should not be temporary organizations but permanent, standing mass organizations' in

---

[7] *PR*, no. 33, 1967, p. 9; *HNA*, 12 August 1966 and 15 December 1967, p. 3, which recalls Lenin's remark about every cook becoming a prime minister.

which 'it is necessary to institute a system of general elections, like that of the Paris Commune' (Point 9). A programme of this sort naturally proclaimed the freedom of opinion and maximum guarantees for minorities, 'because sometimes the truth is with the minority' (Point 6). As we can see, this official document gives its blessing to ideas developed in various speeches and debates at the end of July and the beginning of August, particularly at Peking University. In the course of this work we shall see how far such ideas were translated into practice.

In the main, therefore, Mao emerged victorious from the Plenum and this was symbolized, so to speak, in the decision to speed up a massive distribution of his works. In some ways, however, the decisions of the Plenum represented a compromise or at least gave the other tendencies a number of assurances – this is obvious in the Sixteen Points themselves, especially where they seem to reflect more directly the clash in the Central Committee. In brief, the critics of the Maoist tendency underlined the risks implied in the mass mobilization of young people whom they still considered immature, warned that cadres and Party leaders might end up in the pillory and expressed the fear that certain attitudes in the cultural field might hold up scientific work and jeopardize production. The Maoists replied generally that the masses would be educated in the course of the movement and that production would increase if the cultural revolution succeeded. More specifically, however, the Sixteen Points laid down that criticizing by name in the press should be discussed beforehand by the relevant Party committee and, in some cases, submitted to the Party Committee at a higher level for approval (Point 11). (It is probably out of formal regard for this decision and because it was difficult to get the assent of the normal bodies that Liu Shao-ch'i was not referred to by name for over a year in official documents and articles.) They also advised special care in dealing with 'scientists, technicians and ordinary members of working staffs' (Point 12) and even made a point of reassuring 'people who have the ordinary bourgeois academic ideas' (Point 5). As for the armed forces, decisions were significantly left in the hands of the Military Affairs Commission of the Central Committee and the General Political Department of the PLA (Point 15).

It should be added that the assault on the apparatus at all levels was considerably weakened by the decision (Points 3 and 8) to divide organizations, leaders and cadres into four categories according to how well they had behaved. The 'great majority' of cadres was seen as 'good' or 'comparatively good' (Point 8), while *Red Flag*[8] claimed that 95% of the cadres would unite with the masses once the centre was won over. More important still, there was no provision for a similar mobilization of the workers and peasants, and the accent was on continuity with the earlier socialist education movement; local Party committees were empowered to act according to their own decision (Point 13).

Although nothing has yet been officially made public, the Plenum must have expelled some members or candidate members, like P'eng Chen, Lu Ting-i and Lo Jui-ch'ing, from the Politbureau and the Secretariat, promoted others, like K'ang Sheng, and more generally reshuffled the hierarchy. Liu Shao-ch'i and Teng Hsiao-p'ing, for instance, remained members of the Politbureau and its Standing Committee[9] but were relegated in the official list put out on 19 August from second and fifth places to seventh and eleventh places respectively.[10] This, of course, was only the first in a long series of growing humiliations. Lin Piao was by now unquestionably second-in-command and T'ao Chu was number four after Chou En-lai. In the group in charge of the cultural revolution Ch'en Po-ta (who had jumped from twenty-third to fifth place in the official list) had the main responsibility and Chiang Ch'ing, Mao's wife, was his deputy; K'ang Sheng, who was described as an 'adviser', also had an important role. Serious difficulties arose after the dispute with T'ao Chu, who was not only adviser to the Cultural Revolution Group but also in charge of propaganda. Despite this first reshuffle, and especially considering the evolution of some leading personages, the situation in the established organizations continued to be rather confused. It was also for this reason that in subsequent months many initiatives were still taken outside the normal channels. (One example of a 'factionalistic' initiative was the mass meeting of art and literature workers on 28 November, an important stage in the internal struggle.) The army in particular grew more and more autonomous and continued to carry out duties which would normally have been the province of the Party. In September this was taken a step further when the political sections of the Military Regions were removed from the authority of the Party's provincial secretariats and in December the public security forces passed from the control of the provincial secretariats to that of the political sections of the army. At the same time the Central Committee Cultural Revolution Group, an important centre of decisions, increased its influence. This whole situation played a large part in generating new difficulties and almost immediately rekindling all sorts of conflicts.

[8] *PR*, no. 34, 1966.
[9] *SCMM*, no. 611, p. 14.
[10] Daubier, *Histoire de la Révolution Culturelle en Chine*, pp. 90–91.

To complete our picture of this period we should mention that the very same day the Plenum opened, the *Liberation Army Daily* published an article, cited above, which insisted on the primacy of politics over technique and gave the first public account of the disagreements in the army during the last fifteen years. The article also renewed the attack on revisionist economic ideas (the economist Sun Yeh-fang was still the main target). Pride of place, however, was reserved for an appeal by Mao,[11] which was mentioned for the first time at the beginning of August. This appeal, while calling on the masses to learn from the army, envisaged putting an end to the traditional division of labour by giving the workers military, cultural, commercial and agricultural duties and doing the same with the peasants. According to the Chinese press it would be possible, by putting Mao's idea into effect, to 'promote the narrowing, step by step, of the gap between worker and peasant, town and countryside and mental and manual labour (and) prevent abnormal urban and industrial development'.[12] Ideas such as these were put forward as a blue print for the construction of communism in tones typical of the first stage of the commune campaign but later abandoned. In practice this was a way of preparing for the prospect of a prolonged war into which the Chinese people might be forced by an attack from American imperialism and in the course of which all production and the life of the country in general would have to revert to forms current during the anti-Japanese and civil wars.

The international factor, even if not decisive, continued to weigh heavily upon China's domestic affairs. Following hard on grave setbacks such as the routing of the Indonesian Communist Party and the political break with Cuba, the Chinese Communist Party was beset by new problems during this period: the break with the Japanese Communist Party (this crisis erupted publicly during the Plenum as the situation in the Gensuiko came to a head), the estrangement of the North Koreans and the constant refusal of the Vietnamese to join in condemning the USSR as an accomplice of imperialism (on the eve of the Plenum an article appeared attacking the supporters of 'joint actions').[13]

The Red Guards

The launching of the Red Guards was accompanied by a more precise definition of the ideological aims of the cultural revolution. On the one

[11] *HNA*, 2, 3, 4 and 5 August 1966, passim.
[12] *HNA*, 2 August 1966, p. 7.
[13] *HNA*, 31 July 1966.

hand it was related to the socialist education movement and on the other represented as a movement which would extend to society as a whole, sweeping away the remnants of the past, uprooting revisionism and lastly creating the conditions for a new leap forward in production. In a speech made straight after the Plenum Lin Piao gave a definition which was afterwards repeated time and time again: 'The great proletarian cultural revolution is aimed precisely at eliminating bourgeois ideology, establishing proletarian ideology, remoulding people's souls, revolutionizing their ideology, digging out the roots of revisionism and consolidating and developing the socialist system.'[14] The Sixteen Points had already said quite concretely that 'the main target of the present movement is those within the Party who are in authority and are taking the capitalist road' (Point 5). Tactics were also clearly laid down – support the left, win over the centre and beat the right.

There are many difficulties in the way of an exhaustive analysis of the Red Guard movement: it is impossible either to examine all the great mass of material produced – much of it probably lost already, due to the flimsy materials and the primitive publishing techniques – or to find one's way through the confused tangle of events. There is no question, however, that it was a most important phenomenon with no precedents in other countries in transition from capitalism to socialism and one that resists any partial interpretation. Its main feature was an extraordinary combination of prompting from above in the interests of a struggle at the top and a movement from below which tended little by little to acquire a dynamic of its own.

The Red Guard movement ('officially' launched 18 August) had its antecedents in groups of Red Guards set up in June and July with no more than a few dozen members;[15] Chou En-lai in a speech on 3 October 1966[16] said that one group had been set up on 29 May at Tsinghua middle school. It was not until August, however, that the sporadic movement of mid-July grew and spread to different parts of China. This would not have been possible if the movement had been restricted to an upsurge from below (of which there had already been signs earlier). The other necessary factor was the instigation from above, which meant that the students could make use of established organizational tools and material and technical means (duplicators, lorries and trains, etc.) put at their

---

[14] *HNA*, 18 August 1966. Lin repeated these ideas on 15 September and on the anniversary of the People's Republic.
[15] *People's Daily* and *Red Flag* editorials, 1 January 1967.
[16] *CB*, no. 819, p. 51.

disposal by the state. Daubier believes that this prompting from on high began much earlier than August,[17] that Mao made contact with rebellious groups on his return to Peking in mid-July in order to encourage their efforts and that it was these contacts that resulted in the presence of the 'revolutionary teachers and students' at the Eleventh Plenum. It would certainly have been impossible for an undirected, spontaneous movement to organize the demonstrations on the 16th (at which Ch'en Po-ta spoke) and the 18th, attended by a massive influx of delegations from different parts of the country.

Why was it above all the student youth that Mao wanted to mobilize? Firstly we must remember, as we made clear in the first part of this book, that a number of tensions existed in Chinese society and that the student youth ran the risk of being the first to feel their effect. For this reason the students were possibly more sensitive to certain appeals and more likely to mobilize, especially if the starting-point were linked in some way to their day-to-day worries and aspirations (criticism of the structure of education, of teaching methods, of the ever-increasing class discrimination, etc.) and if the first blows were aimed at those academic authorities who for various reasons were the object of their resentment. Apart from anti-authoritarianism, which in China as in the rest of the world (making all allowances for specific national situations) was a constant feature of the student upheaval, all the more anger was directed against professors in higher learning institutions because of their relatively privileged conditions. Many of the top-level professors were members of the old ruling classes or had received their training in the old society.[18]

From another point of view the mobilization of the student masses would only have a limited effect on the life of the country and, more particularly, on the economy (one of the chief anxieties expressed during the debate at the Plenum – and frequently in the press – was that production should not be impaired).[19] At the same time the Maoist leadership may rightly have thought that it would be easier to control and channel a movement made up chiefly of young students and that if such a movement did burst its banks the effects would be less disastrous.

More generally, there was no denying that relations between the younger generations and the Party and state leadership presented diffi-

---

[17] E.g. Daubier, op. cit., p. 85.

[18] For the situation in 1959 see *HNA*, 19 January 1959. At that time the overwhelming majority of teachers enjoyed similar privileges. Later there were changes, but on the whole the situation remained the same.

[19] *CB*, no. 819, pp. 18, 20, 25 and 34.

culties. The older generations, who had suffered exploitation and oppression under the old regime, would never call into question the gains of the revolution because of difficulties and contradictions under the new regime. Young people, however, born or brought up after the revolution, saw these gains as a natural heritage and inevitably looked more critically at the shortcomings and imbalances of the new society, whose potentialities they wanted to exploit to the full. It is significant that during the cultural revolution the leadership made every effort to expose the Red Guards to experiences that appeared to be substitutes for those of earlier generations during the anti–Japanese war and the civil war and to make them listen to old people 'speaking bitterness' about China under Chiang Kai-shek and the Kuomintang.

The resolutions of the Plenum, particularly the Sixteen Points, had already given notice of the themes around which the students were to be mobilized and these themes appeared more and more frequently in the following weeks in the different publications and *tatzupao*. The accent was on the key role of the masses, the need for the masses to take in hand the affairs of the state, maximum democracy with full minority rights, freedom of criticism, the need to eliminate everything that is conservative and reactionary, especially in people's minds, and the principle that it is right to rebel.[20] On 3 November Lin Piao gave his own definition of this concept: 'By this extensive democracy, the Party is fearlessly permitting the broad masses to use the media of free airing of views, by character posters, great debates and extensive contacts, to criticize and supervise the Party and government leading institutions and leaders at all levels. At the same time, it is providing the people with full democratic rights along the principles of the Paris Commune.' All these themes, strictly speaking, can also be found in Maoist ideology in other periods – hence the use of quotations from earlier works. But what is more important, they were now to be tried out in practice. Welded together in a single campaign and thrust into the hands of a growing movement, they lent an extraordinary charge to the leadership's new course, the like of which has never been seen in the USSR of Krushchev and Brezhnev or the People's Democracies of Gomulka, Kadar or Ceausescu. In September the government issued two decrees which reaffirmed the broadest democratic rights and stepped up the propaganda in this direction. These decrees upheld freedom of opinion, freedom of speech, freedom of assembly, freedom of the press, freedom to demonstrate, freedom to give

[20] See e.g. *HNA*, 18 September 1966, p. 4; *PR*, no. 45, 1966; *HNA*, 5 November 1966, pp. 3–4; *HNA*, 13 November 1966, p. 28.

out leaflets, freedom to make caricatures and freedom to put up *tatzupao*.[21] At the same time no praise was too high for the Red Guards, who were called China's 'shock force' and whose anti-conservative drive was seen as indispensable for digging out the very roots of the 'bourgeois rightists'.[22] The Maoist leadership even formulated an objective law, on the basis of a few historical analogies, which stated that modern China's cultural revolutions had all started with a mobilization of the students.

The movement was organized primarily by means of huge mass demonstrations, the most spectacular of which were held in Peking in the presence of Mao himself. Between 18 August and 26 November no less than eight such demonstrations were organized in the capital and official estimates say that altogether about eleven million young people took part in them.[23] Note that Mao himself never said anything at these demonstrations, except for a word or two to those standing round about him. This is a good example of the way in which he was stage-managed as a transcendental, mystical figure.

It is hard to say which of the various Red Guard activities were wished by the leadership and which sprang from below. It is certain, however, that the leadership was not so much interested in the iconoclasm that made such a splash in the world press as in fostering the journeys and encounters that gave rise to the mass demonstrations and helped spread the movement, the participation in production and especially the autumn harvest,[24] the 'long marches' and above all the military preparation of the Red Guards. Chou En-lai, for instance, said in a speech on 13 December that the Red Guards should be a combat corps (they fought against the capitalist roaders not only in the schools but in society as a whole, and they constituted the army reserve), a study corps and a propaganda corps.[25] The call to learn from the army recurred regularly.[26] Military preparation naturally implied army participation and control and was related to the dangerous situation facing China due to the worsening of the Vietnam war. Needless to say, many of the Red Guard activities would not have been possible without the approval and direct support of the authorities and the administration, both central and local (think, for instance, of the free travel,[27] the provision of board and lodging for the

[21] See Blumer, op. cit., chapter 10.

[22] *HNA*, 30 and 31 August 1966; 20 November 1966; *PR*, no. 45, 1966.

[23] See Gordon Bennett and Ronald Montaperto, *Red Guard*, London 1971, chapter 4, for a personal account of one such demonstration.

[24] *HNA*, 8 September 1966, p. 8, and 13 September 1966, p. 5.

[25] *CB*, no. 819, p. 40.

[26] E.g. *HNA*, 24 September 1966, p. 11 and 13 October 1966, p. 10.

[27] *CB*, no. 819, pp. 28–29 and 40; *HNA*, 1 September 1966 and 24 September 1966.

great numbers of young people on the move, etc.).

The leadership – particularly the Central Committee Cultural Revolution Group – themselves intervened constantly in the schools and universities (and had done so ever since July) in their efforts to direct and channel the movement into the desired direction. (This must be seen in conjunction with the possibilities inherent in the army's role, to which we have already referred.) And in the last analysis 'the Party centre and Chairman Mao', projected almost obsessively as the supreme authority, had the final say. The leadership stressed the importance above all else of loyalty to the Party and at times did not hesitate to state quite bluntly that leadership should take precedence over the masses. There are many instances of this sort of thinking in the speeches of the leadership, and we cite only a few of them. In his speech on 13 September Chou En-lai said that the final decision on how to assess certain groups lay with the Party centre and with Mao.[28] Earlier in the same speech he said that it was right to rely on the masses and follow the line of the masses, but 'reliance on the masses and the mobilization of the masses presupposes the existence of a leadership'.[29] In another speech on 3 October, he declared that 'leadership organs in large and medium-size cities are key points of the cultural revolution' and that Mao and the Politbureau should settle the slogans for demonstrations.[30] Another leader, Ch'en Po-ta, said in a remarkable speech at Peking University on 24 August that only those texts of Mao circulated by the *People's Daily* and the official agency should be published, and that anything else should be withdrawn.[31]

Once it had got going, however, the Red Guard movement tended to acquire a momentum of its own which the leaders, using traditional organizational methods, were powerless to stop. From the very first it was clear that the Red Guards, or a part of them, were going beyond the objectives laid down by the leadership. When it came to destroying symbols of the past, changing – 'revolutionizing' – the names of streets, districts and public places, snipping off counterrevolutionary haircuts and knocking down old monuments, the Red Guards were probably still acting within the framework of their official promoters. However, the Red Guards, eager to move beyond the 'Destroy the Four Olds' campaign, began slowly to strike out at the bureaucracy as well: they requisi-

[28] *CB*, no. 819, p. 44.
[29] Ibid., p. 43.
[30] *CB*, no. 819, pp. 54 and 65.
[31] *CB*, no. 830, p. 36.

tioned apartments, surrounded cars and refused to let them past, invaded offices, turning everything upside-down, and made incursions into luxury quarters frequented not only by survivors of the old regime but also by government bigwigs and their foreign guests.[32] According to a statement by Liu's Maoist daughter,[33] *tatzupao* went up on 24 August attacking Chou En-lai, Ch'en Po-ta, Chiang Ch'ing and even Mao himself. That the Red Guards went further than they were meant to is shown by the leadership's repeated calls to order, the early denunciations of excessive and even violent behaviour and the limitations set to the movement. Students were forbidden, for instance, to search Party and state officials, for this could result in documents falling into the wrong hands. Students were also accused in the press and in the speeches we have already referred to (late August, early September) of acting like hooligans, of destroying goods that could have been put to other uses, of putting dunce's hats on people up for criticism and of trying to get into the Soviet Embassy. (The role of moderator was mostly played by Chou En-lai, but Lin Piao and K'ang Sheng also made appeals in their own speeches.) At the same time the leadership repeated again and again that the workers and peasants were not to be involved in the movement so that production would not suffer; it also limited, or tried to limit, the migrations of young people.

Appeals from above only had a limited effect. The Red Guards did nothing to diminish their campaign, on the contrary they even began to choose as their targets men (like Li Hsueh-feng, P'eng Chen's replacement in Peking) who had been given their posts after the cultural revolution had started, and ignored the warnings set out in the Sixteen Points. Many opposed and conflicting tendencies began to take shape and real confrontations and clashes developed outside the traditional circuits, even though these were distorted and confused by the practice of paying ritual homage to Mao's thought. These developments brought about the rapid collapse of the Communist Youth League's castle of cards, which had never shown much life anyway and for which the events of the 'Fifty Days' had been the coup de grâce. Eventually the Red Guards succeeded in taking over the entire space that in theory the League should have occupied, at least among the students.

[32] For the actions of the Red Guards see e.g. *HNA*, 24, 25, 26, 27, 28 and 30 August 1966, passim; 9 September 1966, p. 21, and 11 October 1966, pp. 13–14. There are references to luxury living in *HNA*, 24 August 1966, pp. 11 and 24, and 21 September 1966, p. 26. More generally, see *Red Guard*, chapter 3.

[33] *CB*, no. 821, p. 19.

Generally speaking, the Red Guards met with little success in their attempts to build contacts with the workers. Jean Daubier talks of some support in offices and factories mostly among apprentices.[34] Neale Hunter refers to a minority of factory-workers who were openly sympathetic to the Red Guards.[35] The most interesting and detailed testimony of all is that of Dai Hsiao-ai, the former Canton Red Guard, who in early September went with a team of students to the Tsangku Warehouse near his school in order to 'get the Great Proletarian Revolution in the factories under way'.[36] Dai makes clear that he took this step without any promptings from the press or leadership and after hearing 'by word of mouth' about activists who had unsuccessfully launched criticisms against their factory leaderships. Several other Canton schools took similar local initiatives. After twenty days 'living in' at the warehouse, Dai and his friends considered they had had a limited 'catalytic' effect and decided to leave the workers to themselves. One reason for their decision to leave was the hostile attitude of the warehouse management. Another was the *People's Daily* editorial of 7 September, which they interpreted as a warning to keep clear of the factories.[37] Looking back on his experiences, Dai considers that the Red Guards' small success in fostering rebellion among some workers was a factor in the later polarization into 'two big factions'.[38] His view is that although the Central Cultural Revolution Group showed a clear 'lack of encouragement' towards the move into the factories, the students succeeded in keeping alight the 'fire of the rebel worker-enterprise leader struggle'.[39] Neale Hunter, writing about Shanghai and the small groups of pro-Red Guard factory-workers, comes to the same conclusion: although they were at first a 'minimal' force, 'they became most important when (they) entered the movement with a vengeance in November'.[40]

One of the obstacles in the way of worker-Red Guard cooperation was interference and obstruction from middle-ranking cadres and management.[41] The Red Guards, eager to help the workers 'contest' their managements, were in many cases attacked or criticized by workers mobilized by and in support of the established middle leadership. Neale

[34] Daubier, op. cit., p. 86.
[35] Op. cit., p. 104.
[36] *Red Guard*, p. 57.
[37] Ibid., p. 59.
[38] Ibid., p. 62.
[39] Ibid., p. 63.
[40] Op. cit., pp. 104–105.
[41] See Blumer, op. cit.; Daubier, op. cit., p. 112; Hunter, op. cit., chapter 5.

Hunter brings a number of cases to light.[42] By October there were reports of an Army of Red Workers in Peking who allegedly attacked radical Red Guards in the so-called Third Headquarters and criticized Chiang Ch'ing and Ch'en Po-ta.[43] Mao, in his directive of 7 September, says that six hundred peasants were brought into Peking to defend the position of Kuo Ying-ch'iu, Vice-Chancellor of the People's University.[44] This directive shows that by early September Mao was greatly alarmed at the growing antagonism between the Red Guards and the worker and peasant masses. In order to lessen this antagonism he asked for articles to appear in the press and took steps to have his directive circulated to all provincial committees.[45] The articles urged workers and peasants not to attack the students and instructed the Red Guards to let the workers and peasants make their own revolution.[46] However, at least in Canton a 'sizeable minority' of students defied these instructions and maintained their links with rebel workers.[47]

It is true, then, that the Red Guards – either because they were naturally estranged from the workers in the factories, because the management manoeuvred to discredit them, because some sections of the workers felt loyalty for their leaders and others were wary or apathetic,[48] or because of a combination of all or some of these reasons – provoked more hostility than sympathy. However, the events of late 1966 and early 1967 suggest that Dai Hsiao-ai was right to claim that the Red Guard excursion into the factories had a catalytic effect, especially among the younger workers. Generally it is hard to say what the attitude of the Maoist leadership was to student–worker cooperation at this stage, although it is clear it reacted sharply in September to the threat of large-scale strife.

We have talked about a Red Guards 'movement'. In fact, it was not a genuine national organization with branches and groupings at a local level but a movement containing many different groups and tendencies which sometimes developed along parallel lines and sometimes clashed fiercely – the most familiar insults were 'fake Red Guards', 'royalist Red Guards', 'reactionary Red Guards' and so on. There were admittedly several 'all-China' organizations (such as the Third Headquarters), organizations with some links in other cities (such as the *Lientung* or

[42] Ibid., pp. 98–102.
[43] Daubier, op. cit., p. 119.
[44] Jean Esmein, *La Révolution Culturelle*, Paris 1970, p. 125.
[45] *Red Guard*, p. 61.
[46] Esmein, op. cit., p. 125–126.
[47] *Red Guard*, p. 62.
[48] E.g. *Red Guard*, p. 60.

United Action Committee), and numerous city-wide groupings, and later in this chapter we will give a short description of them. A constant feature of such federations, however, was that the local sections professing allegiance to them were mostly weak and isolated.[49] The splintering, flowering and multiplication of the different groups was on such an extraordinary scale that there is no room in a work of this length to give even an approximate classification. The leaders frequently refer to such divisions in their speeches and Chou En-lai clearly accepted the situation as inevitable, at least for a certain period, provided the groups recognized the Party's leadership and Mao's thought.[50] In spite of repeated attempts at conciliation from above the group rivalries persisted for a long time and inserted themselves into the more general splits and struggles that grew up later. In some institutions, such as Peking University, this situation lasted until July 1968 when the 'workers' Mao Tse-tung thought propaganda teams' were sent in to restore order.

The outbreak of arguments among the Red Guards gave rise to the expression of dissension in forms that no one could control. Moreover, one of the main features of the rise of the movement was the flood of *tatzupao*, not subject to any form of censorship, and the spreading of various sorts of publications – leaflets, articles, pamphlets, etc. – that promoted a whole range of different opinions. These were published on cyclostyles and duplicators generally belonging to the universities, but in the circumstances few people dared to forbid the students to use them. The anti-bureaucratic rebel spirit that pervades many of these documents emerges clearly from the handful of articles republished by *Hsinhua News Agency* and *Peking Review* towards the end of 1966. It is clear at once from their lively and authentic style that we are dealing with something other than the usual editorials and documents.

This diversity of attitudes and actions was nurtured by the very nature of the appeals, the agitation and the propaganda issuing from the Maoist leadership, and the same was to happen later when the workers and peasants were mobilized. On the one hand, the raising of democratic-revolutionary and egalitarian themes and the denunciation of 'capitalist roaders' in top Party and state positions encouraged the movement, or part of it, to direct its blows against the apparatus as a whole and against top government leaders and to embark upon a decisive campaign against the bureaucracy. On the other hand, the rather general character of the propaganda, the lack of information about the real differences at the top

[49] See Esmein, op. cit., p. 138.
[50] *CB*, no. 819, p. 45.

and the absence of any real concrete objectives confused the Maoist ranks,[51] with the result that when faced with definite choices they took to squabbling and factionalism.

New differentiations and new conflicts

There was a fresh wave of difficulties soon after the conclusion of the Plenum – Chiang Ch'ing said on 28 November that new problems had arisen a few days after the 18 August demonstration.[52] In the first place there were differences of opinion over how to put the decisions of the Plenum into practice. Because of the existence of a centrist grouping, which was quite large judging from the number of times it was attacked,[53] those who had emerged beaten from the Plenum still had some room to manoeuvre. The words and actions of the Red Guards must also have created new disagreements about what stand to take. This situation arose because the Red Guards, as we said earlier, disregarded some of the instructions of the Plenum which a whole part of the Central Committee and the apparatus in general probably saw as essential guarantees. (*Red Flag* no. 13, 1966, admitted that in some areas and in some units the struggle between the two lines was still very acute and very complex; the editorial in the next issue also talked of comrades understanding the work of the cultural revolution very badly and of the 'enormous task' of rooting out the influence of the reactionary bourgeois line.)[54] Besides, it was deeply ingrained in these 'apparatchiks' to look on the Party, and more concretely the apparatus at various levels, as the main instrument for applying the Plenum decisions and the cultural revolution line. They were therefore alarmed to see that the driving force was more and more the Red Guard movement, which had overthrown the Communist Youth League and was continually coming into conflict with the Party apparatus itself. Those who in the top-level discussion from June onwards had warned of the dangers of an uncontrolled movement from below and who had been accused of fearing the masses now considered that they had more than enough cause to return to the attack. The leaders of the group Mao had singled out for criticism understandably thought that if things carried on this way all would be lost. They therefore naturally fought back against the mobilization measures, either by calling for a return to 'normality' (i.e. respect for traditional Party and state conventions) or by

[51] There is a good illustration of this in *Red Guard*, p. 144.
[52] *PR*, no. 50, 1966.
[53] E.g. *HNA*, 1 November 1966, p. 4.
[54] *PR*, no. 45, 1966.

trying to gain a foothold among the Red Guards, who were becoming even more deeply divided. There are many references in the Chinese press to this attempt to gain support among the masses. *Red Flag*,[55] after discussing the cases of a number of people who had committed mistakes (with the clear intention of salvaging most of them), admitted that a section of the masses had been temporarily hoodwinked by the wrong line. The opposition was accused again and again of stirring up conflicts among the masses and in particular among the students.[56] Because of the margins for manoeuvre and the amount of support they were given, some of the old leaders were able to minimize their self-criticisms and refuse to act as scapegoats. Liu Shao-ch'i, for instance, in a self-criticism made before a Central Committee working conference in October, admitted making mistakes during the Fifty Days, but added: 'At that time, if we had not considered the requests for work teams or if we had not sent work teams to schools and government organs, in what other way could we have acted?'.[57] Despite its reticence, Liu's statement already shows clearly how weak his position was. He did not wish to act as a scapegoat, but because he did not dare to call Mao's positions into question he made important admissions. For this reason he was more or less disarmed and could only delay his downfall.

Another major source of difficulties were the excesses, the rivalries and the divisions of the Red Guards, which ran the risk of unleashing all kinds of centrifugal tendencies and blunting the weapon that the Maoists themselves intended using. Not only because different groups or individuals could have tried to gain a foothold in the Red Guards, or because an increase in tension might have neutralized both Maoists and opposition, but also because it was often the fragmentation and confusion of languages that lay behind the frequent clashes between the Red Guards and the worker and peasant masses.

It is difficult to make any satisfactory analysis of the Red Guards during this period, at least if one refuses to accept the apologist propaganda that simply divides Red Guards into 'true', 'fake' and 'reactionary'. It seems that the differences arose over the tendency to overstep certain limits, the struggle still being waged in the top echelons of Party and state and the question of what attitude should be taken towards the Party apparatus and the cadres. As everyone claimed to share certain basic principles (Mao's thought, the leading role of the Party, the need to

[55] *PR*, no. 45, 1966.
[56] E.g. *HNA*, 4 November 1966, p. 6; *PR*, no. 1, 1967, p. 10.
[57] *Collected Works*, p. 358.

struggle against the restorationists, etc.) the differences mainly arose over concrete episodes and practical questions of attitude (whether this local leadership was truly applying the line of the cultural revolution or merely carrying out covering operations, whether that cadre was or was not a 'right-wing restorationist', and so on.) As one of the most frequent charges was that one's opponent was dissembling or 'waving the red flag to oppose the red flag', it is clear that all sorts of suspicions were nurtured and all sorts of dissension arose, giving birth to a multitude of polemics that outsiders find difficult to understand. The work teams were another cause of division, especially since even the Maoist leaders thought that some of them had acted correctly: long discussions flared up about whether or not to annul certain decisions that had been taken. One particular *casus belli* were the dossiers or 'black books' drawn up during the Fifty Days. The dossiers, which were in the custody of the Party apparatus, contained accounts of criticism meetings, positions taken up, etc., and many people, fearing future reprisals, demanded their destruction. (A Central Committee circular of 16 November 1966 declared these dossiers null and void and ordered them to be burned in full view of the masses.)[58] Another critical issue was how much importance to attach to the social origin of the young students. Some were for excluding everyone who had a counterrevolutionary family, while others thought the most important thing should be what position a person adopted. The bitter controversy had its origins in a decision taken by the Communist Youth League at the beginning of the cultural revolution. This decision divided people into two groups according to family origin or 'lineage' – militants from working-class backgrounds were separately organized and were expected to play an active part in the proletarian revolution. Chou En-lai took up a flexible attitude to the question in his speech on 1 September.[59] Later Chou is said to have denounced the 'reactionary theory of family lineage' and the concept of 'naturally red' and Chiang Ch'ing declared: 'Chairman Mao and our Party have always opposed both the tendency to disregard a person's class origin and the "theory that only class origin should be taken into account".'[60] In the long run, then, with a measure of elasticity and empiricism, the tendency prevailed not to judge people solely according to their 'family lineage'.

One organization that championed the doctrine of 'family lineage' was

[58] See Blumer, op. cit., chapter 9; Hunter, op. cit., chapter 6; *SCMM*, no. 617, p. 1; *CB*, no. 852, p. 24 (this last document may not be authentic).
[59] *CB*, no. 819, p. 18.
[60] *PR*, no. 14, 1967, p. 13.

the *Lientung* or *United Action Committee*. This organization was set up in early October. Daubier claims that it embraced the pupils of the special schools for cadres' children, since abolished. Blumer writes[61] – again without giving references – that its members were exclusively the children of Party officials and soldiers and that it set up the same hierarchical organization as existed in the Party. The sons of Li Ching-ch'uan (the 'warlord' of Szechwan, toppled in 1967 by Red Guards), Li Li-feng and a son of Ch'en Yi were all said to have been members.[62] The aims of the *Lientung* were allegedly to defend Liu and Teng and criticize Lin and Chou: its opponents link the date of its formation with the scaling up of the attacks on Liu and Teng on 3 October. Daubier mentions photocopies of documents claiming to show that the *Lientung* 'received large sums of money from certain high officials'.[63] The *Lientung* had a reputation for violence and was accused of taking prisoners in the course of its campaigns[64] and killing members of the Third Headquarters.[65] The *Peking Chingkangshan* accused it of murder, of openly supporting Liu and of attacking the Cultural Revolution Group.[66] In March 1967 the *Lientung* was officially declared a reactionary organization after 139 of its supporters had been arrested by the security forces. These were later released on 22 April after protests from other Red Guard groups.

Daubier and Esmein both link the First and Second Headquarters (two Peking-based federations with groups in the provinces) with the moderate or conservative wing. Esmein says the Second Headquarters served as a rallying-point for reactionaries in the provinces.[67] Jean Daubier, who as usual reproduces every snippet of propaganda as if it were hard fact, declares that the 'conservative' line of the First and Second Headquarters can be traced to the influence of T'ao Chu.[68]

Probably the most radical of the Peking-based federations was the Third Headquarters, which was set up mainly by groups at Tsinghua University, the Institute of Aeronautics and the Institute of Geology at the beginning of September.[69] It was said to have had the discreet support of Mao himself. Nieh Yuan-tzu's *Chingkangshan* participated in

---

[61] Op. cit., chapter 10.
[62] Esmein, op. cit., p. 140.
[63] Daubier, op. cit., p. 118.
[64] Blumer, op. cit., chapter 10.
[65] Daubier, op. cit., p. 117.
[66] *SCMP*, no. 3905, pp. 13–17 and Esmein, op. cit., p. 140.
[67] Esmein, op. cit., p. 137.
[68] Daubier, op. cit., p. 114.
[69] Daubier, op. cit., pp. 114–116.

setting it up.[70] There were reports in the Japanese press in late 1966 that the Third Headquarters and the Peking Institute of Aeronautics were 'playing the role of a guardian' and keeping the leadership in power with their money and their ability to mobilize forces. The same report mentions a group with the bizarre name 'We can do it while we are alive; but we can do nothing if we die' which accused Chiang Ch'ing of failing to criticize the behaviour of the Third Headquarters.[71]

It is clear from official sources that serious difficulties arose in relations between the Red Guards and the workers and peasants.[72] Apart from small minorities of apprentices and younger workers in the larger cities, the worker and peasant masses felt estranged from a movement in which they did not participate and whose aims they did not understand. Added to that, many of the older workers and heads of families (as Dai Hsiao-ai discovered) were wary or apathetic, and expressed fears that the cultural revolution would be 'no different from the 1957–58 anti-rightist struggle'. They therefore advised their sons to avoid doing anything rash that they might afterwards regret when things returned to 'normal'.[73] In some cases the dispersal of Red Guards to the factories provoked bitter ripostes from the factory cadres, while some of the propaganda methods used by the Red Guards must have caused much annoyance. The Maoists admit that the workers sometimes reacted angrily, out of a sense of loyalty to the Party, when cadres who probably came from the same background as themselves were attacked. More generally, they were probably not immune to that distrust of students which is not peculiar to China and which in other countries only began to vanish after the great struggles of the student movement. Clashes took place, some of them very bitter, and in a number of cases the incidents led to a suspension of work.[74]

To conclude, in the months immediately following the Plenum the situation was in many ways still uncertain, confused and not without bitter conflicts. The broad masses of the people were still standing to one side and there was the possibility that their neutrality would become transformed into active opposition to the movement. The Maoists, hav-

[70] Esmein, op. cit., p. 137.

[71] See *BBC Summary of World Broadcasts (Far East)*, FE 2379/Cl.

[72] See, for example, *CB*, no. 819, pp. 18 and 34; *People's Daily*, 7 September 1966 and 1 October 1966.

[73] *Red Guard*, p. 60.

[74] *PR*, no. 1, 1967.

ing won an initial victory in August, could not afford to close their eyes to the situation, which was crying out for new initiatives.[75]

[75] Chou En-lai spoke of hostility towards the Red Guards and of the distrust of the young for the older workers (*CB*, no. 819, p. 18); elsewhere he called on workers and peasants not to interfere in the students' movement (ibid., p. 34). The *People's Daily* of 7 September asked the students in their turn not to meddle in the peasant movement. On 1 October it spoke of antagonism between a section of the workers and peasants and the Red Guards. On 8 October K'ang Sheng talked of conflicts, which he attributed to subversion, between workers and students (*CB*, no. 819, p. 25). One frequently-quoted article mentions production-stoppages (*PR*, no. 1, 1967).

8
The Height of the Crisis

The appeal to the worker and peasant masses

In spite of the upheavals it had provoked, the mobilization of the Red Guards was in itself not enough to bring about that renewal and re-organization of the Party apparatus which was more and more clearly emerging as the objective of the Mao Tse-tung tendency. The groups and individuals defeated at the August Plenum, although seriously weakened, were still very much in evidence and big difficulties had arisen in rela-tions with the workers and peasants. The supporters of the cultural revolution therefore had no choice but to bring up the big guns. This meant renouncing the caution and restraints of previous months and making an appeal to the workers and peasants.

It is not clear from the documents published so far when and by what body the decision was taken. However, the editorial of *Red Flag* no. 15, explicitly setting forth the new course, was circulated on 13 December. Although the article claimed that 'the handful of individuals within the Party who were in authority and were taking the capitalist road' had not resigned themselves to defeat and were trying to split the masses and incite them to oppose the cultural revolution, it also applauded the fact that the 'revolutionary worker masses had plunged themselves into the movement of the great proletarian cultural revolution and (that) the revolutionary students had joined forces with the workers, marking a fresh start for the movement'.[1] On 26 December the *People's Daily* published an editorial which said: 'Now, a new upsurge of the great proletarian cultural revolution is taking place in industrial and mining enterprises throughout the country. The Chinese working class is the leading force and the most active factor in this revolution for which it has particularly great responsibility. It is very good that tens of millions of

[1] *HNA*, 14 December 1966, p. 3, and *PR*, no. 51, 1966.

workers rise up to carry out the great cultural revolution. This trend is inevitable. No force whatever can stop this . . . The working class should firmly observe the decision of the Party's Central Committee concerning the great proletarian cultural revolution, and let the masses elect cultural revolutionary groups, committees or congresses that can represent them. Members to these organizations must not be appointed from above nor is behind-the-scenes manipulation allowed. A system of general elections must be instituted in accordance with the principles of the Paris Commune.'[2]

Similar ideas were expressed in a joint editorial in *Red Flag* and the *People's Daily* on 1 January. After repeating that it should be possible through the mobilization of the masses to crush the capitalist roaders, the editorial went on to call for the broadest democracy and democratic rights and declared that the revolution in culture and in the schools could only be brought to a conclusion once the revolution in the factories and the countryside was complete (compare this with the different emphasis in previous statements from May onwards). More explicitly it declared that further growth in production depended on the successful conclusion of the cultural revolution. *Red Flag* no. 15 (already quoted above) published an article entitled *The dictatorship of the proletariat and the great proletarian cultural revolution*, one of the most comprehensive analyses made up to then. The three authors of the document, Wang Li, Chia Yi-hsueh and Li Hsin, first dealt with the degeneration of the USSR and the other collectivist states and then redefined the cultural revolution as 'a struggle to prevent the usurping of the leadership by counter-revolutionary revisionism'. They stressed the need for the broadest possible mobilization of the masses and called on the masses to make full use of all their democratic rights.[3] The general line remained the same as that elaborated in the Sixteen Points, with the difference that it was now extended to the worker and peasant masses.

The dangers and the unknowns, which had fed the reasoning of a whole section of the leadership and had up to now induced even the Mao tendency to limit the movement to the student youth, were still clearly an important factor, even if the logic of the struggle itself demanded bold and decisive action. In the first place a genuine mass movement could not help but affect production. Secondly, such a movement would be even more likely to overstep the limits set by the leadership and pose an even greater threat to the system. And above all an invitation to the masses to

[2] *PR*, no. 1, 1967, pp. 20–21.
[3] *PR*, no. 52, 1966.

take state affairs into their own hands, to make their own will felt – an invitation which, under the circumstances, would not stop at mere propaganda – would have much more concrete implications for the workers. In practice, it would sound to them like an invitation to press through long-standing claims and aspirations in all fields, from wages to relations inside the factories, that had previously either been stifled or deflected into harmless channels. In the case of the workers the leadership would be unable to fall back on substitute experiences such as long marches, trips to Peking and huge demonstrations because of the effect these would have on production and the everyday life of the country.

Naturally we do not know what solutions Mao and his supporters originally envisaged for a problem whose implications they most certainly grasped. But by the second half of December and the beginning of January they found themselves faced with dramatic choices: the movement was gathering speed and strikes and demonstrations were spreading to different parts of the country and threatening to get completely out of hand.

The wave of strikes

At Shanghai, which has China's biggest concentration of workers, things had been tense for some time. At the beginning of November some 2,500 Revolutionary Rebels, bitter opponents of the Shanghai Municipal Committee, had decided to take their demands to Peking in what proved to be a foretaste of the events of December and January. Their action sparked off incidents. Like the students, they wanted to be transported free, but the train they were on stopped after local leaders intervened. The railway was blocked, and all but a thousand returned to Shanghai. The Shanghai Municipal Committee must then have contacted Peking, for a telegram arrived from Ch'en Po-ta (head of the Central Cultural Revolution Group) telling the workers to go back to their jobs. However, before the Municipal Committee could read the telegram to the workers Chang Ch'un-ch'iao, former Secretary to the Municipal Party Committee and now a Vice-Director of the Central Cultural Revolution Group, turned up at Ant'ing (where the train was blocked) and dealt the Municipal Committee a hard blow by signing the Rebels' demands. The discrepancy between Ch'en Po-ta's and Chang Ch'un-ch'iao actions seems to show that the incident provoked a split in the Central Cultural Revolution Group. Another important split took place in the ranks of the rebels themselves, and this was perhaps the first beginnings of what later developed into a ferocious faction struggle. 474 of the rebel workers (they called themselves a 'protest-brigade' and wanted to continue their journey to confront Ch'en Po-ta about his 'repressive' telegram) pressed on to Soochow and extracted Chang Ch'un-ch'iao's signature for five more demands before agreeing to return to Shanghai. The leader of these 'ultra-rebels', Keng Chin-chang, later became famous as the leader of an extreme left group in Shanghai.[4] It is worth noting, in view of the later polemics, that the Shanghai authorities had not in any way approved of the workers going to Peking and that, as we have seen, the workers concerned were sympathetic to the Maoist tendency. (According to Hunter[5] they belonged to an organization, the Shanghai Workers' Revolutionary Rebel Headquarters, which was formed under the impact of the Red Guard movement, which first 'functioned underground' and which had an inauguration rally attended by 20,000 people on 9 November.[6]) This was probably the first case, therefore, of a group going beyond the objectives set by the top leadership and clashing not only with the old apparatus but also with the new bodies leading the cultural revolution.

The tension in Shanghai increased after Red Guards and local leaders clashed over a leaflet the Red Guards wanted distributed with *Liberation Daily*, the local newspaper. This happened in early December. The Red Guards then occupied the newspaper offices and *Liberation Daily* did not come out for several days, reappearing only after a fresh intervention from the Central Cultural Revolution Group. But the incidents continued and on 24 December, during a large demonstration, the Mayor, Ts'ao Ti-ch'iu, was forced to make a public self-criticism and undergo humiliation at the hands of the Red Guards, in spite of the Maoist leadership's orders to the contrary. By that time deep splits had also appeared in the local Party organizations. (One of Anna Louise Strong's letters[7] refers to 'battles' in Shanghai, but as Blumer points out these are clearly exaggerated.)

The great crisis broke towards the end of December and lasted until the middle of January. It is clear even from the official sources that these movements were of exceptional importance.

The movement first took the form of initiatives like the one in early November, when delegations travelled to Peking and groups of workers toured other cities and regions in order to make contact and 'exchange experiences'. The example of the Red Guards could not help but catch

---

[4] This information about the Ant'ing incident is taken from Hunter, op. cit., chapter 7.
[5] Op. cit., pp. 136–137.
[6] See also *SCMP*, no. 4145, p. 2, and Blumer, op. cit., chapter 11.
[7] No. 52, 23 October 1967.

on and it was difficult to convince the workers that what was permissible for the students was not permissible for them. This partly explains why the administration and Party officials not only allowed the workers to move about but even granted them the same sort of facilities (free tickets, subsidies, permits, etc.) as they had the Red Guards. Quite apart from any factional manoeuvres, which were inevitable given the situation within the Party, how could any official have risked rejecting demands from below at a time when any member of the administration who tried to place obstacles in the way of the Red Guards was vehemently criticized? (There is a good example in Bennet and Montaperto's book of how Red Guards used threats of violence to extort money from local officials.)[8]

As resistance began to take shape the workers, roused by the appeals to mobilize, were forced to resort to what, even in a transitional, post-capitalist regime, is still a basic means of struggle: the strike. From the second half of December to the beginning of January, Shanghai witnessed a wave of strikes of a magnitude probably unprecedented in a country where capitalism has been overthrown. Transport, water and electricity supplies were paralysed and many factories stopped work.[9] No trains ran for ten days: in the early hours of 30 December the two main lines connecting Shanghai with Nanking and Hangchow came to a halt and many goods and passenger trains were stranded at small stations.[10] The port was paralysed for several days and official organs described the situation there as harmful to China's international prestige.[11] Groups of people at the same time occupied public buildings and houses. At a later date, workers in the food and commerce sectors of industry went on strike for no less than forty-three days.[12]

It goes without saying that a movement of this size would have been impossible without the participation of the widest sections of factory, transport and even office workers. Official sources said that the worker detachments of the militia and even Red Guard groups played an important part in the movement. There is no reason to doubt that this was so: small groups such as these, which had the rudiments of an organizational structure, probably came together with workers' organizations formed after the extension of the cultural revolution. There is no mention

[8] *Red Guard*, pp. 124–125.
[9] *HNA*, 10 January 1967, p. 6; 24 January 1967, p. 5; 10 March 1967, p. 11; and 27 February 1967, p. 2.
[10] *HNA*, 17 January 1967, pp. 5–6, and 10 February 1967, p. 11.
[11] *CB*, no. 582, pp. 16–19.
[12] *SCMP*, no. 4293, p. 6. For the strike wave generally see *HNA*, 10, 11, 12, 13 January 1967 and 2 February 1967, p. 41.

at all of participation by the official trade unions, but later there were fierce attacks on trade-union-type organizations formed in Shanghai and elsewhere.[13] It is hard to say if organizations of this sort were active in the strike movement, but the general drift of these initiatives is obvious: because of the fruitlessness of the traditional organizations, the workers in general tried to create new instruments through which to defend their interests, even though this inevitably meant the emergence of trends towards sectionalism.

As for the objectives of the movement, the workers were calling for higher wages, better social security, improved working conditions and shorter hours.[14] In some cases they demanded payment of wage arrears and protested against the higher rates paid to students working in production. The objectives of this movement were clearly both economic and political in character. Later official accounts have sometimes sought to present the January storm as a purely 'economist' deception of the masses by the group around Liu Shao-ch'i. Certainly there is evidence that workers put forward many economic demands; for improved working conditions, for the abolition of contract labour, for a reduction of differentials and the abolition of managerial privileges and for higher wages and better social security provisions. But in these demands themselves and in others that were raised there was also a clearly detectable drive for an undiluted workers' power within the factory and in the various organs of government. As we shall see, workers replaced the management of their factory with elected committees responsible to the assembly of workers and sought to link up these actions on a local and even national scale. As soon as this aspect of the movement became clear there were to be repeated denunciations of worker groups addicted to 'ultra-democracy'. The rhetoric of the cultural revolution group with its appeals to the Paris Commune stimulated the political aspirations of the masses and encouraged them to seek concrete solutions to their problems. In the popular revolts that followed economic and political goals were both combined and confused. Often the authorities conceded on the economic front only later to denounce the whole movement as economist – having meanwhile safeguarded the authoritarian political structure.

For a whole number of reasons, both structural and conjunctural, Shanghai was in the vanguard of the movement and the most typical

[13] *HNA*, 15 March 1967, pp. 14–15.
[14] The repeated calls by the Maoists for the retention of the 8-hour day seems to confirm that there were demands for shorter hours. See *HNA*, 12 January 1967, p. 5, 16 January 1967, p. 27, and elsewhere.

expression of certain trends. Many other cities, however, witnessed similar events at more or less the same time. The day after the Shanghai events were officially made public, the news came of stoppages in some factories in Chekiang Province.[15] There were strikes during December at Chungking, in south-western China.[16] Incidents broke out in Kiangsi over the sending of delegations.[17] The workers exerted pressure (although we do not know the exact form it took) even in the Taching oil fields, constantly held up as a model of how to apply Mao's thought.[18] In Shansi 'big crowds' had come on to the streets, clashing fiercely with orthodox Maoist groups[19] and at Tsingtao there were attempts to 'overthrow the revolutionary order'[20]: in some factories administrators, technicians and workers had stopped work.[21] In Kweichow Province there were stoppages in both factories and transport, producing almost total paralysis.[22] Serious incidents also took place in Harbin, where transport was partially brought to a halt.[23]

In the North-East steel workers struck for three days at the end of 1966.[24] In the coal-mining area of Hsinwen, in Western China, some workers stopped work.[25] In Peking itself some factories ground to a halt during January as a result of 'exchanging experiences' with workers from different parts of China.[26] Groups of building workers from Liaoning flowed into the capital for a meeting to denounce temporary and contract work; more generally, workers from the poorest categories, who were demanding permanent jobs and the payment of arrears backdated to 1958, organized what were considered to be illegal demonstrations and even occupied premises belonging to the Central Committee.[27] At Pengpu, in Anhwei, the railways came to a halt.[28] Later, in the spring, there were strikes and conflicts in Inner Mongolia.[29]

[15] *HNA*, 11 January 1967, p. 31.
[16] *HNA*, 12 January 1967, p. 7.
[17] *HNA*, 15 January 1967, p. 11.
[18] *HNA*, 20 January 1967, p. 24.
[19] *HNA*, 26 January 1967, p. 3.
[20] *HNA*, 31 January 1967, p. 5.
[21] *HNA*, 14 February 1967, p. 17.
[22] *HNA*, 2 February 1967, p. 9.
[23] *HNA*, 1 February 1967, p. 7, and 28 March 1967, p. 41.
[24] *HNA*, 2 March 1967, p. 7.
[25] *HNA*, 26 March 1967, p. 7.
[26] *HNA*, 15 March 1967, p. 13.
[27] *SCMP*, no. 3868, pp. 14–15, and no. 3913, pp. 1–6.
[28] *People's Daily*, 15 January 1967.
[29] *HNA*, 1 November 1967, p. 10. Information on strikes could be gathered from provincial radio broadcasts.

According to the Maoist interpretation, repeated day after day in the official press, all these movements were mainly due to the incitement and corrupting influence of that tendency accused of preaching the restoration of capitalism. The interpretation of the bourgeois commentators, leaving aside the significance they gave the events, was not much different: the events in Shanghai and the other cities were proof of the enduring influence of men like Liu Shao-ch'i, Teng Hsiao-p'ing, etc., and implied a criticism of the cultural revolution and of Mao's thought.

From the point of view of method, the official interpretations belong to the classical police school of thought, which reasons like all true conservatives that the broad masses are easy prey for clever agitators and subversives, who corrupt them and exploit their innocence.

In actual fact the great flood of accusations against the 'capitalist roaders' posed a number of difficult questions. For example, if they had corrupted the masses with wage-rises, allowances, travel permits, and so on, why then did the workers have to go on strike? There again, to organize such a vigorous and widespread movement would have needed an overall plan and complex practical coordination such as only a politically cohesive faction, solidly organized throughout the country, could possibly have conceived and carried out. However, although the groups opposing Mao and Lin Piao still held important positions and could manoeuvre within the space afforded by the presence of centrist groups, they had nevertheless taken very hard knocks, especially at the highest levels, were unable to organize systematically and had taken up defensive positions in their few surviving centres of power. Moreover, a concerted action would have left behind some trace of itself, but there has been no concrete evidence forthcoming to back up the official interpretation which is tirelessly trotted out in tones all too reminiscent of factional polemics.

That does not mean to say that some sections of the apparatus or more likely individual cadres did not have a hand in the movement, helping it along in whatever way they could. The experience of similar movements in other workers' states, from East Germany in 1953 to Czechoslovakia in 1968, shows that the apparatus characteristically splits in the face of an attack from below and that part of it attaches itself to the forces opposing the bureaucracy. There is no reason why the same should not have happened in China where, in spite of all the bureaucratic distortions, broad layers of cadres have still maintained close links with the masses and where the leadership was engaged in an energetic campaign of appeals and admonishments insisting on the need to multiply these links and place oneself at the service of the masses themselves. At a time when the overloading, not to say the total jamming, of the normal transmission mechanisms often made it difficult for middle and lower-ranking cadres to grasp immediately the intentions of the leadership, let alone how it would subsequently judge specific episodes, it is not surprising that individual cadres and sections of the apparatus not only did not oppose a number of the masses' demands but even helped the movement along. It was probably also true that people who in previous months had clashed with the Red Guards or lost ground and felt themselves threatened now hoped – out of opportunistic or factional considerations – that they could recuperate or reconsolidate their positions by supporting the movement among the workers.

The case of Shanghai, which was by far the most important, deserves particular attention. Given the size of the movement, there might have been some grounds for suspecting incitement if all or most of the leaders and the apparatus had taken part in the operation in opposition to the central power of Mao and the Cultural Revolution Group. But Shanghai could in no way be considered a stronghold of 'capitalist roaders'. As we have seen, at the beginning of the cultural revolution Mao relied on Shanghai to oppose the Peking group; Yao's famous article on Wu Han was approved by the Shanghai Party Committee before being published there. Even in May 1966 Shanghai took the initiative in publishing articles that were considered to be of fundamental importance. The city was also held up as a model of how to realize the cultural revolution on the economic plane, and the language used to celebrate these achievements was much the same as that used a short time afterwards to celebrate the consequences of the 'taking of power' in Shanghai.[30] In reality the case of the great industrial metropolis is also typical inasmuch as it shows how in the course of events differentiations and splits took place among those who initially were in the vanguard of the campaign.

Movements like the one in November, when the local leaders certainly did not support the sending of workers' delegations to Peking,[31] could only help to deepen the splits. With the workers on strike and pressure coming up from below, the leaders in Shanghai and elsewhere were on the horns of a dilemma: should they make concessions or should they firmly oppose the movement, with the inevitable recourse to repression?

[30] *HNA*, 17 July 1966, passim.
[31] The Shanghai group had already changed its attitude towards 'exchanging experiences' by October (*HNA*, 2 February 1967, p. 41). Dissent had arisen because some wanted to make a distinction between open and internal criticism, while others were opposed to such a distinction (*HNA*, 12 January 1967, p. 8).

In the circumstances, not a few were inclined towards the first alternative, either because they thought that this was the correct interpretation of the line, or because they did not feel like opposing the masses, or because they wanted to take the opportunity to increase their influence. In many cases this was the course they actually took: they put up wages, paid out wage arrears, improved welfare benefits and gave out travel grants. The concessions must have been quite big, at least in Shanghai, for there are reports in the Chinese press of a drain on local finances[32] and shortages in various fields.[33] These were due not only to the higher wages, benefits and arrears paid out to the workers, but also to the vast sums spent on Red Guard travel, propaganda and reception of travellers. During the middle of September, for instance, there were a million Red Guards in Shanghai catered for by 150,000 full-time reception workers at 1,500 reception stations.[34] As for the wage rises, it should be remembered that the end of the year is traditionally the accounting time in Chinese industry. The various shortages, which resulted from the flow of money and a subsequent rush on consumer goods, also hit Peking, where according to Jean Daubier the sale of bicycles, radios and other costly goods was suspended in order to put an end to the 'economist wave'.[35] The reason people were so anxious to buy in a hurry was probably that, given the abnormal situation, they feared that the steady flow of goods into the shops would be interrupted. Whether or not the original decisions of middle-ranking cadres to bow to the demands of the workers were justified, they certainly had nothing to do with a plot to restore capitalism.

It is possible, then, that individual interests, moves by the bureaucracy and opportunist manoeuvres may have crept into the movement. But – and here is the core of the question – this could not make any fundamental difference to what was largely a spontaneous mobilization of the vast mass of the people, who, interpreting in their own way or taking literally the appeals launched from above, were beginning to fight for their own aspirations. If we consider the social tensions existing in China at the end of the first fifteen years of the new regime, and the persistent shortcomings in the conditions of the working-class analysed in the first part of this book and confirmed by the polemics of 1966–67, it seems quite understandable and legitimate that the workers should have de-

---

[32] *HNA*, 19 January 1967.

[33] *HNA*, 20 January 1967, p. 22.

[34] Shanghai Radio, 7 March 1967, quoted in *Problems of Communism*, January–February 1968, p. 13.

[35] Daubier, op. cit., p. 140.

manded wage increases and, more generally, changes in their favour in the management of the economy. Neither is it surprising that people without a roof over their heads, or people housed under wretched conditions, should try to install themselves wherever they thought there was space available. Indeed, if we bear in mind the Red Guard denunciation of luxury hotels, public buildings and town and country dwellings belonging to top dignitaries, it is even easier to understand this type of reaction. The very appeals of Mao himself and the official documents probably encouraged the workers to take things into their own hands without worrying too much about the consequences.

But as we shall go on to document in this and the next chapter, the more general and fundamental meaning of the Shanghai strikes, the struggles in many towns and in many rural areas, was an assertion of worker and peasant power against bureaucratic encrustation and ideological mystification. Faced with an irreparable split in the old leadership and the crisis and progressive disintegration of the Party and state apparatus at different levels – faced, that is, with a relative power vacuum – the different social forces in the country, conditioned by the situation we have described earlier, began to move, each in defence of its own interests and in order to realize its own aspirations. The movement got out of hand even more rapidly than that of the Red Guards and with much more drastic consequences. The crisis, originally a conflict at the top and in the higher echelons of the state and Party apparatus, had now grown over into a general social and political upheaval. Leaving aside the official slogans and tactical manoeuvres of this or that group, the basic tendencies proper to the transitional phase between capitalism and socialism came into collision with one another.

The movement in the countryside
The general political crisis and the appeals launched in December were not without consequences in the countryside, which, however, judging by the available evidence, was slower to act and did not experience any systematic and widespread movements. The peasants too began to agitate in favour of their own interests and aspirations. Because of the differentiation that still persisted in the countryside and because of the different sorts of pressure experienced by the rural population in the phase after the overthrow of capitalism, it was inevitable that different groups would take shape each with their own distinct aims.

The most important movements we know of took place in areas close to large cities and therefore more exposed to the contagious influence of the urban upheavals.

Once again the scene of the most sensational incidents was the Shanghai region. The first news of these incidents was contained in an appeal to the people of Shanghai (a step in itself spectacular enough to show how serious the situation was) launched by a sort of syndicate of orthodox Maoist groups. As usual, the official press traced back the movements in the countryside to the manoeuvres of 'capitalist roaders' who were supposed to have seduced the people with 'economism' and various sorts of concessions, encouraged stoppages of work, fomented individualism and even deliberately widened the disparity in living standards between town and country in order to set worker and peasant against one another.[36] However, even the official press revealed that the peasants were on the move, that they had adopted the method of sending delegations and 'exchanging experiences' and that they had even resorted to stopping work. Their claims included higher pay and improved welfare, but more generally they called for the elimination or the narrowing of the gap between town and country.[37] (The Chinese press characterized demands of this sort as 'left in form but right in essence'.) On other occasions the peasants demanded a bigger individual share in the distribution of the product and the immediate redistribution of communal funds accumulated in previous years. Another serious problem was that of state delivery quotas and state loans. Where there had already been a rise in income, the peasants aspired to an easier life.[38] Other more special forms of discontent were to be found among rural workers. One vehemently disaffected group were those citizens of Shanghai and other big cities sent down in vast numbers to do agricultural work in isolated and inhospitable regions of China. Another such group were the seasonal or temporary workers and contract workers, assigned from communes on the outskirts of Shanghai and other cities to work under relatively unfavourable conditions in industry. The sackings among these workers (revealed in the *People's Daily*, 26 December 1966) probably had the effect of spreading the most acute forms of unrest to the countryside.

As for the movement outside Shanghai, we have information about unrest and tension in the Wuhan area,[39] at Foochow,[39] in various unnamed villages,[40] in Kiangsi province, where there are said to have been

[36] *HNA*, 22 January 1967, p. 3, p. 13 and passim.
[37] See also *HNA*, 2 February 1967, pp. 32–33.
[38] *HNA*, 24, 27, 28 January 1967; 2 February 1967, and *SCMP*, no. 3868, p. 22.
[39] *HNA*, 24 January 1967, p. 3.
[40] *HNA*, 29 March 1967, p. 4.

attempts at sabotage as well as stoppages of work,[41] and in Heilungkiang, where some of the peasants shared out funds, moved into the towns and started disputes over the right to use the land.[42] In several places tensions reportedly arose at the beginning of spring.[43] Conflicts, including strikes, sending delegations, distributing grain reserves from previous years, even broke out in the famous model brigade of Tachai in Northern Shansi.[44] There were reports on Radio Peking Domestic Service, 28 September, that peasants were distributing all the crop among themselves and thus starving the government of grain procurements. The same broadcast revealed that in some areas a very serious situation existed, with peasants 'snatching' the harvest from neighbouring brigades, teams and communes because they held different points of view. The gravity of the situation at the beginning of the year and the anxiety felt by the Maoist group is confirmed in an 'urgent notice' circulated on 3 February by various Shanghai organizations. The notice denounces the manoeuvres of the opposition, urges people to mobilize to the full in order to boost production and stresses the need to form a great alliance. The Central Committee itself spoke up on 21 February, anxious for normal working during the spring harvest and eager to clarify the correct attitude towards cadres: the overwhelming majority of cadres should not be attacked,[45] even if it was necessary to prevent cadres purged during the socialist education movement from obtaining unjustified rehabilitations. (The reason for this qualification was that during the socialist education movement some of the work teams sent into the countryside had been accused of acting unjustly and summarily. Hence the requests – apparently on the increase in this period – for a review of the sentences.) One particular accusation brought against the opposition was that they had incited young peasants to go into the cities to take part in the movement developing there and had celebrated traditional feasts, thereby increasing consumption.[46]

Later, sections of the peasantry, especially in suburban areas, started up movements which took the form of demonstrating in the cities, blocking communications and struggling against contingents of Red Guards and Revolutionary Rebels. This happened particularly in the

---

[41] *HNA*, 11 October 1967, p. 5.
[42] *HNA*, 9 February 1967, p. 21.
[43] *HNA*, 27 December 1967, p. 20.
[44] *HNA*, 6 March 1967, p. 13.
[45] See also *HNA*, 22 February 1967, p. 3.
[46] *HNA*, 6 February 1967, p. 7.

tense areas of Wuhan[47] and Canton.[48] In Canton a 'conservative' organization of remarkable size had been set up as early as February. Incidents such as these were reflected in Ch'en Po-ta's and Mao's attacks on those who wanted to extend the theory of the countryside surrounding the towns to the cultural revolution.[49] The Central Committee itself found it necessary to intervene in mid-July with a particularly urgent instruction.[50]

Leaving aside its more obscure episodes and particular features, the crisis of early 1967 confirmed the acuteness of the tensions in the countryside and the survival and recurrence of typical – and at least in part contradictory – peasant aspirations which are immune to mere political or propaganda campaigns if their objective roots remain intact. Basically the crisis revealed the peasants' desire to emerge from the conditions of backwardness in which they still found themselves. The easiest way of achieving this, as they saw it, was to increase their individual shares of the product, bring in the free market and allocate more time to work on private plots. More generally, the root cause of the discontent was the absence of any means whereby the peasants could effectively influence basic economic decisions and hence the destination of the surplus product.

Mao's counteroffensive

There was no official indication of the Maoist leadership's attitude to the initial outbreak of the strikes and the autonomous movements from below. The very fact that for some weeks a policy of concessions was fairly widely applied suggests that there was uncertainty, or even temporary paralysis, at the top. There is also evidence that the Maoists themselves were not above supporting the 'economist' campaigns of sections of the working class when it was in their interests to do so. This was particularly true in the case of the so-called temporary and contract workers. These workers lived a second-class existence: they were denied the welfare, pension, unemployment and housing rights enjoyed by the permanent workers, they were not eligible to join trade unions and they often had to draw their rations from the communes of which they remained members.[51] It seems that the heaviest concentrations of these 'worker-

[47] *SCMP*, no. 4041, p. 10.
[48] *SCMP*, no. 4030, pp. 14ff., and no. 4026, p. 12.
[49] *SCMP*, no. 4023, p. 20, and no. 4070, p. 6.
[50] *CB*, no. 852, p. 135.
[51] See particularly *FEER*, 8 May 1968 and *Current Scene*, 15 March 1968.

peasants' were to be found in freight-handling, on the railways, in the mines (where they constituted two-thirds of the labour force) and in stevedoring. The introduction of temporary workers into industry was clearly also a threat to the security of permanent workers. During the winter of 1965–66, for instance, 7,800 workers in the sugar refineries were sacked and replaced by a peasant work-force.[52] We can assume that many of the town-dwellers dispatched to the remote frontier regions had been displaced under the same system. As the cultural revolution gathered momentum it seems that many factory managers, anxious for their positions and eager to build a basis of support among the permanent workers, attempted to exploit these fears and tensions and buy themselves popularity by sacking large numbers of temporary workers.[53] There are indications that these sackings began as early as June 1966.[54] The effect of these actions, at a time when the Maoist leadership was calling on the working class to voice its grievances and 'take a firm hold of revolution', was to goad the temporary workers into defending themselves. 'Hundreds of thousands' of them attended a rally in People's Square, at which, according to Radio Shanghai, they 'pledged themselves to smash the unreasonable system under which they are employed, and to set up a new labour system in line with Mao Tse-tung's thinking'. The rally further declared that 'the system of hiring temporary and outside workers is a remnant of the labour system of capitalism'.[55] The unrest spread far beyond Shanghai. In Shensi, for example, one article said that 'over 95% of the workers in our construction brigade . . . are temporary and contract workers and we have suffered just as bitterly as our comrades under the old society'.[56] At first, as we said earlier, the Maoist Revolutionary Rebels gave their backing to the campaign and called for the abolition of the entire worker-peasant system. Even the *People's Daily*, which strongly condemned the sackings, seemed to be sympathetic towards the temporary workers. There was a wave of reports that Chiang Ch'ing herself received a delegation of these workers and denounced the Ministry of Labour and the trade unions for allowing such a system to exist.[57] Radio Peking appeared to support the granting of differential pay increases to temporary workers.[58] However, the tide of sympathy was

[52] See *Current Scene*, 15 March 1968, p. 5.
[53] *People's Daily*, 26 December 1966.
[54] See *Current Scene*, 15 March 1968, p. 9.
[55] Quoted in *Problems of Communism*, January–February 1968, p. 15.
[56] *Current Scene*, 15 March 1968, p. 11.
[57] Ibid., p. 9.
[58] Ibid., p. 13.

soon to turn. First the *People's Daily* and then the Shanghai *Wen-hui pao* retreated from the positions they had taken up, and by mid-February the Maoist leadership outlawed the organizations set up to defend the interests of the worker-peasants and officially announced that there could be no economic equality for workers in this category.[59] The brief period of unity between the Maoists and the most oppressed part of the Chinese working class was over. Into its place stepped the ubiquitous legend of subversion and incitement by the 'handful'. This and other episodes, in short, would suggest that the leaders did not send out precise orders in advance of the wave of unrest in Shanghai. If they had done so, and if the orders had not been carried out, it would have been in their interests to give publicity to such incidents in support of their own version of events, at least in later reconstructions of what happened.

(An American publication in Hong Kong has reproduced two draft documents issued by the Central Committee which lay down guide-lines on how to carry out the cultural revolution in the factories and in the countryside. There is no way of saying for certain whether or not these documents are authentic, even though from their content and style they would seem to be. They are for that reason interesting, even though only draft projects. The factories document insists on the Sixteen Points and the need to 'make revolution and stimulate production'. It recommends workers not to stop producing and to proceed to the setting up of revolutionary organizations. It further recalls the importance of sticking to the eight-hour day and suggests cutting down on the size of delegations to Peking, and calls for the rehabilitation of the victims of earlier struggles. The document on the countryside has a similar line, but puts the emphasis on the continuity between the cultural revolution and the earlier socialist education movement.[60])

It seems that the Maoist centre did not react immediately even at the height of the Shanghai crisis. It is impossible to say whether this was to gain time in order to avoid taking an open stand against the movement among the masses or because it was blocked by internal conflicts. The 4 January 'Message to all the people of Shanghai', issued by eleven organizations aligned with that part of the local leadership opposed to concessions, was published the next day by the Shanghai *Wen-hui pao*, which had been taken over by Maoist Rebels on 3 January.[61] It is no accident, however, that it was not until 9 January that the *People's Daily*

[59] *FEER*, 8 May 1968.
[60] *CB*, no. 852, pp. 29–32.
[61] *HNA*, 11 January 1967, pp. 25ff., and 20 January 1967, p. 10.

reprinted the article, adding its own approval of the contents. We know that on other occasions similar delays were explicitly attributed to the existence of serious differences of opinion. It would be foolish to suppose that this time the delay was a matter of chance, especially since four days is a long time in a situation of extreme tension. There are indications that the reaction in Shanghai to Peking's decision to republish the appeal was one of relief, as if the leadership's delay in taking a stand had caused anxiety.

After this interval, however, the position of Mao and his direct supporters clearly took shape. They intended to take firm steps to block and deflect the movement, which was escaping all attempts at control from above and developing a momentum of its own.

They vehemently attacked the Shanghai leadership for its policy of concessions, even though they omitted to call for its complete overthrow. (Even the 'Urgent Notice' – issued 9 January by the Revolutionary Rebel Headquarters and thirty-one other organizations[62] – called not only on the police but also on the Municipal Party Committee to act upon the programme outlined.) The Maoist leaders further voiced warm approval of the Rebel groups' appeal, not only in the *People's Daily* editorial of 9 January but also in a special 'Message of greetings to Revolutionary Rebel organizations in Shanghai' of 11 January, jointly signed by the Central Committee, the State Council, the Military Affairs Commission of the Central Committee and the Cultural Revolution Group.[63] (This list is very significant, because it indicates the real centres of power, whose authority the leaders wanted to stress in a particularly dramatic situation. We need hardly remind readers that the Military Affairs Commission of the Central Committee was equivalent to the leadership of the army.) They firmly denounced the strikes and the unrest and ordered the workers to return to work at once, to stop sending delegations and recall those already sent and to vacate all occupied buildings. The Shanghai General Headquarters of the Revolutionary Rebels (as they were by now commonly called) intervened directly in a number of different ways in order to normalize the situation. They occupied the railway head offices,[64] for example. Other measures aimed at stabilizing the situation were the decisions to freeze accounts, to gather in sums of money paid out, and so on. At the same time the Rebels threatened to take and actually took

[62] Text in Robinson, op. cit., pp. 101–105.
[63] Text in ibid., pp. 105–106.
[64] *HNA*, 16 January 1967, p. 39.

various repressive measures, without bothering too much to camouflage them.

It is worth pausing here, especially as in general it is still very difficult to form any exact idea of just how much repression was actually carried out during the cultural revolution. That violence and repression were carried out by various bodies and organizations is shown by the fact that the leadership repeatedly warned against the use of brute force, arrest, mistreatment and torture. For example, as early as 18 November the new Peking committee issued an 'important communiqué' saying that 'no factory, mine, school, organization or other unit is permitted to set up a detention house and court, and arrest and torture persons without authority'.[65] To return to the events with which we are immediately concerned, the 'Urgent notice' of the thirty-two organizations, which had obtained official blessing, made a distinction between people opposed to Mao and the cultural revolution and people who aimed at undermining the social order or committing actual crimes, but it still ordered the immediate arrest of both categories. The Revolutionary Rebels of Shansi and Kweichow issued a similar order in a communiqué published on 25 January.[66] The document circulated by the Central Committee, the State Council, the Military Affairs Commission and the Cultural Revolution Group on 11 January also called for action against the strikes and the Central Committee and the State Council announced decisions to strengthen public security in a circular two days later.[67] It is strange that those people who never tire of holding up the cultural revolution as a triumph for proletarian democracy, basing themselves on one or two quotes from the Sixteen Points or other appeals and documents, have completely ignored this evidence, which proves that repression was directed not against counter-revolutionaries but against critics of the leadership's line.

It was precisely at this point, during the January unrest, that the Maoist centre stepped up the use of the army in support of the Maoist 'revolutionary left' and that Mao directly appealed to the army to engage in the cultural revolution. Previously the role of the army had been restricted – one has only to think, for example, of the cautious approach embodied in the Sixteen Points. It is significant that the Maoist group in Shanghai, which had been so responsible for initiatives in the early stages of the cultural revolution, were unable to control the course of events in

[65] *CB*, no. 852, p. 28.
[66] *HNA*, 2 February 1967, p. 9.
[67] *CB*, no. 852, pp. 39 and 44–45.

their own city. Chang Ch'un-ch'iao, one of the main leaders of this group together with Yao Wen-yuan and Wang Hung-wen, was able to use his influence at the centre to secure the support of the police and the PLA. According to Hunter, Chang and the 'Workers Headquarters' were by this time hard pressed by the political challenge coming from more radical organizations, especially the group known as the Second Regiment and led by Keng Chin-chang. (See pp. 122–3, above.) The alliance of forces around Keng seems to have been more radically opposed to the Municipal Committee than Chang, who after all had long been a pillar of the local Party establishment as Director of Propaganda, a member of the Municipal Committee and a protégé of the former Mayor K'o Ch'ing-shih. According to the attacks upon them, Keng and the Second Regiment became the focus for an alliance of organizations with more than half a million members, both workers and students. Even the most slanderous attacks did not charge this grouping with being 'economist' and they were clearly projecting radical political demands for seizing power from the Municipal Committee. According to Hunter: 'The important thing about the Second Regiment, and about Keng Chin-chang's rivalry with Chang Ch'un-ch'iao, was the revelation that Workers Headquarters – a group whose fame spread far beyond Shanghai and even the frontiers of China – was, by the end of January, a mere shell. The power and the numbers in the Shanghai workers' movement lay elsewhere.' (op. cit., p. 228) He goes on to describe Chang's attempt to regain control: 'Chang Ch'un-ch'iao was aware of his unpopularity, but he was confident of support from the Cultural Revolution Group in Peking. He decided therefore to clamp unity on Shanghai before it became impossible. He scheduled a meeting of the Rebels for January 26th, to "prepare for the formation of the Shanghai Commune". The implication was clear: it would be a Shanghai Commune run by Chang Ch'un-ch'iao, with the assistance of his lieutenant, Yao Wen-yuan.' (p. 235)

Hunter quotes Maoist accounts of the attempted first meeting of Chang's 'Shanghai Commune' which allege that it was successfully opposed by Keng, the Second Regiment and other forces hostile to Chang: 'On January 26th, Keng Chin-chang brought his fourteen organizations and noisily interrupted the preparatory meeting of the Shanghai Commune. In front of delegates from every Rebel group in the City, he wrangled with Wang Hung-wen and other representatives of Workers Headquarters. Because of his obstructionism the meeting could not go on and had to be recessed. Later, he attended a meeting of Workers Headquarters leaders, where he had the temerity to declare: "This preparatory session was actually an attempt to discredit the Second Regiment!" He then stalked off in high dudgeon to his Regiment, where he wrote an abusive telegram to Wang Hung-wen. In this way, the preparatory meeting for the Commune was completely blocked.' (p. 237) Hunter points out that even accounts such as this which were deliberately designed to discredit the 'extremists' also indirectly reveal the fact that they enjoyed sufficient mass support to disrupt the Maoist plans: 'Workers' organizations like Keng Chin-chang's Second Regiment were able to defy Chang Ch'un-ch'iao precisely because they had put down the deepest roots among the people.' (p. 244) However Chang had other means of enforcing his line, in the form of motorized PLA units, police and Red Guard groups drafted in from outside Shanghai. Thus one of the groups opposing Chang at this time had its headquarters raided at night and all its equipment and vehicles seized. (p. 235) When Chang wished to rescue three officials of the Writers Union who had been detained by another group which opposed him, the Red Rebels, Chang was able to summon up a task force of 'eighteen three-man motorcycle outfits, four trucks – two full of soldiers, one loaded with police, and one empty (possibly for use as a paddy wagon). There was also a car carrying a staff officer and a political commissar.' (pp. 238–39) Among the Red Guards groups from outside Shanghai who played a role in breaking the opposition to Chang and the Workers Headquarters were the Harbin Rebels. Such organizations would have had less knowledge of the real nature of the movement under way in Shanghai and were used both to swell the list of Chang's supporters and also to act as a strike-breaking force. When the Harbin group left Shanghai at the end of February, after the defeat of Chang's main opponents, they issued a communiqué which ended: 'We also wish to thank the land, sea and air forces of the Shanghai garrison for the help and support of their commanders.' After quoting this Hunter adds: 'In this polite acknowledgement must lie the key to many an unsolved mystery of Shanghai's Cultural Revolution.' (p. 267)[68]

Though Chang was able to defeat his opponents through the adroit use of the blessing of the Chairman combined with a modicum of armed force, the resulting political structure was to be known as a Municipal Revolutionary Committee and not a Commune: the latter name was, it seems, too

[68] Another reference to army intervention in Shanghai appears in William Hinton, *Hundred Day War*, New York 1972: 'In the Shanghai Diesel Engine Plant armed PLA forces intervened with guns to put down what was regarded as a "mutiny".' (p. 195.) Both Hunter and Hinton are sympathetic to the Cultural Revolution. See also Evelyn Anderson, 'Shanghai Upheaval', *Problems of Communism*, January–February 1968, which gives a similar picture of the Shanghai events based on official sources.

closely associated with the radical democratic principles of the Paris Commune.[69]

In other towns (starting with Harbin in Heilungkiang on 23 January) the army played a crucial role. It was on 23 January that two documents were circulated, one by the four top centres of power mentioned above and the other by the Central Committee,[70] calling for PLA intervention. The latter document declared that the army should take the situation in hand where the 'proletarians' were unable to do so. Three days later, on 26 January, control of airports and civil aviation was entrusted to the army.[71] (There are Japanese reports[72] that this step provoked protests among the Revolutionary Rebels in the civil air-lines, but that the PLA ignored such protests and sent in soldiers to disperse protesting mobs.) These decisions were accompanied by a reshuffle of the army Cultural Revolution Group and the reopening of attacks on military groups considered revisionist and conciliationist, probably because they were opposed to throwing themselves too wholeheartedly into the struggle. The reshuffle, decided by the Military Affairs Commission of the Central Committee, was announced in the army newspaper on 12 January. The new group was headed by Hsu Hsiang-ch'ien, and Chiang Ch'ing was appointed as its 'advisor'; Hsiao Hua, Yang Ch'eng-wu, Wang Hsin-t'ing, Hsu Li-ch'ing, Kuan Feng, Hsieh T'ang-chung and Li Man-ts'un were deputy-heads. Some of these were later to come under attack and lose their front-ranking positions. On 14 January the army newspaper published an important editorial which said, in part, that the struggle between the two lines not only existed in the army, but was bitter and complex. During this period there was reportedly a rash of posters attacking top military leaders and probably inspired by radicals in the leadership – another indication of the scale of the struggle going on in the army's upper echelons.[73] We can conclude, therefore, that although the

[69] Opposition to the name Commune came from both Mao and Chou En-lai. Chou is reported to have said in February 1967 that before Commune-style elections could be held it would be necessary to have achieved 'the integration of the revolutionary organizations with the mass of the people', to have isolated the ultra-leftists and to have united with the 95% of the cadres who were basically good: 'We are far from having reached this stage at this point.' *Hung-se chan-pao*, 17 February 1967, quoted together with other cautionary remarks from both Chou and Mao in John Bryan Starr, 'Revolution in Retrospect: the Paris Commune through Chinese Eyes', *China Quarterly*, no. 49, January–March 1972, p. 119. We will discuss further implications of the Shanghai Commune episode in the next chapter. See also Schram, *Mao Tse-tung Unrehearsed*, p. 278.

[70] *CB*, no. 852, pp. 49–50.

[71] Ibid., p. 53.

[72] Quoted in Esmein, op. cit., p. 205.

[73] *Current Scene*, 7 December 1970, p. 9.

battles of the previous year and the January 1966 conference noticeably strengthened the influence and controlling power of the Lin Piao group, they had evidently not removed the difficulties or solved all the problems that had arisen. After January, however, the army's role grew and it intervened effectively in the most bitter struggles as a repressive force. We shall deal with this at a later stage in this study.

The Maoist group's counteroffensive in the political and ideological controversy took the form of a campaign against economism[74] – this became a major theme of the later stages of the cultural revolution – and an insistence on the need to 'take a firm hold of revolution and stimulate production (thus attacking the agitators and strikers, who were slowing down production)'.

A joint editorial in *Red Flag* and the *People's Daily*, published on 12 January, described economism in the following terms: 'What kind of stuff is economism? It is a form of bribery that caters to the psychology of a few backward people among the masses, corrupts the masses' revolutionary will and leads the political struggle of the masses on to the wrong road of economism, inviting them to disregard the interests of the state and the collective and the long-term interests, and to pursue only personal and short-term interests. Its aim is to strangle the great proletarian cultural revolution, to disintegrate the dictatorship of the proletariat and the system of socialism.

'This economism sabotages social production, the national economy and socialist ownership. It promotes the tendency towards the spontaneous development of capitalism and encourages revisionist material incentives in a vain attempt to destroy the economic base of socialism . . .

'In a word, this economism uses bourgeois spontaneity to replace proletarian revolutionary consciousness, uses bourgeois ultra-democracy to replace proletarian democratic centralism and proletarian sense of organization and discipline, uses bourgeois reactionary illegalities to replace proletarian dictatorship and the extensive democracy operating under it, and uses capitalist ownership to replace socialist ownership. Economism is a new aspect of the big counter-attack launched by the bourgeois reactionary line on the proletarian revolutionary line.'[75]

An article in the *People's Daily* of 23 January quoted historical examples to show that economism represented the interests of the upper layers of the proletariat and the labour aristocracy, while for the phase following

---

[74] E.g. *HNA*, 11, 13, 16, 17, 18, 21, 22, 23, 27 January 1967, and 2, 10, 22, 26 February 1967.
[75] *HNA*, 13 January 1967, and *PR*, no. 4, 1967.

the conquest of power it repeated the demagogy in the editorial quoted above.

It is clear from the passage quoted above that this interpretation is very loose and at variance with the classical Leninist definition (we shall return to some of these points in the last part of this book). It is entirely legitimate to criticize economic incentives in the forms in which they developed in the USSR since the 1920s. But in this particular case the target of criticism were the workers who, hard-pressed because of a long period of wage-stagnation and affronted by the style of living of the old and new privileged layers of society, began to struggle for higher wages and other fringe improvements as soon as they felt their bonds begin to loosen. Obviously we cannot rule out the possibility that the absence of economic margins and possible unfavourable effects in the medium or long term for the masses themselves might counsel against concessions. In such a case, however, any decision should be backed up with closely-reasoned political arguments and the workers should have the opportunity of directly checking the evidence. By falling back on the language of ideological terrorism, the leading groups and strata showed their authoritarianism, sectarian intolerance and set hostility towards any movement from below which begins to develop in its own way.[76]

The 'seizure of power'

But Mao and the group in charge of the cultural revolution could not afford to restrict themselves to a policy of denouncing, attacking and repressing a movement with a mass character and obvious radical aspects. (Apart from denunciations of incitement by 'capitalist roaders', there were also cases of attacks on left extremism.[77]) Such an attitude would inevitably have led to a break with broad sections of the workers, which would have been dangerous for the stability of the regime as a whole. In any case it would have meant the end of the entire political operation which was the official purpose of the cultural revolution; it would have forced Mao to give up the fight against powerful groups at all levels of the Party for certain general policies and ideas which he considered necessary, for the reasons we have given elsewhere.

Therefore, even when the offensive against the strikes and unrest began, the attacks and denunciations were tempered with a note of moderation

[76] Note that even the 'Urgent Notice' did not rule out wage rises in principle; it said they were objectively impossible at the moment, but would be dealt with at a later date.

[77] See, for example, the 4 January 'Message to all Shanghai people' and the joint *Red Flag* and *People's Daily* editorial of 12 January.

and caution. The instructions contained within the 'Urgent Notice', for example, were qualified in such a way as to avoid aggravating tensions (for example, it gave those who had occupied buildings a week to move out, announced that repayments could be made by instalments, excluded transport charges from these repayments, avoided rejecting wage rises out of hand, and even established a category of 'special cases' which might be dealt with immediately). Overtures were made to what were pictured as sections of the masses led astray by provocateurs, and a similarly cautious attitude was adopted towards the cadres.[78]

But even more important, Mao simultaneously relaunched the cultural revolution, not only laying great emphasis on the themes put forward in recent months but above all clarifying and widening the scope of the campaign under the pressure of events. Hence the launching of the 'seize power' slogan, which from mid-January through the whole of the following period became the dominant theme. On 15 January, for example, a *Red Flag* editorial stated the problem of power and said, in part, that 'Marxism-Leninism, Mao Tse-tung's thought teaches us that the basic question of a revolution is that of political power'. The headline of a despatch dated 25 January was 'Revolutionary Rebels all over China resolve to seize power in all fields'.[79]

Judging strictly by the categories and principles of Marxism-Leninism (and of Mao himself, in so far as he used them in his previous writings), the use of this formula in the context of the cultural revolution was totally inappropriate. Marx and Lenin, especially in their writings on the Commune and in *State and Revolution*, did not leave room for even the slightest confusion on this question. The 'seizure of power', which involves the smashing of the old state machine (including the army), means social revolution, the overthrow of one ruling class and the coming to power of a new class. Now, not even the most far-fetched accounts present the processes at work in China in the period up to 1965–66 as an actual reconstruction of capitalism. They see them at the most as preparing the way for such a reconstruction in particular spheres (there is no need to point out the metaphorical value of the expression 'capitalist restoration' in connection with a university or a particular department). The reference to Marx and Lenin was, therefore, sheer propaganda. In any case these 'seizures of power', far from being a revolutionary qualitative leap, were a gradual process, ending with the last 'seizure of power' in the last remaining region as late as September 1968; during certain

[78] *HNA*, 10 January 1969, pp. 3–4, and 13 January 1967, p. 5.
[79] *HNA*, 25 January 1967, p. 3.

periods the process was deliberately suspended and each 'seizure of power' required recognition from the supreme authorities. At the beginning of March, for example, the peasants were invited to suspend the 'seizure of power' during the harvest.[80] On 27 January Mao declared in a speech that accounts of 'seizures of power' should be submitted to the State Council for approval.[81]

In effect the question of 'seizing power' (and its practical application, to which we shall return later) enables us to grasp the essential meaning of the Chinese crisis: it was not a revolutionary break, but rather an admittedly profound movement of reorganization and reform, or rather an unprejudiced attempt at self-reform. Throughout the period up to January 1967, even after the August Plenum and after the appeals to the worker and peasant masses, Mao had conceived the cultural revolution as an instrument of pressure through which to restore the general political line which he believed had been abandoned or dangerously watered down, and to bring about the downfall of groups dug in at all levels of the Party. But neither the Sixteen Points nor the December documents saw the elective bodies of which they spoke as substitutes for Party and state institutions. The decisive turning-point did not come until January, when Mao sent out his appeal to 'seize power', which meant setting up new bodies to take the place of the old ones. In other words, he went so far as to specify how to set about restructuring the apparatus, which he saw by this time as a large-scale operation. To attain this goal, fresh demonstrations and massive mobilizations were organized, this time under the aegis of the 'Revolutionary Rebel' organizations. At the same time, as we have said, the democratic-revolutionary and anti-bureaucratic themes already proclaimed in the Sixteen Points were taken up again, while the official press tirelessly played on the grudges and resentments harboured by the masses against the apparatus, that hotbed of privilege, abuse of power, wastefulness and administrative disorder.[82] Thus we read in the report of the Kweichow 'seizure of power': 'The duration and extent of the brutal bourgeois dictatorship exercised by the handful of counterrevolutionary revisionists within Kweichow Provincial Committee and Kweiyang Municipal Committee over the people was rarely paralleled in China . . . The former state organs were oversized and redundant and were a kind of bureaucratic organ. In handling a

[80] *HNA*, 13 March 1967, p. 16, and *HNA*, 22 March 1967, p. 10.
[81] *Le Monde*, 5–6 February 1967.
[82] See for example *HNA*, 16 January 1967, pp. 9ff.; 17 January 1967, p. 3; 20 January 1967, pp. 5 and 12; 1 January 1967, pp. 3ff., and *PR*, no. 5, 1967, pp. 17ff.

matter, they pushed it around like a ball. The documents often had to take a long journey. This was against the glorious traditions of our Party during the period of the revolutionary war and against Chairman Mao's consistent teaching of better troops and simpler administration. These bureaucratic organs moulded themselves solely on Soviet revisionist organs. They were used by the handful of reactionaries to form cliques for private ends, to place their aides and to rule the people. They must be reorganized thoroughly today.'[83] Nieh Yuan-tzu, the authoress of the famous *tatzupao* broadcast on Mao's orders on Radio Peking in June 1966, gave Anna Louise Strong an interview in which she attempted to account historically for the strength of the counterrevolution in China. After recalling that power was seized 'only at the top' in 1949, she listed a combination of three factors which had produced a greatly swollen apparatus, more and more detached from the masses. These three factors were: the elements of the old state machine, the ideology of the surviving bourgeoisie and revisionism.

In line with the new instructions, revolutionary committees of various kinds began to appear and were given front-page coverage by the press. The Revolutionary Rebels who carried out the 'seizures of power' at the lower levels of industry frequently had to deal with a special set of problems resulting from strikes and journeys to the capital by large numbers of workers. The 'seizure of power' formula was seen as a way of resolving these problems. Shanghai Radio gave a report of Revolutionary Rebel dockers pledging themselves to replace strikers and continue working 'even if there is only one single person left'.[84] Rebel nuclei mobilized 'revolutionary staff members . . . , retired workers, revolutionary students and army men'[85] to 'oppose economism' or, in blunter language, to break the strike.[86]

Paradoxically, the 'seizures of power' also brought into being new and democratic forms of management. In Shanghai, for instance, 'production committees' were set up by the staff in the Yangshup'u power station and the naval shipyards. On 27 December 1966, the Shanghai Glass Machinery plant had set up the first of these revolutionary production committees, which reportedly functioned according to the principles of the Paris Commune: the committee had ten members who were elected by secret ballot and subject to recall at all times. It is interesting to note

[83] *SCMP*, no. 3892, pp. 10–11.
[84] Quoted in *Problems of Communism*, January–February 1968, p. 16.
[85] *PR*, no. 8, 1968.
[86] E.g. Hunter, op. cit., p. 219.

that official propaganda did not emphasize this aspect of the experiment.[87] However, cases such as these, where the workers overstepped the pre-ordained limits of the movement, were frequent. Daubier (a fervent supporter of the Maoists) remarks of the 'transfers of power' at lower levels that 'the masses seem to have spontaneously gone much further than anticipated', thereby upsetting the smooth course of events.[88] In line with the new instructions, revolutionary committees of various kinds began to appear and were given front-page coverage by the press. The Revolutionary Rebels in a Wuhan Light Industry Dies and Moulds Plant seized power.[89] In Kiangsu province they formed production committees in commercial and financial departments after 'seizing power'.[90] Poor and lower middle peasants took over the leadership of a Hangchow commune in Chekiang Province.[91] Rebels seized power in a Peking chemical factory,[92] a Tientsin paper industry.[94] and a Kwangsi printing house,[93] Finally, in advance of Shanghai and Peking, the Shansi Rebels were the first to 'seize power' in Party and state organizations on a provincial scale, after a bitter struggle in which the army intervened in strength.[95]

The Shansi experience acquired considerable significance because it was taken as a model and because it enabled the Maoist leadership to give more precise shape to the question of 'seizing power'. Although, as an obvious precautionary measure, the news of the Shansi events was withheld until 25 January, the decisive action had already taken place on 12 January and it was not until after that date that the new campaign got under way: the demands now were for a great alliance of the revolutionary groups, who were beginning to fight among themselves,[96] and the triple alliance, i.e. a bloc between the three main components in the new organs of power, army, masses and 'good' cadres.[98] The Maoist leaders, with the experience of the crippling factionalism of the Red

---

[87] For the information on Shanghai, see Esmein, op. cit., p. 196. For the Glass Machinery Plant see *PR*, no. 5, 1967, p. 12; *HNA*, 16 January 1967, p. 15, and 24 January 1967, pp. 4–5.

[88] Daubier, op. cit., p. 149.

[89] *PR*, no. 5, 1967, p. 23.

[90] *HNA*, 25 January 1967, p. 3.

[91] Ibid.

[92] Ibid., p. 4.

[93] *HNA*, 27 January 1967, p. 15.

[94] *HNA*, 28 January 1967, p. 10.

[95] *HNA*, 26 January 1967, pp. 3ff.

[96] *HNA*, 15, 16, 17 January 1967, passim.

[97] *HNA*, 5 February 1967, p. 4.

Guard movement behind them, were obviously interested in uniting the various organizations that were beginning to form, so as to control and steer them more easily. Moreover, they must have seen the triple alliance as the inevitable solution, as events revealed to them the nature of the intervention of various forces in the conflicts and the need from the very first to guarantee elements of balance and stability. In Shansi groups of Maoist Revolutionary Rebels, more than 20,000 strong according to Japanese sources,[98] surrounded the provincial committee in T'aiyuan, an industrial and mining town and capital of the province. The workers reportedly countered with a wave of strikes called by a T'aiyuan workers' alliance,[99] with the result that the 'seizure of power' could only be carried through thanks to the resolute intervention of the army. The combination of these two elements, the Revolutionary Rebels and the army, in the new power formula therefore seemed to reflect the balance of power and to represent the logical outcome of the conflict that had taken place. Moreover, some of the old cadres had taken part in the struggle from the inside and the central leadership had every interest not only in drawing these cadres into the restructuring of the apparatus but also in winning back as many as possible of those who had taken a different path or wavered. Hence the formula of the triple alliance, which was shortly to be confirmed by the Heilungkiang and Shantung experiences. (Note that the Shansi revolutionary committee was only officially constituted on 18 March. Looked at in this way, the Heilungkiang and Shantung committees – set up on 31 January and 3 February respectively – were the two earliest.)

This solution carried with it many difficulties. In the first place, to the extent that Mao reacted to the events of late December and early January by giving a new thrust to the cultural revolution and issuing fresh appeals to the masses, there sprang up new differentiations, rivalries and un-governed currents: that is to say, the new wave would also inevitably develop according to its own inner dynamics and with a strongly anti-bureaucratic charge. As early as mid-January the Rebel onslaught was directed not only against conservative groupings but also against the 'anarchists' and the proponents of ultra-democracy, who were even discovered amidst the ranks of the Maoists and in the brand-new revolutionary committees.[100]

Reinstating the cadres was easier said than done, either because many of the young Rebels distrusted and hated the apparatus as a whole or

[98] Quoted in Esmein, op. cit., p. 240.
[99] Ibid., and Dutt, op. cit., p. 145.
[100] *HNA*, 11 January 1967, pp. 4–5, 29 January 1967 and 31 January 1967, p. 3.

because they feared that some cadres were manoeuvring for positions and were insincere in their attitudes (it was not long before the arguments about 'false seizures of power' began). Especially during the next period all these problems were to be sharply posed, but it is significant that they clearly took shape from the very first.

January 1967 was undoubtedly a crucial juncture in the cultural revolution and from the point of view of the mobilization of social forces and the clarification of Maoist policies marked the peak of the movement. The month closed with the publication of the editorial of *Red Flag* no. 3, which was meant to generalize the experiences of the 'January storm' and sum up the ideas and the basic line of the leadership: the struggle against restorationist trends, the struggle for power, the great alliance and the elimination of all traces of departmentalism and sectarianism, the struggle against degeneration in the new organs of power, the absolute supremacy of Mao's thought, integration with the masses, recognition of the essential role of the cadres and the need to win them over in their overwhelming majority (for the purposes of conquering and retaining power), 'taking a firm hold of revolution and stimulating production', the creation of new organs of power, and the struggle against heretical organizations and strike-organizers, using repression if necessary.

9
The Formation of Revolutionary Committees

The development, composition and functioning of the
Revolutionary Committees
It is not easy to grasp all the different phases and variants in the process of rebuilding and restructuring the political apparatus, which was progressively extended to all the country's provinces and to the various levels of the administrative subdivisions and social and economic units. Roughly speaking, however, the sequence was as follows: Revolutionary Rebel groups were set up, bodies were formed linking these groups, great alliances were welded between the various Rebel organizations (which either converged and fused or coexisted on a common basis), preparatory committees of various sorts were set up and provincial Revolutionary Committees (or Municipal Committees in big cities like Peking and Shanghai) were proclaimed. At the same time organizations sprang up whose specific aim was to boost and rationalize production and stop the cultural revolution harming production. These bodies were called 'front-line commands'.[1]

In one of his statements Mao gave the following definition of a Revolutionary Committee: 'The basic experience of Revolutionary Committees is this – they are three-fold: they have representatives of revolutionary cadres, representatives of the armed forces and representatives of the revolutionary masses. This forms a revolutionary "three-in-one" combination. The Revolutionary Committee should exercise unified leadership, eliminate redundant or overlapping administrative structures, follow the policy of better troops and simpler administration and organize a revolutionized leading group which keeps in contact with the masses.'[2]

---

[1] See, for example, *HNA*, 12 February 1967, pp. 11–12; 13 March 1967, p. 6; 4 March 1967, p. 13; 17 March 1967, p. 4, and 20 March 1967, p. 19.
[2] *PR*, no. 14, 1968, and *HNA*, 30 March 1968 (reprinted from a joint editorial in *People's Daily*, *Red Flag* and *Liberation Army Daily*).

These themes later reappeared again and again, in countless different forms. Those features of the Revolutionary Committees given most prominence by the leadership were that they were, in historical terms, a new type of institution, that they enabled the three major constituents to join together, that they guaranteed constant control by the masses and the expression of the will of the masses, and finally that they functioned more flexibly and less bureaucratically than past bodies. Consequently the Revolutionary Committees were said to be less likely to degenerate or become estranged from the masses.

The first formally constituted committee on a provincial level was, as we said earlier, the one in Heilungkiang. The Heilungkiang Red Rebels collaborated with P'an Fu-sheng, first secretary of the Party Provincial Committee, who is said to have confessed his errors personally to Mao after the August Plenum and was now fighting a tough battle within the apparatus. The army gave its support to the Red Rebels, who were hard-pressed by other Rebel groups such as the *Jung-fu chun* or *Glorious Veterans' Army* (demobilized soldiers sent to work in the bleak north of the province), the *War Preparedness Army* (youths from Harbin and elsewhere sent to work at the frontier or in the mountains) and the *Red Flag Army* (Harbin industrial and transport workers fighting for shorter hours and a better wages system).[3] The response of the army was to dissolve these organizations and jail their leaders. If it had not been for this determined intervention it is unlikely that the Red Rebels, who even according to the official press were in a minority,[4] would have had sufficient forces to 'seize power'. An important element in their success, in the Red Rebels' own estimation, was the combination between 'internal and external forces'. It was P'an Fu-sheng himself who went with the military leaders to the headquarters of the Red Rebels in order to discuss the 'seizure of power'. The Red Rebels invited P'an and the commander-in-chief of the Heilungkiang Military Region, Wang Chia-tao, to sit on their committee and this was the basis of the formation of the Provincial Revolutionary Committee.[5] P'an was subsequently made chairman of the Committee – a choice that symbolized the compromise between the old apparatus and the Rebel forces, and was as such opposed by some of the Red Rebel leaders in the province.[6]

In Kweichow the Revolutionary Committee was set up on 13 February

---

[3] See *Current Scene*, 1 June 1968, pp. 4–6.
[4] Ibid., p. 6.
[5] *HNA*, 11 February 1967, pp. 3–6.
[6] *Current Scene*, 1 June 1968, p. 8.

after a 'seizure of power' on 25 January. On 2 February one section of the Rebels, the First Headquarters, called for elections among the Revolutionary Rebels for a provisional Revolutionary Committee, but on 25 February Li Tsai-han, first political commissar of Kweichow Military District, offered himself as leader to the Rebels and became chairman of the Committee.[7] The meeting held on 13 February to celebrate the setting up of this committee approved the following declaration: 'The old Kweichow Provincial Communist Party Committee, the old Kweichow Provincial People's Council and a handful of Party people in authority taking the capitalist road have been overthrown. The Kweichow Provincial Revolutionary Committee, the provincial organ of power through which the proletarian revolutionaries exercise power, now declares its formal establishment. Until the new Provincial Party Committee comes into being, this Revolutionary Committee exists as the leading organ with full power. It exercises the power of party, governmental, financial and cultural leadership in Kweichow.'[8]

In Shansi the Provincial Committee was formally constituted on 18 March. The proclamation was preceded by a seven-day meeting attended by more than 4,000 delegates from revolutionary organizations, the Party, government bodies at various levels and the army. A committee of 245 members was elected, of whom 118 or 48% came from various revolutionary organizations. The standing committee had twenty-seven members.[9]

The formal proclamation of the Shanghai Municipal Revolutionary Committee on 24 February was part of a complex chain of events and fierce struggles that was to continue for over a year. Shanghai more than any other Chinese city was the scene of countless local initiatives and competing groups and organizations. As we have seen, even in the first moments of its existence, during the November train-hijacking, the original Rebel organization had split into at least two different tendencies, one of which was ready to follow the orders of Chang Ch'un-ch'iao, the Shanghai protégé of the Cultural Revolution Group, and the other of which rallied to the fierce and intransigent Keng Chin-chang. By early February the Rebels under Chang Ch'un-ch'iao and his associate Yao Wen-yuan, author of the attack on Wu Han and former editor-in-chief of Shanghai's *Liberation Daily*, were busy preparing to proclaim the Shanghai People's Commune. Information on the structure of this

[7] See Esmein, op. cit., p. 239.
[8] *HNA*, 22 February 1967, p. 6.
[9] *HNA*, 23 March 1967, pp. 28–30.

Commune is partly contradictory. Jean Esmein[10] maintains that it was established on the basis of the workers' committees set up earlier in the factories and that it progressed from lowest to highest levels. He admits, however, that the 'democratic discussions' that prepared the way for the Commune may not have satisfied every organization in the city. Among those for whom there was no place on the Commune's 'provisional committee' was Keng Chin-Chang and his refractory Second Regiment, although Keng and his allies in fourteen separate workers' organizations had over half a million followers, even by the admission of their opponents.[11] Another organization opposed to Chang Ch'un-ch'iao was the so-called Workers Third Headquarters, which Chang's supporters put at several hundred thousand strong.[12] (Chang's own organization, on the other hand, seems at best to have had only modest support, much of it from outside Shanghai.[13]) The Commune was undemocratic in one other important way: the leadership was in effect chosen not by the Commune's constituent organizations but by the central leadership in Peking. Chang Ch'un-ch'iao did not try to hide this. On the contrary, he said quite openly: 'Fortunately we then had a "trump card" in our hands for the Centre designated myself and Comrade Yao Wen-yuan to be members of the Shanghai People's Commune.'[14] Even so, the Maoist centre withheld its approval from the Shanghai experiment. According to Chang Ch'un-ch'iao himself, Mao had told him that the idea of a Commune was premature and the term itself inadvisable. Use of the term Commune implied that this was an entirely new organ of power based on the masses and replacing the existing bureaucratic structure. It was necessary to seek allies in the army and among the cadres.[15] The Shanghai Commune, despite Chang's manipulations, in no way fulfilled these requirements. Its committee was made up of seven workers, three students, two peasants, two cadres and two army men.[16] For these reasons, and because it tended to overstimulate the political aspirations of the rebel mass movements elsewhere, the idea of a Commune was dropped and in its place arose the Shanghai Municipal Revolutionary Committee. However, the Commune was not without echoes in other parts of China. A group of Rebels from the Harbin Military Engineering

[10] Op. cit., pp. 189 and 200–201.
[11] See Hunter, op. cit., pp. 225–226 and 224.
[12] Ibid., p. 229.
[13] Hunter, op. cit., pp. 228 and 256.
[14] *SCMP*, no. 4145, pp. 6–7.
[15] Hunter, op. cit., pp. 261–2. See also references in note 69 of previous chapter.
[16] Esmein, op. cit., p. 200.

Institute were in Shanghai during this period.[17] It was probably this group that carried the idea north to Harbin, in Heilungkiang, where a Commune was proclaimed on 16 February. It too was abandoned, after pressure from Peking.[18]

There were also preparations for a Commune in Peking itself, where two groups of Red Guards and Revolutionary Rebels (fifty-eight organizations in all) came together to form a 'preparatory committee of the Peking People's Commune'.[19] Here too the formula eventually enacted was that of the Revolutionary Committee. The preparatory phase leading up to this committee included convening congresses of the different social groups. On 21 March, a peasants' congress, attended by 2,500 delegates from thirteen different *hsien* and from the outskirts of Peking, closed after electing delegates for the Peking Municipal Revolutionary Committee as well as a standing committee of the congress. On 22 March, representatives of the revolutionary workers and leaders in industry held a similar conference. On 25 March the turbulent Red Guards of the secondary schools held their congress, under the watchful eye of Hsieh Fu-chih (Minister of Public Security) and the army;[20] in this case the minutes contained no specific mention of the election of delegates. On 20 April, the Municipal Revolutionary Committee was proclaimed; it had ninety-seven members, of whom only seventeen were army men and thirteen cadres. There were twenty-four workers, twenty students, thirteen peasants, six members of cultural associations and four citizens.[21]

In August the Tsinghai Provincial Committee was formed: from then onwards reports of the setting up of committees follow a sort of fixed pattern – description of the ceremony, brief notes on the preparatory phase, summaries of the speeches, the names of some of the leaders and the text of the message to Mao. The first proclamation of the Tsinghai committee said: 'All party, government, financial and cultural power in the province comes under the committee.'[22]

At factory level the triple alliance was first conceived differently, at least in some cases, from the provincial committees. To take a few examples, in the Peking Postage Stamp Printing Works the old norms were abandoned with the seizure of power and there was an 87% daily

[17] Hunter, op. cit., p. 263.
[18] *Current Scene*, 1 June 1968, pp. 6–7.
[19] Esmein, op. cit., p. 240.
[20] Ibid., pp. 240–241.
[21] From a Japanese source quoted in Esmein, op. cit., p. 242. See also *HNA*, 22, 25 and 28 March 1967 and 21 April 1967.
[22] *HNA*, 14 August 1967, pp. 3ff.

increase in production, thanks partly to the non-sectarian attitude adopted towards members of organizations defined as conservative (four of the leaders of the Revolutionary Rebel organization *The East is Red* came from the ranks of other organizations, while the former deputy-manager was put in charge of production). There was also the case of the Kweiyang cotton factory, where all the Revolutionary Rebels, formerly divided into a dozen different groups, came together in the *Mao Tse-tung thought 1 March fighting regiment* and set up a revolutionary committee as a 'temporary organ of power'. The committee members, described as 'servants', were elected by secret ballot and put in charge of the factory, but continued to take part in production; new norms were laid down in place of the old.[23] One Kweichow machine factory explained in detail how the triple alliance was different: it consisted of 'an alliance of revolutionary leading cadres, revolutionary ordinary cadres and representatives of the revolutionary mass organizations'. The committee was made up of three workers, two deputy managers and two ordinary cadres. In the Shanghai No. 2 Camera Plant the administrative post of departmental manager was abolished and representatives were elected to supervise production groups. Among the rules that were abolished was one requiring that the transfer of a worker from one job to another be approved at different levels.[24]

Very soon, however, even the triple alliance in the factories began to conform to a set pattern and include army representatives. On 18 March the Central Committee of the Party decided that the army should 'make a great effort to help civilians and support their work in industrial production' and invited 'the revolutionary workers and cadres . . . to cooperate effectively with the comrades from the People's Liberation Army'.[25] An editorial in *Red Flag* on how to treat cadres spoke of representatives of the militia taking part in the triple alliance in factories. For Party and government organs it envisaged a combination of revolutionary leading cadres, revolutionary intermediate cadres and revolutionary masses.[26]

The official press gave particular prominence to the experience of the factories in Tsingtao, where, in the Ssufang Rolling Stock Plant for example, the practice of submitting all finished products to a manager for approval was ended, on the grounds that it might hamper the creative powers of the workers. Most factories set up command posts, answerable

---

[23] *HNA*, 5 March 1967, pp. 3–5, and 9 March 1967, pp. 3ff.
[24] *HNA*, 18 March 1967, p. 3, and 18 February 1967, p. 16.
[25] *HNA*, 19 March 1967.
[26] *HNA*, 24 February 1967, p. 4.

to the Revolutionary Committee, to supervise production. In general there were large cuts in the administrative staff: from forty-four to sixteen persons in one metallurgical factory, for instance. In the great steel centre of Anshan the process of forming the 'new revolutionary leadership' was fairly slow and painful: the great alliance was set up on 25 and 26 December 1967, but the municipal committee did not make its appearance until the middle of April 1968 after a decisive intervention by the army. In the Peking General Knitwear Mill, where a triple alliance committee was set up in November 1967, the workers put an end to the old system of individual responsibility and introduced collective responsibility for controlling the machines. The administrative staff was slashed from 229 to twenty-four (out of a total of about 2,000 workers) and these twenty-four did manual labour three days a week. The revolutionary committee had nineteen members, almost all of whom continued on production and only two of whom – the chairman and the vice-chairman – were administrative cadres.[27]

There is a good deal of documentation on the committees set up in the schools, where events took the same course as in the factories. At the beginning of March an article announcing the re-opening of the elementary schools in Peking and Shanghai described the triple alliance as a coming together of revolutionary teachers, non-teaching staff and students, and revolutionary leading cadres.[28] But already on 7 March a directive from Mao, taking the experience of a Tientsin middle school as an example and launching the struggle-criticism-transformation campaign, laid down the principle that the army should intervene directly in schools at all levels and provide a political and military education. So triple alliance committees began to spring up in the schools too, and included not only students and revolutionary teachers but also leading revolutionary cadres and representatives of the army. The congress of Peking secondary school Red Guards was one example of this; by the middle of July committees had been set up in 130 schools in the capital. At the beginning of August a Revolutionary Committee came into being at the Academy of Sciences.[29]

A number of documents held up as models by the official press give us some idea of how these committees worked. At Tientsin, the first plenary

[27] *HNA*, 29 August 1967, p. 26; 9 December 1967, p. 5; 4 January 1968, p. 15; 29 September 1968, p. 12.

[28] *HNA*, 7 March 1967, p. 3.

[29] *HNA*, 8 March 1968, p. 3; 28 March 1967, p. 13; 15 July 1967, p. 14; 4 August 1967, pp. 5–7. For the Tientsin text, see *CB*, no. 852, pp. 97–99.

session of the Municipal Revolutionary Committee drew up an eight-point programme for its own 'revolutionization'. The eight points were: '1) Place the creative study and application of Chairman Mao's works above everything; 2) Establish the concept of confidence in and reliance on the masses and master the work method of "from the masses, to the masses"; 3) Conscientiously implement the Party's policy of democratic centralism; 4) Establish the style of self-criticism; 5) Strengthen unity between old and new cadres with "fight self-interest, repudiate revisionism" as the guide; 6) Persevere in the practice of cadres taking part in collective productive labour; 7) Be models in publicizing and implementing the Party's principles and policies, maintain high revolutionary enthusiasm, step up investigation and study and improve work efficiency; and 8) Always retain the characteristics of an ordinary labourer.'[30]

Earlier the Shantung Provincial Committee had drawn up a document of regulations on style of work. These regulations were adopted by other provincial committees. After stipulating that cadres must always remain 'ordinary workers' and oppose any preferential treatment that might divorce them from the masses, the document said: '1) It is forbidden to shower praise on members of the Revolutionary Committee. Big character posters and slogans praising members of the committee are forbidden. In cases where such posters and slogans have been put up, efforts should be made to persuade the masses to have them covered over immediately. 2) No member of the Revolutionary Committee should make a public speech on behalf of the committee unless it is discussed collectively beforehand by the committee. No speech of a member of the committee should be recorded or printed without the approval of the committee. 3) When members of the Revolutionary Committee set out for a place or attend mass gatherings, there should be no formal welcomes and send-offs and no applauding at their arrival or departure. Members of the committee may not be photographed or filmed without its approval. 4) Members of the Revolutionary Committee must devote a definite amount of time to doing physical labour. 5) Members of the Revolutionary Committee are not allowed to present gifts in their own name or accept gifts. 6) Generally, the names of Revolutionary Committee members should not appear in the press. Where it is necessary for their names to be printed in a newspaper, this must be done according to the stipulations set out by the Party Central Committee. 7) Members of the Revolutionary Committee should live simply. Extravagance is forbidden. They are not

[30] *PR*, no. 52, 1967, p. 27.

allowed to use for private purposes motor cars belonging to the organization. They should pay attention to economy when using cars on public business. 8) Members of the Revolutionary Committee should set aside a certain amount of time for interviews with the masses and should personally deal with the letters from the people. 9) Members of the Revolutionary Committee should go among the masses regularly and, with an attitude of willingness to be pupils of the people, call fact-finding meetings and forums to invite people's opinions and criticisms. 10) The Revolutionary Committee should undertake small rectification campaigns at fixed intervals (for instance, every two months). Representatives of the mass organizations should be invited to participate in each rectification campaign as and when necessary.'[31]

An example of how this worked in practice: of the eighteen members of the revolutionary committee of the Chingkang Mountains, in Kiangsi province, the majority belonged to the production team and during periods of intense activity took the office with them into the fields, to avoid interrupting their physical work. In ten months, five open-door rectification campaigns were held, in the course of which the masses put forward more than a hundred suggestions which the committee either adopted or commented on in writing.[32]

In partial anticipation of the concluding chapters of this book, we here note that the main consequence of the upheaval at the end of 1966 and the beginning of 1967 was the emergence of a considerable number of new cadres who had been pushed to the fore by a vast movement from below, a movement of which they had been part and whose aspirations they attempted to interpret. This change-over, despite its limitations, had a significance that was objectively far more democratic than the normal change-overs in the past, which were more or less a question of coopting newcomers into the workings of an already existing structure. It is likely, therefore, that cadres took a much more consistent and effective part in production than before: the effect of this was to begin the process of renewal of a connective tissue that had been progressively shrivelling up. Finally, at the lower levels of the factory committee or rural commune, the rank-and-file could take advantage of the climate that had developed to voice their demands and criticisms and impose their will: during the most turbulent months this was also true, though to a lesser extent, at the higher levels.

---

[31] *PR*, no. 27, 1967, p. 32.
[32] *HNA*, 31 January 1969, p. 5.

All this should not, however, lead us to ignore or neglect many essential elements in the situation which, in this case as in others, can easily be unravelled by a careful reading of the official press.

In the first place the triple alliance itself, which was a basic principle in the rebuilding of the administration, had the conservative effect of channelling the movement onto a more moderate course. It is no accident that right from the start this formula had to be defended both against the conservative right wing and a left wing which saw it as a compromise solution. Although the most important documents on the subject stressed that the representatives of the mass revolutionary organizations should play their rightful part in the 'great mass movement from below under the leadership of the Central Committee', they put no less emphasis on the indispensable role of the cadres, the 'nucleus and backbone' of the new bodies, the overwhelming majority of whom were to be reinstated;[33] the army was presented as the main pillar of the dictatorship of the proletariat.[34] In a speech passing on instructions from Mao, Chang Ch'un-ch'iao particularly insisted that young people should learn from the old cadres for many years.[35]

The influence of the army and the old cadres was decisive in the provincial bodies, that is, in the higher bodies created during the movement to rebuild the administration. We are not referring so much to their numerical representation. In fact, in the autumn of 1968, representatives of the new mass organizations accounted for about half the 4,000 or so members of the provincial and municipal committees: in some important cases, for example in Peking, they were in a majority; in Shansi they constituted 48%, as against 23% army men and 29% cadres.[36] These proportions changed radically, however, as one ascended the ladder. In Peking, where the mass organizations were well represented even on the standing committee (nine military men, eleven representatives of mass organizations and three cadres)[37] the chairman was General Hsieh Fu-chih, Minister of Public Security and a Vice-Premier; two cadres, two army men and only one representative of the mass organizations (Nieh Yuan-tzu) were the committee's vice-chairmen. At a rough estimate – some names seem to have two descriptions and others none at all – out of a total of twenty-nine revolutionary committees the army could count on

[33] *HNA*, 1 March 1967, p. 4.
[34] *HNA*, 11 February 1967 and *PR*, no. 12, 1967.
[35] *SCMP*, no. 4147, p. 4.
[36] *HNA*, 13 May 1967, p. 35.
[37] *People's Daily*, 21 April 1967.

at least nineteen chairmanships, as against ten for the cadres and none at all for the mass organizations. The army had seventy-nine vice-chairmanships, the cadres seventy-six and the mass organizations thirty-nine, and this picture would not change substantially even if the great majority of the fifty-one vice-presidents of unspecified background came from the mass organizations. In the factories too it was often the old secretaries or vice-secretaries of the Party committees who became chairmen, vice-chairmen or heads of the new bodies, and even in pilot experiments the workers were in a minority.[38]

How were the Revolutionary Committees chosen? We have seen how in some cases delegates and committees were actually elected: and sometimes strict rules were laid down defining the jurisdiction of the elected bodies and giving the assembly the right to decide on basic questions.[39] References to the election of committees became increasingly rare, however, until finally a theoretical justification was hatched for rejecting the principle of elections. 'Blind faith in elections is also a form of conservative thinking', we read in *Red Flag* no. 4, 1968. 'Revolutionary committees . . . (are) . . . established not by elections but by relying directly upon action by the broad revolutionary masses.'[40]

In reality the revolutionary committees, especially the provincial ones, were the result of agreements between the different component parts. The process of agreement was supervised by the Maoist centre, which always had the final say. According to a text by Mao, quoted above, the new bodies should have been ratified by the State Council: what is certain, however, is that they had to be formally approved by the Central Committee, which demanded to see all relevant reports before any public pronouncements could be made.[41] The top Party authorities, who dealt with the problem province by province and city by city (in the case of the larger cities), continually intervened in the formation of the committees, sending communications and representatives and meeting delegations in Peking, where the main role fell to Chou En-lai and to leaders of the Cultural Revolution Group like Ch'en Po-ta, K'ang Sheng and Chiang Ch'ing. It appointed and gave recognition to the preparatory committees and strongly influenced the formation of the committees even before the conclusive stage was reached. Particularly in the more difficult cases,

---

[38] See *HNA*, 16 December 1967, p. 3 (a Tsingtao cotton factory); 23 June 1968, p. 15 (a Shanghai electrical workshop); and 18 March 1967, p. 3 (an engineering factory in Kweichow).

[39] *HNA*, 14 February 1967, p. 6.

[40] *PR*, no. 43, 1968, p. 7.

[41] See *CB*, no. 852, p. 89, and Chiang Ch'ing's speech in *SCMP*, no. 4069, p. 2.

where the resistance was greatest (Kwangtung and Hupeh, for example), a decisive role was played by the army, which directly controlled the situation until the committee was formed. In the case of Shanghai the intervention of Chang Ch'un-ch'iao and Yao Wen-yuan was decisive. Chang and Yao, as we have already said, were nominated by the Maoist centre.[42] Chang became chairman of the Municipal Committee and Yao a vice-chairman. On the occasion of the proclamation of the Peking Committee it was specifically announced not only that Mao had controlled the operation, but that the Central Committee had given its approval.[43]

Since this point is crucial for an appraisal of the cultural revolution, which is frequently interpreted as a spontaneous or semi-spontaneous affair, we will give some specific examples. In the case of Szechwan, the Central Committee nominated the heads of the preparatory committee on 7 May 1967 and later, on 28 May, the Central Committee, the State Council, the Central Military Commission and the Central Cultural Revolution Group approved the preparatory committee's report on the setting up of the Revolutionary Committee, as well as the names put forward for the standing committee.[44] On 12 November 1967 these same four bodies also approved the formation of the Kwangtung preparatory committee, a decision announced two days later by Chou En-lai.[45] On 13 April 1967 the Central Committee intervened in Inner Mongolia, replacing some military leaders and designating their successors to those responsible for the preparatory committee.[46] The Central Committee also took a special decision approving the military control committee's report of 10 April 1968 on the setting up of the Anhwei Provincial Committee and ratifying the names of the members of the committee itself and of the standing committee, the chairman and the vice-chairmen.[47] Chou En-lai, Chiang Ch'ing, K'ang Sheng and other top leaders held a meeting on 18 March 1968 authorizing the setting up of the Chekiang Committee: the list was not then complete, but some problems of detail were reportedly settled on the spot.[48]

It is much more difficult to assess the situation at lower levels because of the shortage of information. For the *hsien* committees, however, a

[42] See *SCMP*, no. 4147, p. 2, and *SCMP*, no. 4145, pp. 6–7.
[43] *HNA*, 21 April 1967, pp. 14–15.
[44] *CB*, no. 852, p. 128; *SCMP*, no. 4220, pp. 1–2.
[45] *SCMP*, no. 4080, p. 9, and no. 4085, p. 7.
[46] *CB*, no. 852, p. 118.
[47] *SCMP*, no. 4195, p. 1.
[48] *SCMP*, no. 4182, pp. 2–4.

vertical structure was gradually re-established and instructions transmitted from the top downwards.[49]

We can therefore conclude that even during the most dynamic phase of the formation of Revolutionary Committees, control from the top was not lacking. The leadership tirelessly reaffirmed that such control was a matter of principle, and strove constantly to put that principle into practice. The official propaganda was fairly explicit on this point. For example, an article on the experience of Tsingtao Municipal Committee extolled the education of young cadres by the army on the basis of the principle 'following the above and relying on the below'. And did not one document, already mentioned, speak of a 'mass movement from below under the control of the Central Committee of the Communist Party, led by Chairman Mao'? This may seem a stereotyped phrase, but it is a useful clue for interpreting the cultural revolution, which was characterized precisely by the combination – and opposition – of a movement from below and orchestration from above.

In the last analysis the reformist nature of the operation was also confirmed by the strict limits imposed on the 'seizures of power', from which not only the central bodies and the Central Committee but also regional authorities (for example the Regional Bureaux) deemed to be on the same level as the Central Committee were exempted, we might say almost by definition. Chang Ch'un-ch'iao said as much in his 24 February speech: 'The Central Committee indicated that the power of the secretariat of the East China Bureau cannot be seized because it is a representative organ of the Party Central Committee, and seizure of its power is tantamount to seizure of power from the Party's Central Committee' (*SCMP*, no. 4147, p. 3). One reflection in the field of terminology of the limits of the new structure was the Central Committee's decision (taken on 19 February 1967[50] and reported in Chang Ch'un-ch'iao's Shanghai speech of 24 February)[51] to oppose calling the new bodies 'communes' and to enforce the use of the term 'revolutionary committee'.

Finally, we should add that in an important intervention Chou En-lai put the Central Committee Cultural Revolution Group on the same footing as the Party Secretariat, thereby confirming the paramount role of this body at a time when the statutory structure was in crisis.[52] Chou further declared that the Central Committee and Central Committee

---

[49] E.g. *HNA*, 7 April 1968, p. 7.
[50] *CB*, no. 852, p. 89.
[51] *SCMP*, no. 4147, pp. 7–8.
[52] *SCMM*, no. 611, p. 10.

Cultural Revolution Group were the 'main components of the head-quarters of Chairman Mao'.[53]

The multiplicity of groups and organizations: twenty months of struggle
A brief glance at the setting up of the Provincial Revolutionary Committees from the point of view of chronology is enough to give us some idea of the difficulties met by the Maoist leadership in its nationwide campaign to restructure the administration. Between 31 January and 18 March 1967 four Provincial Committees and one Municipal Committee were set up, followed closely by the Peking Municipal Committee on 20 April. In the four following months no new committees were set up, and only three between April and the end of the year. All the others were set up between 5 January and 5 September 1968. The chronology is as follows:

1967
Heilungkiang, 31 January.
Shantung, 23 February.
Shanghai, 24 February (Shanghai Commune, 5 February).
Kweichow, 12 February.
Shansi, 18 March.
Peking, 20 April.
Tsinghai (Chinghai), 12 August.
Inner Mongolia, 1 November.
Tientsin, 6 December.
1968
Kansu, 4 January.
Kiangsi, 5 January.
Honan, 24 January.
Hopeh, 3 February.
Hupeh, 5 February.
Kwangtung, 21 February.
Kirin, 6 March.
Kiangsu, 23 March.
Chekiang, 24 March.
Hunan, 8 April.
Ninghsia, 10 April.
Anhwei, 18 April.
Shensi, 1 May.

[53] Ibid., p. 14.

Liaoning, 10 May.
Szechwan, 31 May.
Yunnan, 13 August.
Fukien, 19 August.
Kwangsi, 26 August.
Sinkiang, 5 September.
Tibet, 5 September.[54]

The unevenness of this process reflected the diversity of situations and relationships of forces in the different provinces and the ups and downs of the movement itself. On several occasions more optimistic deadlines were set: Chou En-lai, for instance, estimated that the process would be over by the end of 1967 or the spring of 1968. There were frequent references to areas in which opponents of Mao were said to have dug themselves in and continued the struggle; there were reports of occasional setbacks and of all kinds of fresh difficulties, even where the 'seizure of power' had been carried through. We have already mentioned the difficult situation in Shanghai: a year after the setting up of the committee, in February 1968, a 'bitter and complex' struggle was still going on; in Heilungkiang affairs had taken such a turn that Chou En-lai found it necessary to speak of a second 'seizure of power'; in Shantung the overthrown authorities reportedly counterattacked three times;[55] a *People's Daily* editorial[56] said that in Shanghai the great alliance 'failed to materialize in a number of spheres, industries, districts and grass-roots units'; and the record of a Kwangtung Provincial Committee session reveals some of the difficulties and tensions to be found more generally throughout the country.[57] Finally, there were cases in which the centre, fearful that an intervention might provoke difficulties, tactically encouraged the spinning out of the struggle in order to play for time.

There is mention in a whole series of documents, including the communiqué of the Central Committee Plenum of October 1968, of an 'adverse current' which took shape in February 1967 (according to Lin Piao's report to the Ninth Congress it was in existence even at the end of 1966). There were later reports of an 'evil wind' in the spring of the following year, whose aim it was to rehabilitate those connected with the 'adverse current'. The 'adverse current' is an obscure passage in the

---

[54] Taken from Jürgen Domes, 'The Role of the Military in the Formation of Revolutionary Committees, 1967–68', in *The China Quarterly*, no. 44, October–December 1970, pp. 112–145.

[55] *HNA*, 23 March 1967, pp. 26–27, and 29 February 1968; *SCMP*, no. 3955, p. 3.

[56] *HNA*, 19 September 1967, p. 3.

[57] *SCMP*, no. 4234, pp. 1ff.

cultural revolution. The background to it was the so-called 'January Revolution', which in Peking involved among other things a wave of 'seizures of power' in the public services and ministries, carried out by groups of Revolutionary Rebels. The chief 'villain' of the 'adverse current' was T'an Chen-lin, Minister of Agriculture and a member of the Party Secretariat since the Eighth Congress. T'an, according to the testimony of K'ang Sheng, opposed handing over the initiative to the masses. In order to prevent his own domain from falling to the Rebel organizations he allegedly mounted what came to be called 'false seizures of power' in those spheres (Agriculture, Meteorology and Forestry) where his jurisdiction ran. This entailed promoting the cause of tamer and more moderate organizations and mobilizing against the radicals. According to Czech and Japanese reports, T'an also took the opportunity to rehabilitate a number of cadres who had lost their positions in previous purges. If we are to believe Japanese sources quoted in Esmein's book, the spirit of resistance – encouraged by and embodied in the stand taken by T'an Chen-lin – spread to two of the highest bodies in China: the Central Committee and the Politbureau. One report (officially denied by the Chinese) said that after T'an had defended his stand at an enlarged March conference of the Politbureau, there was a majority of only one vote. Another report, dating from February, said that the Central Committee had considered setting up a large council, which would include individuals who had been criticized, to replace the Central Committee Cultural Revolution Group. Finally, it seems that 'false seizures of power' were carried out not only in Peking but also in the provinces. To our knowledge there is no evidence, however, that these were directly linked or jointly organized.[58] To sum up, then, the 'adverse current' mainly took the form of a counterattack by a section of the bureaucracy in league with cadres purged during the campaign that preceded the cultural revolution and an offensive against the Rebel groups. It is likely that after the attack on such a notable part of the leadership many people really did believe that the time had come to take their revenge; it is also likely that after the disorders of January many thought it was necessary to revise the principles of the cultural revolution and restore the authority of the old apparatus. We must ask ourselves whether the order of events (the

---

[58] The information for this brief account of the 'adverse current' is taken from Esmein, op. cit., pp. 168–172; Daubier, op. cit., pp. 153–163; and Philip Bridgham, 'Mao's Cultural Revolution in 1967: The Struggle to Seize Power' in *The China Quarterly*, no. 34, April–June 1968, pp. 15–16. See also *SCMP*, no. 4168, pp. 4–9, *HNA*, 30 March 1967, p. 10, and 3 April 1967, p. 6.

'adverse current' in February followed by the open attack on Liu Shao-ch'i on 1 April) does not point to a relationship of cause and effect. It is possible that the events of those weeks made Mao's group decide to settle accounts with the old leader once and for all, either because Liu had really attempted a come-back or because the Maoists wanted to make him the scapegoat for this affair too. They certainly charged Liu Shao-ch'i and Teng Hsiao-p'ing with responsibility for the 'evil wind' of spring 1968, which was defined in April as follows: 'The present right deviationist trend of reversing correct decisions aims to reverse the verdict on China's Krushchev and the rest of the handful of capitalist roaders in the Party, on the bourgeois reactionary line and on the landlords, rich peasants, counterrevolutionaries, bad elements and rightists. It opposes the proletarian headquarters with Chairman Mao as the leader and Vice-Chairman Lin Piao as deputy leader. It opposes the Chinese People's Liberation Army and undermines the newly established revolutionary committees. It negates the great proletarian cultural revolution and the previous political–ideological movements and the dictatorship of the proletariat.'[59]

The phase we are examining, however, was characterized not only by the conservative resistance of those who were defending acquired positions, criticizing the scale of the offensive and denouncing the immaturity of the young troops,[60] but also by serious difficulties and tensions inside the ranks of the Maoists themselves. *Red Flag* recognized this explicitly when it wrote: 'Contradictions also exist among different mass organizations of the left.'[61]

Right from the very start of the campaign there were attacks against 'false seizures of power'. Some of these were attributed to groups inside the bureaucracy who proceeded to set up supposedly 'new' bodies in a completely administrative fashion, but others were the work of groups the leadership considered not sufficiently representative or responsible.[62] But even in the wake of a recognised 'seizure of power' the difficulties persisted and even multiplied. The official commentators either tried to show (perhaps with a reference to the universal law of 'the one that divides into two') that such developments were inevitable or gave some sort of psychological or moralistic interpretation, e.g. the new structures degenerated as the old ones had done because the new cadres became

---

[59] *HNA*, 27 April 1968, p. 6.
[60] *HNA*, 23 March 1967, p. 22.
[61] *HNA*, 20 May 1967, p. 3.
[62] See *HNA*, 3 March 1967, p. 3 (Shantung), and *CB*, no. 866, p. 6 (Canton).

swollen-headed and arrogant and were animated by a wish to excel.[63] However, vague statements such as these were followed by more precise criticisms. As early as the end of January 1967 the *Red Flag* published an article denouncing small-group mentality, dispersion of forces (excessive decentralization), contempt for discipline, ultrademocracy, liberalism, subjectivism and individualism and opposing the tendency to deal too severely and indiscriminately with cadres.[64] As the campaign got under way, more and more prominence was given to the attacks on what were said to be 'anarchist' trends and a series of articles against anarchism appeared: on 26 April 1967 the *People's Daily* published an editorial entitled 'Down with anarchy!' and on 11 May Jen Li-hsin's article 'Anarchy is a punishment for the sins of opportunism'. (Among the more specific allusions was an attack on anarchist trends in a mine.)[65] The same paper published an article on 13 August 1968 accusing some people of inventing speeches or documents and interpreting Mao's instructions in their own way – a point we emphasize because the vagueness of many of Mao's statements certainly encouraged differing interpretations. More generally, the roots of 'anarchism' were attributed to the persistence of petty-bourgeois attitudes, from which not even the workers were exempt.

We have no reason to doubt that particularist and sectarian tendencies did make themselves felt: international experience shows that such manifestations are inevitable when powerful social forces come into play and an old ruling group is toppled without a new political and ideological coalescence of forces to provide an alternative leadership and a victorious outlet for the movement. But the reasons for the differentiations and the antagonisms were similar to those at the root of the troubles in the Red Guard movement, even though their practical implications were necessarily much greater. The leading group in the cultural revolution paid the price for their democratic-revolutionary propaganda, which recoiled on them like a boomerang: currents began to form whose aim was to sweep away the entire panoply of bureaucracy, destroy the old apparatus root and branch and create new bodies which would express more authentically and more completely the aspirations of those social forces (working class and peasantry) that were pressing from below.

Currents of this sort – they proclaimed that 'all rebellions are justified' – were not inclined to accept the limitations set to the 'seizures of power'

[63] See *HNA*, 28 June 1967, p. 5.
[64] *PR*, no. 6, 1967, p. 12. See also *HNA*, 5 February 1967, p. 4; 16 February 1967, p. 7; 10 March 1967, pp. 7–8; 23 March 1967, p. 20, and 28 March 1967, p. 13.
[65] *HNA*, 25 May 1967, p. 17.

and the rooting out of the old cadres; nor were they inclined to welcome the setting up of the triple alliance, which in their eyes trammelled the movement from below, and the intervention of the army, even though it was initially in a position to favour them. These contradictions, which given the conditions could hardly manifest themselves in an explicit and generalized form, trickled through in particular conflicts which seemed to limit themselves to the question of how to appraise this individual or that organization. It could not be otherwise. On paper it was relatively easy to say that good cadres should be won back and that the overwhelming majority were in this category; the trouble started when it was a question of bringing the general theory down to earth. The formula of the 95% good cadres, which in itself showed the limits the leaders intended to set to the reorganization of the apparatus, clashed with the hopes and feelings of the most advanced sections of the masses, whose distrust and hostility were directed not only against the 5% who were to pay for the operation, but more generally against the bureaucratic structures of the Party and the state.

The movement from below, with the conflicts that characterized it both during the Red Guard movement and the troubles of early 1967, gave birth to an extraordinary blossoming of groups and organizations which was one of the most striking aspects of the cultural revolution and had no precedent in a workers' state in a period of transition. There is probably no one, even in China, yet in a position to make an exhaustive survey of this phenomenon, but there is no doubt that thousands, if not tens of thousands, of organizations and groups sprang up, from groupings like that of the Shanghai Rebels (which at one time boasted a million members) to tiny cores of a handful of militants. The overwhelming majority were local and sectional organizations trying to link up on the level of one town or city or one particular trade, industry or profession. There was also a tendency to seek out links in other towns and provinces and in some cases nation-wide organizations did take shape.

We have already seen how the Shanghai appeal of 4 January was signed by eleven organizations, while the subsequent 'Urgent Notice' was signed by thirty-two and the 'Urgent Notice' to the peasants (also at Shanghai) by thirty.[66] In the universities the groups sometimes ran into hundreds. In the university for teachers at Peking various groups continued to clash with one another even after the army had rushed to the aid of the *Chingkang Mountains Commune*, which was considered the main

---

[66] See *HNA*, 10 January 1967, pp. 4–5; *PR*, no. 4, 1967, pp. 7–9; no. 5, 1967, pp. 14–16.

organization. At Tsinghua the struggle only came to an end after the intervention of a group of workers and soldiers on 27 July 1968. The situation in the secondary schools was no different: to give only one example, in the Yenan Secondary School at Tientsin, which had a total of 1,300 students, no less than forty-eight organizations sprang up with a membership of from three to over a hundred.[67]

Just to give some idea of the situation we will pause here for a brief survey. In a Shenyang (Mukden) railway office there were already a dozen revolutionary groups in January 1967. In Shansi, after the events of January, twenty-three Revolutionary Rebel organizations and seventeen revolutionary organizations held a meeting and on 16 January representatives of 370 groupings or organizations joined together for a demonstration in Harbin. On 22 January 1967 the *People's Daily* published an appeal by twenty-two organizations in the Peking and Shanghai publications sector. More or less during the same period there were over 300 organizations in Lhasa, Tibet, and twenty-five organizations set up a head-quarters in T'aiyuan, capital of Shansi province. At Tsinan, in Shantung, over thirty organizations held a conference, while the seizure of power at Tsingtao was due to the initiative of twenty-three rebel groups. In Kweichow Province the Revolutionary Rebels set up their headquarters on 25 January 1967 with the participation of forty organizations: in the same period some twenty workers', peasants' and students' organizations were active in Tientsin. At Canton in the summer of 1967 there was (according to Chou En-lai) a hard core of five Rebel organizations, while a further five were authorized to send representatives to Peking; other names are mentioned in various publications. Some months later, on 2 November, more than forty organizations or groupings signed an agreement in the same city, and in June 1967 forty-six workers' and students' organizations signed a protest against the assassination of a Red Guard. As for Wuhan, a Central Committee message of 27 July 1967 calling for a struggle against the organization known as the *One Million Warriors* also listed seven organizations loyal to Mao's thought. Later the leaders of various mass organizations agreed to publish a joint newspaper called *The Wuhan Worker*. In Tsinghai province in June 1967 there were many groups in the mass organizations (the military decided at a certain moment to support the organization known as *18 August*). In Shantung province a number of organizations continued in existence throughout the summer of 1967, three of them quite large. At Shenyang, in Liaoning

---

[67] *HNA*, 17 April 1967, pp. 9–10, and 29 June 1967, p. 35.

province in the north east, three main groups were active during the same period: the *Liao-lien* (Committee of the Revolutionary Rebel Great Alliance of Liaoning), which claimed more than half a million members, the *31 August Group*, reportedly some 150,000 strong, and the *Liao-ke-chan* (Liaoning Proletarian Revolutionary Liaison Station) which claimed 600,000 militants.[68]

As for factories and places of work, in Kweiyang, capital of Kweichow province in the south west, seventeen different organizations were set up in a cotton-mill and twenty were active in the financial and trade departments in February 1967. In the first phase of the cultural revolution a Shenyang factory working for the army had over twenty organizations, which later fused into nine (some had two hundred or so members, while the smallest had three). There were reports of one Shanghai factory which had more than a hundred different groups. In the same city there were five organizations in the naval shipyard 'The East is Red' in June 1967. During the same period there were four main organizations in the literary and artistic circles of the capital. These were: *The united committee of Revolutionary Rebels to smash the old ministry of culture*, the *Revolutionary literary and art Rebel headquarters in the capital*, the *Worker-peasant-soldier literary and art commune in the capital* and the *Literary and art circles' Red Rebel headquarters in the capital*. At the Academy of Sciences there were about fifty organizations. At Tsingtao, early in 1967, there were ten organizations in a railway factory, the biggest of which (*Study-work* and *1 August Command*) fought bitterly with each other. The Iron and Steel Works at Paotow, in Inner Mongolia, had no less than two hundred organizations. To conclude on a picturesque note: three opposing groups clashed with each other even on a train in which Mao was travelling. There is hardly any need to add that the providential intervention of Mao himself quickly put an end to the unpleasant situation – two hours after leaving Peking an alliance was set up.[69]

The organizations and groups gave voice to their opinions in various kinds of publications. This phenomenon, which had begun with the Red Guards, took on even greater dimensions after January 1967. The editors

[68] *HNA*, 16 January 1967, p. 12; 20 January 1967, p. 23; 23 January 1967, p. 6; 25 January 1967, p. 4; 26 January 1967, p. 4; 28 January 1967, p. 9; 31 January 1967, p. 3; 2 February 1967, p. 13; *SCMP*, no. 4041, p. 12; no. 4046, p. 8; no. 4082, pp. 10–11; no. 4219, pp. 4–5; no. 4041, p. 9; *HNA*, 5 January 1968, p. 8; 12 June 1967, p. 7; 20 July 1967, p. 7; *SCMP*, no. 4091, pp. 7ff.

[69] *HNA*, 1 March 1967, p. 9; 16 March 1967, p. 5; 20 March 1967, p. 23; 17 March 1967, p. 7; 12 June 1967, p. 7; *HNA*, 1 November 1967, p. 13; 19 March 1968, p. 2; *SCMP*, no. 4088, p. 9; *SCMP*, no. 4145.

of these sheets enjoyed every kind of facility, such as free paper and ink, materials for making *tatzupao*, and access to printing houses.[70] According to Yao Wen-yuan, Szechwan province held the record for the number of small-format newspapers. The *Fan-tao-ti* organization is said to have published thirty different types.[71] The fact that these groups were dependent on the consent of national or local leaders might have meant that what they wrote was conditioned in one way or another. However, effective control was probably impossible on account of the size of the phenomenon in a country as large as China. However hard they tried, the leaders were unable to exercise strict vigilance. This was true, moreover, not only of publications but also of the more general situation, especially since the normal channels of transmission were blocked (it is striking, for example, how often the leaders admitted in their speeches to having only limited information or to knowing nothing of specific situations).

We need not conclude, however, that absolute freedom was permitted. 'When some of the papers proved to be under the control of a few persons in authority in the Party taking the capitalist road, that is, in the control of those trying to push China towards revisionism and finally bourgeois restoration – said Epstein in an interview with the *Hsinhua* Agency – these papers were taken over by the revolutionary people, including revolutionaries on their own staffs.' Similarly, organizations which adopted positions considered unacceptable by the leading group were dissolved and outlawed (some continued their activities underground). A number of these organizations became the object of violent polemics. As early as 16 January 1967 the *Army of the Defenders of the Red State Power*, whose actions were attributed to the conservative tendency, came under fire. A little while later attacks started up on the Harbin *Jung-fu Chun*. Among the Shanghai organizations attacked were the *Workers' Scarlet Guard*[72] and the *Lu Hsun Corps*, which was accused in a student *tatzupao* of conceiving the purge in too administrative a way. Particularly intense and bitter campaigns were waged against the *Lientung* and the *5.16* or *16 May Group*.

There were also cases of sensational rehabilitations. The *1 August Combat Corps*, for example, was denounced by the Kwangtung district command, but a campaign (referred to by Chou En-lai himself) was later started up to rehabilitate it. No formal measures were taken, but the

---

[70] *HNA*, 28 March 1967, pp. 39–40 (Israel Epstein's evidence).
[71] *SCMP*, no. 4181, p. 2.
[72] Hunter and Esmein, especially the former, provide a mass of material on this organization and the role it played in the events at Shanghai.

sentence was completely reversed.[73]

The organizations that came under most fire were those attempting to set up links in different towns and build a nation-wide structure. As early as 12 February 1967, the Central Committee and the State Council denounced 'a large number of national organizations' which had sprung up in Peking and other parts of the country, declaring that they did not recognize them and announcing their immediate dissolution. Ironically, these organizations were reproached for not being 'democratically elected from the lower level to the higher level on the basis of genuine revolutionary alliances' – as if this were the procedure in those committees that received formal recognition! On 17 February the Central Committee put out another directive which annulled and declared illegal a joint communication circulated on 2 January by the *National Rebel General Corps of Red Labourers*, the Ministry of Labour and the trade unions. It forbade temporary workers, contract workers, rotation workers and piece workers to set up independent organizations and declared the *National Rebel General Corps of Red Labourers* dissolved. Certain categories of workers who in the course of their jobs moved around the country were forbidden to take part in the cultural revolution in other localities (this was stipulated, for example, in the text of an agreement for a great alliance among one section of Canton railway workers). Other organizations which at least in theory were nation-wide were also bitterly denounced. They included the *National headquarters of the Rebel corps of the army for the elimination of bourgeois ideology*, the *National Red Rebel state farm corps*, the *National Revolutionary Rebel Corps of educated young people who go into the mountains and the rural areas* and the *Chinese section of the international Red Guard army*. On 2 March 1967 Tsingtao revolutionary committee condemned those organizations that were tending to spread horizontally into various commercial sectors and departments.[74]

Some of these organizations and other groups were characterized as left 'deviations' (the recurring formula was 'left in form, right in essence'). As early as February 1967 the leaders condemned 'extremist seizures of power' and, more particularly, the tendency to want to hit out too radically at too many cadres. As we pointed out above, tendencies defined as 'anarchist' (the Kwangtung *Red Tumult* group, for example) were attacked, and more general criticisms were aimed at those who rejected any sort of authority and called on people to 'doubt everything' and 'deny

[73] See *SCMP*, no. 3905, 4041, 4081, 4009, 4082 and 4085.
[74] *CB*, no. 852, p. 75 and 83; *SCMP*, no. 3913, pp. 1–3; no. 4082, p. 14; *HNA*, 7 March 1967, p. 9.

everything'. Extreme left groups were also denounced in specific situations (in Inner Mongolia in August 1967, for example, when the revolutionary committee was reportedly accused of following a neo-bourgeois line) and on a general scale, especially during the summer and autumn of 1967. The far left's attack on 'conciliationism', which implied distrust and open criticism of the triple alliance, sometimes took the form of attacks on Chou En-lai, whom the left considered a man of compromise and the champion of the apparatus they were attacking as a whole.[75] Attacks were also launched from the left on the army, particularly in those areas in which it was given control. At first the slogan 'drag out the handful of power holders in the army' was put out, but this was later considered to be wrong.[76] Anxiety about left-wing tendencies was fairly wide-spread among the leadership. Mao himself reportedly said that 'the left wing will turn to the extreme left if it is not educated' and also remarked: 'Have some posters been put up? Don't arrest the people (i.e. the extreme left), let them put up more posters: the masses will stop them. You must not arrest any people.'[77]

Wuhan and Canton

The continuation of the conflicts at various levels provoked serious incidents, deepened the paralysis and partial decomposition of the state and administration and encouraged centrifugal tendencies that caused anxiety about the very unity of the country. Speaking during an inspection tour of Hunan, Mao is reported to have said: 'The Provincial Committee, the People's Council and the authorities of the military district, the region and the administrative district are paralysed . . .' In a reference to the overall situation, he is even said to have compared China to a country divided into eight hundred principalities.[78]

The most dramatic incidents took place in Wuhan and Canton in the summer of 1967. We will here give a brief account of the Wuhan incident and the events leading up to it, for it is crucial to the whole subsequent development of the cultural revolution and posed an unprecedented threat to the control of the Maoist centre.[79]

The army, which first intervened in the cultural revolution in January

[75] See, for example, Esmein, op. cit., pp. 293ff.
[76] *HNA*, 23 February 1967, p. 8; *SCMP*, no. 3979, pp. 1–3; *HNA*, 6 March 1967, p. 6; 25 April 1967, pp. 4–5; 4 November 1967, p. 16; 17 January 1968, p. 3; *SCMP*, no. 4168, p. 8; *HNA*, 3 March 1967, p. 4; *SCMP*, no. 4003, pp. 4–5; no. 4088, p. 2; 4066, p. 5; 4006, pp. 4–5; 4066, pp. 1ff.; 4068, pp. 16–19.
[77] *SCMP*, no. 4070, p. 10.
[78] *SCMP*, no. 4070, p. 11, and 4088, p. 17.

1967, after the conflicts and disorders provoked by the 'January Revolution', played a decisive role in the events of Wuhan and ignored the restrictions imposed by the leading group on the activities of the regional commands. Earlier, in the areas where the Rebels had failed during the 'first wave' to set up revolutionary committees (Wuhan itself was one such area), the army was instructed by the leading group to declare military control. One effect of this move was to increase the weight of the 'army factor' in the complex struggle between the different factions of the masses and the Party.

In Wuhan the clash of the 'two big factions' during early 1967 almost took on the proportions of a small civil war. Japanese sources claim that over 50,000 (Taipei sources say 500,000) workers took part in armed clashes in and around May 1967.[80] The 'two big factions' themselves, here as elsewhere, split broadly along 'conservative' and 'radical' lines. The 'conservative' faction embraced organizations such as the *One Million Warriors*, said to include in its ranks both workers and managers, and the *Kung-chien-fa*, said to consist of cadres working in law and law enforcement. The 'radicals' were in general younger: the *San-hsin* was an organization of student Red Guards, the *San-kang* represented some workers at the Wuhan Iron and Steel Company and the *San-lien* represented middle-school Red Guards. The 'radical' faction, which reportedly numbered more than 400,000, had outside student support.

It is clear from the way in which the conflict in Wuhan developed that much turned upon the unusual degree of autonomy assumed by the Wuhan Military Region District Headquarters, headed by Ch'en Tsaitao. Between February and April, Ch'en is said to have suppressed over three hundred Revolutionary Rebel organizations and arrested more than 10,000 people. He openly ignored the 6 April directive forbidding the army to take sides or suppress organizations without permission from the centre and gave his backing to the 'conservative' *One Million Warriors*. He enabled this organization to link up with organizations in other parts of China, such as the *Industrial Army* in Szechwan and others in Honan and Kiangsi.

The Revolutionary Rebels and Red Guards fought back, and the tension reached its peak in July when they attacked the headquarters of the *One Million Warriors* and allegedly arrested a number of leading officers.[81]

[79] The chief sources we have used are: Thomas W. Robinson, 'The Wuhan Incident', in *The China Quarterly*, no. 47, July–September 1971, pp. 413–438; Esmein, op. cit., pp. 281–286; *HNA* and *SCMP*.

[80] Robinson, loc. cit., p. 418.

[81] Jürgen Domes, 'Revolutionary Committees 1967–68', loc. cit., pp. 127–128.

Peking took alarm at these developments. Chou En-lai himself investigated the situation. He judged in favour of the 'radical' *San-kang* and *San-hsin* organizations, branded the *One Million Warriors* as 'conservatives' and rebuked Ch'en and the Military District for supporting the latter. Two more senior Maoists, Hsieh Fu-chih and Wang Li, arrived in Wuhan on 14 July and carried out a further investigation which backed up the conclusions Chou had reached. Even before they made their judgement public, Hsieh and Wang's presence gave rise to violence and unrest: on 15 July, for example, during the course of a procession to welcome the visitors from Peking, bitter clashes broke out between rival groups, leaving dead and wounded. On 19 July, Hsieh and Wang announced their decision to back the Rebels and denounce the *One Million Warriors*. This provoked violent protests. In the words of the New China Engineering College, a 'counterrevolutionary armed revolt, which shook the whole country, broke out on 19 July'. The *One Million Warriors* marched to the hotel where Wang and Hsieh were staying. Soldiers of the 8201 Unit joined forces with them and put on *One Million Warrior* armbands. Ch'en told Wang and Hsieh that the situation was no longer in his control, and he did nothing to intervene as workers and soldiers entered the hotel and kidnapped Wang, killing his secretary. The *One Million Warriors* and their army allies now took over part of the triple city, seizing key points such as the railway station, the radio station and the airport. Peking lost no time in hitting back with an airborne division, the 15th Army and five gunboats. Chou En-lai once more flew to Wuhan. After reports that Ch'en and the *One Million Warriors* intended to kidnap him, he landed at another airport south of Wuhan. Wang and Hsieh eventually flew back to Peking on 22 July, where they were given a heroes' welcome.

The *One Million Warriors*, who despite strong military and political pressure retained the support of some of the local army, continued to resist until the first week of August. Other incidents (apparently not directly connected with those in July, but in any case indicative of a continuing state of tension) are said to have taken place on 7 September, when armed bands attacked a group of 'educated young people' going to an 'employment office' for 'answers to their questions', and killed and wounded some of them.

Later, in June 1968, one publication printed a confession by Hsia Shao-ch'ing, described as one of the leaders of the *One Million Warriors'* clandestine headquarters. The details add up to a murky portrait of the person: he is said to have admitted that in the three difficult years he was in contact with internal and external class enemies and confessed to an episode in which he tried to get into a women's lavatory. The whole confession seems to be built on clichés and for that reason is hardly credible.[82]

In conclusion, the Wuhan incident signalled grave warnings to the Maoist leadership. Once again China was faced with the threat of centrifugal tendencies in the provinces; and this perennial problem was now aggravated by the apparent presence in the army of units and high-ranking officers who from the point of view of the Maoist centre were politically unreliable. In this sense it is accurate to call Wuhan a 'turning-point' in the cultural revolution,[83] for in its wake flowed a number of decisions (the first of which was the extension of the purge to the army itself) which deflected the course and in the long run helped to determine the outcome of the cultural revolution. (This remark is developed in the next section.)[84]

Canton also witnessed serious incidents which paralysed the organs of public security. The centre followed the situation very closely and on 14 and 16 August Chou En-lai received representatives of the Canton Revolutionary Rebels in Peking. The story is that groups of peasants got into the city, carried out thefts and blocked goods traffic; inmates of the reformatory are said to have got away in the confusion. It seems that there were strikes too, and the railways were paralysed for about a fortnight. Capitalist roaders in the Military Region were blamed for this situation. The Canton military commander, General Huang Yung-sheng, allegedly supported the old Provincial Party Committee against Rebel attacks and used the army to clear local newspaper offices of Rebels on 28 February.[85]

Agreements reached in Peking between rival groups did not prevent fresh incidents, clashes and outrages. On 13 August a group belonging to *District Headquarters* is said to have clashed with a group of Red Guards in the port, fired on them on the pretext that they were escaped prisoners and killed about fifteen youths. On 19 August the same group is said to have provoked another bloody incident, this time involving a *Red Police Headquarters* patrol, in which two died and nine were seriously wounded. On the morning of 20 August armed workers and peasants ambushed a

---

[82] See *SCMP*, no. 4223.

[83] See Robinson, loc. cit., p. 435, and *Current Scene*, 7 December 1970, p. 16.

[84] Other sources used include: *PR*, no. 33, 1967; *HNA*, 11 October 1967, pp. 12 and 13; *SCMP*, no. 4023, pp. 21–22; 4042, pp. 1ff.; 4043, p. 15; 4048, pp. 12ff.; 4043, pp. 1–18; 3995, p. 2; *SCMP*, no. 4041, pp. 8–10, and 3998, pp. 1–3.

[85] Domes, 'Revolutionary Committees 1967–68', loc. cit., pp. 128–129.

group of Red Guards travelling in lorries through a suburban area: a Red Guard newspaper claimed that 150 were killed and some taken prisoner. On 23 August the *Canton Joint Committee to repudiate T'ao Chu* and the *Canton Combat Corps* reportedly tried to assault the city's military command.

Huang Yung-sheng was temporarily forced to remain neutral during the outbreak of factional violence in late July and August. This spell of inactivity coincided with the Central Cultural Revolution Group's onslaught, led by Chiang Ch'ing, against the 'tiny handful' in the army. Canton's Red Guards, encouraged by the centre's campaign against Ch'en Tsai-tao, mounted their own attacks on 'Canton's Ch'en Tsai-tao'.[86] However, the campaign against the army was short-lived, and Huang himself was back in favour as early as mid-August.[87] The army was once more in a position to intervene in the factional struggle: Canton Radio reported clashes on 2, 11 and 17 September in which the army intervened in strength against the 'radicals'.[88] On 2 September a serious incident occurred at the T'aiku Warehouse at Whampoa, where Red Guards were killed by two other groups. Reports say that on 11 September six people were killed and a hundred or so wounded in clashes provoked by groups of peasants who were incited by followers of T'ao Chu. On 2 October there was a further clash, also leaving dead and wounded, in the Kwangtung Engineering College. On 19 October the situation was still tense and Revolutionary Rebels from Canton Technical Institute clashed with a group of Red Guards which an investigation team described in its report as revisionist. Finally, we should note that the Party Committee of the Canton Military Region Command admitted having made many mistakes since the end of January and in particular having improperly disbanded certain Revolutionary Rebel groups and mass organizations.[89]

Difficult situations also existed in other provinces, although to a lesser extent than in Wuhan and Canton. Bitter struggles took place in Sinkiang, 80% of whose population belong to national minorities. Relations between army and people were severely tested. Moreover, the aspiration towards greater autonomy on the part of Wang En-mao, Sinkiang's military chief, aggravated relations with the centre in Peking. Despite

[86] See *Red Guard*, pp. 200–201.

[87] Domes, 'Revolutionary Committees 1967–68', loc. cit., p. 129.

[88] Ibid.

[89] *SCMP*, no. 4041, pp. 11–13; 4088, p. 4; 4026, p. 12; 4045, pp. 8–9; 4017, p. 7; 4272, pp. 1–6; 4040, pp. 7–8; 4059, pp. 1ff.; 4090, pp. 1ff.; 4064, pp. 1–12; 4082, pp. 1–5; 4204, pp. 1ff.; 4020, pp. 1ff.

propaganda campaigns against him, Wang survived the cultural revolution as a vice-chairman of Sinkiang revolutionary committee and First Political Commissar. Of the seventeen members of the Sinkiang standing committee, there were only two from the region's national minorities.[90] Incidents also occurred in Kwangsi, especially at Wuchow, where, according to some accounts, there were 'massacres' and 2,000 buildings were reduced to rubble. Matters became so serious at one point that there was disruption of regular supplies bound for Vietnam.[91] In an appeal dated 13 June 1968, the Central Committee, the State Council, the Central Military Affairs Commission and the Central Cultural Revolution Group insisted that it was important to avoid such disruption.[92]

In many of the descriptions we have mentioned, there has been no lack of exaggeration, hyperbole and misuse of metaphors to achieve the required effect. It is plain, however, that these reports were not mere inventions, for much of what they say is borne out by the most sober official publications. Furthermore, they often give precise references, and indicate not only the names of those killed, but also their ages, the schools they attended, the groups they were members of, etc. The fact is that the tensions had reached breaking point, the stakes were high and there was no lack of fanaticism, provoked in part by the arguments and the tone of official propaganda. In these circumstances, clashes were inevitable and, since many groups had managed to get hold of weapons, such clashes inevitably ended in bloodshed. (The authorities frequently condemned the seizure of arms and called on people to hand over any they had in their possession.) Violent and repressive measures were used on a considerable scale, including arrests and acts of lawlessness. There were occasions on which the victims of such maltreatment committed suicide.[93] Mao himself forbade the extortion of confessions by violent means.[94] The victims often made self-criticisms in order to escape ill-treatment and there are some fairly clear examples of interrogations in which the accused first denied the specific charges only to end up by admitting that he was a criminal or an 'archcriminal'.[95] Sometimes local leaders made mass arrests: reports say that they reached 100,000 in Szechwan and that Chou En-lai criticized the state of affairs.[96] It was not merely the constituted

[90] Domes, 'Revolutionary Committees 1967–68', loc. cit., p. 141.
[91] *HNA*, 1 January 1968, p. 3; *SCMP*, no. 4213, pp. 4–5.
[92] *SCMP*, no. 4226, pp. 1–3.
[93] *CB*, no. 864, p. 29.
[94] *PR*, no. 1, 1969.
[95] See, for example, the case of Ch'en Tsai-tao, *SCMP*, no. 4089.
[96] *SCMP*, no. 4181, p. 4.

authorities, both old and new, who made use of such methods. Many of the organizations that sprang up during the cultural revolution itself resorted to arbitrary arrests, mock trials, imprisonment and even torture. Even in the hospitals the wounded were sometimes subjected to odious discrimination.

The role of the army

We have already mentioned how, when the struggle reached a certain pitch, the weight and power of the army grew and it was called upon to intervene in the most difficult situations. In the political and social crisis situation which crippled or seriously disorganized the political apparatus in all its forms, in the relative power vacuum which obtained and in the face of the growing movement from below, the army (the only section of the old apparatus to maintain, despite the difficulties, a quite remarkable degree of cohesion and efficiency) tended almost naturally to take command and to carry out functions normally outside its sphere of competence.

As early as 23 January 1967 the Central Committee, the State Council, the Central Committee Military Affairs Commission and the Central Committee Cultural Revolution Group ordered the army actively to intervene, annulling 'all past directives concerning the army's non-involvement'. On the same day the Central Committee decided that 'when the proletarian revolutionaries are still unable to control the situation and the protection of the People's Liberation Army is called for, the armed forces should at once enforce military control'.[97] In many provinces military control was not only established, but lasted for a long time – even the revolutionary committees later set up in these areas had more military members than elsewhere. For example, according to a speech by Chou En-lai military control was declared in Kwangtung in the first months of 1967, on the decision of Mao and the Central Committee. According to another speech by Chou, in September 1967 the revolutionary committees were in a preparatory phase and military control commissions existed in eight provinces and large communes; the situation in other provinces, some of which were also under military control, was under discussion in Peking. Chou also said in this same speech, delivered on 26 September, that 'under the Party Central Committee and the proletarian headquarters headed by Chairman Mao, the overwhelming majority of the comrades responsible for and taking

[97] *CB*, no. 852, pp. 49–51.

the leading role in the various provinces, municipalities and regions are army personnel . . . It means that our People's Liberation Army is not merely a fighting force, a work force and a propaganda force as we said in the past, but is charged with the monolithic leadership of the Party, the government and the army. Had not such leadership been implemented during the war of resistance against Japan?' At the same time he recalled that the army's first rule was 'obey orders in all your actions' and called on people not to interfere in decisions taken by the army.[98]

The army, which controlled the airports, also took over control of the railway network, at least when there were strikes or when traffic ceased to flow. And since the public security forces were disintegrating, the army tended to take over more and more of the responsibility in this field too. As we remarked at the beginning of this chapter, the army was soon called upon to intervene in the factories and took part in the triple alliance even in the schools: 'From the top to the bottom – wrote *Red Flag* – in all the departments where power must be seized, representatives of the armed forces or of the militia should take part in forming the three-way alliance.' It was therefore logical that the army was considered to be 'the most solid and the surest guarantee that it will be possible to carry through the cultural revolution to the end'.[99]

Some specific examples of intervention, other than those already mentioned. In Shantung, army action was seen as decisive at a crucial moment in the struggle. In Kweichow military support was a vital factor in the 'seizure of power', as it was in Tsinghai (where military control was set up in 'vital sectors') and in Inner Mongolia. As for the factories, the military intervened, for example, in one dispute in T'aiyuan, deciding which faction to support and arresting 'counterrevolutionaries'. According to Revolutionary Rebel sources, the army played a crucial role in various Peking factories (in particular in a big printing works, where a group of six soldiers was sent in on Mao's direct instruction to sort out a complicated situation). It also intervened in a Kiangsi mine and a Tientsin factory. As for the schools, the army carried out a difficult task at the Universities of Nanking and Peking. It helped to form alliances and overcome conflicts in a Tientsin secondary school and in the teachers' training college and secondary schools in Peking. Finally, as we shall see, in the summer of 1968 the action of groups of workers and soldiers was considered indispensable to put an end to the quarrels among the students

[98] *SCMP*, no. 3979; *SCMM*, no. 611, pp. 8–11 and 17.
[99] *SCMP*, no. 4088, p. 18; *SCMM*, no. 611, p. 16; *HNA*, 11 March 1967, p. 5, and 17 August 1967, p. 4.

and among the intellectuals.[100]

In spite of the successes achieved by Mao and Lin Piao since the end of 1965, there was resistance and opposition when the army's role in the cultural revolution was defined and when it actually intervened. It is true that the leadership, even after casting aside its initial cautiousness, was still careful to avoid too much disruption: above all, it set strict limits to the sphere within which 'seizures of power' could be carried out inside the army (these limits are laid down in a document of the Military Affairs Commission of the Central Committee, dated 16 February 1967; Mao once said he was concerned that the army should not be confused).[101] Nevertheless, crises and dangerous situations did arise.

One such crisis clearly lay behind the shake-up in the army's Cultural Revolution Group, announced on 12 January and accompanied by violent polemics. These controversies flared up again and again and led to the dismissal both of men who had held senior posts in the past and of others promoted since the beginning of the cultural revolution. A typical example of the first group was Ho Lung, who played a prominent part in the revolutionary wars, was elected to the Central Committee at the Seventh Congress, even became a member of the Politbureau at the Eighth, was an authoritative spokesman for the leadership and a highly influential political figure up to 1965 and yet disappeared from the scene and became the object of scathing attacks which did not even spare the most intimate and grotesque details of his private life.[102] An example of the second group was Yang Ch'eng-wu, who took over as Chief of Staff after the fall of Lo Jui-ch'ing and played a big part in the cultural revolution up to the second half of 1967. Yang was accused (in a speech by Chou En-lai, for example) of having committed 'extremely serious errors', of having later carried on a series of intrigues to make sure of his control over the army and of being one of P'eng Chen's men. One of the themes of the controversy was an article by Yang published prominently in all the Peking newspapers under the headline 'Establish in a thorough-going way the absolute authority of our great supreme commander Chairman Mao, and of his great thought'. According to some extremists, whose views were voiced by a Fukien soldier in a letter to the author, the

---

[100] *HNA*, 2 March 1967, pp. 3–6; 13 April 1967, p. 3; 22 September 1967, p. 16; 2 November 1967, p. 20; 9 April 1967, p. 9; 29 August 1967, p. 34; 22 September 1967, p. 24; 29 October 1967, p. 9; 9 December 1967, p. 17; 5 April 1967, pp. 3–4; 3 June 1967, p. 6; 29 June 1967, p. 35; 29 November 1967, p. 16; 15 August 1967, p. 15; 13 September 1967, p. 20; 18 October 1967, p. 21; 10 September 1968, p. 6, and 26 August 1968, p. 4.

[101] *SCMP*, no. 4201, p. 6.

[102] *CB*, no. 859, contains some Red Guard articles attacking Ho Lung.

very title of the article was a mistake – what need was there to establish Mao's thought when it was already deeply rooted? Mao was also said to have criticized the article, though with which arguments we do not know. In fact, Yang's article, much of which was aimed at Lo Jui-ch'ing, even tried to provide a theoretical basis for the cult of Mao, recalling some of Lin Piao's more brazen panegyrics ('a genius such as Mao will remain unique for hundreds of years in the world and for thousands of years in China') quoting Engels and Lenin and dismissing almost with contempt the idea that Mao and Lin could, as senior party leaders, be put on the same level.[103] Finally, it is worthwhile recalling that among those accused was Hsiao Hua, who was chairman of the military conference at the beginning of 1966 – a landmark in the first phase of the cultural revolution.[104]

The army's interventions, especially some of the more serious episodes, could not help but strain its relations with the forces mobilized in the cultural revolution and, more generally, sections of the masses. In fact, there emerged a fairly widespread tendency to criticize army control and its bias towards some organizations and against others. The leadership realized it was necessary to oppose this tendency and deal on the spot with the dangers inherent in it. Hence, for example, the two campaigns on the theme 'support the army and cherish the people' and on the need for the army to support not this or that faction, but the left in general. (Official propaganda also took up the role of the militia,[105] but sections of the militia on various occasions adopted unorthodox standpoints and the opposition was accused of exploiting it for its own ends.)[106]

The contradictory role of the PLA

The army's activity throughout the second half of 1966 was restricted to giving logistic support and political guidance to the student Red Guards. Even at this date its attitude towards the mass movement was a moderating one. This is not to say, however, that the PLA was a monolithically conservative body. At all levels and in many regions it had an important complement of radicals: at the national level these were reflected in the powerful but ambiguous figure of Lin Piao. But the radicalism of the PLA seems to have been a characteristic expression of the army's historical role of being the military cutting edge of a revolution based on the

[103] *SCMP*, no. 4168, pp. 1ff.; 4213, pp. 1–3. Yang's article was reported in *HNA*, 4 November 1967, and *PR*, no. 46, 1967.
[104] *SCMP*, no. 4168, p. 8.
[105] *HNA*, 17 March 1967, pp. 3ff.
[106] *HNA*, 7 August 1967, p. 7.

exploited and the oppressed. Military radicals might be expected to pursue an intransigent left line in foreign policy and to be responsive for the need for an egalitarian style of work in domestic affairs. But nothing in the military tradition would push the PLA radicals to welcome untrammelled expressions of popular power or untidy mass movements. When the PLA was permitted to intervene it saw its natural task as that of restoring order by suppressing popular initiative rather than by consolidating it. Moreover if the military radicals could exercise a certain influence at national level, in many of the regions the radicals seem to have been in a small minority. It should be remembered that in the two decades since liberation the army had been involved in administrative tasks in the closest cooperation with Party and state bodies. In many areas outside the capital it intervened in an unambiguously conservative sense reflecting the strong conservative urge inherent in any body of armed men separate from society and pledged to preserve that society's institutions. PLA men – both officers and soldiers – have a relatively privileged position in Chinese society, in access to education and in the distribution of certain goods. Apart from the multiple relations between the army command at each level and its counterpart in the civilian administration, we should also bear in mind that the party organization in the army was generally sheltered from the storms of the cultural revolution. For all these reasons we should not be surprised that the PLA – whose tolerance may well at one point have made the cultural revolution possible – should at the same time have played a consistently moderate role when confronted by the mass movement. Enthusiasm for the people's war, Spartan ways and unremitting hostility to US imperialism could quite easily be combined with support for commandist and authoritarian structures wherever these were challenged. In some instances the army became a sort of rallying point for conservative forces in the civilian world – the *Lientung*, for example, seems to have asked that 'all organizations be placed under the leadership of the Military Affairs Commission of the Central Committee'.[107]

As we have already noted, the army's direct intervention began with the so-called January Revolution of 1967. It was first reshuffled, as described in the preceding section, and then called upon to intervene in

[107] Esmein, op. cit., p. 183. Harvey Nielsen ('Military forces in the Cultural Revolution' in *China Quarterly*, no. 51, July–September 1972) analyses the PLA in terms of a division between *regional forces* who tended to support the conservatives in the Party on account of their established local ties, and *central main corps units*, who were used when necessary to supplant the administrative roles of conservative regional forces where this was possible.

support of the flagging campaign to 'seize power'. But it seems that the military command, despite the earlier shake-up, still had doubts about the course the Maoist leadership was pursuing. The child of this union between the army and the Cultural Revolution Group was not an invigorated Commune, but a Revolutionary Committee based on the compromise formula of a triple alliance: a mechanism that ensured a majority of military men and 'good cadres'. But because the movement unleashed in January in many places still retained much of its initial momentum and because of the particular set of circumstances obtaining in each local area, the six committees set up between January and April – the first wave – were strikingly different in composition from those set up in later waves. The main difference was in the relatively high level of representation (32.9%) achieved by the mass organizations on the standing committees of these new bodies, compared to 35.4 'revolutionary cadres' and 31.6% military men. From the point of view of the mass organizations, the situation was to worsen considerably in later months.

After the substantial failure of the first attempt at a transfer of power (a mere six Revolutionary Committees had been formed out of a possible twenty-nine) the army's new role was defined as filling the administrative and political vacuum in those areas where up to now there was no Revolutionary Committee in existence. In these areas so-called 'frontline production commands' were set up. These bodies had the outward trappings of a triple alliance but were in fact firmly under the control of the army. The army's task was to shepherd these bodies from the stage of tutelage to that of independence. But it seems to have had no enthusiasm for this task, for after the Peking Municipal Revolutionary Committee was set up on 20 April there was no new committee until mid-August. The army was in reality often more concerned with suppressing than with supporting the radicals. In mid-March the radical wing of the Central Cultural Revolution Group, angered by the attitude of the army, counterattacked with a propaganda campaign against specific actions and particular military leaders. On 6 April the Military Affairs Commission issued an important directive forbidding the army to act on its own initiative against any mass organization and generally reducing its role to a minimum. The Wuhan incident came closely afterwards, in July, and greatly strengthened the hand of the radicals in the Central Cultural Revolution Group. In the weeks immediately following Wuhan, the cultural revolution veered sharply to the left and decisions and actions were taken which had a crucial effect on its subsequent course. Chiang

Ch'ing, a leading radical member of the Cultural Revolution Group, issued an unprecedent call to 'drag out the handful of capitalist roaders from the army'. Red Guards and Rebels began openly to raid the army for weapons, and extremism and factional violence grew.[108] In Peking various 'ultra-left' groups were becoming more and more daring and the Ministry of Foreign Affairs was reportedly seized by extremists. Moreover, the army itself was said to be losing its patience and ready to hit back.

Clearly the central leadership needed to take decisive action both to head off the opposition building up in the army and to check the extremists. The first conciliatory step was the purging of Wang Li and other alleged extremists. The second was a sensational speech, delivered on 5 September by no less than Chiang Ch'ing, condemning extremism and violently denouncing the 'armed struggle' against the army.

The army, back in favour, was now entrusted with responsibility for disarming the Red Guards and supervising the reconstruction of the apparatus. Its main task was once more to bring into being Revolutionary Committees in the areas it controlled. We have already seen, in an earlier chapter, how the Shanghai Commune model – itself a bureaucratic perversion of the original Paris Commune – was abandoned for the compromise formula of the Revolutionary Committee based on the triple alliance. This long march backwards was taken one stage further in August 1967–March 1968, during which months twelve more Revolutionary Committees were set up. The standing committees of those bodies set up in the first half of 1967 were, as we saw, divided in roughly equal proportions between the army, the cadres and the mass organizations. In this second wave, however, over a half or 53.3% of the members of the combined standing committees were military men, while the share of representatives of the mass organizations was down to a miserly 21.1%. Clearly, the moderates were now in the ascendency. But the radicals still had an important power base in the mass organizations.

From the point of view of the distribution of power, there was now the distinct danger of an imbalance in favour of the army. The central leadership, anxious at the way things were developing, once more swung briefly – and cautiously – behind the radical wing of the Cultural Revolution Group and began to talk of a revival of the 'February adverse current' of 1967. This was in March 1968. It was also in March that Yang Ch'eng-wu, Acting Chief of General Staff, was purged. The events surrounding this episode are obscure, but one of the official accusations was that Yang had sought to launch a 'rightist current'. At the same time

Fu Ch'ung-pi, the commander of the Peking garrison, was purged for allegedly using his troops against the Central Cultural Revolution Group. It seems, therefore, that the aim of the central leadership was to redress the balance of forces in the new power structure at the expense of the army. That is not to say, however, that the intention was to repeat the experience of summer 1967: the leadership was this time very careful to avoid launching an assault on the army. Furthermore, there are indications that Yang's purging was not only part of an anti-rightist campaign but also the culmination of a power-struggle within the army itself, and for that reason a popular move for at least one section of the military hierarchy. Certainly the appointment to Yang's post of Huang Yungsheng, the scourge of the Canton Red Guards, must have helped to allay the fears of many senior army men. March 1968 therefore represented the first step in a cautiously executed readjustment in the balance of power in favour of the mass organizations. This shift was possibly reflected in the composition of the eleven Revolutionary Committees set up after April 1968. Their combined standing committees included 46.7% military, 32% mass organizations and 21.3% cadres.

The radical revival of early 1968 was short-lived. Not only was the struggle once more threatening to burst its narrow banks, but armed factional warfare was in full swing. On 28 July the central leadership once more backed away from the precipice with Mao's order dissolving the factions and authorizing the army to intervene. In August the 'worker-peasant Mao Tse-tung thought propaganda teams' were in action, re-imposing discipline on the Red Guards. (Such teams, despite their names, were under the guidance and control of the army.) Millions of students and intellectuals were dispatched to the countryside in a massive *hsia-fang* campaign, one of whose effects was the dispersal of a large part of the radical forces. Spring 1969 saw a last resurgence of the 'revolutionary masses' in which the radicals were briefly mobilized in yet another attempt by the leadership to readjust the equilibrium. After the familiar burst of violence and 'extremism' this campaign too was wound up.[109]

[108] See *Red Guard*, chapter 10, for an interesting account of this period.

[109] Much of the information used in the foregoing was taken from the following sources: Ellis Joffe, 'The Chinese Army in the Cultural Revolution: the Politics of Intervention', in *Current Scene*, 7 December 1970, pp. 1–25; Esmein, op. cit., pp. 181–184; Domes, 'Revolutionary Committees 1967–68', loc. cit., pp. 112–145; Philip Bridgham, 'Mao's Cultural Revolution: the Struggle to Seize Power', in *The China Quarterly*, no. 41, January–March 1970, pp. 1–25; Melvin Gurtov, 'The Foreign Ministry and Foreign Affairs during the Cultural Revolution', in *The China Quarterly*, no. 40, October–December 1969, pp. 65–102.

10
The Final Phase and the Ninth Congress

The reorganization is concluded: the October Plenum

The autumn of 1968 marked the beginning of the end of the great upheaval of the cultural revolution. In September the reorganization of the apparatus came full circle with the setting up of the last revolutionary committees on a provincial level. The Central Committee sat from 13–31 October to sanction the changes that had come about in the Party, expel Liu Shao-ch'i and convene the Ninth Congress.

Before we come to analysing the Congress we should briefly recall some of the characteristic features of this phase, in particular as they emerge from the more significant documents of autumn 1968 and early 1969.

1) The reconstruction of the political and administrative apparatus through the extension of revolutionary committees to every province in China made the process of restabilization and 'pacification' easier and above all reaffirmed the control and power of the top leadership. The authorities therefore felt they could relax their policies towards former cadres, more and more of whom were rehabilitated. They even offered a way out to the minority of die-hard 'capitalist roaders' and the 'bourgeois technical experts'.[1] Rules were drawn up for dealing with all the complex cases that arose and *ad hoc* offices were set up to put them into practice. A Kwangtung revolutionary mass organization called *Reversal of verdicts and criticize-the-bourgeoisie* compiled an interesting collection of documents in which there is a description of the competent offices and the record of a question-and-answer session in which cadres from various levels of the hierarchy gave answers based on an examination of the instructions issued by the Central Committee and other leading bodies.[2]

[1] *HNA*, 6 September 1968, p. 3, and *PR*, no. 1, 1969, pp. 8–9, which reprints a directive from Mao recommending caution even towards 'counterrevolutionaries'.
[2] *SCMM*, no. 617.

Thus, while stressing the need to boost production and mobilize the masses to this end, the leadership frequently referred to an instruction from Mao recommending people to 'see to it that there is enough leeway'.[3] But above all it insisted on the need for a strict centralization of leadership: 'The whole Party, the whole army and the Revolutionary Committees at all levels must continue to hold aloft the great red banner of Mao Tse-tung's thought (and) unite closely around the proletarian headquarters with Chairman Mao as its leader and Vice-Chairman Lin as its deputy leader.' The theory of 'many centres' and of various 'leading nuclei' was firmly rejected.[4] An instruction from Mao on unification said: 'The revolutionary committees should exercise unified leadership.'[5]

2) One of the leadership's main concerns was to avoid a deepening of the differentiation in the working class, which was reflected in the multiplicity of groups and of Rebel organizations. After a certain date the leadership waged its campaign for the great alliance and the triple alliance on the additional grounds that there were no objective reasons why the working class should split into two opposing organizations. (But note that this did not refer to the opposition between Mao and his (presumed) opponents, but to two opposing factions in the ranks of the Revolutionary Rebels and the Red Guards.) The leadership saw the healing of this breach as indispensable if the working class were to exercise universal hegemony and therefore – in the words of the official documents – 'enter into the superstructures'. Mao proclaimed this hegemonic role in one of his usual infallible formulations[6] which Yao Wen-yuan afterwards illustrated at greater length in *Red Flag* no. 2, 1968.[7] In other words, the leaders had initially decided to concentrate on mobilizing the students not only for the reasons given at the time but also because they considered them less infected by conservatism. They had now changed this decision and were concentrating more on sections of the working class, who they considered more loyal to the Party and to themselves, in order to counterbalance the critical and centrifugal tendencies in the schools, universities and intellectual circles generally.[8]

3) The situation among the students continued to be marked by deep splits and disagreements. The most significant example was that of Tsinghua University, where on 27 July 1968 a team of workers and

[3] *HNA*, 21 February 1969, p. 5.
[4] *HNA*, 26 August 1967, p. 3; *PR*, no. 43, 1968, p. 6; *PR*, no. 44, 1968, p. 7.
[5] *PR*, no. 1, 1969, p. 8.
[6] *HNA*, 17 August 1968, p. 1.
[7] *HNA*, 26 August 1968, pp. 3ff.
[8] *HNA*, 15 September 1967, p. 3; 16 September 1967, p. 13; 18 October 1967, p. 18, etc.

soldiers made a symbolic entry. In the secondary schools, both in Peking and elsewhere (Shanghai, for example), the situation was much the same. Divisions and difficulties of every kind made it difficult for the students to resume their studies, and they repeatedly put off doing so. Some of the students, in spite of repeated warnings, continued to move from one place to another 'exchanging experiences'. For their part, the teachers were paralysed with fear and uncertainty, which, all considered, was quite understandable.

The solution finally adopted was to send teams of workers, peasants and soldiers into the schools and universities and all organizations and institutions which had not completed the tasks of struggle-criticism-transformation, i.e. had not set up a triple alliance in accordance with the line as laid down. (Note that these teams did not automatically resolve the difficulties; in Tsinghua University, for instance, a team was sent in at the end of July 1968 and yet no revolutionary committee was set up until 25 January 1969.)[9] Mao issued another of his instructions on the subject. 'The facts show – wrote Yao Wen-yuan – that under such circumstances it is impossible for the students and intellectuals by themselves alone to fulfil the task of "struggle-criticism-transformation" and a whole number of other tasks on the educational front; workers and people's liberation army fighters must take part, and it is essential to have strong leadership by the working class.' One of the results of this new course was that the Red Guards, who after mid-1968 were mentioned less and less frequently, were more or less put on one side. It is interesting, for example, to compare the difference in tone between the article written on the first anniversary of the Red Guards with that written on the second.[10] It was left to Chiang Ch'ing, at a meeting to celebrate the setting up of the last provincial revolutionary committees, to make a speech in which, after recalling the 'extraordinary contribution' made by the Red Guards in the opening and intermediate stages of the cultural revolution, she denounced their mistakes and their divisions and proclaimed the need to subject them to discipline.[11]

In the same period the leadership relaunched the campaign to send young people into the countryside. Mao declared on 23 December: 'It is very necessary for educated young people to go to the countryside to be

[9] *HNA*, 30 January 1969, p. 3.

[10] *HNA*, 19 August 1967 and 18 August 1968.

[11] *HNA*, 10 September 1967, p. 7. More generally see *HNA*, 18 October 1967, pp. 21–22; 7 March 1967, p. 3; 3 September 1967, p. 18; 29 October 1967, pp. 14–16; 29 August 1968, p. 6.

re-educated by the poor and lower-middle peasants. Cadres and other people in the cities should be persuaded to send their sons and daughters who have finished junior or senior middle school, college or university to the countryside . . . Let us mobilize. Comrades throughout the country-side should welcome them.'[12] This campaign corresponded to both political and tactical requirements; but, in the last analysis, it revealed that the bottleneck in the urban and industrial economy, which made it difficult to absorb school-leavers and graduates, had not been broken. This was sometimes admitted quite openly. Shanghai's *Wen-hui pao*, for example, replying on 25 February 1968 to readers' letters, made it clear that there was no chance of a job in Shanghai (or even in less remote parts of the countryside) for young people who had returned from Sinkiang.[13]

4) The October Plenum of the Central Committee, which to judge from its duration did not go smoothly, was the last stage in that 'great Party reshuffle' which was one of the main aims of the cultural revolution. It sanctioned the changes at the top and the wide-ranging shake-up at various levels. Shortly before the Plenum there appeared an article the contents of which are clear from the title: 'Take in fresh blood from the proletariat: an important question in Party consolidation.'

Contrary to many interpretations apparently influenced by the theory of spontaneity (and generally characterized by a complete lack of any real analysis), the official propagandists never tired of repeating that the Party's role was to lead and that authority was vested in the leadership and in the formally constituted organs of the Party, however badly shaken by the upheaval. We have shown again and again how at critical points in time it was precisely in the name of the Party's supreme organs that decisions were taken and appeals and proclamations published. In the phase we are now dealing with, the leadership's main concern was not so much to re-affirm notions that it had never given up or to confirm the authority of the Party's leading organs; it was rather to restore the Party to a position in which it could carry out its tasks as the supreme instrument of leadership. The Congress was convened with this aim in mind. It was no accident that the article on the need to 'take in fresh blood' opened with the declaration: 'The great proletarian cultural revolution is an open Party consolidation movement.'[14]

---

[12] *PR*, no. 52, 1968.

[13] *SCMP*, no. 4146, pp. 15–16.

[14] *HNA*, 16 October 1968, and *PR*, no. 43, 1968. Note that the English version of the article quoted has 'rectification' and the French version 'consolidation'. However, in Lin Piao's report the English text also has 'consolidation' (*HNA*, 28 April 1969, p. 16).

The Ninth Congress

There is little information about the preparatory phase of the Congress, but there were certainly lively discussions both before and during the October Plenum. Different views were expressed on when to call the Congress, how to choose the delegates and how to use the Congress in the struggle against leading members of the groups that had fallen into disgrace. In autumn 1967, for example, there were some who thought that the Congress should be held fairly soon – in May or June, or before the 1 October celebrations at the latest. They wanted a large number of delegates (seven or eight thousand) and even considered the idea that some of the 'renegades', like Li Li-san and Wang Ming in the past, should be 'allowed to remain, although without real power' as negative examples. There were also discussions about whether to organize the Congress 'from the top downwards' or 'from the bottom upwards'.

Apart from Lin Piao's report and the text of the new Party Constitution, the only documents officially issued in connection with the Congress were three short communiqués. In his 28 April speech to the First Plenary Session of the Ninth Central Committee, held immediately after the Congress, Mao explained to delegates that this procedure had been adopted as a security measure. He said: 'We adopted the method of issuing a communiqué so that foreign newsmen could no longer get our news.' (Ironically enough, a copy of the speech, which both from internal evidence and in the light of subsequent developments seems authentic, was passed on to foreign journalists.)[15] We do not know the text of Mao's first speech to Congress, although its importance has been emphasized. Nor do we possess the texts of the speeches by Chou En-lai, Ch'en Po-ta and K'ang Sheng, not to mention lesser fry. It is worthwhile recalling, for the purposes of comparison, that on the occasion of the 1956 Congress fairly full accounts of all the main speeches were published in China and abroad.

As the first communiqué shows and as was to be expected after some of the theories put forward in the months leading up to the Congress, the delegates – 1,512 in all – were not elected but unanimously chosen 'through full democratic consultation' at various levels of the Party. This means that the Congress was concerted from above, in keeping with the tradition whereby delegates were nominated and not elected (the same procedure was followed from the Second Congress to the Seventh – the

[15] The speech is reprinted in *Issues and Studies*, November 1969, pp. 91–92, and *Tokyo Shimbun*, 27 October 1969.

Eighth was an exception). Hsieh Fu-chih, in the course of a speech that contains much information on the preparatory stage, told Peking Revolutionary Committee on 26 October 1967 that organizing the Congress 'from the top downwards' would guarantee a majority of 'Rebels', i.e. supporters of the Maoist tendency.[16] Naturally, it is not at all strange that the 'normal' functioning of an apparatus should encourage the more conservative elements. But the method of appointing delegates from above has just as many drawbacks and is basically inspired by paternalism and authoritarianism.

In spite of this, however, the Congress was marked by various discussions and differences of opinion: these inevitably reflected the subdivisions and differentiations that had arisen within the Maoist ranks. The official communiqués spoke of 'numerous and excellent proposals for additions and modifications' to Lin Piao's report; almost a fortnight elapsed between the reading of Lin's report and its acceptance, which would seem to indicate that a real debate took place. The debate on the composition of the new Central Committee also went on for some time (from 15 to 24 April). Apart from methods of selection (indicated in the final communiqué), delicate and complex problems of apportionment arose: what proportion should be allotted to each of the constituents that had emerged from the cultural revolution? Significantly, both the 2 April communiqué, which spoke of the delegations present, and the final communiqué, which announced the 'election' of the highest leading body, took care to underline that all layers and sections of the Chinese Communist movement were represented. But accounts with members of the opposition had been settled in advance. They had been dismissed or expelled at the October Plenum or earlier and the Congress could only ratify these decisions in retrospect.

The new Central Committee was largely renovated. It now consisted of 170 full members (97 in 1956) and 109 alternate members (109 in 1956). Of these 279 members, only forty-two were survivors of the Eighth Central Committee. The new Committee was built more or less on the lines of a triple alliance. It consisted of roughly 40% army representatives, 30% 'revolutionary cadres' and 30% representatives of the 'revolutionary masses'. Significantly, the representatives of the 'revolutionary masses' included very few Red Guards or radical figures. Nieh Yuan-tzu, for example, was only made an alternate member. One observer put the number of peasants and workers on the new Committee

[16] *SCMP*, no. 4097, p. 2.

at sixty-three, or 23%.[17]

The Politbureau went up from twenty to twenty-one members (after the 1956 Congress there were only seventeen), plus four alternate members (as against six previously); there were twelve new members, and two more – Ch'en Po-ta and K'ang Sheng – were previously alternate members (this meant seven full members stayed on from the old Politbureau). The new members included the chairmen of the Revolutionary Committees of some of the most important provinces or those where the most difficult situations had arisen: Hsu Shih-yu, the military chairman of Kiangsu committee, Ch'en Hsi-lien, also an army man and chairman of Liaoning committee, army chief-of-staff Huang Yung-sheng, who on 21 February 1968 was made chairman of Kwangtung Committee, and two high-ranking members of the Party and state apparatus, Chang Ch'un-ch'iao, chairman of Shanghai Committee, and Hsieh Fu-chih, chairman of Peking Committee. The alternate members included Li Teh-sheng, an army man and chairman of Anhwei Committee, and Li Hsueh-feng, first secretary of the North China Bureau, who at the beginning of June 1966 had taken P'eng Chen's place in Peking. Alongside the 'old' military men like Lin Piao and Chu Teh, there were quite a few 'new' military representatives (obviously men like Ho Lung and P'eng Teh-huai had disappeared). A former stranger to the top hierarchy who rapidly made his mark was Yao Wen-yuan, vice-chairman of the Shanghai Committee and now a member of the Central Committee and the Politbureau. There was not even one representative on the Politbureau of those genuinely 'new' cadres who during the cultural revolution had emerged from the mass organizations. At first sight the overall weight of the army in the Politbureau was greater than in the Central Committee or in the previous Politbureau: ten of the twenty-five (in addition to Lin Piao and his wife) were directly associated with the army. It is important, however, not to draw hasty conclusions from this. It has been pointed out[18] that, of these ten, two (Chu Teh and Liu Po-ch'eng) were inactive and four others (Huang Yung-sheng, Wu Fa-hsien, Ch'iu Hui-tso and Li Tso-p'eng) were close associates of Lin Piao and central political figures in the cultural revolution. Here are the complete lists for the 1956 and 1969 Politbureaus:

[17] Klein and Hager, 'The Ninth Central Committee', in *The China Quarterly*, no. 45, January–March 1971, p. 41. See also Bridgham, 'Mao's Cultural Revolution', loc. cit., pp. 13–18; *The China Quarterly*, no. 39, July–September 1969, pp. 144–146 (Documentation).

[18] Bridgham, 'Mao's Cultural Revolution', loc. cit., pp. 15–16.

1956	1969
Mao Tse-tung	Mao Tse-tung
Liu Shao-ch'i	Lin Piao
Chou En-lai	Yeh Chun
Chu Teh	Yeh Chien-ying
Ch'en Yun	Liu Po-ch'eng
Teng Hsiao-p'ing	Chiang Ch'ing
Lin Piao	Chu Teh
Lin Po-ch'ü (died 1960)	Hsu Shih-yu
Tung Pi-wu	Ch'en Po-ta
P'eng Chen	Ch'en Hsi-lien
Lo Jung-huan (died 1963)	Li Hsien-nien
Ch'en Yi	Li Tso-p'eng
Li Fu-ch'un	Wu Fa-hsien
P'eng Teh-huai	Chang Ch'un-ch'iao
Liu Po-ch'eng	Ch'iu Hui-tso
Ho Lung	Chou En-lai
Li Hsien-nien	Yao Wen-yuan
alternate members	K'ang Sheng
Ulanfu	Huang Yung-sheng
Chang Wen-t'ien	Tung Pi-wu
Lu Ting-i	Hsieh Fu-chih
Ch'en Po-ta	*alternate members*
K'ang Sheng	Ch'i Teng-kuei
	Li Hsueh-feng
	Li Teh-sheng
	Wang Tung-hsing

(K'o Ch'ing-shih, Li Ching-ch'uan and T'an Chen-lin were reportedly brought in later as full members and Po I-po as an alternate member. Note that the 1956 list is in the official order of listing, whereas the 1969 list is in stroke – the equivalent of alphabetical – order after Mao and Lin.)

In the Standing Committee, which is in reality the highest organ of power, the change-over was less drastic. Of the seven pre-Congress members (six were nominated after the Eighth Congress, but Lin Piao was not at that time a member) three remained: Mao, Lin Piao and Chou En-lai. The aging Chu Teh only stayed on in the Politbureau, while Liu Shao-ch'i and Teng Hsiao-p'ing naturally left; Ch'en Yun regained a place on the Politbureau but not on the Standing Committee. Ch'en Po-ta and K'ang Sheng, leaders of the Central Cultural Revolution Group, joined this body, which was thus reduced to five members.

Turning to the Constitution, we should first of all remember that the Chinese Communists have always been fairly empirical in this respect. They have tended to adapt each one largely to suit the specific needs of the phase they happened to be passing through, as can be seen above all from the preambles. The result was that every Congress had to adopt a new Constitution or at least introduce big changes, especially considering the long intervals between Congresses. Thus, one Constitution was adopted in 1938, another in 1945 and a revision was made in 1956. The 1969 Constitution was no exception to this rule: it was inspired directly by the needs of the cultural revolution, the themes of which are set forth in its first chapter. The only difference is that it is shorter than the others.

According to Lin Piao, the Central Committee had received 'several thousand drafts' from November 1967 onwards. At the October Plenum a draft was presented which was described as 'the product of the integration of the great leader Chairman Mao Tse-tung's wise leadership with the broad masses'. The Plenum approved it in its entirety and then discussed it; the centre was charged with making the final draft to put before the Congress, taking into account the opinions expressed.

There are roughly a dozen changes between the October draft (if the version we possess is accurate) and the one passed by Congress. Some of these differences are secondary – in the editing, for example, or in the order of the sentences.

More important, however, is the change introducing a two-year maximum period of candidature – this provision had been included in the previous Constitution, but omitted from the draft passed by the October Plenum.[19] (We should specify that the 1945 Constitution provided for a candidature period varying, according to the candidate's social origin, from a minimum of six months to a maximum of two years.) An explicit reference to the army as one of the organs of proletarian state power which had to accept Party discipline was added to Article 5, while Article 6 ended with the phrase: 'The convening of Party congresses in the localities and army units and their elected Party committee members are subject to approval by the higher Party organizations.'[20] In so far as they had any importance, these modifications were in a conservative direction. (The official English translation of the Constitution contains

[19] *HNA*, 29 April 1969, printed the final text; *SCMP*, no. 4334, printed the draft. Though writing after the Congress, Blumer (op. cit., p. 477) refers to the abolition of the candidature period but not to its re-introduction. This confirms that his information is unreliable.

[20] The text of the Constitution is in *PR*, no. 18, 1969, and *The China Quarterly*, no. 39, July–September 1969, pp. 164–168.

one important mistranslation which needs to be cleared up. Article 5 says in part: 'The leading bodies of the Party at all levels are elected through democratic consultation.' In fact a more accurate translation would have 'produced' in place of 'elected'.)[21]

The new Constitution did not differ in basic principles from that of 1945 or the revised version of 1956: this is particularly so of the right to criticize, the rights of the minorities and the right to appeal to higher levels without going all the way up the hierarchy – here the changes were more of form than of substance. Congresses were once more fixed for every five years, but a change was incorporated which involved limiting their powers: the new Constitution omitted a provision introduced in 1950 to hold one session of Congress annually. Compared with 1945, when the term was set at three years, the interval between Congresses was longer.

This is a very important point. Ignoring for one moment the fact that such deadlines are not kept to (the Constitution had its escape-clauses in the past, too) the intervals are too long for the Congress to be able to exert any effective control on the activities of the leadership. Article 6 defined the Congress as the 'highest leading body of the Party' and according to the monocentric Maoist conception 'the organs of State power, of the dictatorship of the proletariat, the People's Liberation Army and the Communist Youth League and other revolutionary mass organizations, such as those of the workers, the poor and lower-middle peasants and the Red Guards, must all accept the leadership of the Party'. In the light of this, the failure to respect Congress deadlines has all the appearances of a reflection on the constitutional level of a bureaucratic authoritarianism and paternalism which concentrates power in the hands of the leading groups. This was confirmed, moreover, by the canonization of Mao's thought as the supreme principle. It is reflected not only in the shrill restatement of certain phrases used in 1945 and abandoned in 1956, but also and even more importantly in the formal and constitutional recognition of Mao's chairmanship and Lin Piao's right of succession, which was an indisputable innovation. (One rarely remarked detail that nevertheless indicates a certain method and a certain mentality: except on rare occasions, Mao was called Chairman and not comrade.)

Mao's speech to the Central Committee, which we examine below, showed that from the point of view of the leadership there were still unresolved conflicts. In general, however, the Congress was intended to

[21] See Bridgham, 'Mao's Cultural Revolution', loc. cit., pp. 14–15.

mark the end of a process. This was most apparent in Lin Piao's speech (contrary to past procedure, no resolutions were put to the vote, or at least not publicly). Lin's report introduced nothing new, but limited itself to drawing up a balance sheet. It is significant from the point of view of content, methodology and style that the report was built up around more than sixty quotations from Mao Tse-tung. Thus Lin Piao returned to the idea of the inevitable persistence of the class struggle (between bourgeoisie and proletariat) in the phase following the conquest of power; went back into the past to find examples of Liu's mistakes and 'crimes' (mixing together real disagreements, plainly concocted charges and Stalinist-type smears); described the main events of the cultural revolution, its antecedents and origins – all in his own way, of course, without pausing to examine, say, the huge strikes at the beginning of 1967, which he instead summarily included in the 'adverse currents' formed between winter 1966 and spring 1967; and recalled the internal struggles in the Maoist group and the polemics against every sort of right or left deviation up till the reconstruction phase, brought to a conclusion in October 1968 (even making sallies into the Party's remotest history).

As for the main topics, Lin emphasized that the apparatus should not detach itself from the masses (he reproved Liu for having prevented Mao's instructions from reaching the broad masses) and stressed the fundamental role of the army. He touched only in summary form on economic problems, referring to a relatively favourable situation and confirming the general line adopted in the period of readjustment: 'agriculture as the foundation and industry as the leading factor' (this also deserves noting). He repeated the official view, as propounded since June 1968, that students and intellectuals should accept the direct control of the workers and peasants (which meant in effect the control of the reconstituted apparatus, led by the army) and that it was the duty of young people to go into the countryside and the mountainous regions. He also confirmed the regime's more tolerant attitude towards its opponents. Finally, it is worth recalling that Lin Piao admitted in relation to internal problems that in some places the great alliance had not yet been set up while in others the campaign of rectification and purification had not yet started. In the section on international policy he also took up recurrent themes, affirming in particular that the Chinese were ready to negotiate with the USSR on the border question. It would be extremely interesting to know the terms of the debate on the report, and in particular the additions and modifications in the published text with respect to the original one. But the fact that the leading group published nothing but a handful of brief communiqués hardly squared with the need to keep the mass fully informed.

Mao's 28 April speech to the First Plenary Session of the new Central Committee (if the document at our disposal is an authentic one) is very different in its tone and contents from Lin's report. His overriding theme was unity. He frankly admitted that 'the revolution has not yet ended' and that unity had not yet been achieved in every factory or every province. In the provinces the problem 'lies in the military, and the problem of the military lies in work'. He went on to urge self-reliance in preparation for war – a theme prompted both by the drive for unity and the clash with the Russians on the Ussuri, which took place shortly before the Congress began. He also reproached the Central Committee, in passing, for being 'bureaucratic'.

The general 'problem of the military' seems, from contemporary references in the press, to refer to army arrogance and the use of coercion. The particular 'problem of the military' in Mao's speech refers to the situation in Shantung, which is one of a minority of provinces where the chairmanship was in the hands not of the army but of a 'leading cadre'. Mao revealed in his speech that relations between the civilian chairman and the military first vice-chairman were 'of the kind between enemies and us'. He went on to speak of 'personal grudges'. Underlying this antagonism was probably the more general tension between the army and the two civilian components of the new power structure. After the Congress, campaigns to rehabilitate 'leading cadres' and revive Red Guard organizations were launched, probably with the intention of setting up a counterbalance to the strength of the army.

But the result of this campaign was other than the leadership intended. The Red Guards, unwilling or unable to act as a tool of the centre, set out once more on the path of political struggle. There soon followed a flood of denunciations of sectarianism, anarchism, ultra-democracy and other forms of 'extremism' in Kweichow, Anhwei, Inner Mongolia, Fukien and other areas. The furies unleashed by the cultural revolution had not yet been laid to rest.

11
The Dismissed Leaders and the New Opposition

In the course of its criticisms and attacks, the group that eventually emerged victorious attributed a number of positions to its opponents. We now intend to examine how far these imputed positions corresponded to the actual ones.

Since we only have very limited access to material on the series of discussions held at the various levels of the leading bodies, and since those who were defeated had no means of making public their own version of the facts or replying to the avalanche of attacks on them, it is very difficult to find out the truth. However, we will do all we can to unravel the tangle, making the most of the facts at hand and analysing the principles, the contents and the internal logic of the factional polemics. Here, then, we pause to examine the leaders of the dismissed opposition, in the order in which they were attacked.

Teng T'o
Over the past fifteen years, Teng T'o had occupied a special place in the affairs of the Party. Editor of the *People's Daily* during the 1957 rectification campaign, he intervened directly in the polemics of that time with important articles and even took the liberty of censoring Mao's statements.[1] It is probably not purely coincidence that the most radical antibureaucratic criticism of that period came from an associate of his, Lin Hsi-ling (mentioned in the first part of this book), who once defined her friend as an 'unorthodox' Marxist.

In 1959 Teng T'o was removed from his post. He took up journalism again two years later, contributing to *Frontline* (whose editorial staff he joined), the *Peking Daily* and the *Peking Evening News*. *Frontline* was the organ of the Peking Party Municipal Committee, which put Teng in

[1] *HNA*, 3 September 1968, p. 37.

charge of political and cultural work. He not only published widely read articles, but also embarked upon rash ventures such as the publication of articles refused by other newspapers. In later years his work on these papers became the subject of fierce attacks. Teng's writings, as far as we can judge from the very incomplete evidence, showed a sound talent, an effective sense of satire and the versatility of an intellectual and a scholar capable of dealing with problems ranging from literary history to economics. One of the items that was to call forth the wrath of his opponents and the accusation that he wanted to poke his nose into everything was his praise for the 'miscellaneous scholars', i.e. intellectuals whose broad education equipped them to play a leading role in society. He is even said to have thought of starting up a special magazine for these intellectuals in which 'every word written must be like a cannon shot'.[2]

It is not easy to form any precise idea of what Teng T'o's beliefs were. He felt compelled above all to criticize exaggerated propaganda and excessive emphasis on psychological factors. More concretely, he condemned the excesses of the Great Leap Forward, including the irrational use of the labour force, which was subjected to what was in the long run an unbearable strain (even though he talked in some articles of the need to 'translate Mao's thought into practice' on the agricultural production front).[3] His polemical broadsides against any claim to omniscience were later interpreted as a criticism of the much-lauded universality of Mao Tse-tung's thought.

We might loosely define Teng as a 'liberalizer', in the sense that he seemed to look forward to a regime that would wield its power in a more flexible and less bureaucratic way (one of the metaphors he used was that the royal road was preferable to the tyrant's road). He was also said to be in favour of a change in the way in which polemics were conducted in the international communist movement (and to have spoken not of Krushchev's 'crimes' but of his 'mistakes', expressing the view that they could be set right). He frequently returned to the theme of the distortions of post-revolutionary society, and he seems to have been interested in Djilas' book on the new class (it is not clear from the source we are using whether he had read it or merely supposed that it contained interesting material). In October 1963 Chou Yang asked Teng to make a speech on anti-revisionism at a meeting of the Academy of Sciences' Philosophy and

---

[2] *HNA*, 13 February 1967, p. 7; *People's Daily*, 21 May 1966, quoted in *CB*, no. 792, p. 65. This issue of *CB* includes the most important articles against Teng.

[3] *People's Daily*, 24 October 1960, in *SCMP*, no. 2375.

Social Science Department, but we do not know what he said.[4]

Teng T'o once wrote: 'The *Book of Rites* had long ago this to say: "When rites, music, punishment and administration are implemented without conflict, conditions are available for the rule of right." According to this interpretation, what is called rule of right is in fact a certain attitude and action taken by people at a certain historical period to deal with all problems in accordance with the human affection and moral standards of society prevailing at that time on the presupposition that the political and judicial systems then in force are not violated. On the other hand, if power and influence are used . . . to carry out things in a barbarous and forceful way, to issue unreasonable orders arrogantly, and to implement seizure by trick or force, this is what is called rule of might. In terms of our present point of view and in our language, what are after all rule of right and rule of might? What is called rule of right can be interpreted as the honest way of thinking and method of work that stem from the mass line, while what is called rule of might may be interpreted as the reckless way of thinking and method of work based upon subjective dogmatism.'[5]

Teng's approach to the internal dialectics of post-revolutionary society is evidently not the usual bureaucratic one. But is this a right-wing attitude, as Teng's critics insinuate? Apart from the fact that it is not easy to express such characterizations in the abstract (their real meaning can only be given in the context of a concrete situation), the author, when he says that one should start out from the premise that 'the political and juridical system are not violated', is affirming the basic idea that every internal dialectic of the new society should be within the framework of the new economic and social foundations. All of which has nothing to do with the restoration of capitalism or the preparations for such.

Lu Ting-i

Lu Ting-i, a veteran of the Long March, was given top-ranking assignments in the fields of propaganda and culture after liberation and was later chosen as Minister of Culture in place of Mao Tun; he was a leading figure in the 1956 Hundred Flowers campaign and was elected an alternate member of the Politbureau by the Eighth Congress, entering the Secretariat at the September 1962 Plenum of the Central Committee. In a speech on 26 May 1956, which was widely circulated abroad as well as in China, he attacked the dogmatists for their oversimplifications, vigorously affirmed the rights of minorities in scientific, literary and

[4] *CB*, no. 792, p. 70; *HNA*, 12 January 1967, p. 32.
[5] *CB*, no. 792, p. 9–10.

philosophical debates and invited historians to get down to work without waiting for inspiration from the Party. A speech of this nature obviously became a target for attack during the cultural revolution, but we should not forget that Lu was voicing the general trend prevalent at that time (and repeatedly and openly appealed to the authority of the Central Committee).

On 30 October 1959 Lu, who had not fallen into disgrace in 1957, delivered a speech at the National Conference of Outstanding Groups and Workers in Socialist Construction in which he attacked the right-wing and spoke of the need for 'uninterrupted revolution'. In 1960 he wrote the article commemorating Lenin's birth, which marked an important stage in the polemics with the Soviet Union, and in the same year he was part of the Chinese delegation to the Moscow conference of the eighty-one Communist Parties. He joined the Secretariat, as we said, in autumn 1962; in 1964, when a number of bitter polemics (including an intervention from Mao made public at a later date) had already taken place in the cultural field, he wrote an article on the cultural revolution among the national minorities which was circulated internationally. In 1965 he is said to have attacked Stalin at length on two different occasions.[6]

The chief accusation levelled against Lu during the cultural revolution was that he had not taken into consideration the criticisms made by Mao since 1954 of certain cultural trends and had left things unchanged for no less than twelve years. In 1962, with the approval of Liu Shao-ch'i, he is said to have put about a 'sinister document' slandering the creative study of Mao's works as 'oversimplification, vulgarization and pragmatism' (from which we could conclude that he took up some of the themes of the rectification campaign in an attempt to oppose the canonization of Mao Tse-tung). In the same year he is said to have had published the biography of an historical figure, Emperor T'ang T'ai Tsung, and to have exclaimed at a Central Committee working conference that 'even the old emperors allowed oppositions'. One report has it that on another occasion he even dared to say: 'All the text books on Chinese language in every middle school grade begin with something by Mao Tse-tung . . . what servility!' This would explain the criticism that Lu had openly professed 'opposition to dogmatism' and was opposed to the 'absolute leadership' of Mao's thought: and it is also plain why he was reproved for opposing censorship.

[6] *The National Conference of Outstanding Groups and Workers in Socialist Construction*, Peking 1960; *PR*, no. 49, 1964; *CB*, no. 842, pp. 30–31.

Several of the attacks on him related to the question of education and schools.[7]

It is very likely that among the more immediate reasons for Lu Ting-i's fall was his support for the document drawn up by P'eng Chen in the name of the cultural revolution Group of Five. The reader will recall that this document was attacked in the Central Committee circular of 16 May 1966.

P'eng Chen

P'eng Chen, for many years one of the senior Party leaders, a member of the Politbureau even before the Eighth Congress, head of the Peking Party and mayor of the capital, and a prominent figure in the trade unions, was one of the Party's most authoritative spokesmen during the crucial years of the polemics with the USSR. For example, his speech at the Aliarcham Academy of Social Sciences in Jakarta, Indonesia (25 May 1965), trenchant in style and more effective than any stereotyped text, was one of the most thorough expositions of the Chinest point of view and one of the most bitter denunciations of Krushchevite revisionism. At the time of the reform of Peking opera (the high point of the rectification campaign prior to the cultural revolution) P'eng gave a speech complete with all the ritual references to Mao's works. In 1965 he was given the task of commemorating the anniversary of the founding of the People's Republic.

Later this speech attracted the attention of commentators eager for some indication of what the ex-Mayor of Peking's views might have been. Blumer points out, quoting from the text distributed to the guests, that P'eng spoke not simply of 'dogmatism' but of 'modern dogmatism' and says that this expression was used in public 'only by P'eng Chen and only on this occasion'. However, apart from the fact that the expression was punctually reported in the Chinese press,[8] P'eng himself used it again in a speech to the Japanese Communists on 26 March of the following year. Other commentators give prominence to a passage which said: 'In these circumstances it is all the more necessary for cadres at various levels to be able to listen to the opinion of the masses and to allow full expression of different opinions. We must know how to listen to what is right, and also to what is not right; to words of approval, and also to words of dis-

[7] *PR*, no. 15, 1967, pp. 5–6; *HNA*, 13 October 1967, p. 22; 13 November 1967, pp. 3–4; 23 September 1967, p. 7; 7 September 1967, p. 17; 14 December 1967, p. 17; 10 January 1968, p. 4.

[8] See *PR*, no. 40, 1965.

approval. We should and surely can create on a national scale a political climate in which there exist simultaneously centralism and democracy, discipline and freedom, unity of intentions and a state of mind full of life and ardour in each individual.'

Arguments of this sort were put forward fairly frequently even then. However, certain differences in emphasis show in what ways P'eng's position tended to differ from those of other members of the leading group. Besides, didn't his opponents reproach him for saying that 'everyone is equal before the truth, that even the Chairman of the Party's Central Committee is no exception', that Mao was studied in a formalistic and philistine manner and that comrades should avoid the despotic methods of bourgeois experts and scientists? As for the famous circular of 16 May, one of the main charges brought against the then head of the cultural revolution Group of Five was that he had written that 'it is necessary not only to beat the other side politically, but also really to surpass and beat it by a wide margin, by academic and professional standards'. At least on this point, for those who look on Marxism as a science and not a catechism or a metaphysical system, there is no doubt that P'eng was right.[9]

The accusations brought against P'eng after spring 1967 were broadly the same as those brought against all the other leaders who fell into disgrace. They insinuated that for many years the Peking Committee had been a centre for reactionaries and that P'eng Chen had plotted to restore capitalism by putting into effect the plans of P'eng Teh-huai (in the same way as the Maoist propagandists brazenly accused Krushchev of carrying out Trotsky's designs some tens of years after they were first formulated). There was no shortage of references to the most distant past: P'eng was accused of being in favour of conciliation and negotiations in 1945, when he held a leading position in North East China. In 1947 he was supposed to have deviated in a different direction, wanting to sweep away the rural cadres who were holding up the attack on the landowners and putting out the slogan 'Throw out the base-level cadres!' As for his policy in the countryside after liberation, he was accused among other things of providing State aid to model production teams around Peking without getting any positive results. In the trade-union field, he was reproached for having wanted to make the unions an 'independent kingdom' (i.e. calling for their relative autonomy) as well as having said in 1964 that former

[9] *HNA*, 4 September 1967, p. 5; *CB*, no. 842, p. 28; *PR*, no. 21, 1967, p. 8. P'eng was also accused of anarchism, but his 'anarchist' attitudes were said to be in stark contrast to his despotic methods (*HNA*, 15 July 1967, p. 5).

reactionaries should no longer be discriminated against or excluded.[10]

It has been suggested that P'eng's fall was mainly linked to the question of united action against imperialism in the interests of the Vietnamese revolution. In this connection we should bear in mind that P'eng's Jakarta speech attacked the Soviet Union for its conception of united action, while expressing the hope – usual at that time – that the CPSU would change course and return to Marxism-Leninism. According to Korean and Japanese sources quoted by members of the Italian Communist Party in March 1966, a Chinese delegation which included Liu Shao-ch'i and Teng Hsiao-p'ing as well as P'eng Chen agreed with the Japanese Communists on a declaration in which the question of united action was couched in terms acceptable to the latter. On their return to Peking some time later, the Japanese were told by a new Chinese delegation that the original text had been turned down because Mao considered it a capitulation. Some Maoist sources accused Liu and Teng of having been in liaison with the Japanese Communists.[11]

Chou Yang

In May 1957, during the course of the rectification campaign, Chou Yang, already mentioned in another part of this work, gave a sensational interview in which he recognized the right to strike and to protest in other ways and called for a redistribution of income such as to avoid creating excessive inequalities. At that time this was the line of all the leading group and Chou was only acting as its spokesman. For that reason, when the rectification campaign changed tone, it was still Chou who gave a speech to the Communist writers (16 September). This speech not only attacked Ting Ling, Ch'en Ch'i-hsia, Hu Feng and Feng Hsueh-feng, but even put forward the argument that the 'rightist' intellectuals intended setting up a Chinese Petöfi Circle under the cover of the *Movement for a New May 4* and were in reality attacking the socialist system when they called for freedom of artistic creation. Again, he accused the 'rightists' of despising works produced by the masses and taking over important positions of control (including a newspaper), denounced crimes stretching back to a now distant past and, finally, railed at some people for having spoken of an imminent 'thaw'. Plainly, there is a very close parallel between this speech and the identical criticisms later brought against the intellectuals (including Chou himself) attacked in the first

[10] *HNA*, 17 April 1967, p. 3; 22 July 1967, p. 4; 15 July 1967, p. 5; 6 December 1968, p. 3; 10 August 1968, p. 5; 13 October 1968, pp. 3–4; 14 June 1968, p. 5.

[11] *CB*, no. 834, p. 26.

stages of the cultural revolution. Published in the same volume as Chou Yang's speech[12] is an article by Shao Ch'uan-lin (also attacked in 1966) criticizing an article by Chin Chao-yang entitled *The broad path of realism*. It is interesting to see that the groups under attack in 1966 were also accused of characterizing realism in this way. (Note that the speech and a note in the same volume contain Chou Yang's version of the controversy over the two slogans 'a literature of national defence' and 'a mass literature for the national revolutionary war'. This version also appeared in an edition of Lu Hsun's works, and was afterwards attacked as biased and even false in July 1966. Lu Hsun's widow joined in the attack.[13] The attack on Chou Yang was conducted in the manner of a factional polemic. One example: Chou was rebuked for having said in 1959: 'What is socialist culture? It is the culture of the whole people', thereby associating himself with Krushchev's theory. Apart from the method, which consists in wrenching one sentence out of its context, the expression 'the whole people' was not used by the CPSU until the Twenty-second Congress, i.e. after 1959.[14] All this shows that some of the arguments and some of the epithets used against Chou Yang and others had more in common with factional abuse than honest representation.

Six years later, in October 1963, Chou Yang was asked to make another speech to the enlarged plenum of the committee of the Philosophy and Social Science Department of the Academy of Sciences. Once again what he had to say was inspired by the most rigid orthodoxy. His speech contained a fairly systematic summary of the main arguments in the controversy with the Soviet Union (including a criticism of the 'state of the whole people' formula and the idea of material incentives). He argued against those who interpreted the hundred flowers as a 'liberalization policy', confirmed the well-known theory that all things split into two and strongly attacked humanist tendencies. At the end of 1965, he addressed the national conference of non-professional writers: once again he argued the Maoist line and gave no hint of the motives later attributed to him. He actually said that the battle on the literary and artistic front was a battle between the working class and the bourgeoisie and between the socialist and capitalist roads, quoted all Mao's major writings, underlined the bourgeois training of intellectuals, referred to the 1961 and 1962 literary offensives by 'feudal and bourgeois forces', pointed out the need to write about 'important' figures and heroes who had 'risen from the ranks of our

[12] *A Great Debate on the Literary Front*, Peking 1958.
[13] *HNA*, 20 October 1967, p. 9.
[14] *HNA*, 7 July 1966, p.9; 19 July 1966, p. 12; 22 September 1966, p. 3.

workers, peasants and soldiers', criticized the 'use of material incentives, with the thirst for fame and profit to the fore' and once again rejected the 'liberalizing' interpretation of the hundred flowers. The criticisms later made of this speech rested not on what it said but rather on the fact that it did not contain an explicit criticism of Wu Han's play.[15]

We have already spoken elsewhere of the accusations brought against Chou Yang in July 1966. How shaky their foundations were is shown by an interview Chou gave Karol not long before the beginning of the cultural revolution.[16] For example, Chou, who was accused of having praised eighteenth and nineteenth century bourgeois culture as the 'pinnacle of human culture', made an identical accusation against Lukács, who he said was a 'veteran of revisionism'. Soviet art and culture, which he was accused of slavishly imitating, he described in the following drastic terms: 'Soviet art and literature count for nothing . . . They are dull and lifeless, unviewable and unreadable.'

But it was Yao Wen-yuan who took it upon himself to show how Chou Yang's orthodox positions, which were well-known even outside China, were nothing but a camouflage for his double-dealing. The first issue of *Red Flag* in 1967 carried a long 'documented' article by Yao. In this article he attacked Chou's 1965 speech for the reasons given above and declared that Mao's article of 27 June 1964 was aimed mainly at Chou, although Chou himself allegedly tried to weaken its effect in a speech he gave immediately afterwards. Secondly, Yao once more set about analysing Chou's positions during the artistic and literary polemics of 1951 (in connection with the film *The Life of Wu Hsun*, which Mao criticized but which Chou, as vice-director of the Central Committee Propaganda Department, had allowed to be shown – it was not until later that he made a self-criticism); of 1954 (in connection with an academic study of *The Dream of the Red Chamber*, which Mao also criticized); of 1954 and 1955 (Yao claimed that Chou actually supported Hu Feng, and that his supposed attacks on the latter were in reality attacks on Mao); and of 1956 and 1957 (Yao accused Chou of saying in September 1956 that China should learn from the capitalist countries and of attacking dogmatism and the resulting simplifications, while in 1957 he allegedly called a series of meetings 'to incite the rightists to hasten the coming of "spring", namely the restoration of capitalism'). Thirdly, Yao took Chou to task for certain positions he was said to have held in 1959 (underrating the scientific work of the previous ten years at an army seminar and for-

[15] *PR*, no. 13, 1966, pp. 11ff.
[16] K. S. Karol, *China, the other Communism*, New York 1967, p. 276.

getting Mao's great works); in 1961 (ridiculing plays for thanking Mao 'not just once but even three or four times', more generally opposing 'talking of Chairman Mao every day', praising 'the spirit of Hai Jui' and publishing the 'Ten Points on Literature and Art', which criticized a 'narrow, one-sided and incorrect understanding . . . of how to make literature and art serve politics'); and in 1962 (continuing his double-dealing in spite of criticism by the September Plenum, and presenting the situation in the literary field in over-optimistic colours). Finally, in 1963, Chou was said to have hindered the reform of Peking Opera, attacked an article by Ch'i Pen-yu and dwelt at too great a length on the problem of historical heritage in his above-mentioned report to the Department of Philosophy and Social Science of the Academy of Sciences, when he also encouraged 'revisionists' to dominate the discussion; in 1964, he was supposed to have tried to play down the mistakes of the Ministry of Culture, claiming that they were 'not necessarily a mistake of line'.[17]

It is all too clear that Yao's method consisted essentially of scrutinizing all sorts of past statements in the light of present polemics and attributing to single sentences, almost always wrenched from context, meanings that they mostly did not have. He made full use of all the tricks of factional warfare, ranging from artful hinting at the meaning of certain omissions (actual or presumed) to passing over crucial aspects of the texts under attack (for example, his criticism of the 'Ten Points' tried to obscure the fact that Chou at no point argued against the doctrine of 'politics in command'; he also failed to point out that in his 1963 speech Chou gave first place to 'the synthesis of experience and the study of the problems of contemporary revolutionary struggles'). Finally, Yao is a master of demagogy: for example, he attacks Chou Yang's alleged aversion to 'talking of Chairman Mao every day' with the cry: 'We do want to talk of Chairman Mao every day, read his works every day, review his instructions every day and study his thoughts every day.'[18]

As for the accusations about Chou's activities in the thirties, it has been rightly pointed out that Chou's critics hushed up the fact that the dissolution of the League of Left-wing Writers and its replacement by united associations of Chinese writers was part of the more general turn towards the popular front, encouraged by the Comintern.[19]

---

[17] *HNA*, 9, 10, 11 January 1967, and *Chinese Literature*, Peking, no. 3, 1967, pp. 24–71.
[18] Ibid., p. 50.
[19] *World Outlook*, 10 March 1967, p. 261. In the opinion of the Chinese Trotskyist Ch'en Pi-lan, Chou was pretending to adhere to Maoist views which in reality he did not share (ibid., 14 July 1967, p. 675).

T'ao Chu

T'ao Chu's case is particularly interesting in that he was one of the main protagonists of the first phase of the cultural revolution. He was First Secretary of the Central-South Bureau of the Central Committee. He took Lu Ting-i's place on the Politbureau on 1 June 1966, joined the Central Cultural Revolution Group and the Standing Committee of the Politbureau and jumped from ninety-fifth to fourth place at the August Plenum, after Mao, Lin Piao and Chou En-lai. He was at the very fore in many of the most important demonstrations of autumn and early winter. T'ao disappeared from the scene suddenly between the end of December and the beginning of January (on 29 December he was still in second place on the list of those present at a demonstration in the capital but on 11 January a violent attack on him appeared in *Peking Ching-kang-shan* and others followed almost immediately).[20]

For many years a senior Party leader, T'ao had often written widely circulated articles representing the point of view of the leadership. In 1964 *Red Flag* published an article by him on agricultural questions and on the lessons of the commune experiment in Kwangtung. There was nothing strikingly different about the ideas expressed in this article. It reaffirmed the line that agriculture was the foundation of the economy and justified self-reliance in the socialist countries mainly by pointing to the existence of the imperialist bloc. After summarizing the limits and internal contradictions of the cooperatives, it concluded that the passage to communes was necessary as a 'concrete path of transition from collective property to property of the whole people'. It reaffirmed basic principles and listed the types of property prevalent at that time (rather cautiously adding that it would take a 'relatively long' time for the brigade to replace the team as the basic accounting unit and a further period still for the commune to do so). It reiterated the idea that the struggle in the countryside was being fought between the socialist road and the capitalist road and presented socialist education as a 'long-term task', to be carried out along the lines of 'politics in command'. In August 1965, when the infighting that was to develop into the great crisis had already begun, T'ao once again wrote an article for *Red Flag* celebrating the anniversary of Mao's essay on cooperation. Here too he repeated the current line on economic policy and stressed the need to combine the theory of revolution in stages with the theory of uninterrupted revolution in order to guide the socialist transformation of agriculture. He also criticized the

[20] *CB*, nos. 824 and 825 contain a collection of attacks on T'ao Chu.

rightists, who favoured the 'four big freedoms', referred to the idea that cooperation should precede mechanization and to the contradiction in a socialist society between the relations of productions and the productive forces and ended up with a ritual attack on Krushchevite revisionism.[21]

Between June and August 1966 T'ao was present in the universities, receiving student delegations and making frequent speeches. For example, on 1 July he spoke at Peking University and on 2 August at the People's University, insisting on the need for democracy and posing as the champion of the rights of minorities. On 23 August, at a meeting in Peking with students from different universities, he discussed an incident which had taken place at Tientsin. His tone on this occasion was not without touches of demagogy: however, his main theme was to invite the students to struggle against the Party committees wherever they followed a wrong line, while supreme authority was to remain firmly in the hands of Mao and the Central Committee. Two days later he brought up the same ideas in a speech at the Central Committee Propaganda Department, where he also dealt with the problem of the composition of the Red Guards and the exchanges of experiences between different cities and reaffirmed that Mao – like Lin Piao, the chief standard-bearer of Mao's thought – was not to be attacked.[22] (Later criticisms seem to reprove T'ao for having defended the authority of the Party at all levels, but this does not tally with the statements in those of his speeches known to us.)

Once he had fallen into disgrace, T'ao became the object of furious attacks that lasted for two years. In many cases he was included in the more general attacks on old leaders and accused of 'white terror', of working for the restoration of capitalism ever since liberation and of sabotaging the early stages of the cultural revolution through his agents, sometimes from the right and sometimes from the 'left'. More particularly, he was accused of having formed a bloc with Hsiao Wang-tung and having feigned an attitude of harshness towards P'eng Chen and Lu Ting-i.[23]

But in his case too, the more sensational settling of accounts was left to Yao Wen-yuan, who as usual sifted through his victim's past and put a new and factionally-inspired interpretation on it. He drew his evidence mainly from two books T'ao had published in 1962 and 1964, called

[21] *PR*, nos. 15 and 16, 1964; *HNA*, 7 August 1966, pp. 7ff.

[22] *CB*, no. 330, pp. 14–15, pp. 20, 30 and 34; no. 819, pp. 11ff.

[23] *HNA*, 23 February 1968, p. 4; 24 February 1968, p. 6; 5 September 1967, p. 8.

Ideals, Integrity and Spiritual Life and *Thinking, Feeling and Literary Talent.*

It is neither an easy nor a pleasant task to attempt to extract anything of substance from Yao's article. Its distortions are apparent even to someone who is unable to make a point by point check of the sources and its view of the political and class content of art and literature is expressed in a crude, obsessive form bordering on the grotesque, not in the Leninist but in the most obtusely Zhdanovian tradition. However: Yao accused T'ao of having said in 1957 that 'by and large the classes have now disappeared' and 'the role of the dictatorship should be weakened'. T'ao was also supposed to have voiced a similar idea in November 1965, when at the height of the controversy over Wu Han's play he allegedly wrote in the Literary and Art Gazette (*Wen-i pao*): 'I think that at the present stage, the task of reflecting the contradictions among the people should be put in the most important position.' He is also said to have lacked a class analysis, saying that 'the idea of socialism is to use every means to ensure rapid national industrialization', whereas industrialization considered in the abstract had been made possible in the United States by taking the capitalist road. (Apart from the obvious sophistry of this argument, Yao seems to have been unaware of the fact that capitalist industrialization – as experience shows – is impossible in underdeveloped countries.) T'ao's critics also condemned as aberrant and individualistic the idea that communism will mean the full satisfaction of consumer needs. On the cultural level, the former Kwangtung leader was said to be opposed to Mao's thought and to support revisionist ideas, and from the point of view of method to underestimate the dynamism of the subjective factor with his claim that 'existence is primary while thinking is only secondary, the objective is primary while the subjective is only secondary'. Taking up a fashionable theme, Yao finally criticized T'ao ('an ultrarightist one minute and on the extreme "left" the next') for continually oscillating from one extreme to another. In conclusion, however, he insisted that from a certain moment onwards T'ao Chu had presented himself as an 'extremist anarchist' and had claimed that it was right to suspect everyone and oppose everyone. For this reason in particular he denounced him as being behind the *16 May Group*, to which we will return later.[24]

On a number of substantial points, above all the view that the contradictions taking shape were mostly 'contradictions among the people', i.e.

[24] *HNA*, 8 September 1967.

internal to the dialectics of post-revolutionary society, T'ao Chu's ideas were after all not all that uncommon and in any case had nothing to do with Krushchevite ideas (in the USSR, under Krushchev and Brezhnev, as under Stalin, all those who do not entirely accept the policy and ideas of the leadership are still considered capitalist agents). In the final part of the article, the main charge was one of 'extremism' and 'anarchism', and this was confirmed in other articles attacking T'ao.[25] But if T'ao's real or presumed positions in previous years really were revisionist and Krushchevite, and this was the real reason for the attack, how can we explain the fact that it was precisely after the start of the cultural revolution that T'ao was called to the top?

It is worthwhile pausing at this point to take a look at the methods of Yao Wen-yuan, who as chief polemist of the cultural revolution was given the job of settling accounts with Wu Han, Teng T'o and Chou Yang.

We have already seen how Yao twisted a statement by T'ao on the need to industrialize, giving it a totally false meaning. In some cases he descended to sheer insult, as when he wrote: 'Would you like to know what kind of spiritual life is extolled in these two books? No need to read too far, just to get the essence is enough. It is the reactionary Kuomintang philosophy plus the flunkey's mentality.' (Blumer boldly declares that Yao Wen-yuan 'honoured the best sarcastic tradition of Friedrich Engels'.[26] One wonders whether he has misread Yao or not read Engels...) Elsewhere he made an attempt at 'demonstration': after remarking that T'ao Chu made use of a quotation from Sun Yat-sen which also appears in one of Chiang Kai-shek's lectures, he concludes triumphantly: 'T'ao Chu shamelessly proclaims that he was a student of Chiang Kai-shek.' There is no need for any comment. There is need for comment, however, on a later passage where Yao condemned the 'plain historical distortion' whereby T'ao ascribed the victories during the first period of the revolutionary war to the Kuomintang and not 'to the correct leadership and policies of the Communist Party represented by Mao Tse-tung'. T'ao was in fact probably speaking of military victories and in this sense there was some basis for what he was saying; in any case, the leadership itself admitted (though not until later) that the Party's policy at the time of the first revolutionary war was wholly wrong. Besides, it is quite plainly an anachronism to talk, as Yao does, as if Mao were already the leader during the mid-twenties.

Yao found it scandalous that T'ao Chu had one day written that even

[25] E.g. an article in *Liberation Army Daily*; *HNA*, 11 September 1967.
[26] Op. cit., p. 98.

the sun has its 'black spots' and praised the pine tree because it protects us from the sun's rays in summer. The remark about the sun was seen as 'invective' against the Party and its leader, while the remark about the pine tree was seen as a covert attack on the 'brilliance of Mao Tse-tung's thought . . .'. And what can we say when Yao declares that T'ao's remark about Party members cherishing sentiments for all but 'counterrevolutionaries' in fact means 'love for all', i.e. 'love for the exploiting classes and the renegades'? As for T'ao distributing his books at public expense, this may be proof of his ambition and his tendency to abuse power, but not necessarily of his desire to prepare public opinion for the restoration of capitalism, as Yao claimed. Finally – and this is one more example of the method of seeking a scapegoat for more general responsibilities – Yao rebuked T'ao for having said in September 1959 that men like P'eng Teh-huai should change course and return whole-heartedly into the ranks of those who were building socialism. Our diligent critic forgot that the Lushan meeting decided that P'eng and his supporters should remain members or alternate members of the Central Committee or Politbureau and that the resolution explicitly said that their conduct would be re-examined at a future date.

Some days after Yao's article, the *People's Daily* dedicated an entire page to the polemic against T'ao.[27] As for the past, there was once again criticism of his calls for changes and relaxations in the way the proletarian dictatorship was exercised; there was a new and interesting accusation that T'ao, arguing from the idea that the exploiting classes had more or less been eliminated, issued warnings against the growth of a bureaucracy. It was also said that he criticized the pace of development in 1958–59, emphasized the need to boost production and declared that there was no need unduly to fear the growth of spontaneous forces because at the worst only a few 'pedlar capitalists' would pop up. In the cultural field, he was accused of interpreting the hundred flowers idea in a liberal way and sabotaging the publication of the article against Wu Han in the newspapers under his control. Finally, he was taken to task for saying in 1959 that there should be no objections if some members wanted to leave the cooperatives, as legally they were quite within their rights. Here we can clearly see the prejudice and artfulness behind these attacks: the idea that joining the cooperatives should be voluntary was, at least in principle, common to the whole Party and Mao himself had written, in the essay

[27] *HNA*, 13 September 1967. When Blumer says he knows of no articles on T'ao except that of Yao Wen-yuan (op. cit., p. 335), he once again reveals the inadequacy of his sources.

quoted above, that members had not only the right to leave but even to disband the cooperatives.

The attacks in the official press were preceded by attacks in Red Guard and Revolutionary Rebel publications in T'ao's own region (some of these are reprinted in the above mentioned issues of *CB*). These slashing attacks anticipated some of the arguments taken up by Yao and the other polemists. But sometimes they argue their cases in more detail and quote T'ao at greater length, which gives us a better understanding of his real positions.

First of all, these articles confirm that T'ao had dwelt at length on the theme of bureaucratization, saying: 'The danger of bureaucratism is very great and is of a universal character . . . As far as we are concerned, bureaucratism of today is still a kind of ideological tendency . . . If we do not clearly explain and pay attention to this question, it is possible that we shall degenerate and become bureaucrats and a special class divorced from and finally spurned by the people.' As for economic problems, which were said to be his special field of interest, he allegedly criticized the 'violation of objective laws', the 'violation of the law of planned and proportional development and the law of value', and the neglect of 'economy and business procedure in planning work'. He was also accused of listing the following main causes of China's temporary economic difficulties: 'Highness – too high a speed; bigness – all things run on a large scale; equality – communist style; urgency – over-eagerness for accomplishment without seeking truth from facts; dispersion – manpower and material resources are dispersed on too long a front; confusion – maladjustment of proportions.' On communes, he reportedly said in October 1961: 'In regard to the question of productivity and production relationship, the production relationship has moved too far, as is reflected in the people's commune.' T'ao's opponents also accused him of forcing three communes to combine in 1959, when he allegedly stamped out peasant opposition and favoured the brigade in which he was working, giving it state aid and backing up worthless cadres. On the other hand, during the socialist education movement in 1964 he was accused of hitting cadres too hard and indiscriminately. In 1958 and in the spring of 1959 he was accused of demagogically increasing consumption by offering people three meals a day, with the result that supplies ran out. In the readjustment period he had done an about-turn, encouraging private plots and material incentives and declaring that 'undernourished people are backward'. Heartened by what was happening in the countryside, he had – at the prompting of the Chancellor of Chung Shan University –

even supported the idea of special types of incentives for intellectuals. He had also said that intellectuals 'formed a stratum and not a class'. As for the period of the cultural revolution, he was accused of being behind a circular of 22 June 1966 which insisted on the leading role of the Party and the need to send work teams to schools where the Party committees were not in a position to carry out their duties. Other documents in January 1967 took up the same arguments in less detail, and included additional attacks on the incredible luxury and wastefulness of T'ao and his court – a confirmation of the gap in living standards between the masses and the bureaucracy.

Not even these attacks – some of which, at least, applied to the whole leadership (the circular of 22 June was certainly not a personal initiative) – really prove that T'ao was a right-wing revisionist and a capitalist roader. On the contrary, some of the statements attributed to him show that he was inclined towards the left and clearly perceived some of the crucial problems of the transitional phase between capitalism and socialism.

Teng Hsiao-p'ing

The personal history of Teng Hsiao-p'ing, who joined the Communist Party as an immigrant worker in France in the early twenties and was for many years its General Secretary, still remains relatively obscure. Even the attacks on him very rarely became intense and when the Central Committee dismissed and expelled Liu Shao-ch'i in October 1968, it said not a word – in public, at least – about Teng.

In May 1966, Teng made a speech in Shanghai to a visiting delegation from Albania which was given prominence in the press.[28] In it he attacked 'some people' who thought that the new Soviet leaders had changed course, and said that Marxist-Leninists should not look for unity or compromise with the Krushchevites, but struggle against them to the very end, rejecting any centrist or eclectic position. Although he came out in favour of the united front, he added quite clearly that the Soviet leaders 'naturally could not be included in this united front'.

At the end of July and the beginning of August, Teng was among those following events at Peking University. On 2 August he spoke up for the withdrawal of the work teams and the election of committees of students, teachers, leading personnel and university workers. He continued to be mentioned, though lower down in the official listings, even after the August Plenum, and received students and teachers from the college for

[28] *HNA*, 7 May 1966.

international relations, occasionally stepping in to smooth over disagreements or set up a committee with representatives of the various
tendencies. On that occasion he declared that 'the Party Central Committee and Chairman Mao have turned over the power to you'.[29]

When Liu came under fire in April 1967, Teng was charged with similar offences. His opponents accused him of a long list of crimes: he had
opposed Mao for years, encouraged material incentives and the use of
capitalist commercial techniques, opposed cooperation, accused the
government of wanting to shoot ahead with the communes, stimulated
private property and the market in the agricultural sector, opposed Mao's
thought in the field of literature, preached the theory of the dying out of
the class struggle, tried to cut aid for the revolutionary struggles of other
peoples and favoured unleashing an offensive against 'a great number of
cadres'. Another article accused Teng of responsibility for the 1959
Tibet revolt. Some of these attacks – in particular one made against him
at a meeting in Shanghai – were typical examples of the procedure by
which an incriminated person is accused of a whole assortment of crimes,
with the aim of making him into a general scapegoat, a convenient Aunt
Sally.

It is worth recalling that when, at the Eighth Congress, Teng Hsiao-
p'ing spoke on the reform of the Constitution, he went to some length to
criticize the personality cult (he was careful, however, to point out that
Mao himself had suggested concrete steps in this direction as early as
1949). Also that, on the tenth anniversary of the People's Republic, it fell
to Teng to write a commemorative article for *Pravda* defending the
Great Leap and the communes, condemning right-wing deviationists and
praising the 'socialist initiative of the masses' in the economic construction of the new society.[30]

Though many patently false accusations were launched against Teng
during the cultural revolution, his position as General Secretary of the
Party certainly meant that he was a linchpin of the bureaucratic system.
That this arch bureaucrat should subsequently re-emerge in the top
leadership is thus of great significance for evaluating the outcome of the
cultural revolution.

Liu Shao-ch'i
The grand onslaught on Liu Shao-ch'i began publicly on 1 April 1967,

[29] *CB*, no. 819, pp. 4 and 72.
[30] *HNA*, 7 April 1967, pp. 3–4; 9 April 1967, p. 5; 17 July 1968, p. 3; *PR*, no. 12, 1968,
pp. 25ff.; *SCMP*, no. 4086, pp. 6ff.

with an article by Ch'i Pen-yu in *Red Flag*. A good part of this article was taken up with a polemic on an old film (*Inside story of the Ch'ing court*) which Mao had criticized as 'a film of national betrayal' and which Liu is said to have praised as 'patriotic'. It ended with a series of questions anticipating in summary form almost all the main charges that were to be repeated hundreds of times in publications of all sorts.

The article provided no evidence that Liu had actually called the film 'patriotic'. Indeed, we have a categorical statement from Wang Kuang-mei (Mme Liu), who in the course of her 'trial' on 10 April 1967, while admitting that her husband had made serious mistakes and expressing her agreement with Ch'i Pen-yu's criticisms of the film in question, denied that Liu had ever used the words attributed to him. One of the supposed facts upon which the polemics were based therefore appears to be very doubtful. (The documents on the 'trials' of Wang Kuang-mei, together with a letter and a self-criticism by her, can be found in a pamphlet published by a Tsinghua University group and reprinted in *CB*, no. 848. One of the interrogators claimed that Liu's remark about the film was revealed by Chou Yang in a self-criticism, but we have no knowledge of this.)

We can compare the charges in Ch'i's concluding list of questions not only with Wang Kuang-mei's evidence, but also with three documents by Liu which contain a list of answers. (Liu made his first self-criticism at a Central Committee working conference on 23 October 1966; the following summer first a 'confession' and then a second self-criticism were circulated.) Let us look point for point at the main arguments of both prosecution and defence.[31]

1) *On the eve of the war against Japan Liu authorized some political prisoners to make 'anti-communist statements' to get out of prison.*

Liu replied that in March 1936, when he went to Tientsin as a delegate of the Central Committee, K'o Ch'ing-shih had asked him to decide whether some imprisoned militants who had served their sentences should agree to perform certain formalities in exchange for their release.

[31] Apart from the article by Ch'i Pen-yu, here is a list of the main articles against Liu: *HNA*, 9 April 1967, 12 April 1967, 8 May 1967, 15 August 1967, 22 August 1967, 25 August 1967, 26 August 1967, 27 August 1967, 20 September 1967, 21 September 1967, 8 November 1967, 24 November 1967 (almost all taken from *PR*); we shall quote other articles as we come to them. The October Plenum resolution may be found in *HNA*, 2 November 1968, and *PR*, no. 44, 1968; another document of the same Plenum, not officially published, is in *SCMP*, no. 4334, pp. 5–10. *CB*, no. 834, reprints a savage biography. In many cases the direct quotes are taken from personal conversations reported at a later date (e.g. *HNA*, 15 August 1967, p. 12; 17 September 1967, p. 3; 4 September 1968, p. 7); they are therefore very unreliable.

He had consulted the Central Committee, who told him that it was up to K'o Ch'ing-shih to make the decision, which is what happened. Liu knew nothing about the details of the case and even less about what the formalities were. The day-to-day business of the Central Committee was at that time in the hands of Chang Wen-t'ien (Lo Fu), who according to Liu did not consult Mao about the problem. (Wang Kuang-mei repeated much of Liu's version during her 'trials'.) Finally, Liu conceded that he was partly to blame, but rejected the basic charge.

2) *After the victory over Japan, Liu had 'raised the capitulationist line of a new stage of peace and democracy'.*

In his first self-criticism, Liu admitted having cherished illusions about peace in 1945, but Wang Kuang-mei pointed out that he was not alone in this. The words 'peace and democracy' were clearly written into the armistice agreement and this was why Liu had used them.

Quite apart from what the individuals involved said, only someone ignorant of the policies of the Communist Party between 1944 and 1946 could believe that Liu was the only or the principal inspirer of a policy which was in fact personally carried out by Chou En-lai and by Mao himself. We need only recall, for example, that on 10 November 1944 Mao and the American General Hurley signed an agreement, full of phrases taken from the so-called Atlantic Charter, on the setting up of a coalition government to establish justice, freedom of conscience, freedom of the press, freedom of assembly and association, etc. Mao also personally took part in the Chungking negotiations: the joint communiqué of 10 October 1945 provided for a national assembly and a constitutional government. Later the Communist leaders accepted – after much hesitation – an invitation to attend a consultative assembly and again and again gave evidence of their desire to come to terms. The later break was Chiang Kai-shek's fault and in no way a deliberate strategic choice by Mao and the rest of the leadership. In his speech to the Seventh Congress, Mao openly called for a coalition government, spoke of civil war as the least favourable course and declared that 'what China urgently needs is the establishment, through uniting all political parties and groups and non-partisan leaders, of a democratic, provisional coalition government, so that democratic reforms may be instituted, (and) the present crisis overcome . . .'.[32] As for the economic order under the New Democracy, Mao said he accepted the principles of Sun Yat-sen, and denied that 'the Chinese Communists are opposed to the development of individuality,

[32] Mao Tse-tung, 'On Coalition Government', in Brandt et al., *A Documentary History of Chinese Communism*, Harvard 1952, p. 295.

the development of private capital and the protection of private property'.[33] He reaffirmed his readiness to negotiate with the Kuomintang
and to work together, in the framework of a coalition government, with
all parties, political groups and even 'business circles'. Quite apart from
whether this political strategy was correct or not, it is clear that certain
perspectives and certain tendencies were by no means the exclusive
property of the unfortunate Liu Shao-ch'i.[34]

3) *After liberation, Liu opposed the socialist transformation of industry
and of commerce, opposed agricultural cooperation and considerably reduced
the number of cooperatives.*

These arguments were later set out in more detail and repeated again
and again: Liu had 'praised exploitation', urged the capitalists to increase
their profits and looked forward to a long-term collaboration with the
so-called national bourgeoisie. He had preached the 'four big freedoms'
in agriculture (freedom to lend at interest, freedom to engage manpower,
freedom to buy and sell land and freedom of private enterprise) and after
having done his best to stop the changeover from mutual aid teams to
cooperatives, he wanted to disband 200,000 cooperatives in 1955.

Liu's reply was that he now recognized that certain of the positions he
had taken up (his position on the change-over from mutual aid teams to
cooperatives in Shansi, for example) were wrong and that certain of his
perspectives (particularly his hopes of peace in 1946) were illusory. He
blamed himself for not having opposed the actions of others in connection
with the disbandment of the cooperatives. Wang Kuang-mei said that
Liu was in agreement with the views of Teng Tzu-hui, but added that at
that time it was thought that things should move at a slower and steadier
pace. As for the charge that Liu had encouraged the capitalists, in particular during a speech at Tientsin, Wang replied that some of Liu's remarks
had been wrong while others were 'correct but not properly presented',
and that some of the remarks attributed to Liu in wall-posters were
inventions. Liu had actually gone to Tientsin to put right a 'left' deviation
on the part of those who wanted to wipe out the exploiting classes
immediately, but he had been sent there by Mao himself. (Kenneth
Lieberthal, writing in no. 47 of *The China Quarterly*, shows how Liu was
in fact applying Mao's own principles at Tientsin and that the real 'split'

[33] Ibid., p. 303.
[34] Various documents on this period are to be found in the *United States Relations with
China*, published in 1949 by the U.S. State Department. See also J. Guillermaz, *History of
the Chinese Communist Party 1921–1949*, London 1972, and the previously cited article by
K. Lieberthal in *China Quarterly*, no. 47.

was not between Mao and Liu but between the Party leadership, which wanted to stabilize the situation in order to increase production, and the 'leftist' lower-level cadres, who wanted to import the class struggle immediately from countryside to town.)

Here again, then, Liu, even though he may have deviated here and there or occasionally put the wrong emphasis, was in the main carrying out the Party line, as we pointed out in the first part of this book. Mao himself, with the speech on coalition government in which he sketched out the perspectives for the period of New Democracy, prepared the way for the policy of moderation and cautious gradualism which at a later date was also to characterize his report of March 1949 to the Central Committee.

4) *After the socialist transformation of industry and commerce was completed, Liu preached the theory of the dying away of the class struggle and even foresaw its abolition.*

In the first place, this appears to contradict another accusation brought against Liu, though with reference to a different period. Immediately after the beginning of the cultural revolution he is alleged to have said: 'So far as all humanity and the whole world is concerned, the taking of the socialist road is still in an experimental stage. We too are experimenting, uncertain of what is in store for us in the future . . . (that China will take the socialist road) is not yet a foregone conclusion.'[35] We do not know the context in which this remark was made, but it is hard to see how the remark itself, especially the first part, can be faulted, considering the painful experiences of the different countries that have entered into the transitional phase.

In his 'confession' Liu admitted that there were contradictions in his report to the Eighth Congress and mistakes in the final resolution. For example, he said at one point in his report that in China the struggle between socialism and capitalism had already been fundamentally settled. Further on, however, he contradicted this by saying that 'class struggle will go on until socialist transformation is completed. Even after that, there will be struggles between socialist and capitalist stands, viewpoints and methods over a long period of time.' The resolution, which was approved unanimously, said: 'A decisive victory has already been won in (the) socialist transformation. This means that the contradiction between the proletariat and the bourgeoisie in our country has been basically resolved, that the history of the system of class exploitation,

---

[35] *SCMP*, no. 4048, p. 7; *HNA*, 19 October 1967, p. 3. The two differ slightly and the quotation is integrated from both.

which lasted for several thousand years in our country, has on the whole been brought to an end, and that the social system of socialism has, in the main, been established in China.'[36] He said that Mao had criticized these mistakes, but there had been no time to put them right. It is all too obvious, however, that the leading bodies and therefore Mao himself would have approved the report beforehand, and that they would have found time to correct the presumed mistakes if they had really considered them serious. Wang Kuang-mei commented: 'However, the document was released long ago. Chairman Mao and the Party Central Committee did not say anything.'

It is worth quoting what Liu said on other occasions about this subject. In a report on the work of the Party Central Committee to the second session of the Eighth Congress (5 May 1968), he described the rectification campaign as 'a decisive struggle between the socialist road and the capitalist road' and spoke of four classes in China, two of them exploiting classes (the pro-Kuomintang right-wing bourgeosie and the national bourgeoisie) and two of them toiling classes (the workers and the peasants). In the same year he denounced both extremist and opportunist ideas on what attitude to take up towards the bourgeoisie and – what is more relevant – openly rejected the idea that the socialist revolution was already completed. He actually based his remarks on a formula from Mao Tse-tung which was afterwards continually used against him in the cultural revolution.[37] In a speech at the end of June 1961 he said: 'The struggle as between the socialist and the capitalist road has not ended with the basic completion of the socialist revolution in the ownership of the means of production and this struggle will go on for a long time, especially on the political and ideological fronts.' On 12 May 1963 he said even more clearly that class struggle was inevitable throughout the period of transition and that the question of whether socialism or capitalism will win could be 'finally solved only through a protracted struggle' which would be 'complicated, tortuous and sometimes very sharp'. Some months later, at Pyongyang, he again criticized 'any denial of the existence of class difference and class struggle in a socialist country'.

5) *During the three difficult years, Liu had attacked the 'three red flags' (the Party's general line for socialist construction, the Great Leap Forward and the People's Communes), had called for 'the extension of plots for private use and of free markets, the increase of small enterprises with sole responsi-*

---

[36] *Eighth Congress*, vol. I, pp. 72 and 115.

[37] Liu Shao-ch'i, 'The Victory of Marxism–Leninism in China', 14 September 1959, in the *Collected Works of Liu Shao-ch'i*, Union Research Institute, Hong Kong 1968.

bility for their own profits or losses, the fixing of output quotas based on the household' (the so-called *san-tzu i-pao* campaign) *and the 'liquidation of struggle in our relations with imperialism, the reactionaries and modern revisionism, and reduction of assistance and support to the revolutionary struggle of other peoples'*.

More specifically, he had hinted that the communes were introduced too hastily and that this had prejudiced the support of the masses. He was alleged to have said that 'it is impossible to carry out agricultural socialization by relying on mutual aid teams, cooperatives and labour-exchange teams. This is a kind of Utopian agricultural socialism; it is erroneous . . . Without industrialization, it is simply impossible to realize agricultural collectivization . . . Collective farms without machines cannot be consolidated.'[38]

On the first charge, Liu's reply went straight to the point: 'During the three years of difficulty I did not attack the Three Red Flags.' As for the communes, Liu had been one of their firmest supporters. In the 1959 article quoted above ('The Victory of Marxism-Leninism in China') he not only defended them all along the line but openly contradicted those who said that they were 'set up much too soon', were 'in a mess' and 'outstepped the level of social development and the level of the people's political consciousness'. He confirmed this stand on various occasions (for example in a speech at Moscow on 7 December 1960 and in his speech on the fortieth anniversary of the foundation of the Party). On the other hand, he admitted not having opposed Teng Tzu-hui's ideas in 1962 and having been generally inclined towards the right at that time. Wang Kuang-mei denied the more specific charge against Liu regarding the *san-tzu i-pao* campaign. She maintained that Liu had in fact considered it 'a big retrogression in history' and added that 'his mistake lay in his not bringing it to the attention of Chairman Mao or acting too late'. Liu was also accused of having criticized the peasants during the difficult years because they held up regular food supplies and of having proposed raising the prices of industrial goods in retaliation.[39] This seems like an obvious attempt to make Liu the scapegoat for measures that the peasants naturally disliked. (Note that several months after his 'confession', Liu's statement that he had not attacked the communes during the difficult years was described as 'shameless'.)[40]

On industrial development, Liu's 5 May 1958 speech set forth the

[38] *HNA*, 22 August 1967, p. 22.
[39] *HNA*, 7 September 1967, p. 17.
[40] *HNA*, 24 November 1967, p. 8.

prevailing line of simultaneously developing industry and agriculture while giving priority to heavy industry and rejected the arguments of those who opposed moving too quickly. The following year he firmly supported the Great Leap Forward, defending it in the face of the reservations and criticisms of others.

On international problems, leaving on one side the paradoxical phrasing of the charges, we should remember that Liu, even according to the Maoists themselves, was at the height of his power during the very years when the Sino-Soviet conflict was working up to the final break. It is difficult to find one single speech by Liu which contains ideas or expressions at variance with those of the rest of the leadership at that time (or even later, for they remained substantially unchanged during the cultural revolution).

True, the charges against Liu were later elaborated. He was criticized for statements he made during his journey to Indonesia, for his praise of Sukarno and the Nasakom formula (the union of nationalist, religious and Communist elements) and for approving of the Indonesian Communists' collaboration with the government; and Wang Kuang-mei was even rebuked for flirting with Sukarno. Liu was similarly accused of collaborating with the Burmese President Ne Win.[41] But if there ever was a case of setting up a scapegoat, this was it. The Indonesian débâcle, which flowed inevitably from what was at root a shortsighted and opportunist policy, was a very severe blow to the entire leadership. Why, then, should they not give in to the temptation to heap the blame on Liu and pass over the fact that he was merely supporting the line of the Indonesian Communist Party (long hailed by Peking as a model of non-revisionism) and that much more important than Wang's alleged coquetry was the prolonged political flirtation between the Chinese leadership, including Mao, and the head of Indonesia's so-called 'national bourgeoisie'?

According to Liu's critics, he said in 1965 that it was hard to arrive at any conclusion as to the nature of the Soviet Union and the CPSU and considered that Soviet aid was necessary for China's nuclear development. On the more burning question of the united front and unity in action, contradictory evidence exists. Liu is said to have declared that 'it was not possible for the USSR and the United States to unite on fundamental questions' (if this referred to problems in which opposing class interests are at stake, the statement was not so strange after all), but right

[41] *HNA*, 15 July 1967, pp. 15–16; 18 August 1967, p. 20; 14 October 1967, p. 5; *CB*, no. 848, p. 7; *HNA*, 15 August 1967, p. 9; 18 August 1967, p. 20.

up to his last public statements he always came out clearly against united action with the 'modern revisionists' over Vietnam. We should bear in mind, however, that according to the sources quoted above, in March 1966 Liu joined together with P'eng Chen and Teng Hsiao-p'ing in presenting the Japanese Communists with a draft declaration on this problem which the Japanese accepted but which was later annulled because of opposition from Mao and Lin Piao. It is hard to say, of course, how important this episode really was and how far it influenced relations between Mao and Liu. In any case, Liu did not fall in the hierarchy until after the Fifty Days, by which time other problems had arisen.

6) *In 1962 Liu republished his book 'How to be a Good Communist', which 'does not advocate revolution, class struggle, the seizure of political power and the dictatorship of the proletariat, opposes Marxism-Leninism, Mao Tse-tung's thought, preaches a decadent bourgeois world outlook and the reactionary philosophy of bourgeois idealism'.*

More particularly, the book was said to have inculcated into Party members the principle of servile obedience and to have encouraged individualism, ambition and careerism. What is more, the 1962 edition was a touched up version of the original 1949 edition.

Judging from the information at our disposal, Liu said nothing about the book in his 'confession' or his self-criticisms, even when he listed all the mistakes he was supposed to have made. Wang Kuang-mei, while agreeing that the book was idealistic, declared that she 'could not think of anything to justify the allegation that it rejects the dictatorship of the proletariat'.

The book in question is certainly not a masterpiece of Marxist litera-ture. It suffers from a pedantic, text-book approach and is heavily influenced by the Stalinist ideas in vogue when the first edition came out (and which the second edition failed to remove). Liu quotes one of Stalin's most banal and catechismal statements to define Lenin's thought, and his paean to the Party is also in the Stalin school: 'the most con-scientious, progressive and healthy people in the world, who have the highest sense of morals and virtues'. His views on the identity of aims between Party and individual and the need to subordinate the latter to the former if they should come into conflict are moralistic and almost melodramatic. But it is absurd to suggest that he ignored the class struggle, the dictatorship of the proletariat, Mao's thought, etc. Quite apart from the fact that the book was meant to cover only a limited amount of ground, the author starts – albeit schematically – from the premise of class society, refers explicitly to the proletarian revolution, repeatedly

quotes Mao, warns against the influence that the ruling classes will continue to have long after their downfall and explicitly condemns individualism and careerism several times. One interesting detail: in a
speech on 1 February 1942 Mao criticized tendencies towards egoism and
departmentalism and quoted as an example a statement by none other
than Liu Shao-ch'i. This quotation appeared in the first edition of the
famous little red book. It was left out of subsequent editions both of the
red book and of Mao's works, which only goes to show that certain practices die hard.[42]

7) Liu had '*put forward and put into effect the "left" in form but right in
essence opportunist line in the socialist education movement to sabotage it*'.

The more concrete charge was that as early as 1964 he had taken advantage of his wife's visit to T'aoyuan brigade to put into effect his policy
of making all cadres responsible for mistakes and hitting them hard. At
the same time he is said to have encouraged the tendency to seek state aid
instead of urging the on-the-spot mobilization of forces.

In his self-criticism he replied, 'I said that to make it effective, the
Four Clean-ups campaign should be launched in a mass movement. When
I said so, I thought that the investigative meetings that Chairman Mao
wanted to hold would be insufficient. In reality this negated Chairman
Mao's thought.' Once again Wang Kuang-mei was more outspoken: in
her view, 'the T'aoyuan experience had more merits than demerits'. If
we are to believe a statement by Liu P'ing-p'ing (Wang's daughter), Liu
Shao-ch'i shared this opinion.[43] Liu was also accused of wanting to
counterpose T'aoyuan to Tachai as a model.[44]

It is still difficult to form an exact opinion on the events of 1964, which
were fairly confused. Bear in mind, however, that Liu's position was
considered a 'left deviation'. He had also been accused of a 'left deviation'
in connection with events that had taken place in 1947, when, 'trying to
sabotage the agrarian reform, he proposed a reactionary line, "left" in
appearance but right in essence, giving out these slogans: Let the masses
do what they want!, Let them keep out of the Party cell, throw out the
cadres!'. At that time Liu had made concessions to the masses, who
wanted to carry through the agrarian reform to its end, rectifying the
previous moderate line. In connection with these events he was also

---

[42] *HNA*, 8 April 1967, pp. 5 and 16; 2 September 1967, p. 27. For some variations in the
different editions of Mao's works, see F. Charlier's article in *Quatrième Internationale*,
July 1969.

[43] *CB*, no. 848, pp. 21 and 42; *HNA*, 3 March 1968, p. 3.

[44] *HNA*, 9 September 1967, pp. 26ff., and 10 September 1967, pp. 5ff.

accused of upholding the theory of 'spontaneity' (a charge that was conveniently extrapolated to account for the events of 1927). This contradicted, at least in part, the accusation that he trusted the apparatus more than the masses, whom he wished to keep under rigid control.[45]

8) *He had 'colluded with another top party person in authority taking the capitalist road in the course of the great proletarian cultural revolution in putting forward and carrying out the bourgeois reactionary line'.*

In later and more detailed accusations, he was given the main share of responsibility for the line put forward during the Fifty Days, for sending out the work teams and for his policy of striking cadres indiscriminately and dividing the masses. Together with Wang Kuang-mei he was blamed for the serious incidents at Tsinghua University.

On this latter question, we have already seen how Wang Kuang-mei resolutely denied that her husband had labelled the student K'uai Ta-fu as a 'counterrevolutionary' or given out the slogan 'suspect everything'.

On the more general issue, Liu said in his first self-criticism that he had neither understood the cultural revolution nor trusted the masses. In his confession he said he did not understand how he could have made mistakes and that so far no article had explained it to him. In his second self-criticism he specified that he had only realized his mistakes on 5 August after reading Mao's big-character poster: his mistakes during the Fifty Days had been against 'principle and Party line', but others had shared the responsibility for them. His main mistakes had been trying to limit the actions of the masses (by distinguishing between Party members and non-members, forbidding people to demonstrate or paste up *tatzupao* in the streets, etc.) and supporting the work teams.

In speeches made at the beginning of August Liu said it would have been better not to send in the work teams, suggested allowing non-members of the Communist Youth League to also attend meetings, warned against over-criticizing cadres and Party members, came out against discrimination on the basis of 'family lineage' and recommended that no arrests should be made until all the necessary proof had been gathered. He defended the majority of the Party and League members, declared that students should be allowed to make noisy demonstrations (the schools had been closed for this very reason), called for fresh elections and confidence in the Party organizations and said: 'The Chinese Communist Party is Marxist. It is not justified to rebel against the Communist Party. If the Party becomes a revisionist Party, then we should

[45] *PR*, no. 42, 1968, pp. 27 and 31; *HNA*, 15 March 1968, p. 4; 28 July 1968, p. 4; 15 July 1968, p. 4.

rebel against it!' And turning to the work teams: 'You are afraid of mass democracy and mass movements to undermine our order. The order of the revolutionary mass movement will not take our subjective framework as the main factor.'

In conclusion, there are a few other points that we should bring out.[46]

The first of these relates to Liu's 'misdeeds' in the now long distant past. He is said to have revealed his true character as early as 1922 in the course of a famous strike; still in the early twenties, he showed himself to be an opportunist when he said conditions were not ripe for a seizure of power and went along with Ch'en Tu-hsiu's line; in June 1927, at Wuhan, he had ordered workers to break up their pickets and hand in their rifles and ammunition. Once again his accusers chose to forget that here too Liu was following the Party line and that the same criticisms could have been made against those leaders who were still at the top even after the cultural revolution. They should have blamed not the old Chinese leaders but Stalin, for he was the firmest supporter of the opportunist line and of the compromise with the Kuomintang, even though Maoist propaganda continues to paint him with the aura of an intransigent revolutionary.[47] (In the *Resolutions on Some Questions of our Party History*, voted by the Central Committee on 20 April 1945 but drawn up by Mao himself, Liu is twice referred to as an example of correct work in 1927.[48] The new editions of Mao's writings have once again been suitably censored.)

The second point regards the nature of the Party: Liu was accused of demanding a spirit of servile obedience from the militants and a passive and unconditional acceptance of the line as laid down; at the same time he is said to have not wanted to admit that the internal struggles in the Party were nothing but an expression of the class struggle.

A Communist Party, expecially if it is the only party in power, is inevitably subjected to various pressures from the social forces around it and it is therefore legitimate to look for the social roots of its different lines and tendencies (provided, we hasten to add, that the investigation is carried out along strict lines and does not degenerate into a police frame-up). This is not to say, however, that there is no internal dialectic

---

[46] Others we shall omit, although they are not without importance (e.g. *HNA*, 8 November 1967 – on questions of methodology; *HNA*, 26 August 1967, p. 11 – on the concept of journalism; *HNA*, 14 March 1968, p. 3 – on women's problems; and *HNA*, 13 October 1967, p. 23 – on the omission of references to Mao).

[47] *HNA*, 15 August 1967, p. 4; *PR*, no. 47, 1968, p. 7.

[48] See also Lieberthal, op. cit.

in an organization which is engaged in building a new society and which, at least in theory, embraces the vanguard of the class in whose interests it is working. Liu has grasped this aspect of the inner-Party struggle and is attempting to define its ambit when he says that 'in substance and content, it is fundamentally an ideological struggle . . . As the Party members see things differently, they settle problems with different methods . . .'. In the last analysis, we could say that Mao's own distinction between antagonistic and non-antagonistic contradictions also moves in this direction.

It is also right to say that no one should unconditionally accept the Party line: it was Liu himself who said that if the Party became revisionist, it would be right to rebel against it. But the principle according to which the majority position is accepted when it is right and rejected when it is wrong is not very helpful in the abstract, since minorities always form, if they are in good faith, because they hold the majority position to be mistaken. It is true, however, that the Maoists have given their position a very concrete content: it is right to rebel if the majority belongs to Chairman Mao's tendency, otherwise it is wrong.[49]

(Note that in his essay *On the Intra-Party Struggle* (2 July 1941), Liu Shao-ch'i strongly emphasized that the Party was subject to the influence of classes hostile to or other than the proletariat and declared that 'the intra-Party struggle is a reflection of the struggle outside the Party'. The article's main reference was Stalin and it several times mentioned that 'Trotskyist spies' were infiltrating the Party.)[50]

Liu was also accused of encouraging profits and material incentives, putting the emphasis on 'expertness', and maintaining that it was necessary to learn from the capitalists about management methods, adopt economic criteria and reach production efficiency so as to be able to settle accounts with capitalism. During the readjustment period he was said to have insisted on the seriousness of the situation, coming to the defence of P'eng Teh-huai and calling for priority to be given to the development of the chemical industry, 'following the path of Germany and Japan'.[51]

As we have seen, in his self-criticism Liu admitted inclining towards the right in 1962 and also admitted accepting some of Ch'en Yun's mistaken views.

[49] *HNA*, 26 October 1967, p. 7; *PR*, no. 46, 1968, p. 20; *HNA*, 10 August 1968, p. 5; *CB*, no. 842, p. 4.

[50] See Brandt et al., op. cit., pp. 356–372.

[51] *HNA*, 22 August 1967, pp. 15–16 and 17; 26 August 1967, p. 19; 25 March 1968, pp. 19–20; 7 September 1967, pp. 18–19.

We need not here examine the advisability of giving priority at any given moment to the development of the chemical industry, or how far the retreats proposed by some economists were necessary. These are problems that must be stated or re-examined in the framework of precise historical analyses rather than tacked on to the end of an already long list of accusations. There is no doubt that some of the ideas ascribed to Liu were not without foundation. For example, his claim that the three difficult years were more the result of bad policy than bad weather was largely true and it was certainly no flight of fancy to say that the communes were launched too hurriedly. As for certain opinions of Ch'en Yun, which Liu was said to have shared ('we shall need more than five years to recuperate'), events have shown that they were not over-pessimistic. And we fail to see what is wrong with reaffirming the basic idea that socialism will only triumph if it succeeds in reaching a higher level of production efficiency (that is, unless we intend returning to the same Utopian ideas that Marxism has rejected since its earliest days).[52]

Liu was also attacked for his ideas on the trade unions. He is said to have thought that the unions should concern themselves with production and the workers' welfare, 'protect the material interests and democratic rights of the workers and staff' and avoid organizational dependence on the Party. He was also said to have 'dreamed of setting up a workers' soviet that would place the trade unions above the Party and the government'. Here again, it would be a mistake to consider this statement out of context (the age-old experience of the workers' movement shows, for example, what different meanings the demand for trade-union autonomy can assume). But why should the trade unions not protect the material interests and the democratic rights of the workers? Was not this the sense of Lenin's stand in the famous controversy in the early twenties? And why should we begin by rejecting in principle the need for a clear-cut differentiation between the Party and the unions or the idea of soviets conceived as organs of a working-class democracy, distinct both from the unions and the Party?[53]

Finally, some of Liu's positions on a whole range of problems should lead us to examine more carefully the basis of many of the attacks on him. In his speech of 1958 (cited above), after emphasizing the participation of cadres and leading technical personnel in manual labour, he said: 'The Central Government and local authorities at all levels must . . . firmly

---

[52] *CB*, no. 834, p. 20.

[53] *HNA*, 8 October 1967; 14 June 1968. The latter refers to the splits in the USSR during the twenties, but cheerfully lumps together Trotsky, Bukharin and the Workers' Opposition.

oppose capitalist ideas in management, and any tendency to localism or departmentalism. At the same time, whether in national or local industries, in giant enterprises or small and medium-sized enterprises, it is necessary to oppose resolutely any tendency to chase only after the latest technical equipment, while failing to make full use of all that is on hand: oppose any tendency to overemphasize the role of experts to the disparagement of the great role that can be played by the workers and peasants in developing new production techniques.' On another occasion he said: 'Essentially "Politics in Command" means insistence on leadership by the Party and the correct carrying out of the Party's mass line.' Still in 1958, he said: 'It is undoubtedly wrong to imagine that a single rectification campaign can settle all questions at a single stroke and that there will be no more twists and turns or ups and downs in the struggle. That is why from now on the method of the rectification campaign, the method of criticisms and self-criticism through full and frank airing of views, great debates and posting *tatzupao* must be made the regular method of reforming ideology and improving work. All-round rectification campaigns should be launched at set intervals to handle systematically the contradictions among the people and other contradictions that may have come to light at that time.' The Maoists were to formulate identical or similar ideas during the cultural revolution. Liu later emphasized that a 'very long time was still required to build China into a great socialist country with modern industry, modern agriculture and modern science and culture, and a long historical period (was) required to realize the transition from socialism to communism' (30 June 1961). Dealing at Pyongyang with another fundamental problem, he said in September 1963: 'Everyone understands that self-reliance definitely does not mean a closed-door policy and rejection of external aid. But every country in its revolution and construction must rely mainly on its own efforts and seek external assistance as a supplement . . . In any case international division of labour and cooperation in production must not be used as a pretext for opposing the principle of self-reliance. The essence of the controversy does not lie here. Those who are opposing us are not actually adhering to proletarian internationalism or sincerely wanting to increase the might of the entire socialist camp through international division of labour and cooperation in production which cater to each other's needs and benefit each other. They are merely using this so-called international division of labour as an attractive cloak to cover their own practice of profiting themselves at the expense of others, a practice characteristic of relations among the capitalist countries, so as to obstruct the efforts of the economically underdeveloped socialist countries to develop an independent national economy and to make these countries economically dependent on them and politically come under their control.'

One last important point. Whereas the Maoists tended to lump all their opponents together, Liu took pains to distinguish between the different positions. On 3 August 1966 he attacked Teng T'o and Wu Han as people who had burnt their bridges. The next day he took his distance even more clearly from P'eng Chen: 'P'eng Chen had been on the stage for so many years! It only took us two years to liquidate him.' Wang Kuang-mei, who was also anxious to draw the necessary distinctions, declared for her part: 'Liu Shao-ch'i is different from P'eng Chen, Lu Ting-i, Lo Jui-ch'ing and Yang Shang-k'un. He is basically not a double-dealer – he is basically not such a kind of person.'[54]

Because of the lack of information, any conclusion we come to will necessarily be tentative and approximate. Having said that, though, it seems fair to say that the so-called 'traitors' who were accused of coming together in a big plot and setting off delayed-action mechanisms had in reality travelled different roads and represented different tendencies. The figures that emerge from the polemics have very little to do with reality: they are more like grotesque individuations of all those ideas and attitudes against which the Maoists were campaigning. Scapegoat number one was the unfortunate Liu Shao-ch'i, who was found guilty of all the deadly sins and raised to the level of a dark, negative myth, as against the sunny, positive myth of Mao Tse-tung's thought. The aims of this operation transcend the events of these years. An obvious effort was under way to re-write the Party's entire history from the visual angle of the cultural revolution, attributing to the insidious infiltration of the enemy and the actions of the various Lius, P'engs and T'aos all those episodes and aspects of that history which are hard to defend from the later Chinese position (and even more so from a strictly Maoist position), which may give rise to doubts and questions (especially among the younger generations, who tend to be free of inhibitions and taboos in their approach to the past) and which, moreover, obstruct the myth of Mao as the supreme and omniscient authority.

We are not suggesting that the positions of the most representative and the most powerful core of the group under attack are generally more progressive than those of the Cultural Revolution Group. All told, Liu

[54] We would remind readers that Liu's statements are mostly taken from Liu Shao-ch'i, *Collected Works 1958–1967*, Hong Kong 1968.

Shao-ch'i and Teng Hsiao-p'ing probably stood for the more traditional – and more inherently bureaucratic – view of the role of Party and state, best expressed the middle levels of the apparatus and for that reason tended towards a greater empiricism in the formulation and tackling of problems. (For example, Liu was a fervent supporter of the Great Leap Forward and the communes as long as they seemed to offer the possibility of spectacular short-term progress, but when they proved unsuccessful he became one of the most convinced supporters of a systematic retreat and a change in economic policies, not as an emergency measure but as a long-term choice.) In every situation they attempted to carry out the Party line with the utmost consistency and firmness. It was for this very reason that they did not at first oppose the launching of the cultural revolution, which they saw as an extension or a revival of previous rectification campaigns, to be conducted in the usual way and under the control of the central decision-making bodies. But when events – as we have seen – took an abnormal turn and the movement from below looked like bursting its banks, they felt compelled to sound the alarm about the danger to the regime as a whole (experience has shown that this was no delusion) and to reaffirm the need to preserve the basic structures and traditional procedures of the Party and state apparatus. They would never have dreamed of calling into question these structures and procedures, just as they never called into question the propagandistic ideological cement of Mao Tse-tung's thought. It was because of this, and not because of any tactical ruse – or not so much because of any tactical ruse – that, even though they tried to defuse some situations and exploit others, they failed to make any serious challenge to the charismatic leader's hegemony, and actually helped to keep the cult going. Hence their great weakness. As they had no clear line and did not dare to take a clear stand on the most burning issues, they gave the impression of hedging and manoeuvring and only seemed interested in saving their own skins. They were quickly thrown on to the defensive and proved incapable of moving into a counter-attack against the group led by the person they would never have dared to overthrow. Their dogged resistance, which was also translated into a refusal to make the self-criticisms demanded by the Maoists, was not sufficient, for the crisis spread from the various levels of the apparatus to society as a whole and the great masses had begun to move. This, combined with Mao's offensive at the top, was the death-blow to a group which could not, in the last analysis, hope to gain from a movement from below and which either would or could not challenge the authority of the leader. (Liu's self-criticisms were not only described as inadequate, but were even seen by the leading group as a counter-attack.[55] In late November 1967 Liu was accused of being 'adamant' in his refusal to admit his mistakes and before that, in June, he was supposed to have said according to the testimony of his daughter Liu P'ing-p'ing: 'I am not a counter-revolutionary. Notwithstanding my shortcomings and mistakes, I am a revolutionary.'[56])

We cannot rule out in advance the possibility that, as a result of developments at present unforeseeable, more men defeated in the cultural revolution may re-emerge in positions of high responsibility at top levels of the Party and the state. But it will certainly not be these men who set in motion a democratic and revolutionary renewal of the system and promote a qualitatively new policy. Moves in this direction are more likely to come from groups which emerged during the three years of the cultural revolution, which made no secret of their disappointment with the way the movement ended up and which began the task of building from below a new left opposition.

New opponents on the left
Groups and organizations formed during the cultural revolution are often accused of being ultra-left. On several occasions they have been more specifically accused of Trotskyism, and one *tatzupao* reportedly took K'ang Sheng to task for defending the 'Trotskyist' T'an Li-fu, arrested in December 1966.[57] Opinions on T'an, who was vice-chairman of the Cultural Revolution Preparatory Committee of Peking Technical University and whose father was head of the People's Procuracy until his death,[58] are violently contradictory. According to 'Dai Hsiao-ai',[59] T'an defended the work teams, upheld the 'conservative' principle of the Five Kinds of Red and had the support of the Party apparatus in distributing one of his speeches. T'an was also accused of being a friend of Ho Lung.[60] Esmein, on the other hand, classifies T'an as a 'libertarian' who criticized everyone, including Chiang Ch'ing, Ch'en Po-ta and even Lin Piao. He quotes a Japanese newspaper which claimed that printed copies of T'an's quotations were sold in their thousands.[61]

A Canton Red Guard publication of August 1968 spoke of a 'Trotsky-

[55] *HNA*, 22 July 1967, p. 3; 25 July 1967, p. 3.
[56] *CB*, no. 848, p. 42.
[57] This information is taken from a *France Presse* despatch from Peking.
[58] *Red Guard*, pp. 137 and 243.
[59] Ibid., pp. 137–8.
[60] Ibid., p. 244.
[61] Esmein, op. cit., pp. 118 and 145–147.

ist' called Wei Po, but at the same time described him as a Kuomintang major-general and a secret service agent.[62]

One case about which we have some details is that of Wu Ch'uan-p'in, a Red Guard leader who joined the Kwangtung Revolutionary Committee when it was set up on 21 February 1968. He is said to have criticized Lin Piao and even Mao himself, opposed the decisions of the leading group and aligned himself with those who 'doubted everything'. He was also accused of attacking the very committee of which he was a member, calling it 'a group of soldiers in power', and of defending the slogan 'Drag out the small handful in the army'. He is even said to have tried to usurp the power of the Canton garrison by setting up the 'red garrison command' and to have gone on hunger-strike during the international fair to attract the attention of the foreign guests.[63]

Esmein records the case of two students – Yi Lin and Ti Hsi – who wrote an open letter criticizing Lin Piao for having said that Mao was greater than Marx, Engels, Lenin and Stalin and pointing out that such conclusions were 'contrary to historical evolution'.[64]

One Canton Rebel publication attacked a left-wing group which had published a document with the suggestive title of *The Gotha Programme Today*. The document, which we have not been able to see, is supposed to have been a 'product of ultra-left ideas'.[65]

One of the most frequently attacked organizations was the *16 May Group* (also called the *5.16 Group*) which had its biggest following in Canton and Peking. It also spread to other towns, including Harbin.[66] At the beginning of September an enlarged session of the Peking Revolutionary Committee declared it to be 'counter-revolutionary' and outlawed it. The attacks continued during the following days. On 26 August a rally was held in Peking to celebrate the capture of a certain Chang Chien-chi, said to be *5.16*'s 'ringleader'. But this was not the end of the story. On 6 September a further announcement claimed that a *16 June Group*, said to be the true headquarters of *5.16*, had been crushed at the Peking Foreign Languages Institute. A speech on 5 September by Chiang

---

[62] *CB*, no. 866, p. 7. For other references to Trotskyism, see *CB*, no. 844, p. 12; Hunter, op. cit., pp. 233 and 238; *Red Guard*, p. 175.

[63] *SCMP*, no. 4303, pp. 7ff.; see also *Red Guard*, passim.

[64] Esmein, op. cit., p. 147.

[65] *SCMP*, no. 4125, p. 3.

[66] Our sources for the *5.16 Group* are: *SCMP*, no. 4136 and no. 4088, p. 3; *HNA*, 3 September 1967, p. 18; 8 September 1967, p. 14; 12 September 1967, p. 14; 18 September 1967, p. 4; *SCMP*, no. 4069 and no. 4072, pp. 4–6; *CB*, no. 844; *Current Scene*, 7 August 1971, pp. 12–16; Esmein, op. cit., pp. 292–296.

Ch'ing included renewed denunciations of ultra-left tendencies which had opposed Chou En-lai. Later an entire pamphlet was taken up with the Peking *5.16 Group*, which was accused of attacking Ch'en Po-ta and Chiang Ch'ing as well as Chou, and even of drawing up a sort of black list of information to use against Mao. The supporters of this group held that Nieh Yuan-tzu and Chang Pan, rebels from the first hours, had turned conservative.

According to what purports to be a chronology of events connected with the *5.16 Group*, its supporters pasted up *tatzupao* demanding the right to criticize the Cultural Revolution Group, attacked Mao and Lin Piao and criticized Mao's call for a great alliance. There are also accusations that they attacked senior army leaders and, more specifically, led a campaign against the Canton Military Region.

We should be very wary, however, of believing all that is told us about the *5.16 Group*. Although it was formally set up on 3 August 1967 – after a first Congress on 1 July – it has been accused of 'crimes' committed in late 1966. One Revolutionary Rebel group (cited in Esmein, p. 295 fn.) claimed that those who were later behind the *5.16 Group* set up a 'group to investigate the Central Committee' in March 1967.

There are also unsubstantiated allegations that the *5.16 Group* had considerable support in the highest ranks of the apparatus. Ch'i Pen-yu, T'ao Chu, Wang Li, Lin Chieh, Kuan Feng and Mu Hsin were all accused of having special links with the organization, which was also said to be at the head of the Rebels in the Institute of Foreign Affairs. The official campaign against the *5.16 Group* was briefly revived during 1971.

But among the most interesting of the publications that sprang up during the cultural revolution are those of the *Sheng-wu-lien* (a shortened form for Hunan Provincial Proletarian Revolutionaries Great Alliance Committee). The *Sheng-wu-lien* programme, published in March 1968 by the Canton Printing Red Flag,[67] is worth quoting at length.

'1) The victorious initiation of the great proletarian cultural revolution marks the entry of the international communist movement into a new age with Mao Tse-tung's thought as its great banner. . . .

'In the new historical stage, the criterion for a revolutionary is to recognize not only the class struggle and the dictatorship of the proletariat, but also continuous revolution under the dictatorship of the proletariat (of course, not remaining at the stage of making revolution in words).

'2) To carry out a great proletarian cultural revolution under the

[67] Text in *SCMP*, no. 4174.

dictatorship of the proletariat is similarly "a violent action of over-throwing one class by another". This means that the proletarian revolutionaries overthrow the newborn and yet decadent privileged stratum of the bourgeoisie (which constitutes the bourgeois headquarters headed by Liu and Teng) and smash the old State machinery which serves the privileged class of the bourgeoisie. In the 18 years after the founding of the State, the majority of cadres have embarked on or passed through the capitalist road, a very few of them consciously while the majority of them unknowingly. Judging the problem through a historical point of view on a long-term basis, most of them will follow Chairman Mao and take the socialist road when they have awakened. However, to awaken is a course of pain and reversals. This is a thorough transformation of world outlook and will inevitably meet with setbacks. The very few who consciously embark on the capitalist road are the privileged stratum which has to be overthrown.

'A quotation from Lenin is very applicable to our State machinery: "Our State machinery . . . is in a very big degree a remnant of the old machinery which rarely goes through serious transformation. This machinery has been renovated only superficially and, as long as other aspects are concerned, is still the most typical State machinery of the old type." As the principal component parts of the State machinery, the army, the prisons, the courts of justice and the police – with the exception of the Army which was led by Deputy Supreme Commander Lin in and after 1960 and is basically in the hands of the proletariat – have long been occupied by Lo Jui-ch'ing and have become totally decadent.

'The emergence of the privileged class indicates that some relations of production have degenerated. Though the economic foundation looks generally to be socialist, yet the whole of the huge superstructure can only be basically capitalist. The relations of production seriously impede the development of the productive forces, and the superstructure forms a serious impediment to the development of the economic base. As a result, the socialist transformation of the economic base under way in China has been carried out by peaceful means and the transformation has not been thoroughgoing. The superstructure has been touched in a still smaller degree. Therefore, the socialist revolution at present – the great proletarian cultural revolution – is in essence a genuine beginning of a socialist revolution in China.

'3) The great proletarian cultural revolution is still at its beginning. The greatest achievement made in the great cultural revolution in the past year and more is that the masses are mobilized and the authority of

Chairman Mao and Mao Tse-tung's thought is established.

'However, because the privileged stratum of the bourgeoisie make use of the power still in their hands to fool the masses and interfere with the dissemination of Mao Tse-tung's thought and, particularly, Chairman Mao's theories about the great proletarian cultural revolution, and because of the influence of the reactionary socialist habitual forces, a large part of the masses still do not understand the target of the great cultural revolution. Their resistance against the privileged stratum remains at the stage of an effort to change their position of being the oppressed.

'Notwithstanding the criticism and repudiation of the bourgeois reactionary line last year, the criticism and repudiation was restricted to the disclosing of the crimes of individuals and seldom touched either the class roots of the reactionary line or the bureaucratic organs serving the reactionary line.

'Although the storm of January this year had lifted the curtain on the struggle to seize power from the bourgeois headquarters, the seizure of power was regarded as dismissal of individuals from their offices and not as the overthrowing of the privileged stratum and the smashing of the old State machinery. Moreover, the proletarian revolutionaries were childish. As a result, political power is still in the hands of the bureaucrats, and the seizure of power is only a superficial reform.

'Although battles on varying scales have taken place in various parts of the country since May this year, they are generally regarded as armed struggles and not as battles between revolution and counter-revolution, big-scale civil wars inevitably resulting from a political revolution, and revolution by violence which the proletarian revolutionaries must make to seize and consolidate political power.

'Therefore, the great cultural revolution in the past year and more can only make the broad masses acquire perceptual knowledge of it. Generally speaking, the movement is still at the spontaneous stage, and the historical task of the great cultural revolution is still far from being accomplished, as the first step has just been taken in a long march of 10,000 *li*.

'6) Opportunist ideas show their greater danger at the moment of change. At the present moment of change from retreat to counter-attack, the opportunist ideas demoralize the revolutionary ranks and make the counter-attack decentralized or even impossible.

'Effort must be made to shake off the trammels by the leaders who have been corrupted by opportunist ideas, and to overtake them so as to make revolution.

'It is necessary to eliminate the influence of opportunist ideas. If we do not eliminate opportunism, opportunism will eliminate us.

'7) The importance of strengthening theoretical study is shown more clearly at the moment of change.

'"Without a revolutionary theory there is no revolutionary movement." To raise the movement from the plane of spontaneity to a higher plane, to realize the hope placed by Chairman Mao's proletarian headquarters on the proletarian revolutionaries in Hunan, and to carry the great proletarian cultural revolution through to the end, it is necessary to grasp the revolutionary theory and Chairman Mao's theory of making revolution under the dictatorship of the proletariat.

'The initiation of the great proletarian cultural revolution is the beginning of the new era in which the revolutionary masses directly grasp Mao Tse-tung's thought. Through practice in the revolution, the broad revolutionary masses have learned, understood, applied and grasped Mao Tse-tung's thought and will eventually unmask the distortion of Mao Tse-tung's thought by the bourgeois privileged stratum for maintaining its rule and fooling the masses, shake off the trammels of the habitual forces and carry the revolution through to the end.

'"The world has come to a moment when the whole of mankind consciously remould themselves and remould the world; that is an age of world communism." The initiation of the great proletarian cultural revolution has unveiled a bright future before us.'

(Passages we have omitted speak of the situation in Hunan and instructions from Lin Piao and Chiang Ch'ing which, in the opinion of the authors, had opened up a new phase. They claimed that whereas 'reform had been the keynote of the Party Central Committee's attitude to problems in various provinces and municipalities in the early stage', the latest instruction was 'a change from reform to thoroughgoing revolution'. The Hunan preparatory committee was described as 'a reprint of the old political power'.)

The *Sheng-wu-lien* programme attracted the attention of the Central Cultural Revolution Group and in particular K'ang Sheng, who in one of his speeches (reported in February 1968 in a Canton publication) attacked it at length, quoting from it the passages he found most scandalous. He said that such a document could not have been drawn up by middle-school or even university students and must have been inspired in high places; the quotation from Lenin involved a considerable distortion of its actual meaning, and as for Hunan itself, Lin Piao's instructions had been misrepresented; basically, the document was an attempt to diminish the authority of Mao Tse-tung and clashed with the ideas and directives of the Party Central Committee. Nor, of course, could K'ang accept the views expressed by Chou Kuo-hui, a member of *Sheng-wu-lien*, that Mao's thought before the cultural revolution was worn out, antiquated and backward compared with Marxism-Leninism. Another violent attack on *Sheng-wu-lien* was published in a Canton newspaper in a reply to a reader's letter. The *Hunan Daily* and the *Southern Daily* (Canton) also published attacks during January and February 1968.[68]

At the same time as the programme we have quoted, there appeared a more lengthy document setting forth *Sheng-wu-lien*'s platform.[69] The authors asked their readers whether this platform should be adopted as the 'Declaration of the Establishment of the Ultra-left Faction Commune'. Its basic theme is that the true point of arrival of the cultural revolution should be the 'People's Commune of China', and that the revolutionary committees, which represented a fresh usurpation of power by the bourgeoisie, were nothing more than an inevitable transitional stage. But it would be adventurist to repudiate this stage absolutely, without taking into consideration the degree of maturity of the masses. The document claimed that the main achievement of the 'January Storm' was 'that 90% of the senior cadres were made to stand aside' and that the initiative passed from the hands of the bureaucrats into those of the masses. It described Chou En-lai as 'the general representative of China's red capitalist class'. Not even the army escaped severe critisism: it had changed since liberation, and had become at least in part an instrument for suffocating the revolution. This was why one of the 'great pioneering acts' of the August storm was 'the appearance of an armed force organized by the revolutionary people themselves', why it was necessary to hail the 'arms grabbing movement' and condemn the order of 5 September 1967 which nullified Mao's call to 'arm the left' and resulted in the disarming of the working class. But as a result of their experience of struggle and the new stage which had been entered, the political maturity of the Chinese people had reached a higher level. 'A new trend of thought (called "ultra-left trend of thought" by the enemy), including "overthrow of the new bureaucratic bourgeoisie", "abolition of bureaucratic organs", "thorough smashing of the State machine", etc.

[68] *SCMP*, no. 4136. Note that in his speech K'ang referred to a 'counterrevolutionary' *Extraordinary Committee of the Party Central Committee*, which on 1 October had addressed an open letter – reproduced on 3 October in a Peking *16 May Group* publication – to all Party members.

[69] See also Tariq Ali's interview with a Red Guard printed as an Appendix to this book for another radical viewpoint on the cultural revolution.

wandered among the revolutionary people, like a "spectre" in the eyes of the enemy.'

The document concluded as follows, 'The class (of bureaucrats) will be replaced by cadres with true proletarian authority naturally produced by the revolutionary people in the struggle to overthrow this decaying class. These cadres are members of the commune. They have no special privileges. Economically they get the same treatment as the masses in general. They may be dismissed or changed at any time in accordance with the demands of the masses. These new, authoritative cadres have not yet made their appearance. But these cadres will be spontaneously produced following the increased maturity of the political thinking of the revolutionary people. The commune of the *Far Left Faction* will not conceal its viewpoints and intentions. We publicly declare that our object of establishing the "People's Commune of China" can be attained only by overthrowing the bourgeois dictatorship and revisionist system of the revolutionary committee with brute force. Let the new bureaucratic bourgeoisie tremble before the true socialist revolution that shakes the world. What the proletariat can lose in this revolution is only their chains, what they gain will be the whole world. The China of tomorrow will be the world of the "Commune". Long live the doctrine of Mao Tse-tung.'[70]

Although we disagree with many of the authors' political formulations and characterizations and would criticize some of their attitudes (it is hard to say whether they are naïve or tactical) documents of this kind show that the cultural revolution generated forces capable of understanding its dual nature, its contradictions and its intrinsic limitations and capable of showing the way forward to the revolutionary struggle necessary to overthrow the rule of the bureaucracy. The same conclusion can be drawn from the interview with a Cantonese Red Guard published as an Appendix to this book.

[70] *Whither China?*, in *SCMP*, no. 4190, pp. 1–18.

12
Maoism and the Problems of the Transition Period

The cultural revolution provided the Chinese leadership with an opportunity to return to and develop its most radical ideas on the transition period between capitalism and socialism. They can be briefly summed up as follows:

a) In a post-revolutionary society the class struggle, far from dying away, grows even more intense. The statement that 'classes and the class struggle still exist after the socialist transformation of the ownership of the means of production has been in the main completed' was made by Mao 'for the first time in the theory and practice of the international communist movement' (Lin Piao). The period of transition will last for decades and even centuries and only in fifty or a hundred years' time will there begin 'a great age that will see radical changes in social systems all over the world' (Mao). Further cultural revolutions will be necessary to ward off the dangers of degeneration that are bound to spring up in the future.

b) 'The contradiction between the proletariat and other sections of the working people on the one hand and the handful of top Party persons in authority taking the capitalist road on the other is the principal contradiction and is an antagonistic contradiction.'

c) In a context where, in Lenin's phrase, 'small-scale production engenders capitalism and the bourgeoisie continuously, daily, hourly, spontaneously and on a massive scale', the degeneration of the collectivist system comes about through the degeneration of its top political levels: ideology is the main vehicle of this degeneration, since it creates a favourable environment for it. Appeals to egoism and the use of material incentives are particularly insidious and effective instruments of this degeneration.

d) Contrary to their view of the passage from capitalism to socialism, the Maoists believe that 'in the present day world we have . . . the tragic lesson of socialist countries which have peacefully evolved into capitalist countries'. To meet this danger, together with any other tendencies towards degeneration, 'during the entire period of the transition to communism, the dictatorial function of the State apparatus should be strengthened, not weakened'.

e) Wherever the dangers of regression have not been promptly recognized and firmly combated, a restoration of capitalism has taken place. Such is the case in Yugoslavia and in the Soviet Union itself, where profit, material incentives, the laws of the market and the tendency to private accumulation in the countryside are given full sway.

f) The problems of the countryside cannot be solved by making mechanization a precondition of collectivization; on the contrary, it is necessary to harness the energies of the peasantry through social forms such as communes, based on the collectivist principle, before introducing mechanization. Furthermore, sending educated young people into the countryside to work and be re-educated is a 'brilliant policy for building the new socialist countryside, an important measure for narrowing down and eliminating the differences between town and country, between worker and peasant and between mental and manual labour'.[1]

Mao Tse-tung was certainly not the first to discover that classes continue to exist during the transition period. But apart from that, the important point is that as the building of socialism proceeds, the traditional classes left over from the old society are either eliminated or begin to die away, and a new social dialectics takes the place of the old one. Mao's essay on contradictions among the people grasped this basic concept. And yet the version of Maoism that asserted itself during the cultural revolution tended to distort these ideas: while the idea that contradictions with the bourgeoisie can be non-antagonistic continued to be upheld, the contradictions within the Party and leadership of the state that has emerged from the revolution are defined as antagonistic. The two opposed terms of the principal contradiction – see point b) – are heterogeneous. One indicates classes, the other a political group. This is not merely an unfortunate choice of words, it is rather the reflection of a dangerous distortion in analysis and method. True, we cannot rule out the possibility that a group inside the Party may, under certain circumstances, become the expression of hostile class forces. But in that case,

---

[1] *PR*, no. 1, 1969; *HNA*, 30 May 1967, pp. 9 and 19; 28 May 1967, p. 10; *HNA*, 19 June 1967, p. 10; *PR*, no. 33, 1967; *HNA*, 18 August 1967, p. 18; *HNA*, 27 August 1967, p. 4; *HNA*, 9 February 1969, p. 4. For a parallel with the ways in which bourgeois hegemony is established, see *HNA*, 12 June 1966, pp. 3ff.; *PR*, no. 29, 1966.

these forces themselves, and not the narrow political group, would be the other term of the 'principal contradiction'. If there is no mention of these forces, the reason is that it would be difficult to identify them. Is it, perhaps, a question of residues of the old ruling class? But in that case, they should have been clearly defined, on the basis of a concrete analysis.

In so far as the information given throws any light on the matter, the Maoists are referring not to the old bourgeoisie but to a new bourgeoisie growing up on the basis of petty commodity production. We have already recalled the quotation of a well-known passage from Lenin. But vague quotations are of no use unless backed up by an analysis of processes and tendencies in their concrete manifestations and a strict examination of whether or not they imply qualitative structural changes. During the cultural revolution the Maoists took care not to tread on this ground, preferring instead to indulge in vague and summary invective.

To touch on another aspect of the problem, material incentives in themselves imply nothing more than differences in remuneration and therefore different standards of living: actual tendencies towards the restoration of capitalism would arise only if higher incomes were invested for private appropriation of the means of production and not merely for the purchase of consumer goods. But the supporters of the cultural revolution were unable to unearth any such tendencies, either in China before 1965 or in the USSR after 1953. They put the accent not on structural phenomena but on symptoms of degeneration at the subjective level. In their view it is moral and ideological backsliding that opens the first breaches in the system, setting in motion the process of a restoration of capitalism, whereas for a Marxist, ideological and moral degeneration is only the reflection of deeper economic and social processes.

'Lenin – *Red Flag* recalled once again in 1967[2] – showed how small-scale production generates capitalism daily and hourly. This theory is equally applicable to cadres and intellectuals of petty-bourgeois origin who have not been properly re-educated, to cadres and intellectuals with many petty-bourgeois ideas. If they are not willing seriously to re-educate their ideology and place themselves under the control of the masses, they run the risk of becoming bourgeois elements once they come to power.' Here the confusion is transparent: whereas Lenin spoke of a structural process – the consequences of the persistence of small-scale production allowed to develop spontaneously – Maoist theory translates Lenin's analysis into idealist terms, centring it around a process of subjective

[2] *Red Flag*, no. 10, 1967.

corruption. Elsewhere the Maoists outlined the theory that the class struggle takes place in the intimate being of the individual, in the form of a conflict between personal and collective interests, adding that to make a revolution against oneself is the most difficult of all revolutions. Hence the subjectivist and moralistic character of the means and remedies proposed: the asceticism, the ideological intransigence, the classical sectarianism, the absolute enthronement of Mao's thought and the recourse to Zhdanovian-type ideas, the near-fanatical rejection of material incentives, and the constant praise of the spirit of sacrifice (a distinctive feature of the modern Chinese hero, who is generally painted in the most hackneyed edifying terms).[3] Note that the degeneration that occurred after the 'seizures of power' during the cultural revolution was also ascribed to moral causes, such as lax living on the part of the new cadres.

In support of the struggle against the dangers of degeneration, the Maoists proclaimed the need to strengthen the repressive functions of the state. This is a crucially significant point. Marxism has never subscribed to anarchist ideas on the state or denied that the state would have to perform a number of functions during the period of transition. But it has always recognized that this implies profound contradictions. Marx spoke of the inevitable survival of bourgeois right during the first stages of communist society, Lenin commented that this would mean the existence of a bourgeois state without a bourgeoisie and Trotsky located the principal contradiction during the period of transition in the opposition between collective ownership of the means of production and bourgeois norms of distribution. It is essential to grasp these contradictions and even more essential to understand how to overcome them. This does not only mean locating the objective conditions under which they can be overcome (we have nothing to add in this connection to the precise analyses made by Marx and Lenin, except that it is more than ever necessary to recall them now in order to counteract a certain subjectivism and Utopianism that has gained ground among Maoists and their followers). Above all it means establishing some practical way of breaking the circle of contradiction.

Lenin's *State and Revolution* is unequivocal on this question: the proletariat needs a state, but one which immediately starts to wither away, i.e. a state whose every representative is elected, recallable at all times and paid no more than a worker's wages: a state in which each individual has the opportunity of taking part in control and supervision and in which all

---

[3] *HNA*, 10 May 1967, p. 29; 30 June 1967, p. 23.

are 'temporarily bureaucrats'. In other words, Lenin understood that the main danger for a workers' state would be the tendency of the functions of leadership to ossify and of delegated power to estrange itself from its basis. He therefore said that it was necessary for the state to begin to wither away immediately, even though he recognized the need for repressive measures to prevent the old ruling classes regaining power. It is significant that each time the problem has been urgently posed, Lenin's essential and elementary teachings have once more come into their own. The Chinese leadership, for its part, not only put forward the theory of the strengthening of the 'dictatorial function of the state apparatus' but also, after paying lip service to Leninism in its Sixteen Points, forgot all it had written and went on to reorganize the apparatus in a manner quite out of keeping with the principles of the Paris Commune.

One might object that during the cultural revolution the leadership proposed other methods of dealing with the process whereby the apparatus becomes estranged from the masses. Firstly, they put special emphasis on the mass line; secondly, they insisted that cadres take a real and not merely a symbolic part in production, so as to avoid becoming detached from the masses. More generally, the Party itself, as the primary instrument of hegemony, needed to take steps to avoid crystallizing into a bureaucracy: 'The great proletarian cultural revolution', said one of the most important articles on the subject, 'initiated and led by Chairman Mao, solves more fundamentally the question of the links between the Party and political power and the masses, thus guaranteeing that our country will never change its political colour . . . The great proletarian cultural revolution is a great movement in which the revolutionary masses in their hundreds of millions are mobilized to rectify Party organizations.'[4]

As for the mass line, it is clearly not enough just to make abstract proclamations. If our analysis of the cultural revolution is accurate and if all the evidence we have examined is true, the leadership was constantly trying to channel and control the mass movement which it had helped to bring about and to re-establish a relationship with the rank-and-file that was essentially paternalistic and authoritarian. Moreover, it openly declared that the mass movement was the decisive factor, but only on condition that it was 'inoculated' (this is the term most often used) with the thought of Mao Tse-tung: 'The breadth and depth of the revolution depends on the breadth and depth of the mass movement', we read in one

[4] *HNA*, 1 July 1968.

of the main articles against Liu. 'This in turn depends on how deeply the masses have grasped Mao's thought.' And again, 'unless Marxism-Leninism-Mao Tse-tung's thought is instilled into the masses, there will never be a genuine revolutionary mass movement'.[5] This does not mean to say that we support a spontaneist theory or are underestimating the importance of politically educating the working class and its vanguard. But in the formulations of the cultural revolution we often get the impression that Mao's thought has replaced the objective factors as the mainspring of history. The idea that 'inoculation' is necessary had its corollary in practice: when mass movements grew up outside the Maoist political framework – e.g. the strike-wave at the beginning of 1967 – the leadership firmly opposed them, attempting to channel and divert them and resorting wherever necessary to repression.

Direct participation in production by leading cadres can undoubtedly acquire a political and formative value: the Cubans are no less convinced of this than the Chinese. But it would be a mistake or an illusion to idealize or overestimate its significance. It is clear from the controversies of the cultural revolution that the method has many shortcomings. Some top people tried to re-create their usual conditions of comfort in the places to which they were transferred, reduced the amount of work they did to a token contribution and used their influence to obtain state assistance for 'their' communes (they also intervened strongly, for example, in some rectification campaigns).[6] Being sent into the countryside was definitely seen as a punishment in some cases. The peasants themselves, unless they happened to be hoping for some special favours, made no secret of the fact that they were sceptical about the usefulness of people unaccustomed to the environment and lacking any real training in farm-work.[7] The fact that Mao, in his instruction of 27 December 1968 on sending young people into the countryside, found it necessary to urge the peasants to welcome their guests from the towns shows that the attitude of the peasants has not changed. But quite apart from this, there is nothing new about cadres taking part in manual labour and production: it was widely practised, for example, during the Great Leap Forward and dates back to the rectification campaigns of the early forties.[8] Yet it has never succeeded in preventing a crystallization of the apparatus and the

[5] *HNA*, 27 August 1968, p. 3; 15 March 1968, p. 5.
[6] *World Outlook*, 3 February 1967; *CB*, no. 824, p. 16; *HNA*, 10 September 1967, p. 6.
[7] Karol, op. cit., pp. 280–281 and *CB*, no. 824, p. 17.
[8] See, for example, M. Selden, 'The Yenan Legacy: the Mass Line', in A. Doak Barnett (Ed.), *Chinese Communist Politics in Action*, Seattle 1969, pp. 110–111.

privileged layers of society. The rapid reappearance of symptoms of decay in the new bodies and organizations is due partly to the fact that it is difficult to carry out important leadership functions and work in production at the same time and partly to the inevitable tendency of leaders and cadres to seize privileged positions.[9]

Finally, we have already seen how the Party was rebuilt and reorganized along the same lines as in the past. Even if we admit that the renewal of the apparatus and the experiences undergone made it more aware of the needs of the masses, decisions on fundamental matters still lie with the top leadership. After the Ninth Congress there was a vigorously sustained campaign for unity and discipline, i.e. for the concentration of power and control in the apparatus and the supreme organs of the Party. The principle that there should be a plurality of decision-making bodies and instruments for the organization of society has been firmly rejected (for example, in the polemics against any form of trade-union autonomy), whereas it is precisely such articulated structures that could prevent the excessive concentration of power that deprives the masses of their choice and constitutes a powerful vehicle of bureaucratic degeneration. If we accept an apologetic view of the transitional society, the workers appear as the monolithic agents of the revolution inspired by a lucid overall vision of the needs of socialist construction. The interests of the guiding Party and the interests of the working class coincide perfectly and the Party is the supreme and unique synthesis of the proletarian dictatorship. But this view refuses to recognize the fact that the worker is at one and the same time a wage-earner demanding wage-levels in keeping with his needs, a consumer interested in influencing specific economic choices and a citizen-politician intent on participating in basic political decisions. For this reason he needs not only vanguard organizations but instruments to defend his more immediate interests – even against his own state, if necessary – economic management organs where he can make his influence as a producer felt and more properly political bodies in which he can exercise his sovereignty as a member of the ruling class. In other words, the Party's function as guide does not dispense with or replace the functions of the trade unions, the workers' councils and the soviet bodies through which power is democratically exercised. (We can see the difference between Maoism and Leninism particularly clearly when we compare the Chinese views on the unions and those expressed by Lenin in the famous 1921 controversy.) What for us, then, is a fundamental lesson of more than fifty years of experience of the transition period in a

[9] *HNA*, 13 June 1968, p. 5; 19 February 1967, p. 3; 3 August 1967, p. 44.

whole series of countries is for the promoters of the cultural revolution a closed book.

We now come to the relationship between mechanization and collectivization. The first point to bear in mind is that if the revolution had begun in a country with a high productive level where agriculture was run on capitalist lines, the question of priorities would not even have arisen. Right from the start the material conditions would have existed for a collectivization which exploited modern techniques to the full. But since the overthrow of capitalism first took place in economically backward countries, the contradiction was to a large extent inevitable. To create the material basis for mechanization a fairly long period of time would have been necessary. And it was out of the question to expect these countries to restrict themselves during this period to the status quo of an agriculture based on small and middle peasants such as had emerged from the expropriation of the big landowners. In the case of China such a solution would have entailed from an economic point of view the disadvantage of not being able to make use of collectively organized labour, either in production itself or in the creation of the indispensable infrastructure. From a social point of view, it would inevitably have led to an increasingly clear-cut social differentiation and the growth of peasant strata capable of carrying on capitalist accumulation and hence eating into more general accumulation. This was basically the experience of the Soviet Union in the second half of the twenties and, *mutatis mutandis*, of a country like Poland more recently. But it would be wrong to consider the Chinese viewpoint – or its concrete application – as an effective solution of the problem. It is true that from the social and political point of view there have been unquestionable achievements. Collectivization in the mid-fifties was an essential step in the process of eliminating the bourgeoisie and the new capitalist tendencies in the countryside. It is also true that the communes provided an answer to the crucial problem of utilizing underemployed manpower by helping to mobilize and organize a collective effort for massive public works (thus helping towards the creation of a viable infrastructure). Nevertheless the Chinese countryside is still a long way from real and organic collectivist relations. Because mechanization is not widespread and because modern technical means are still in short supply, formally collectivist relations have remained void of real content and the organization of production has fallen back, as we have repeatedly emphasized, to the lowest levels of the collective structure. Most observers tend to pass over this crucial fact without bringing out all its significance.

We have already mentioned the idea of self-reliance as one example of the Maoist method of dangerously generalizing on the basis of evidence that is only valid under certain conditions. That China, which is still subjected to economic discrimination by imperialism and hard hit by the criminal reprisals taken by the Kremlin, should try to exploit all her resources to the full and appeal to her people's spirit of sacrifice, ingenuity and versatility is absolutely natural. This line cannot have been a reason for dissent that broke out in the old leadership, for one of the most relevant statements on this issue came from Liu Shao-ch'i himself when he condemned Soviet calls for a united socialist market and a division of labour among the collectivist countries. But we cannot agree with the Chinese leaders when they advance the theory of self-reliance as an essential component in the building of socialism, thus confirming (though in a different context and in different terms) their support for the idea of socialism in one country. This theory fails totally to grasp the principal contradiction in the process of building socialism so far. While from the point of view of Marxism the qualitatively new element in socialism and its chief claim to historical validity is its ability to go beyond the limits set to economic development and organization by the existence of national barriers, in practice the new society has been developing for a fairly long time now in the general context of a world that has remained capitalist, and no real economic unity or effective integration has come about even in countries which already have collectivist regimes. Therefore economic construction has suffered, and continues to suffer, not only from all the limitations and contradictions that stem from the continued existence of the imperialist system and the world capitalist market but also from tensions and conflicts between the non-capitalist countries. How far this was historically inevitable is open to discussion, but the consequences have been and still are extremely grave. In the final analysis, the essential condition for overcoming the contradictions in which China is caught (as are other countries) is her integration into a world system of workers' states with a qualitatively superior economic potential. (In one article which justifiably criticizes Soviet politics in Comecon, even if it does interpret certain phenomena in an arbitrary way, we read: 'The economists at the service of the Soviet renegades have gone so far as to maintain that "from the point of view of applied technology production has been pushed beyond national frontiers" and "the economic organization of one country is too restricted".'[10] Apart from denouncing the real inten-

[10] *PR*, no. 25, 1969.

tions that are hidden behind the screen of such statements, the Chinese should say whether or not they believe such concepts to be intrinsically correct. For they undoubtedly refer to objective tendencies, and these constitute one of the major premises of socialism conceived as a supranational system. As we have shown elsewhere, the Chinese leaders expect the period of transition to last a very long time and Mao declared, according to Lin Piao's report to the Ninth Congress, that it is impossible to speak of the definitive victory of a socialist country before the victory of the world revolution. This is further proof of the presence of diverse and even contradictory elements in the ideology of the cultural revolution. As we will see the aftermath of the cultural revolution was to witness an abandonment of the radical internationalism which surfaced, partially and ambiguously, during the cultural revolution itself.

Throughout the cultural revolution, starting with the *People's Daily* and *Red Flag* article of 11 November 1965, the theoreticians and propagandists of Maoism declared in ever shriller tones that the degeneration in the USSR had led to a restoration of capitalism.

The idea that the USSR is a capitalist country is not at all new. As early as the twenties theories of this kind were circulating within the workers' movement and on its periphery. However, because of the historical context in which it was formulated and the background of those who express it, the Chinese variant of this thesis assumes special characteristics. Without going back to questions already dealt with more generally, the Chinese arguments can be roughly summed up as follows:

a) The process of degeneration set in after the death of Stalin and the Twentieth Congress and developed along peaceful and evolutionary lines. The persons in authority taking the capitalist road, with the concepts and measures they enforced, made it possible for a new privileged bourgeois stratum to emerge and crystallize, after having prepared the way for this process in the field of ideology and propaganda.

b) This new stratum emerged from the big and little 'bosses' of the Party and government institutions, the heads of state enterprises and collective farms and intellectuals in the departments of culture, the arts, science and technology in the universities and colleges. These people secured for themselves a privileged standard of living thanks to their big salaries, their high bonuses, the sums they received for publications, etc.: 'moreover, they took advantage of their privileges to cruelly exploit the broad masses of the Soviet working people by cheating, taking bribes, embezzling and profiteering'.[11]

[11] *HNA*, 11 May 1967, p. 15.

c) The recent economic reforms introducing profits and upholding material incentives are the most concrete manifestation and the completion of the restoration of capitalism. These reforms have increased the exploitation of the workers and accentuated wage differentials (among the odious forms of exploitation are the abolition of holidays and the lengthening of the working week). At the same time they have re-established the authority of the market. The existence in particular of a free market crowded with customers buying all kinds of goods is 'irrefutable proof of the restoration of capitalism by the Soviet revisionist clique'.[12]

d) In the countryside the Russian leadership has given free reign to the law of value and encouraged the trends towards capitalism by encouraging private plots. In some sectors – market garden produce, cattle, etc. – these account for a high percentage of total output.

e) The regime in the USSR has turned into a social-imperialist regime which exploits other countries in its bloc (by imposing its will through Comecon) and neo-colonial countries (through the mechanism of the world market and by imposing conditions even more unfavourable than those of the world market).[13]

In the first place, two points are enough to defeat the Chinese arguments. The idea of a 'peaceful' transition from socialism to capitalism is an evolutionary concept that has little to do with the dialectical and revolutionary method of Marxism. The rebuilding of capitalism in the USSR or in any other country would necessarily involve an extremely acute struggle and could not possibly be the result of an abstract social dynamic without a direct confrontation between social classes, without a revolutionary – or rather a counter-revolutionary – *break*, without a qualitative leap (in an opposite direction to the leap that had previously taken place). The parallels drawn by the Chinese with the historical development of the bourgeoisie are quite worthless: one elementary difference, as Marxists have frequently stressed, is that the bourgeoisie has owned means of production ever since it first emerged.

The second point regards the dating of the regression. Apart from the precise social and economic significance the Chinese invest in what has

---

[12] *HNA*, 18 July 1967, p. 17.

[13] *HNA*, 4 June 1967, p. 4; 2 November 1967, p. 22; 11 May 1967, p. 15; 28 April 1968, p. 8; 13 November 1968, p. 15; 11 November 1965, p. 16; 8 February 1968, p. 6; 10 April 1967, pp. 21–22; 10 May 1967, p. 19; 18 July 1967, p. 17; 25 July 1967, p. 16; 15 May 1967, pp. 11ff.; 23 July 1967, p. 17; 8 November 1968, p. 11. The Chinese defined social-imperialism immediately after the Soviet occupation of Czechoslovakia (*HNA*, 30 August 1968, p. 2).

happened, it is beyond all doubt that most of the phenomena they denounce arose before the death of Stalin, during the mid-twenties and early thirties. We need only think of the social differentiation and the enormously wide wage differentials that were not only put into practice but even backed up with theoretical justifications. Even under Stalin the principal means of carrying out the plans of production lay in the personal interest taken by the bureaucrats; even then private plots existed and the very year that Stalin died half the cattle production came from such plots.

As for 'social-imperialism', how can we forget the notorious mixed companies set up by the Soviet Union at the end of the war which were the cause of tensions and controversies, starting with the denunciations of the Yugoslavian communists?

The true nature of the Chinese attacks is concealed behind this 'mistake' in dating. For a whole number of basic political reasons, the Maoists are continuing to defend the regime of Stalin and to concentrate their fire on his epigones. They therefore only make peripheral criticisms of the USSR under Stalin, but brand the USSR under Krushchev and Brezhnev as capitalist. The requirements of political polemics take precedence over the requirements of a precise scientific analysis.

Before we move on to examining the arguments advanced by the Maoist theoreticians, it would be useful if we reviewed some of the essential criteria for a proper evaluation of the period of transition, criteria which can be derived from the works of Marx and Lenin.

In the first place, a social class is not defined according to the amount of income it manages to appropriate during distribution (i.e. on the basis of its more or less privileged standard of living), nor on the basis of legal property relations considered in the abstract. The distinguishing feature is its place in the relations of production, from which derive legal relations, political relations and ideological hegemony. In a Marxist and Leninist analysis, the capitalist class is distinguished precisely by its hegemonic position in the productive process, which enables it to exploit the class opposed to it: it is distinguished by its ability, juridically recognized as private ownership of the means of production, to expropriate surplus value. In other words, its privileged position stems from its ownership of the means of production. In the second place, we should remember that the economic mechanism and the categories that distinguish it should not be considered in the abstract but in the context of concrete social and political relations. For example, categories such as profit and the market cannot be taken as absolute, near-metaphysical values: their content is defined *historically*, in the framework of the relations between the different classes which appropriate – or do not appropriate – profit and which in one way or another make use of the market.

In the third place:

a) During the transition period the law of value continues to operate, but is contained and regulated by the Plan, i.e. by the conscious intervention of the political power.

b) The means of production, at least for the most part, are no longer exchange values, commodities that can be bought or sold, and are therefore no longer subject to the laws of the market, but rather to the decisions of the planning authorities.

c) The circulation of commodities is restricted to consumer goods (it only marginally affects means of production, mainly in agriculture); but within this sphere the market develops considerably (in particular in those countries where the vicious circle of agriculture based on direct consumption was only broken by agrarian reform after the overthrow of capitalism).

d) The profitability of an enterprise is no longer established anarchically, *a posteriori*, in virtue of the laws of the market, and strictly economic principles are tempered by the principles of social utility (this does not mean, however, that it is possible to distribute more than the total value produced).

e) On the level of distribution, 'bourgeois norms' remain in force and inequalities are therefore inevitable, whatever specific forms they might take. At the root of this is the persistent shortage of productive forces in relation to the needs of a truly collectivist system; it follows, to quote Marx, that 'the individual producer receives back from society – after the deductions have been made – exactly what he gives to it' (*Critique of the Gotha Programme*). Here – Marx continues – 'the same principle prevails as that which regulates the exchange of commodities', with all the inequalities that inevitably derive from it.

In their own analyses, the Maoists attribute the degeneration of the USSR to ideological and political rather than economic and social causes. It emerges from the description we have quoted that the privileged strata are not strata of the traditional industrial or commercial bourgeoisie who have passed over to the counter-offensive or neo-bourgeois strata produced by the mechanism of petty commodity production, but new strata that spring from the new society itself and acquire a position of privilege not by virtue of an economic mechanism but thanks rather to the exercise of political power at the different levels. If this explanation is correct – and broadly speaking, it is – and if the higher living standards are due to much higher salaries, perquisites of various kinds and even embezzlement, it follows that the privileges enjoyed by these strata stem not from their position in the relations of production or from their appropriation of the means of production, but from the functions they perform and the control they exercise over the distribution of the surplus product. It is entirely possible in theory that this situation might generate or revive a process of capitalist accumulation. But it is necessary to analyse whether this has actually happened, whether the privileged strata manage to acquire means of production, make investments, etc. The Maoists have failed to prove – or rather, they have not even tried to prove – that this has happened in the USSR.[14]

The new Soviet reforms, the introduction of profit and the powers granted to the managers have not brought about any substantial changes. Profit under Liberman's reforms is in fact quite different from profit under capitalism: in the final analysis it is a means of checking profitability. The aim of the reformers was to substitute a (tendentially) objective criterion for the arbitrary criteria and anti-economic and chaotic practices previously in force. The instrument they proposed remains internal to the system and therefore has a quite different economic and social content from that of profit under capitalism. Moreover, the planners are still responsible for basic investment decisions and very strict rules govern how the profit at the manager's disposal should be used. As for the increased role of the market (note once again that this refers to consumer goods and not means of production) here too the aim is to avoid or limit those bureaucratic irrationalities which are the cause of such incredible waste and which in the long run are paid for by the consumers. We have already mentioned that according to Marxism the market in consumer goods does not disappear in a transitional society, and we fail to see why an abundance of goods and purchasers should be 'an irrefutable proof of the restoration of capitalism', unless of course it can be proved that means of production and not consumer goods are being sold. (It is worth recalling that in his report to the Ninth Congress Lin Piao noted with approval that 'the market is flourishing in China'.) There is no doubt that these reforms have strengthened the position of the technocrats both in the field of consumption and the field of decision making (which incidentally explains the caution with which the reform was passed and the diffidence of broad layers of the political bureaucracy); but this by no means represents a qualitative change in the class

[14] In the West there have been sophistical attempts to remedy this deficiency, notably in the work of Charles Bettelheim. For a critique see Ralph Miliband, 'Bettelheim and the USSR', *New Left Review*, 91, May–June 1975.

nature of the regime.

The changes in the countryside were, all in all, even less important. Although the Krushchevite and post-Krushchevite reforms introduced changes with respect to the Stalinist period, they did not affect the basic structures. They aimed essentially at improving the conditions of the peasantry, who carried by far the greatest burden of socialist accumulation, by fixing more remunerative prices and adjusting the principles which regulated relations between the state and the peasants. We can say that in the light of the Soviet experience the Chinese leaders tackled these problems right from the beginning: hence their prices policy and the constant efforts on their part to prevent serious tensions arising in the countryside. (Note that the Chinese, given the practice prevailing in their own country, have avoided using one argument that they could have put forward in support of their thesis that capitalism has been restored in the Soviet Union, i.e. that tractors were given to the *kolkhoz*. But even if this does mean that the means of production have reverted to being commodities, the fact remains that we are dealing with a change in one single sector: the specific weight of the industrial sector is becoming more and more important and the Plan continues to regulate the overall functioning of the law of value.)

As for 'social-imperialism', this is all too obviously a political and not an economic and social category. It has yet to be proved that the USSR needs to export capital and invest abroad for the same organic reasons and by virtue of the same mechanism that cause capitalism to make such investments and imperialism to drain the entire planet for its profits. In the specific case of India, upon which Maoist theoreticians have focussed their attention, Soviet policy may well be questionable and worthy of condemnation (it was quite wrong, for instance, to give military aid to the Indian ruling class for their struggle against the Chinese) but it would be foolish and mistaken to maintain that the USSR invests and makes profits in the same way as British or US imperialism. Given its superior strength, the Soviet bureaucracy constantly tends in its relations with the countries in its sphere of influence to subordinate them to its own interests and to oppress them. But Marxism has never defined every form of domination and oppression of other peoples as capitalistic imperialism. Capitalist relations are connected to an historically determined form of exploitation, the essential traits of which cannot be found, except in partial and formal analogies, in the relations between the USSR and other collectivist countries.[15]

One might object that the USSR profits from its trade with the other

Comecon countries simply because it is the more industrially advanced country. Actually, this is very often not the case, given the nature of the interchange (in fact, it is the USSR that exports raw materials and imports machinery in a relationship with countries that have already attained high levels of production). But whatever the case, imbalances of this kind, with all the necessary implications, are largely inevitable until effective supranational integration is brought about within a socialist system (theories of self-reliance will do nothing to help achieve this end).

As for China's condemnation of deals such as the one the USSR made with FIAT, thanks to the financial intervention of the United States, we fail to see how such operations affect the relations of production and the basic social structure. (China herself had moved onto similar if not identical ground. Since 1962 China has purchased complete industrial installations and high-level technological equipment from capitalist countries. Between 1961 and 1964 she received short- and medium-term loans totalling roughly 1.2 billion dollars.[16] Whereas up to 1960 two-thirds of China's foreign trade was with collectivist countries, by the late sixties about 70% of it was with capitalist countries. The total value was 1.2 thousand million dollars in 1950, 4.3 thousand million dollars in 1959 and 2.7 in 1963; in 1965 it went up again to 3.7 thousand million dollars.[17]) The fact that the USSR has been forced to take such steps is further proof of its backwardness in certain sectors of the economy: and there is no doubt that in the final analysis foreign capitalists receive a part of the surplus value produced by the Soviet workers. But other solutions might prove more costly; and more generally, as long as capitalism continues to exist, the working class of the USSR (like that of China) will inevitably feel the effects of the world market, despite the protective barrier that exists in the form of a monopoly of foreign trade.

In conclusion, we do not deny that tendencies are at work in the USSR that under certain conditions could result in a restoration of capitalism. Mandel writes: 'The contradiction between the non-capitalist mode of production and the bourgeois norms of distribution is the fundamental contradiction of the Soviet economy, as of every economy of the transition era. But due to the bureaucratic management of this economy, the contradiction has been carried to extremes and given

---

[15] Moreover, Soviet economic assistance has been crucial in sustaining the Cuban and Vietnamese revolutions; see Robin Blackburn, 'Cuba and the Great Powers' in *Patterns of Foreign Influence in the Carribbean*, edited by E. De Kadt, Oxford 1972.

[16] *Economic Profile*, pp. xvi, 587 and 602.

[17] Ibid., p. 583.

a sharply antagonistic character. It has developed into a contradiction between the use-value character of capital goods and the exchange-value character of consumer goods, and into a contradiction between the purely accounting role of money in the sphere of capital goods and the role of real equivalent for commodities which money retains in the sphere of consumer goods. The principle of individual profitability of enterprises reintroduces money as a real means of payment in the capital goods sphere. Thereby, a tendency for commodity production and commodity circulation to reappear in the capital goods sphere makes itself felt, with all that this implies – a tendency for planning itself to be disorganized.'[18] When analysing a process, we must never lose sight of its contradictory nature. We must verify analytically and point by point the characteristics of the stage reached. We must avoid substituting an extrapolation of tendencies that are merely potential or categories interpreted metaphysically for the detailed analysis of concrete phenomena.

[18] Ernest Mandel, *Marxist Economic Theory*, London 1968, p. 593.

Part 3
Aftermath of the
Cultural Revolution

13

A Provisional Balance Sheet

In discussing the origins and the functioning of the revolutionary committees, we did not ignore the new elements or democratic and revolutionary themes that inspired the campaign leading up to their formation. We pointed out, however, that in the last analysis these committees were conditioned, controlled and recognized from above and that far from being a genuine expression of the wishes of the masses, they were the outcome of agreements, sanctioned or imposed at top levels, between the constituent parts of the so-called 'triple alliance', with most of the top posts going to army men and, to a lesser degree, former cadres. This disproportion increased towards the end of the cultural revolution and after. Between the spring of 1968 and September 1969, seventeen of the twenty-nine members purged from the standing committees of the various Revolutionary Committees were representatives of mass organizations, ten were revolutionary cadres and only two were soldiers. Twenty-one of the twenty-seven replacements, however, were soldiers and only six were representatives of the mass organizations.[1] The only place where leaders who emerged during the cultural revolution were still in power was Shanghai. The only possible conclusion is that although the apparatus underwent a profound upheaval and was largely reconstituted, its political structure has remained essentially paternalistic and authoritarian. The proclamations put out at crucial moments concerning the elective character of all the new bodies that emerged during the cultural revolution, together with the references to the principles of the Paris Commune, remained a dead letter and even the name 'commune' was at first turned down and then expressly outlawed. The intrinsic weakness of these structures was suggested by frequent charges that the new bodies were rapidly degenerating.

[1] Domes, 'Revolutionary Committees', loc. cit., p. 144.

But even if at the lower and intermediate levels real changes did take place and the balance of forces was adjusted in favour of the masses, no significant change came about at the level of the central political structures. These remained substantially intact, and power was concentrated in those bodies which, as we have seen, intervened punctually at decisive moments in the cultural revolution. Maoist propaganda was quite explicit on this point: 'seizures of power' must go no further than provincial level and must not affect the State Council and the Central Committee (the real depositories of power) or even the regional bureaux of the Central Committee. We repeat: there can be no proletarian democracy, free of bureaucratic distortions, as long as political decisions on key problems and the day-to-day exercise of power on the national level are in the hands not of the workers and peasants, or of bodies directly expressing their wishes and constantly under their control, but of bureaucratic machines which crystallize, perpetuating their power and estranging themselves from the masses in whose name they claim to govern. The situation that existed before the cultural revolution could not be surmounted by a shake-up, however wide-ranging, of the leadership, but only by a qualitative structural change. This did not come about. A decisive role in the cultural revolution was played by the army, which from a certain point onwards emerged as the backbone of the entire apparatus and was tirelessly held up as a model to be emulated in all fields. The regional and provincial military commanders who played such a crucial role during the cultural revolution retained their strong positions on the all-important provincial revolutionary committees. At the Ninth Congress they gained extensive representation on the Central Committee and two places on the Politburo itself.

Dangerous Methods of Political Struggle

For anyone neither ignorant nor forgetful of the fateful consequences that Stalinist methods had on the international workers' movement, the significance of the methods used by the Maoists in the battle with enemies or rivals is all too clear. The accused persons became the object of one-way diatribes and had no chance to defend themselves; their views were systematically distorted; their actions and attitudes portrayed as the Machiavellian intrigues and acts of sabotage of enemy agents within the Party and the state; history is rewritten to fit in with this campaign of 'unmasking'. Quite apart from whether the positions adopted by Liu Shao-ch'i, P'eng Chen or T'ao Chu were valid or not, we cannot admit the principle that any methods are legitimate in the defence of a cause held to be just: those who resort to slander and falsification thereby demonstrate that they are not interested in discussing clearly stated problems or in stimulating the growth of a critical spirit among the broad masses, but prefer instead destructive monologues and ideological terrorism.

True, one of the charges brought against Liu was that he tried to impose on the Party a spirit of servile obedience and spineless acquiescence towards the leaders. But it is impossible to take this criticism seriously when at the same time the supreme principle of obedience to Mao was proclaimed again and again, together with an insistence that Mao's instructions were to be carried out whether their meaning was understood or not. It is unusual to find praise for the spirit of rebellion incorporated into the ideology of any ruling group, and there can be no doubt that this was an important factor in mobilizing the Red Guards. However, the peculiar – one might say, contradictory – nature of this rebellion was involuntarily revealed by one Shanghai Red Guard inscription: 'In a word, we will rebel against anyone who dares to oppose Chairman Mao and his thought.'[2]

Here we come to a crucial ideological mechanism for the bureaucratic recuperation of the cultural revolution – the adoption of Mao's thought as an absolute and unquestionable value: in other words, the affirmation of a centralized leadership as the unique seat of power, with the Mao cult – taken to the most grotesque lengths – as its symbol and quintessence. The idea Mao wanted to establish, or rather re-establish, during the cultural revolution was actually the paternalistic and authoritarian one whereby a small leading nucleus – symbolized by himself – maintained direct contact with the masses without gaps and without intermediaries (i.e. without intermediaries who would refuse to accept the role of mere transmission channels). Obviously, a criticism of the cultural revolution that relied mainly for its effect on deriding the leader cult would have little weight. Praise for the charismatic qualities of the leader has recurred too often in history for us to have to point out the concrete significance of what lies behind the outward forms. But the fact remains that any ruling group or layer that resorts to such techniques in exercising its power and ideological hegemony is necessarily paternalistic and authoritarian, and the same applies to any leadership that mobilizes its forces with methods and appeals that prevent, rather than encourage, the education of the masses. What is more, this method of cementing unity is inherently precarious

[2] *HNA*, 8 April 1967, p. 5; *HNA*, 4 November 1967, p. 16; *PR*, no. 27, 1967; *HNA*, 20 January 1967, p. 13.

and it was clear from the very beginning, despite Mao's prestige and despite the enshrining of Lin Piao's right to succession in the new Party Constitution, that fresh imbalances and fresh crises would sooner or later come to the fore. The use of the Mao cult as an instrument for controlling and channelling the mass movement from below is clearly revealed by the fact that the volume of mindless adulation of the Chairman and his thought was reduced following the closing phases of the cultural revolution. At the height of the cultural revolution the cult reached a pitch scarcely equalled even in Stalin's Russia. Chairman Mao's thought was said to improve the playing of table tennis and the growing of pumpkins. The 'little red book' of *Quotations from Chairman Mao* was invested with magic power; a waving of the 'magic wand' of the Chairman's thoughts could banish enemy plots, 'before the magic mirror of Mao Tse-tung's Thought no monster can escape detection'.[3] Lin Piao did not hesitate to declare that 99% of the time spent studying Marxist classics should be set aside for Mao.[4] It is one of the greatest achievements of the Chinese revolution to have spread literacy and education through the mass of the population in a country where previously eighty per cent were illiterate. But the cult of Mao's thought and similar campaigns exploit and debase these achievements in the narrow interest of the different factions of the bureaucratic group which monopolizes politics. (The ousting of Lin was to lead to a diminution in the ritualistic worship of Mao's thought, but unfortunately it was replaced by an orchestrated mass campaign whose ideological content was to be even more debauched and confusing than any of its predecessors: the anti-Lin, anti-Confucius campaign.)[5]

Culture

As for their cultural policy, the theories adopted and the positions defended by the leadership during the cultural revolution and the initial period of reorganization represented a step backwards in the direction of increased bureaucratic control, compared not only with the situation at the height of the hundred flowers campaign but also with the general atmosphere of the period preceding the cultural revolution, when a series of fairly lively literary and philosophical debates were held and differences of opinion openly voiced. The general line and the methods that came to

[3] See for example *HNA*, 28 December 1966, p. 29; 14 October 1966, p. 3; 25 August 1967, p. 7.

[4] *HNA*, 13 October 1967, p. 22.

[5] See the analysis of the Chinese Trotskyist, W.F.H., 'Behind the "Criticise Lin, Criticise Confucius" Campaign', *Inprecor*, no. 10, 17 October 1974.

dominate the cultural scene, far from representing a revolutionary inno-vation, were in the tradition of that sadly famous Soviet experience known as Zhdanovism. Apart from Mao (the unchallenged authority in this field as in others) the role of supreme controller fell to Chiang Ch'ing, writer of constantly quoted speeches and articles and prodigious dispenser of instructions to everyone from pianists to playwrights. Chiang Ch'ing's ideas and her mentality are clearly revealed in the famous army seminar report, where Stalin, although considered sufficiently severe towards modern art and literature, was condemned for being soft on the classics, both Russian and European. Not so Mrs. Mao. Totally adamant and without a trace of subtlety, she included rock-and-roll, jazz, strip-tease, impressionism, symbolism, abstract art, fauvism and modernism on her black-list of corrupt and decadent bourgeois forms of expression. Indeed, she expressed explicit approval for the excommunication orders against Akhmatova and Zoshchenko and for the repressive measures against Serebrajakova, thus openly defending Zhdanovism.[6]

The logical consequence of this line was that the regime held up as masterpieces and as faithful expressions of the new society and the new revolutionary spirit purely propagandistic and didactic works, 'whole-some' works, such as the celebrated *Red Lantern*, or paintings such as *Chairman Mao on the Road to Anyuan*, which combine the oleographic realism of a Gerasimov with a vein of grotesque mysticism. In the cultural field itself the 'cultural' revolution thus led to an immense impoverish-ment. Less than a dozen novels and less than a dozen films were permitted throughout the whole period 1965–72 and these were mostly rehashes of works that originally appeared in the fifties.

At the beginning of 1972, *after five years or so in which nothing except political texts were published*, a new list of titles came out in Peking – including the re-issue of a 1965 novel, a study of T'ang poetry, three volumes of a dynastic history (prepared in 1966 and not published until now) and a new dictionary.[7]

But it would be foolish to interpret this development as anything more than a slight relaxation, in line with the general retreat from some of the more extreme positions taken up during the cultural revolution. The development of a creative and differentiated culture, such as existed in the Soviet Union in the first years after the revolution, is impossible as long as the perimeter of the 'free discussion' is patrolled by state watch-dogs such as Yao Wen-yuan.

[6] *HNA*, 27 August 1967, p. 7; 3 November 1967, p. 7.
[7] Cf. *Chinese Art and Literature*, 1973, no. 1.

Re-emergence of the Party Committees

One recurrent theme of the polemics over industrial management and leadership during the cultural revolution was the condemnation of technocratic and authoritarian ideas and methods. These had mainly taken the form of individual leadership as opposed to the collective leadership of the Party committee. In actual fact, since the setting up of the People's Republic the system of control has constantly oscillated between these two methods: during the First Five-Year Plan, which largely drew its inspiration from Soviet models, responsibility rested mainly in the hands of the managers, while later on, especially during the Great Leap Forward, control passed into the hands of the Party committee; in 1961 a swing in the opposite direction took place and the managers and technocrats again came to the fore. Following the cultural revolution there was a renewed stress on the primacy of the Party committee.

However, the process of reorganization that led up to the resumption of control in industry by the Party committees was confused and protracted and for some time factory administration stayed in the hands of the revolutionary committees that had grown out of the cultural revolution. These committees, which continued in existence even after the re-establishment of the Party committees, initially had a large proportion of representatives from the rank-and-file workers: in 1969, for example, the Shanghai Textile Factory no. 17 revolutionary committee was composed of 80% workers, while groups set up in base-level units to deal with problems connected with technology and machinery were made up of workers, revolutionary cadres and technicians (a formula also applied more generally).[8] By 1971, however, an adjustment appears to have taken place in the balance of forces in favour of the old cadres. For example, Jack Chen visited a Peking wool mill whose revolutionary committee had seventeen members, six of them representatives of the mass organizations, eight of them representatives of the old cadres and three of them soldiers (smaller sections of the mill had revolutionary groups in which the militia took the place of the soldiers).[9] The Committee of Concerned Asian Scholars talked with representatives from twelve revolutionary committees and found that on average 'ordinary workers' made up 45% of the membership, 'revolutionary cadres' 36% and soldiers 14%.[10] It is

---

[8] PR, no. 27, 1969; HNA, 2 and 3 June, 1969; HNA, 21 February 1969.

[9] FEER, 21 August 1971.

[10] Committee of Concerned Asian Scholars (hereafter CCAS), China! Inside the People's Republic, New York 1972, p. 91.

difficult, however, to draw firm conclusions because of the fragmentary nature of the evidence.

It seems that the revolutionary committees are chosen rather than elected. The choosing involves a combination of discussion and screening by some outside body, such as the army. Any nominee who fails to get the approval of the screening body is automatically dropped from the list of candidates. It is not clear whether any regular period of office is fixed.[11]

As each place of work acquired its own Party committee, the functions of the revolutionary committee came to be redefined. It retained administrative functions, while its leadership functions passed to the Party committee. (The domination of the Party committee is ensured by the fact that 50% or more of the members of each revolutionary committee are also on their respective Party committee.[12]) But it would be wrong to depict the resulting situation simply as a return to pre-cultural revolution days. The revolutionary committees were in many cases responsible for setting up the Party committee (depending, of course, on the approval of higher levels), and in such cases it seems unlikely that the parent body would meekly accept a subordinate role. It also seems that contrary to what some observers expected,[13] the dualism of the revolutionary committee and the Party committee continued for a time. But the position of the mass organizations that sprang up during the cultural revolution is crucial here, for the revolutionary committees could only be said to represent the wishes of the workers as long as the workers have the organizational means to control their 'representatives'. During and immediately after the cultural revolution it was precisely through the different mass organizations that the workers in many factories and industries managed to exercise some form of representation and control, and it was often true to say that a real change had taken place in the balance of power at factory level. One sympathetic observer was even inspired to write that the preservation of the popular organizations was 'more important than the system of revolutionary committees'. He continued: 'Not many revolutionary organizations have been dispersed. To give the renovated Party the popular censors it deserves, Mao Tse-tung took care to preserve political enthusiasm wherever it arose.'[14] All the signs suggested that the mass organizations were subsequently stripped of whatever autonomy they ever had and transformed into transmission

---

[11] ibid., pp. 92–93.
[12] Ibid., p. 91.
[13] E.g. *FEER*, 2 October 1971, p. 21.
[14] Esmein, op. cit., pp. 341–342.

belts for the top Party leadership. Andrew Watson observed that the 'main task' of a mass organization (or workers' congress, as it was called) 'is to lead in the study of Mao's works and the criticism of the Liuist line. It also runs such activities as giving cultural education and organizing teams to sweep the graves of martyrs. It is led by the Party and revolutionary committees and has no power to make decisions.'[15] Clearly, the workers' congresses were fulfilling functions similar to those of the old bureaucratic trade-union organization before the cultural revolution. By 1971 the latter were being rehabilitated and references were once more being made to the All China Federation of Trade Unions,[16] the structure of which was 'hierarchical from factory level congresses up to municipal at least'.[17] Members of the so-called Shanghai group around Chang Ch'un-ch'iao seem to have had special responsibility for re-establishing the trade unions and other mass organizations at national level.

It appears from the official press that the tightening up of controls over the labour force met with some opposition, and that this opposition took the form of attempts to vest more power in the mass organizations than in the Party.[18] During 1971, the *People's Daily* continued to assail 'ultra-leftists' who claimed that 'all systems of management, old and new, aim at achieving supervision, control and suppression of workers'.[19] There was mention of persistent 'anarchism' and ultra-leftism in Fukien docks, on the railways, in Harbin industrial plants and elsewhere.[20]

These attacks on 'anarchism' and 'bourgeois factionalism' were parallelled by attacks on 'commandism' and 'arrogance, complacency and erroneous ways' among cadres. *Red Flag* noted that cadres cut themselves off from the masses 'as soon as they accumulated some experience and scored some successes'.[21] The top leadership attempted to remedy such developments by the usual method of launching special campaigns. 1970 saw a 'Mao Tse-tung philosophy' campaign, the aim of which was to teach erring cadres proletarian thinking. This was followed by the setting up of a hundred or so 'May 7' cadre schools, which belong to Central Committee and State Council departments. These schools were set up to re-educate cadres 'at their posts in rotation' through a combina-

---

[15] *The China Quarterly*, no. 49, p. 148.
[16] See *CS*, 7 April 1971.
[17] *The China Quarterly*, no. 49, p. 148. See also CCAS, op. cit., p. 177.
[18] *The China Quarterly*, no. 43, Documentation.
[19] *FEER*, 2 October 1971, p. 31.
[20] *China News Analysis*, Hong Kong, no. 864, p. 3.
[21] *FEER*, 2 October 1971, p. 20.

tion of study and manual labour.[22] *Red Flag* wrote: 'We must seriously regard the successful and indefinite operation of "May 7" cadre schools as a great plan against revisionism in the next hundred years.'[23] In the long run, however, it is only possible to solve problems such as 'commandism' by means of a deep-going structural transformation of social and political relations that would place control firmly in the hands of the working class and not by the make-shift, pragmatist response of bureaucratically conceived 'campaigns'. The proof of this was the cultural revolution itself. Despite the fact that in one sense it was the most massive campaign of this nature that history has ever seen, most of the tensions that it was meant to resolve resurfaced spontaneously the moment the immediate pressure of the masses was removed.

As for wages, the system remained much the same as that depicted in the first part of this study. The criticisms during the cultural revolution of the system of material incentives, bonuses, special supplements, etc. initially led to the partial modification of such practices, or their combining with other 'political' methods of assessing remuneration.[24] The practical result of this was probably to reduce the range of wages actually paid. By 1971, however, there were unmistakable signs of a tendency to restore the old system. The door was left open to such a tendency even during the height of the cultural revolution since the range of basic income categories (embodying at its limits a ten to one differential) was never officially revised. In October 1971 the *People's Daily* talked of 'rational rewards in accordance with the quantity and quality of labour performed', and the policy of 'to each according to his needs' is ascribed to Liu Shao-ch'i and counterposed to the correct policy of 'to each according to his work'. On another occasion Liu, formerly alleged to be the chief advocate of material incentives as a means of bringing about a restoration of capitalism, was accused of 'whipping up a black wind to abolish rational rewards'.[25]

According to the published accounts of a number of Western visitors to China, workers' wages range through eight grades from 40 to 110 *yuan* a month. The lowest (male urban) wage mentioned is 34 *yuan*, usually paid only to apprentices. Administrative personnel in factories, on the other hand, are covered by over twenty grades ranging from 37 to 200 *yuan*. The average worker's wage seems to be between 50 and 60 *yuan*. (But note that the CCAS unearthed an astronomer who was paid the

[22] *HNA*, 4 February 1971; *PR*, no. 19, 1972, pp. 5–7.
[23] *CS*, 7 June 1971, p. 12.
[24] See, for example, Klaus Mehnert, *China nach dem Sturm*, Stuttgart 1971, p. 232.
[25] See *FEER*, 2 October 1971, p. 26, and *The Times*, 26 June 1972.

suitably astronomical figure of 330 *yuan*.) When it comes to women's wages, the differentials widen. The CCAS found that the maximum a woman at the Hung-ch'iao Commune could earn in a day was $8\frac{1}{2}$ work points, as opposed to 10 for a man. They also discovered that women working under very bad conditions in a so-called Housewives' Factory just outside Peking were paid only 30 *yuan* a month. A recent article in the *People's Daily* advocating equal pay reported that Shantung women farm workers were saying: 'Who would like to sweat more in work when, under the system of equal work but unequal pay, we get only 75% of what men get, even if we removed the T'ai mountain?'[26]

Generally speaking, with a few important exceptions, overall differentials among urban workers seem to have remained in the ratio of approximately three to one. If there has been any narrowing, it is probably due to the attacks on the system of special bonuses and supplements, which tended to favour those at the top end of the scale. (An interesting detail: one observer claims that between summer 1966 and summer 1969, bank deposits were reportedly equal to a third of total deposits. If this is true, it means that the tendencies towards social differentiation have continued, for such deposits certainly do not concern the vast majority of the population.[27]) Mehnert found that some accounts in one suburban Shanghai bank held more than 1,000 *yuan*.[28]

Economic Developments

In his report to the Ninth Congress Lin Piao talked in vaguely optimistic terms about the situation (he stressed in particular that the market was flourishing, prices were stable, and all internal loans had been repaid). Later, Ts'ai Cheng wrote an article drawing favourable parallels with the first years of the People's Republic (he said that the production of grain, cotton, oilseeds and pigs, etc., had doubled or more than doubled and that the total value of industrial production had increased tenfold). At the end of September the official press published figures for different sectors generally comparing them to 'previous' years.[29]

The conclusion to be drawn is that during the years of the cultural revolution the Chinese economy confirmed that it had emerged from the serious crisis of the most difficult years and resumed its upward curve,

[26] *The China Quarterly*, no. 49, p. 149; *China Now*, July 1971, p. 2; Mehnert, op. cit., p. 232; CCAS, op. cit., pp. 135, 189, 272 and 276–278; *The Times*, 26 June 1972.

[27] *Le Monde*, 15 December 1970. In 1971 total urban and rural bank savings were reportedly up by 13.8% – an 'unusual increase' – over 1970 (*HNA*, 24 February 1972).

[28] Mehnert, op. cit., p. 101.

[29] *FEER*, 20 March 1961, p. 531; *PR*, no. 21, 1969; *HNA*, 30 September 1969.

with vigorous growth in some sectors (notably oil). On the whole, however, the development rate was still modest; most of the peaks of the 1958–1960 period were probably not attained. Even when records were actually broken (and such claims always appear to be very cautious and refer only to single sectors) no account was taken of production per inhabitant. The obvious failure of the authorities to supply overall figures and valid comparisons tacitly confirms this supposition. If the results had been spectacular, the leadership would have had every reason to make them public, especially during the twentieth anniversary of the setting up of the People's Republic – a fitting occasion for a general weighing up of achievements.

The leadership attempted to stimulate production through special campaigns and methods, but it was plainly anxious to avoid excessive tensions (we have already remarked on Mao's instruction to 'see to it that there is enough leeway'[30]). The main thing, however, is that the general definition of economic policy (agriculture as the base and industry as the leading factor) remained what it was at the time of the readjustment phase, when Mao's power was at its lowest ebb.

The turmoil of these years led neither to the elimination (which would have been impossible in such a short period of time) nor the attenuation of the tensions that had existed before the cultural revolution. Such increases in production as there were failed to reduce the imbalance between the growth of the economy and the growth in population and to eliminate or reduce in any way the tension deriving from a rise in the general level of culture without a corresponding rise in the number of qualified jobs in the industrial and urban sector of the economy.

The leadership's response to the shortage of urban employment was to revive the *hsia-fang* campaign, which has resulted in the resettlement of vast numbers of educated or unemployed young people in the countryside. The scale of this operation can be judged from the fact that 476,000 educated youth and 105,000 urban residents 'not engaged in manual labour' were sent down to the villages from Honan alone.[31] Chou En-lai told Edgar Snow that the number of people leaving Shanghai for the countryside from 1965 to 1971 approached one million.[32] Some of Mao's

---

[30] It is worth pointing out that a similar expression to the one used by Mao had already appeared in August 1960 in a speech by Li Fu-ch'un and was used once again in an article in 1964 (*FEER*, 20 March 1969, p. 530).

[31] *The China Quarterly*, no. 38, Documentation.

[32] *China Now*, September 1971, p. 6. (Note that the Committee of Concerned Asian Scholars were given the figure of 730,000 – see CCAS, op. cit., p. 171.)

less critical admirers have interpreted policies such as *hsia-fang* as a conscious attempt at shaping 'socialist man'. For example, Wheelwright and McFarlane have written: 'Mao's Chinese followers here seem to be getting back to the earlier Marxist notion of breaking down the distinction between town and country life, and between worker and intellectual.'[33] All we can say in answer to such blatant mystification is that Marx was referring to the generalization of abundance, not the generalization of want (on the basis of a crash deurbanization programme). We would also remind readers that there is nothing new about the idea of resettlement: similar campaigns took place in 1957–1958 and 1963, and the tactic was first developed in the base areas of North China in 1941–1942 as a means of involving cadres in production and injecting new ways of thinking into the villages.

But quite apart from the results achieved up to now, have any new concepts or solutions emerged which are capable of bringing about substantial changes in the future?

We have already seen how Lin Piao's report, while quoting slogans more in keeping with the Great Leap than with the subsequent period, confirmed the basic line adopted at the beginning of 1961. One article, published by *Red Flag* in October 1969 under the title *China's Path for Socialist Industrialization*, vigorously defended the concepts of self-reliance and 'politics in command' and re-echoed the themes of the Great Leap Forward, with a favourable reference to 1958. It then continued with a passage worth quoting in full: 'Priority for developing heavy industry is necessary to obtain socialist industrialization. Only when heavy industry is developed and priority is given to increasing the means of production will it be possible to effect extended social reproduction, provide advanced technical equipment of light and heavy industries and bring into full play the leading role of industry in the national economy.

'There are two ways to develop heavy industry. One is by devoting less efforts to the development of light industry and agriculture, with the result that the people grow dissatisfied and heavy industry will not really be built satisfactorily but will be retarded on account of the slow development of light industry and agriculture. Another way is the one pointed out by Chairman Mao, in which more efforts are devoted to developing

[33] Wheelwright and McFarlane, *The Chinese Road to Socialism*, New York 1970, p. 219. The *hsia-fang* campaign also helped to disperse and demobilize the former Red Guards, an aspect of the movement we shall consider in the next chapter.

[34] See also the pertinent comments of G. Padoul, 'China 1974: Problems not Models', *New Left Review* 89, January–February 1975, pp. 77–79.

light industry and agriculture. When agriculture and light industry are developed, it will be possible to turn out large quantities of farm produce and light industrial goods to satisfy the people's daily needs and to accumulate more funds for building a powerful heavy industry. With the development of agriculture, it will be possible to supply industry with still more ample raw materials and to find an extensive market for industrial goods, particularly heavy industrial products, so that heavy industry will be developed on a still more solid basis.' [35]

This passage is a clear example of a tendency in Maoism to attempt to reconcile contradictory needs with eclectic empiricism, garnished with peremptory aphorisms and solemn declarations of principle. It combines the idea of priority for heavy industry (which in this formulation is a remnant of the Stalinist ideas of the thirties), the idea of the simultaneous development of industry and agriculture (which in practice meant several years' relative priority for agriculture) and the idea that the development of agriculture and light industry is indispensable both to ensure a better flow of raw materials, to widen the home market and to avoid creating tensions with the masses (an idea that has much more in common with Trotsky and the left opposition than with Stalin).

The last paragraph of the article is entitled 'Be prepared against war, be prepared against natural disasters and do everything for the people'. Here we have one more explanatory key: certain decisions, far from having any universal historical value, are taken on the basis of the specific prospects of a determinate historical period (for which in this case there were undeniably good grounds). This also applies to the theme of self-reliance, to which we will return later, and to the idea of combining industrial, agricultural, military and cultural activities (an idea developed mainly after Mao's declaration of 7 May 1966). It is quite legitimate to suggest combining these activities when war threatens and when the productive level of the country is still low; but it is another thing entirely to say that such measures could stimulate the long-term development of production and the modernization of the country. Still less is it a first step towards overcoming the division of labour in the communist phase, for communism will spring not from emergency measures taken by a society forced to struggle for its survival but from the achievement of levels of production and culture incomparably higher than those of capitalism or even of the transitional society just emerged from the womb of the old society based on exploitation and oppression.

---

[35] *HNA*, 18 October 1969; *PR*, no. 43, 1969.

In 1971 the Fourth Five-Year Plan began, but no detailed programme of targets was published. This was probably due to (a) the wider area of tolerance permitted to local areas in interpreting or helping to formulate targets, (b) the continuing state of confusion in the planning bodies as a result of the cultural revolution and (c) differences within the leadership on future economic strategy.

During the course of 1971 it emerged that the Plan's priorities were steel (the 'key link'), iron, coal, cement, electrical power, chemical fertilizer and machinery. Large numbers of town-dwellers were drafted into the mining industry in support of the effort to smash the steel bottle-neck. The size of the problem in this crucial sector of the economy can be judged from the fact that, according to Chou En-lai in his interview with Edgar Snow, average steel output during the last Five-Year Plan veered between 10 and 18 million tons. These figures fall well short of the target of 20 million tons that Mao set for 1967. It was for this reason that steel was given crash priority in 1971. The official end-of-year statistics for 1971 claimed an 18% increase in steel production over the previous year, or a total of 21 million tons though a significant proportion of this was probably of poor quality. (Other reported increases: pig iron, 23%; coal, 8%; cement, 16.5%; mining equipment, 68.8%; metallurgical equipment, 24.7%.) Compared with most backward capitalist states, and especially India, the development of China's industry has been quite satisfactory. Table II at the end of this chapter indicates that the growth of the Chinese steel industry has been something like three times more rapid than that of the Indian steel industry. Moreover the effectiveness of planning in China's nationalized industry enables growth to be more rationally employed. But this does not mean that the Chinese leaders do not face extremely frustrating economic constraints. If the development of China's economy is compared with the economic development of Japan or the Soviet Union then this point becomes clear – some of the relevant indices are assembled in Table II. China's economic development has been vastly outstripped by these powers and there is not even any sure indication that the gap between them is narrowing. The Great Leap Forward had been an attempt to confront this problem and to embark on a programme of crash industrialization. During the cultural revolution there were echoes of this approach and by 1969–70 it seems that a wing of the leadership was profoundly disturbed by China's continuing relative backwardness in the most modern industrial sectors. The grouping around Lin Piao wished to enhance China's military and economic capabilities by a planned concentration of resources on the most modern industrial sectors. This implied tackling another problem: the slow growth of agriculture (see Table I) and the associated system of decentralization and 'self-reliance'. A stress on self-reliance possessed strong attraction to the localistic forces which acquired power during the later stages of the Cultural Revolution. But to the extent that it inhibited a more rapid development of industry it was bound to limit the economic and military assistance that China could extend to the revolutionary movement in Indochina and elsewhere (we will consider some of the further implications of this in a later chapter). The overwhelming emphasis on 'self-reliance' also implied an abandonment of the egalitarian themes which emerged during the Cultural Revolution. It is no secret that big differences in income exist from one commune – or one production team – to the next. Wheelwright and McFarlane, two dogged admirers of Maoist economics, have estimated that whereas the highest daily income in the countryside is about 1.5–1.6 *yuan*, the lowest is about one-third of that.[36] There have been reports in the Chinese press of attempts at democratic management of tractor stations by committees of peasants, cadres from various levels and technicians.[37] It is plain, however, that even if these projects were carried out successfully they would still do nothing to eliminate big differences between communes rooted in variations in soil productivity, in the availability of equipment and technically-trained cadres and in access to markets.

The remuneration system adopted by the famous Tachai brigade did not constitute a real change, since it was applied before November 1965.[38] Moreover, some of the radical aspects of the Tachai system, such as the free supply of grain, vegetables and fruit, were played down by the authorities. The Committee of Concerned Asian Scholars noted in its book that stress on enthusiasm, class consciousness, etc., as opposed to labour power, 'seemed to be given more weight at Tachai than at other communes now following the Tachai system'.[39] The *People's Daily* of 21 March 1971 criticized one brigade for 'not observing the principle of distribution according to labour, thus impairing the masses' activism'. It condemned another brigade for 'abolishing certain systems of reasonable assessment of work and recording of work points'.[40]

[36] Wheelwright and McFarlane, op. cit., p. 194.

[37] *SCMM*, no. 644, p. 7.

[38] *SCMM*, no. 600, pp. 23ff.; *HNA*, 30 September 1968, p. 6; Bettelheim, op. cit., p. 84; *CS*, 7 September 1971, p. 7.

[39] CCAS, op. cit., p. 169.

[40] Quoted in *CS*, 7 September 1971, p. 9. See also Andrew Watson's article in *The China Quarterly*, no. 49, p. 143.

All this means that on the level of the structure of agriculture the tensions at the root of the cultural revolution were neither resolved nor brought nearer to a solution. The contradiction between the objective need to socialize the agricultural surplus and thus accelerate economic development and the political need to carry through this socialization with the active consent of the peasantry was not so much resolved as avoided.

Hence the majority of the top leadership, for all their talk about the need to think in terms of the collective (the peasants' duty to oppose all tendencies towards individualism, etc.), opposed calls for a radical reorganization of agriculture. Examples of this radicalism include the reduction of private plots on southern communes, the nationalization of private plots in Shantung in early 1971 and a whole series of attempts in different parts of China (probably by members of poorer production teams) to transfer accounting and ownership of land from the production team to the larger brigade, as had happened in the much vaunted example of Tachai brigade (clearly the pooling of resources would have worked to the advantage of the poorest teams). *Red Flag* countered such moves with the argument that 'three-level ownership with the production team as the basic unit is fundamentally in step with the level of development of the production forces'. Such attacks were carried on throughout 1972. For example, the *Ninghsia Daily* explained in an editorial broadcast on 10 March that 'it is imperative resolutely to implement the policies of "from each according to his ability, to each according to his work", "exchange at equal value", and to allow commune members to engage in proper family side line production, so as fully to arouse the initiative of the broad masses in developing production . . .' This strongly suggests that the radical wing, at least at lower levels, was not yet eliminated.[41] Lastly, we should note that the leadership has strictly avoided using methods of draining off the agricultural surplus similar to those used in the USSR under Stalin. On the contrary, the state pays the same or an even higher price for any surplus above the state targets.[42]

This policy of moderation inevitably entails the persistence, if not the widening, of differentiations among the peasantry and therefore the perpetuation of those phenomena that have been denounced again and again in the realm of ideology. It also entails a failure to resolve the conflict between the short-term private interests of the peasants and the

---

[41] *The China Quarterly*, no. 50, p. 376; *Red Flag*, no. 2, 1970; *FEER 1972 Yearbook*, p. 46; *The China Quarterly*, no. 38, Documentation.

[42] See *China Reconstructs*, no. 1, 1972, pp. 10–13.

interests of the wider state. For example, government emphasis on the key role of grain sometimes clashed with local emphasis on more profitable side lines, as in the case of the Kwangtung brigade that earned only 51% of its income from grain and the rest from industrial crops, livestock and fish.[43]

Given conditions such as these, it would be foolish to talk of eliminating the tensions that arise from the differences in living standards between town and country. In fact, the authorities rejected the peasants' openly voiced demands for a narrowing of the gap as 'demagogic' and inspired by 'capitalist roaders', while at the same time continuing to oppose any tendency to an exodus towards the towns and encouraging massive transfers into the countryside. (It seems that the temporary and contract workers who during the cultural revolution were to the fore in contesting the established authorities were returned to their rural units.[44])

Without doubt the gravest problem confronting the Chinese leadership is the slow growth of grain output, referred to as a 'key link' in the economy. Grain production in 1970 – officially claimed to be 240 million tons – had still not reached the scaled down figure for grain production claimed after the Great Leap Forward. Between 1952 and 1970 the average rate of growth of grain production calculated on the basis of the official figures was 2.3 per cent a year.[45] This is likely to have been only a little ahead of the rate of growth of the population as a whole. Moreover, as Table 1 shows, the rate of growth of grain production in China has not been faster than the rate of growth in many of the capitalist countries of the Third World. A more effective and egalitarian system of distribution means that China has avoided the famines which periodically devastate India and, as we have pointed out in Part One, China's agriculture was in certain respects already more productive than India's in the early fifties. But nevertheless there has yet to be a qualitative breakthrough with respect to this vital 'key link' in the economy, and China remains a net importer of cereals.

We can sum up the conclusions of this chapter by saying that the immediate aftermath of the cultural revolution suggested that the fundamental problems which had provoked it in the first place had not been resolved. Bureaucratic structures were reasserting themselves at every level, economic inequalities were reappearing on something like their old

---

[43] *FEER*, 2 October 1971, pp. 37–39.

[44] *CS*, 1 June 1970.

[45] See Alexander Eckstein, 'Economic Growth and Change in China: a Twenty-Year Perspective', *The China Quarterly*, April–June 1973, no. 54.

scale and the relatively slow growth of vital sectors of the economy inhibited the attainment of the political objectives that had been proclaimed. As we shall see in the next chapter these developments provided the background to a renewed crisis within the leading group.

Table 1

Grain Production 1952–6 = 100	
Country	1971
China	148
India	155
Indonesia	148
Japan	163
Burma	148
Taiwan	213
Ceylon	173

Source: John Wong, 'Grain Output in China', *Current Scene*, February 1973, vol. XI, no. 2. Based on official Chinese and FAO statistics.

Table 2

Output of Selected Industrial Indicators
(in millions of metric tons; for electricity thousands of Kwh)

Soviet Union	1928	1940	1955	1970
Electricity	5	48	292	993
Steel	3	13	35	154
Cement	2	6	23	103
China	1952	1957	1970	
Electricity	7	19	65	
Steel	1	5	18	
Cement	3	7	17	
India	1949	1960	1970	
Electricity	4	17	56	
Steel	1	2	5	
Cement	2	8	14	

Japan	1952	1960	1970
Electricity	52	115	360
Steel	7	22	93
Cement	7	23	57

Sources:

Soviet Union – M. Kaser, 'Soviet Economics', London 1970, p. 199; UN, *Growth of World Industry*, 1971.

China – Werner Klatt, 'A Review of China's Economy in 1970', *The China Quarterly*, no. 42, July–September 1970; Economist Intelligence Unit, Quarterly Economic Review, *China*, no. 1, 1972.

India – M. Kidron, *Foreign Investments in India*, London 1965, p. 79; EIU, Quarterly Economic Review, *India*, Annual Survey, 1972.

Japan – G. C. Allen, *Japan's Economic Expansion*, London 1965, p. 267; *UN Statistical Yearbook for Asia and the Far East*, 1971.

14
The Fall of Lin Piao

In the early stages of the cultural revolution it was said that P'eng Chen and his black gang had converted the Peking municipality into a 'Three Family Village'. After the Ninth Party Congress it seemed that the leading organs of the Party itself had become a 'Three Family Village', comprising the friends and relations of Mao, Lin Piao and Chou En-lai. It was remarkable enough that the wives of Mao and Lin found themselves on the Political Bureau; the wives of two other members of the Standing Committee of the Political Bureau, K'ang Sheng and Chou En-lai, were in the Central Committee, though at least Chou's wife had always been a political figure in her own right. Of course all members of the Political Bureau were Maoists and Mao was the decisive figure should any divisions appear. As we have seen Maoism encompasses a whole series of elastic formulas which can be given a 'leftist' or 'rightist' twist according to circumstances. Two members of the five-man Standing Committee of the Political Bureau were to disappear in the aftermath of the Ninth Congress (Ch'en Po-ta and Lin Piao) along with five of the other sixteen remaining members of the Political Bureau itself. Both Lin and Ch'en owed their political promotion largely to Mao but both seem to have become overly identified with the leadership line developed during the cultural revolution – it thus became convenient to abandon these men when the time came to abandon this particular line. We will seek to unravel the course of this purge and its consequences for both foreign and domestic policy.

In this study we are not concerned with 'Kremlinological' speculations, but rather attempt to place leadership conflicts in the context of the broad, underlying trends at the level of economic and political relations. Above all we have focussed on the changing relationship between the masses and the decisive institutions of power, on the problems posed by the rhythm of development of the economy and on the pressures exerted by the international context. The interaction of these three different levels invariably forces harsh choices on the leadership and it is around these choices that different political trends emerge within the bureaucracy. No less than the dramatic episodes of the cultural revolution itself, the leadership crisis which erupted in 1971 reflected underlying trends and policy options of this sort. As is always the case the developments in the preceding period set strict limits on the possible outcome of the conflicts within the leading group. In fact it is clear that big shifts in the leadership are produced by changes in the underlying relationship of forces – and at the same time such shifts help to confirm and accentuate the particular trend that produced them. A *fundamental* change could only occur on the basis of an eruption by the masses which broke the power of the bureaucracy.

Between the Ninth Party Congress and the visit to China of President Nixon in 1972 about one third of the members of the Political Bureau of the Party were removed from their posts. First to go was Ch'en Po-ta; he appears to have been dropped in the latter half of 1970. The purge of Lin and his associates seems to have taken place in September of 1971, about a year later. This convulsion in the leading organs of the Party involved a drastic shake-up in the top levels of the PLA: those who disappeared at this time included the Chief of Staff of the PLA (Huang Yung-sheng), the Commander of the Air Force (Wu Fa-hsien) and the chief Political Commissar of the Navy (Li Tso-p'eng), all of whom were members of the Political Bureau. However the regional military chiefs represented on the central bodies remained, for the most part, in place. Some regional commanders who had been notorious opponents of the cultural revolution began to stage a comeback at this time: even Ch'en Tsai-tao, the Wuhan military chief who had blatantly defied the central Cultural Revolution Group in 1967, reappeared at public functions such as Army Day in 1972. There was also a move to rehabilitate Party and state officials who had been disgraced during the cultural revolution – prominent among them the *doyen* of the pre-1966 Party bureaucracy, Teng Hsiao-p'ing. Although Lin's supporters were strongest in the central bodies of both the Party and the PLA, the purge of 1971 did also extend to some provincial leaderships. The Canton regional leadership seems to have been radically changed and prominent leaders in a further five provinces appear to have been dropped, including Liu Feng who had been posted as Political Commissar in Wuhan following the incident there in 1967.[1] Although it cannot be excluded that certain associates of

[1] Documentation in *The China Quarterly*, no. 51, July–September 1972.

Lin will subsequently work their way back into the leadership, it is clear that as a group they have been definitively defeated and Lin Piao himself is dead. This unceremonious dethroning of Mao's 'close comrade in arms' and officially designated heir can only have reflected deep shifts in the underlying relationship of forces and sharply opposed policy options. Before exploring the probable nature of these conflicting options it will be necessary to indicate the sorts of changes within China and in the international context which combined to produce them.

Re-constructing the Party

In the last chapter we have sought to establish that in the two years following the Ninth Congress there was a generalized tendency for bureaucratic structures to reassert their power against the remnants of the popular currents that had emerged during the cultural revolution. It seems likely that the disappearance of Ch'en Po-ta in 1970 was linked to this trend. Prior to the cultural revolution Ch'en had been Mao's secretary and had special responsibilities in the field of economic planning and policy-making. As we have seen Ch'en, with the assistance of Chiang Ch'ing, was leader of the Cultural Revolution Group which took the initiative after the August 1966 Plenum. His main task was to attempt to channel the mass movement in the desired direction, preventing it either from acquiring a dangerous autonomy or from hitting at the wrong targets. This involved Ch'en in repeated attempts to mediate between the forces unleashed by the cultural revolution on the one hand and the established structures of Party and state on the other. Ch'en was able to bring to this role the prestige of his close connection with Mao but in the end it must have forced him into an exposed position. Thus Ch'en played a prominent part in deflecting the 'ultra-left' groups who made such a bitter assault on the Foreign Ministry in 1967. This is unlikely to have endeared him either to the rebels, who were in any case dispersed, or to Ch'en Yi and his officials whom he had allowed to be mercilessly grilled by these young enragés. Order was restored at the Foreign Ministry through the intervention of Chou En-lai, who naturally earned the gratitude of the frightened bureaucrats.[2] At the time of the Wuhan incident it was the Cultural Revolution Group directed by Ch'en Po-ta which promoted a vigorous, but ultimately only half-successful, offensive against the recalcitrant regional military chiefs. It was an editorial in *Red Flag*,

[2] See the account of this episode in Melvin Gurtov, 'The Foreign Ministry and Foreign Affairs during the Cultural Revolution', *The China Quarterly*, no. 40, October–December 1969.

apparently edited by Ch'en at this time, which took the occasion of this resistance to launch the general slogan that it was necessary to 'drag out' the 'handful' of capitalist roaders in the PLA. Under this slogan a number of violent clashes occurred between left groups and local military commanders. Within three weeks of issuing this call the Cultural Revolution Group was having to prohibit the seizure of military equipment by Red Guards. As we have seen it was Chiang Ch'ing who initiated a public reversal of the policy of 'dragging out' the 'handful' in the army when it became clear that it was provoking a strong backlash, based on institutional loyalty, among all sections of the PLA.[3]

Up to August 1967 the Cultural Revolution Group had managed to organize three-way Revolutionary Committees to 'seize power' from the capitalist roaders in only six out of the twenty-nine provinces. After the army was declared off-limits to the Red Guards the formation of Revolutionary Committees speeded up and the role of the military increased in them until they supplied a half rather than a third of the members of the Standing Committees established. The enhanced role of the military can only have encroached on the position of Ch'en Po-ta and the Cultural Revolution Group and made more difficult their central task of enlisting Red Guard enthusiasm for the massive rectification campaign. On the one hand genuinely rebellious Red Guards would not want to compromise with the local military bureaucracy, on the other hand compliant Red Guards were likely to be in the pocket of the local 'conservative' forces. Even though Ch'en and the other members of the Cultural Revolution Group appeared to emerge triumphant from the Ninth Party Congress the basis of their power was, in fact, precarious. Ch'en Po-ta was a member of the five-man Standing Committee of the Political Bureau. However Ch'en still lacked the basis for an independent position of the sort that other members of the Standing Committee possessed (Lin in the PLA, Chou in the state administration). No doubt it was hoped that the Ninth Congress would itself lend a powerful impetus to the reconstruction of the Party and Ch'en would have special responsibilities to see that this was carried through as much in accordance with the original intentions of the cultural revolution as possible. However the formation of new Party Committees at regional level proved even more difficult than the formation of Revolutionary Committees had been. From April 1969 until August 1970 no suitably renovated provincial Party Committees were established despite much propaganda stressing

---

[3] The directive restraining Red Guards is in *SCMP*, no. 4026, 22 September 1967; Chiang Ch'ing's speech of 5 September is in *SCMP*, no. 4069, 29 November 1967.

the importance of 'Party consolidation'. Ch'en Po-ta was dropped from the leadership at the Second Plenum of the Central Committee held in August and September of 1970. Within the next twelve months new Party Committees were announced in every province together with hundreds or even thousands at lower levels.[4] The attacks on Ch'en Po-ta which began to appear after the Second Plenum give a very meagre idea of the reasons for his disgrace. There were no references to Ch'en by name but rather jibes at the expense of 'the "humble little commoner" who is actually a big careerist'.[5] There were also attacks on Ch'en for being a 'know-all' who valued theory and book knowledge at the expense of practice and experience. Ch'en was eventually attacked by name at the Tenth Party Congress in August 1973 in a resolution which called for the expulsion of 'Ch'en Po-ta, principal member of the Lin Piao anti-Party clique, anti-Communist Kuomintang element, Trotskyite, renegade, enemy agent and revisionist'.[6] Apart from the more grotesque slanders involved in such denunciations the main charge against Ch'en is that he was promoting an 'anti-Party clique' together with Lin Piao. (So far as we are aware this empty political category, 'anti-Party clique', was introduced into the vocabulary of the Communist movement by none other than Nikita Krushchev at the time of his defeat of the 'anti-Party' group of Molotov and Zhukov in 1957 – it is ironical that it should have been refurbished by the leaders of the Chinese Party after more than a decade of polemics against 'Krushchevite revisionism'.) In Chou En-lai's report to the Tenth Congress Ch'en and Lin were also charged with believing that China's rate of economic growth was too slow and that it should be a first priority to raise it. The unresolved questions of the Ninth Party Congress would mean that political and economic consolidation would have a high priority for both Ch'en and Lin.

The problems that beset Ch'en in his attempts to reconstruct the Party seemed to have come from both left and right. Throughout the latter half of 1969 and the first half of 1970 there were continuing reports of intransigence from former Red Guard groupings. When the Revolutionary Committees had been formed participation by representatives of the

[4] On the failure to establish Party Committees eighteen months after the Ninth Congress, see The China Quarterly, no. 42, April–June 1970, Documentation, p. 270, and The China Quarterly, no. 44, October–December 1970, Documentation, p. 241. On the widespread setting up of such Committees after the Second Plenum in August–September 1970, see The China Quarterly, no. 46, April–June 1971, Documentation, p. 387, and The China Quarterly, no. 48, October–December 1971, Documentation, p. 789.

[5] PR, no. 27, 1971.

[6] PR, nos. 35 and 36, 7 September 1973.

mass movements fluctuated between a third and a fifth. However even when they were accorded lesser representation this still must have given them some lever on the local power structure, especially at a time when the ideological fanfare of the cultural revolution had done much to discredit the local Party bureaucrats. An article that appeared in the first issue for 1970 of *Red Flag*, gives an idea of the difficulties Ch'en was encountering. The article, rather hollowly entitled 'Triumphantly forge ahead along Chairman Mao's line on Party Building', admonished the left in the following terms: 'Some people, seriously influenced by anarchism and bourgeois factionalism, deny the leadership of the Party from the "Left". They say: "We old rebels are the most revolutionary and the most advanced, we must lead the task of Party consolidation and Party building and we must be regarded as the foundation in this task." This idea is extremely wrong. The Communist Party is the vanguard of the proletariat and is the highest form of organization of the proletariat. The Party should exercise leadership in everything. . . . Some of our comrades have come to regard themselves as "most revolutionary, and most advanced", because they made some contribution during the great proletarian cultural revolution. This shows that they are unable to view themselves correctly, and that they lack the spirit of remoulding oneself. Some other comrades have desperately exaggerated the role of the former mass organizations, incorrectly handled the relations between the mass organizations and the Party, and tried to put them above the Party organizations to contend with the Party for leadership. This is an expression of reactionary anarchism, syndicalism and the "theory of many centres", that is "the theory of no centres". To use them as the foundation to transform the Party means to reduce the Party organizations from the level of a vanguard to the level of a mass organization.'[7] Among other erroneous ideas that it was necessary to overcome was that of those who said, 'we should be admitted into the Party because we are leading members of the revolutionary committee' and 'in recruiting Party members each faction should be represented by one member'. Although by this time most of the Red Guards had been demobilized, it is clear that a number of former Red Guard organizations still existed and that their leaders were pressing for a modification in the Party's political monopoly

[7] This article was signed PLA Unit No. 8341 and was republished in the *People's Daily* on 6 January 1970. This PLA Unit was based in Peking with special responsibilities for guarding the top Party leaders. They had also been detailed to restore order to the campus of Tsinghua University: the attack in this article must have been directed in part at the remnants of a left Red Guard group there; see William Hinton, *The Hundred Days War*, New York 1972.

allowing more autonomy to mass organizations that had emerged in the cultural revolution. The intervention of both the Cultural Revolution Group and the army in 1967 prevented the mass organizations launched by the Red Guards from constituting themselves as the basis of the local institutions of power. They were now being prevented from constituting themselves as the basis of Party reconstruction – in fact they were being denied any significant participation in this process. At the same time Ch'en needed former Red Guard leaders so long as they were willing unreservedly to accept the political direction of the centre. At the same time as he was seeking to discipline the Left he was also seeking to rebuild the Party apparatus in such a way that the former Party bureaucrats who had supported Liu would not again hold the reins of power at local level. An article that appeared in *Red Flag* in July 1970 indicated guidelines for dealing with old Party cadres. According to this article, 'to carry out Party consolidation and Party-building on a sound basis it is necessary not only to grasp ideological consolidation but to grasp it as the central link'. It insisted: 'It is necessary to analyse Party members who have made mistakes, including those who have made serious mistakes. While recognizing the seriousness of the mistakes committed by these Party members, we must also realize that the majority of them are willing to follow Chairman Mao in making revolution; while noting that they have been seriously poisoned by revisionism, we must also consider the fact that they have been tempered in the great proletarian cultural revolution; while recognizing that they fall short of the requirements for Party members stipulated in the new Party Constitution, we must also realize that the majority of them can also play a vanguard role if given help. In carrying out Party consolidation we have come to realize that for those Party members who have made mistakes the starting point for continuing the revolution is somewhat behind that of the others; but they can be changed. . . .'[8] Although there is a conciliatory tone about these judgements they still implied excluding from Party membership those who had made 'mistakes' in the cultural revolution. In fact, Ch'en's efforts to rebuild the Party clearly revolved around the problem of how to make bricks without straw. The new elements thrown up by the cultural revolution were a prey to anarchism, syndicalism and the 'theory of many centres', but at the same time Ch'en was unwilling to hand the Party

[8] Worker-PLA Mao Tse-tung Propaganda Team at Peking University, 'Struggle to strengthen the building of the Party ideologically', *Red Flag*, no. 7, 2 July 1970; also in *People's Daily*, 4 July 1970. The authors of this article would be members of the PLA Unit 8341 mentioned above.

apparatus back to the old cadres. And, of course, there remained the very tricky problem of relations with the army, both the main forces under Lin Piao's command and the local forces under the regional military commands. At the same time as Party reconstruction was being advocated there was a campaign to subordinate revolutionary committees to the Party. Since the army was heavily represented on these committees the delicate question of the fidelity of the army to the wishes of the centre was raised. A directive on these problems seems to have been issued in January 1970, producing such formulations as the following from the *Hunan jih-pao* of 23 January: 'The relationship between the Party Committees and the revolutionary committees is that of the leadership and the led. Only under the absolute leadership of the Party can the revolutionary committees effectively carry out their functions as proletarian organs of power and fully play the part they should.'[9] To drive the point home the Hsin-hua News Agency published touching reports about how PLA representatives had faithfully carried out the directives of the Party even when they personally had put forward different suggestions.[10]

There is much evidence that relations between the Cultural Revolution Group and much of the PLA remained strained after the Wuhan incident, even though the call to 'drag out' the 'handful' in the army had been quickly withdrawn. Army commanders would be likely to feel that the Cultural Revolution Group had recklessly incited the Red Guards in the first place and were thus responsible for the subsequent outrages and excesses whether they sought to disavow them or not. There is evidence that serious incidents continued even after the Ninth Congress had supposedly brought to an end the turbulent phase of the cultural revolution. In July 1969 there were many complaints that 'the trend of anarchism is running rampant' and showed signs of having taken root in young workers. An article in *Red Flag* 6/7, 1 July 1969, on 'The Responsibility of Young Workers' spoke of some young workers who had been led astray by 'harmful books, songs and theories', sometimes showed 'the vacillations of the petty bourgeoisie' and were inclined to say: 'I am also a member of the working class. I do not need re-education.'[11] Since the centre was at this time using contingents of PLA men and workers to restore order in the colleges and universities, the existence of young workers who supported the Red Guard groups posed special

---

[9] *The China Quarterly*, no. 42, April–June 1970, Documentation, p. 173.

[10] *HNA*, 23 February 1970.

[11] Quoted in *The China Quarterly*, no. 40, October–December 1969, Documentation, p. 170.

problems. While the defeat of earlier workers' struggles meant that, as a rule, they could be used against the Red Guards, this does not seem to have been everywhere the case. A remarkable Proclamation issued by the Central Committee in July 1969 had claimed that: 'In Shansi, as in the country as a whole, the situation is fine. But in the city of Taiyuan, and in a few areas of Central and Southern Shansi, a small handful of class enemies and evil people who have infiltrated mass organizations of all tendencies have used bourgeois factionalism to deceive some of the masses into refusing to implement the orders, commands, notices and proclamations successively issued by the Centre and have committed a series of extremely serious counterrevolutionary crimes.' Among these crimes were those of having 'attacked the organization and units of the PLA, seized PLA arms and equipment, beaten up, tied up, killed and wounded members of the PLA. They had incited and threatened workers to cease work and production, incited peasants to enter the towns, struggled by force and wrecked industrial and agricultural production'. They had further: 'used armed force to occupy territory; set up bases for struggle by force . . . practised fraud and extortion against the masses and handed out food and money'. The Proclamation insisted that all ammunition, vehicles and other equipment stolen from the PLA should be returned; trains should be returned to the public transport authorities: 'Those bad people who had threatened workers to quit production or their work posts must be punished according to the law. . . . Those workers and staff who have not returned to their factories and organizations within a month of the publication of this notice will have all their wages stopped. . . . Those who return should be welcomed, their personal security should be assured and there must be no revenge by discrimination or attack.'[12]

That incidents of this sort could flare up at this late stage gives some idea of the formidable problem of disciplining and controlling the former Red Guards. After all, millions of young people, workers as well as students, had been caught up in the mobilizations of the cultural revolution, had been launched against the 'top Party people in authority' and had a gigantic collective experience of struggle and discussion. Such a movement could not just be turned off at will like a tap. The steps taken by the centre to end definitively such renewed outbursts of Red Guard rebellion seem to have been drastic enough. Numerous trials were conducted against those 'criminal' elements who had damaged property

[12] Quoted in *The China Quarterly*, no. 40, October–December 1969, Documentation, pp. 171–3.

during the cultural revolution. The Minister of Public Security at this time was Hsieh Fu-chih, a prominent member of the Cultural Revolution Group. In 1969 and 1970 millions of former Red Guards were sent to the countryside. Reports spoke of 650,000 'young intellectuals' settling down in Heilungkiang, coming from Peking, Tientsin and Shanghai; 800,000 settling down in Liaoning; 100,000 in Sinkiang and 120,000 in Kiangsi.[13] It was reported that, 'units of the Chinese PLA have made outstanding achievements in their efforts to re-educate the college graduates on Army farms'.[14] We have already considered the economic rationale of the *hsia-fang* movement; it seems likely that during the post-cultural revolution phase it had additional political motives since it helped to weaken the striking power of the former Red Guards.

Though there is every sign that Ch'en Po-ta was as much implicated in the decision to demobilize and discipline the former Red Guards and to destroy the left as any other member of the top leadership, in the long run it did not strengthen his position. With the political influence of the left eliminated, Ch'en's special role as the man detailed to control it was undermined. At the same time there is every sign that the army had not forgiven him for his part in promoting and protecting Red Guards in an earlier period and even inciting them to attack the PLA. It seems likely that it was the PLA, in league with local conservative elements, who prevented the establishment of Party Committees in 1969–70. After the dismissal of Ch'en local military men played a prominent part in the Party Committees which were then speedily set up. Of the twenty-seven cases where the First Secretary was named, in eleven cases he was Commander of a Military Region or District and in ten cases a Political Commissar of a military formation (with one case where the First Secretary was both a Commander and a Political Commissar). The published names also show the survival of many former Party and state officials and, apart from Shanghai, *a virtual absence* of new cadres thrown up in the struggles of the cultural revolution.[15] To avoid misunderstanding it must be repeated that the Chinese PLA is no ordinary army but an instrument

[13] *The China Quarterly*, no. 43, July–September 1970, Documentation, p. 176. Hinton, *The Hundred Day War*, reports some of the measures taken against left groups, though his account is partly vitiated by an inability to evaluate critically what he is told.

[14] *HNA*, 5 May 1970.

[15] Details of these appointments based on official sources will be found in *The China Quarterly*, no. 45, January–March 1971, Documentation, pp. 198–199; *The China Quarterly*, no. 46, April–June 1971, Documentation, pp. 387–390; *The China Quarterly*, no. 47, July–September 1971, Documentation, pp. 595–597; *The China Quarterly*, no. 48, October–December 1971, Documentation, pp. 789–791. See also E. Joffe, 'The Chinese Army After the Cultural Revolution', *The China Quarterly*, no. 55, July–September 1973.

of social revolution forged in the course of a bitter civil war. Its commanders were also political leaders. And the Political Commissars must be regarded as Party men at least as much as military men. The point of the above identification is to show that the arbiters of the cultural revolution were precisely the PLA commanders and those Party men who had been embedded in the protective carapace of a military formation, together with a smaller number of Party and state officials with whom they enjoyed good relations. No doubt closer scrutiny of the published lists would enable us to identify provisionally those new Party Secretaries who seemed to be local men and those whose main links were with the centre (either military or political). However such investigations could not make any more emphatic the general conclusion that the cultural revolution resulted in the triumph of some sectors of the bureaucracy against other sectors: and that triumph flowed from their institutional base and not from a political line.

The consolidation and rehabilitation of 'conservative' PLA and Party men was creating an alternative to the group which had been associated with Lin during the cultural revolution. Previously Lin had been one of the few operative army commanders who was present in the highest councils of the Party. With the Ninth Congress military representation dramatically increased until about 140 members and alternates of the Central Committee held military posts out of a total membership of 279; of these military men about three quarters held posts in the provinces. There seems a considerable likelihood that military representation was still further increased by the developments leading up to the removal of Ch'en Po-ta, since in at least seven cases provincial Revolutionary Committee Chairmen seem to have been dropped at about the same time.[16] Whereas Lin and his supporters had been the predominant representatives of the army prior to 1969–70, by this time they were swamped by a host of provincial military chiefs with potentially or actually differing interests and perspectives. During the cultural revolution Lin had been able to use the political weight of the army for his own ends. Even at the time of the incidents in Wuhan and Canton he was still the only active military commander at the highest political level and thus the man best placed to mediate between the Cultural Revolution Group and the PLA. With the Ninth Congress two operative regional military commanders entered the Political Bureau. Since the Political Bureau is a more functional body than the Central Committee this fact was at least as important

[16] *The China Quarterly*, nos. 47 and 48, op. cit.

as the military representation on the latter organ. There is no reason to believe that these new men endorsed the role that Lin had played in the stormy period of Red Guard mobilization. However these new alignments in themselves certainly cannot explain the remarkable reversals of 1971. It seems likely that the failure to reconstruct the Party after the Ninth Congress played a major role in the disgrace of Ch'en Po-ta, since this was the main unresolved question at the time and since it was an area for which he had particular responsibility. With the formation of the provincial Party Committees other problems must have come to the fore, especially the problems of the economy and of the international situation. During the cultural revolution the struggle around the institutions of political power had evidently preoccupied most of the contending parties with economic and international questions taking a secondary place.

Economic Constraints and the International Context

It is possible to compare the performance of the Chinese economy with that of the Indian economy in terms which are broadly unfavourable to the latter. Unquestionably the Chinese example shows that a socialist revolution makes a decisive break with the underdevelopment and dependent development which afflicts the countries of the capitalist 'Third World'. Without economic aid from the advanced countries China has made decisive advances in mobilizing the energies of the entire population for social and economic advance. However China's achievements cannot only be measured against the performance of the backward capitalist states since these states are not the most important contenders China has to confront in the international arena. There is little doubt that in the future Japanese capitalism and imperialism will prove to be more of a threat to China than India. According to all available evidence the Japanese economy has been developing more rapidly than that of China – and, moreover, starting from a much higher level. The Chinese leadership has on occasion shown itself aware of the dangers this portends. A major editorial published in September 1971 pointed out: 'Since the war, Japan has rehabilitated and developed her economy speedily under the patronage of US imperialism and by amassing a huge fortune out of war. Today Japan's economic strength is seven or eight times that of pre-war days and Japan has become an "economic power" in the capitalist world, second only to the United States. The contradiction between the malignant swelling of Japan's economy and her shortage of natural resources and limited markets are even sharper than in pre-war times. This determines that Japanese monopoly capital must seek a way out through expansion abroad. Japanese monopoly capital is sure to protect its colonial interests by armed force and scramble for spheres of influence. An "economic power" is sure to become a "military power" and economic expansion definitely leads to military expansion.'[17]

In the Stalin period the Soviet Union responded to capitalist encirclement with a programme of forced industrialization. Because of the grave deformations of the Stalin regime, and because it was several years late in launching this programme, the Soviet path to industrialization involved a whole series of extremely negative features even in purely economic terms – notably the lasting alienation of the bulk of the peasantry. Yet at the same time it must be conceded that the Five Year Plans did lead to a qualitative expansion of Russia's industrial base which greatly enhanced Soviet military capability. The Soviet Union's emergence as a world power was intimately related to its industrialization. China has certainly achieved significant industrial growth but it has not yet accomplished anything which could be compared to the Soviet Five Year Plans. To cite just one example, the Soviet Union in the thirties built up a strong civil and military aircraft industry virtually from scratch; China at the beginning of the seventies was still dependent on imports from foreign (imperialist) countries so far as modern aircraft were concerned. The fact that China has no significant merchant marine or navy further drastically limits the scope of her foreign policy. However the fact that the peasantry have not been forced to subsidize a crash industrialization programme means that peasant support for the Government remains very strong and this in turn makes China almost invulnerable from a military point of view. As we shall see Lin advocated a more rapid rate of growth for advanced industry with the aim of strengthening China's ability to assist the Vietnamese and other revolutionary movements.

Inside the Factories

A theme which runs right through the post-1968 period is that of combating anarchism and lack of discipline among the workers. Not only were PLA detachments sent into factories to bring rebellious workers

[17] Editorial in *People's Daily*, 18 September 1971, also available in *PR*, 1971, no. 39. This editorial, published at just the time when Lin was being ousted and shortly before the visit to China of the Japanese Premier (Tanaka), contained a conclusion which marked a complete break with the analysis quoted above or, indeed, any Marxist analysis. It declared: 'What Japan should take is another road, the road of independence, democracy, peace and neutrality. That is to say Japan must free herself from US imperialist control, dismantle the US military bases and achieve genuine national independence; she must renounce fascist dictatorship and let the people enjoy democratic rights.'

under control again but a system of 'Red Sentinels' was introduced in 1969 which management could call on when the need arose. However, complaints that groups of workers were taking things into their own hands remained a refrain of official pronouncements; indeed there is the implication that PLA units had sometimes failed to take the right line when confronted with conflicts between workers and managers. The restoration of labour discipline and firm management invariably aroused the enthusiasm of bourgeois visitors to China on their tours of inspection of Chinese factories. There is a whole category of *bien-pensant* 'Friends of China' whose only knowledge of Marxism and the workers' movement comes from such political tourism – they are equally impressed by the genuine achievements and the equally manifest deformations of the Chinese revolution. They yearn for a bourgeois order without a bourgeoisie and without bourgeois excesses and they think they have found it in China. They are particularly impressed by the spectacle of an apparently tame and happy proletariat accepting the puritanical directives of a wise leadership. A good example of this will be found in 'The Shenyang Transformer Factory – a Profile', (Mitch Meisner, *The China Quarterly*, no. 52, October–December 1972, pp. 717–37). In this factory the former manager, who had been attacked during the cultural revolution, had emerged as Secretary of the Party Committee and head of the Revolutionary Committee. The author notes the wide differentials which she insists are not so much 'material incentives' as an expression of natural justice: 'There is a quality of rightness and equity about the payment system that would be brought into question if there was no differentiation of rewards. This is related to the relatively scarce conditions that still prevail, and to the amount of very hard struggle put in by senior workers in both pre-liberation and early post-liberation years.' The disciplining of the 'ultra-left' in the factory with its 'erroneous' egalitarian ideas is also somehow right and natural. At one time such workers were inclined even to question the cadres' right to use a special car but now they understood that it would be of benefit to the factory and to the workers. Also it was clearly convenient that the Workers Representative Congress should be so tightly integrated with the Party leadership, that trade unions should have been abolished, and that the Congress should not be a forum for workers to criticize individual managers – this was a matter to be 'dealt with by a few responsible people in private' (p. 728). Presumably the 'responsible' person would in fact be the Party Secretary who would be in a very good position to judge his colleagues in the factory management. The only fly in all this remarkably emollient ointment was the ambiguous role of the PLA; the author quotes the following confession: 'Class enemies made rumours that the PLA had the right to control the Party organization in the factory.' Although the author acknowledges that 'the grand slogan "the workers are masters of the factory" is elusive in its content' she concludes: '. . . in the Shenyang Transformer Factory, where the cadres seemed powerful and impressive people, the workers also appeared to be pretty "together" people in their own right. And the factory was working as a united community' (p. 737). Of course the author, whatever her naiveté, has grasped one truth – that a factory in China is not a capitalist factory. But because she was not looking for revolutionary democracy she did not notice its absence. Whereas the PLA was the main instrument for encouraging labour discipline in the years 1968–70, by 1972 the Party and factory management were sufficiently restored to be able to assert their authority directly – a point noted and emphasized by Mitch Meisner in the above-quoted report. In March 1972 a keynote article entitled 'Do a Good Job of Enterprise Management in a Practical Way' was published by the *People's Daily*. It declared: 'Due to the influence of the extreme Left trend of thought in society at one time a situation arose in which the management system was like a "gust of wind" while the operational units always acted on their own decisions . . . while criticizing and negating erroneous rules and regulations, it is necessary boldly to reaffirm and adhere to reasonable ones.'[18] The traditional 'New Year Message' published jointly by the *People's Daily* and *Red Flag* on 1 January 1973 defined the line for industry as 'rely on the masses of workers in strengthening the management of enterprises, improving the quality of products, lowering production costs and raising labour productivity'.[19]

Planned Growth versus 'Self-Reliance'
Apart from a certain reinforcement of the trend to strengthen management there were also general shifts in economic policy which emerged by 1972. In the aftermath of the Ninth Congress a new emphasis on central planning began to appear in writing on economic policy. During the cultural revolution only those industries directly related to defence requirements seem to have been under firm central control, with considerable scope allowed to market forces and the law of value in the rest of the economy. The slogan 'Learn from Tachai' emphasized the virtues both of 'self-sufficiency' and of egalitarian measures in making arrange-

[18] *People's Daily*, 2 March 1972.
[19] *PR*, no. 1, 5 January 1973, p. 11.

ments within the Commune and production brigade. By 1969 there were moves both to achieve more centralized planning, even where this meant abandoning the 'self-reliance' formula, and to systematize the egalitarian arrangements at Commune level. Early in 1970 *Red Flag* carried two important articles on economic policy, one boldly arguing for more planning, the other more cautiously advocating 'the mechanization and electrification of agriculture on the basis of agricultural collectivization'.[20] The article on planning even spared the reader the usual catechistic conjugation of policy clichés and allowed itself certain quite direct formulations: 'If "our plan is based on the law of value", as far as the State is concerned, it is impossible for unprofitable national defence industries to develop; it is impossible to establish heavy and inland industries; it is also impossible for districts, provinces and municipalities to build industrial systems under different conditions proceeding from the viewpoint of preparedness against war; it is impossible to develop those industries of low production value, which make little profit on a temporary basis, for supporting agriculture; it is impossible for the State to run and develop certain categories of daily necessities which the people need as subsidy within a certain period of time; and it is impossible in accordance with the proletarian spirit of internationalism, to produce products needed for the struggle of the revolutionary people of the world. . . . The law of value and commodities exists in a socialist society. We use the law of value as a tool in planning work and economic accounting. However, we resolutely oppose making the law of value the basis for regulating production and mapping out the plan. . . . All the enterprises under the system of ownership by the whole people have only one owner. This is the State of the proletarian dictatorship under the leadership of the Party. . . . Resolutely implementing the national economic plan approved by the Party Central Committee will basically ensure the rapid development of our country's socialist development. It is a manifestation of anarchism to neglect the State's unified plan; to start one-sidedly from the needs of one's own department, area and enterprise; to use the planned materials and funds to undertake capital construction not included in the plan; to fail to implement the Party's unified policy, spending the wealth of the State freely for the interest of the few; and to change the direction of production arbitrarily without considering the interests of the State. This will certainly result in scattering our strength

---

[20] 'The Road Forward for China's Socialist Agriculture' by the writing group of the Honan Revolutionary Committee, *Red Flag*, no. 2, 1970.

and in undermining socialist construction.'[21] This article can be read as a response to the dangers of decentralization encouraged by the 'self-reliance' formula. Although these articles were given much publicity at the time there is little evidence that the more rapid and planned development they advocated was effectively followed through. After the dismissal of Lin Piao the ideas contained in these articles were to come under ferocious attack. In general they were attributed to 'sham Marxists' and to 'political swindlers like Liu Shao-ch'i', terms used to refer to Lin and Ch'en.[22] Thus an article in *Red Flag* for mid-1972 declared: 'In their efforts to oppose Chairman Mao's correct line and their schemes to subvert the dictatorship of the proletariat and to restore capitalism, swindlers like Liu Shao-ch'i went to great lengths to undermine the two systems of socialist ownership. They advocated the anti-Marxist viewpoint that the main contradictions within the country were so-called contradictions between the advanced socialist system and the backward productive forces. . . . They also tried to deny the law of value, exchange at equal value and the necessity and inevitability of commodity production in socialist society in a vain attempt to eliminate the distinction between the two systems of socialist ownership and to ignore the difference in degrees of socialist ownership.'[23] What this meant in practice had been spelt out in a number of attacks on the 'Left adventurist line' which 'negated the law of value and the production of commodities and created a trend of distributing everything equally'.[24] Indeed it was said that 'egalitarianism has become the chief obstacle . . . in share-out work in rural areas'.[25] The *People's Daily* (24 August 1972) complained that: 'Some cadres encroach upon the right to self-determination of production teams by setting impractical requirements and rules for them to follow even when they have fulfilled their state plans, and by blindly demanding unified action.' Such deviations usually had their root in the recent past: 'From

[21] 'The Class Struggle in the Spheres of Socialist Construction and Economics' by the writing group of Kirin Revolutionary Committee, *Red Flag*, no. 2, 1970.

[22] Chinese Party polemics invariably refer to the most recently disgraced political current in terms which are a variant of the previously established bogy-man. Thus the Soviet Union was first attacked via virulent polemics against the Yugoslavs and Liu Shao-ch'i was attacked as 'China's Krushchev' despite his many attacks on Krushchev. Apart from generally obscuring the content of political conflicts this practice frequently produces manifest absurdities; thus 'swindlers like Liu Shao-ch'i' were to be accused of failure to expose Liu Shao-ch'i.

[23] 'Learn Some Political Economy', Fang Hai, *Red Flag*, no. 7, 1972.

[24] Heilungkiang radio, 30 October 1971, quoted in *The China Quarterly*, no. 49, January–March 1972, Documentation, p. 186.

[25] Yunnan radio, 11 March 1972, quoted in *The China Quarterly*, no. 50, April–June 1972, Documentation, p. 376.

1968, during the first six months of 1969, some of the communes and production brigades in our region, under the influence of the erroneous line which was "Left" in form but right in essence and which was pursued by swindlers like Liu Shao-ch'i, arbitrarily changed the ownership system and distribution policy for the rural people's communes at the present stage. . . . We discovered that some members in our leading group, under the influence of the fallacy that "politics can oust everything" which swindlers like Liu Shao-ch'i promoted, had erroneously thought that so long as the line was correct, it was all right to go beyond the limits set by policy.'[26]

The new emphasis in agricultural policy was to give much more scope to market forces and to be tolerant of both the peasants' private plots and of all types of subsidiary and sideline production. 'Along with creating conditions for the development of collective economy, commune members should be encouraged to develop side-line occupations in their spare time or on holidays so that their own income will increase and the variety of their commune and brigade products be expanded. Otherwise the enthusiasm of the masses for developing side-line occupations will be dampened. In 1970 we also considered by mistake the weaving of baskets and rain hats by commune members in their spare time to be capitalistic activities, and we refused to accept any of these products. . . . Later on we firmly grasped education in ideology and political line and insisted on performing our work in accordance with Party policies. We drew a demarcation line between the reasonable side-line occupations of commune members and capitalistic tendencies. . . .'[27]

In the towns the service sector was expanded and diversified and the quality and range of available goods increased. All these measures would tend to enhance the features of the Chinese economy discussed in the previous chapter. Inequality between production teams, between communes and between regions would increase, reflecting their different

[26] Hopeh radio, 9 August 1972, quoted in *The China Quarterly*, no. 52, October–December 1972, Documentation, pp. 771–772.

[27] Peking radio, 27 July 1972, quoted ibid., p. 773. It should be remembered that Liu Shao-ch'i had been mercilessly attacked as a 'renegade, scab and traitor' for allegedly plotting to restore capitalism by promoting side-line production and encouraging the peasants to cultivate their private plots. Now policy was switched and the above distinctions drawn. According to circumstances encouragement of market forces and of private production may or may not be a good idea. What is quite wrong is to so manipulate the scientific terminology of Marxism that petty capitalist tendencies are only called by their right name when it suits the Party leadership. This is in strong contrast to Lenin's clear formulations about the necessary risks entailed in encouraging petty capitalism at the time of the New Economic Policy.

natural endowment and their differential access to important markets. Industry would be able to develop in the big centres such as Shanghai but in other regions there would tend to be a wasteful duplication of small, inefficient industrial plants. Above all, the surplus produced by the well-endowed and well-placed areas would not be used to generalize development over the whole economy. To mention only one decisive factor, the further development of agriculture is likely to demand ever larger industrial inputs (machines, fertilizers, etc.). If these are mainly to come from small, backyard plants in every commune, then all the advantages of scale will be lost and the rate of growth retarded. Such practices may appear to have powerful advantages in the short run, since they respond to the strong localistic sentiments of the peasants, but what they do in the long run is to undermine the rationality of the transitional, non-capitalist economy. In a capitalist economy there is not only a market in consumer goods but also in producer goods – whatever its imperfections the market in producer goods will lead to their profitable employment in capitalist terms. In the transitional economies there is some sort of a market in consumer goods but no market in the means of production which are owned by the state. This opens up the possibility for a conscious and rational deployment of economic resources by the planning authorities – but if these possibilities are not utilized then there is no automatic mechanism which will measure the efficacy of investment in one area against that in another. Of course even a decentralized transitional economy such as that of China or Yugoslavia still entails a measure of planning at every level but they dilute it with irrationalities and rigidities.[28]

An issue which seems to have been central to the economic programme associated with Lin was the necessity of dynamically expanding China's electronic industry. At all events shortly before Lin's disappearance the following attack appeared in the *People's Daily* (12 August 1971): 'After composing some fairy tales about developing the electronics industry, Liu Shao-ch'i and company said that the development of the electronics industry and electronics technology "would not only advance the development of the national defence industry but also the national economy as a whole". They also said: "The development of a modern

---

[28] For valuable evidence on this aspect of China's economy, see 'China's Cellular Economy: Some Economic Trends Since the Cultural Revolution', Audrey Donnithorne, *The China Quarterly*, no. 52, October–December 1972, pp. 605–619. For a general assessment, see Roland Lew, 'China and the Crisis of the Capitalist World', *Inprecor* 27–28, June 5 1975.

electronics industry will bring about a big leap forward for our industry and it will be a starting point for a new industrial revolution in the history of China." The rapid popularization of modern electronic technology "will make China the first newly industrialized socialist power with first-rate electronic technology". . . . The sinister aim of sham Marxist political swindlers, who preach that the electronics industry should be made the centre, is the vain attempt to undermine the principle of taking steel as the key link as well as our country's socialist construction. . . . Political swindlers like Liu Shao-ch'i discovered from the publications of a monopoly capitalist class in a bourgeois country the "theoretical basis" of the "electronics industry being the leading industry" which would lead to a "second industrial revolution". They also discovered from the publications of another country the way to apply the theory that "the electronics industry should occupy the leading position" so that it will become the "centre of the whole national economy". These discoveries came to them like rare treasures with which they concocted the "theory of making the electronics industry the centre". This theory enabled them to bluff and deceive people everywhere. This fully proves that these political swindlers are none other than imperialist slaves. Their purpose in adopting the "theory of making the electronics industry the centre" from the bourgeoisie was only to lead us onto the wrong path of capitalist restoration.'

Debased polemics of this sort are presumably designed to drill into the heads of the Party cadre the vileness of the heresy of the moment and give only a rough and ready indication of Lin's strategic conceptions for economic policy. Taken with other such indications, however, it seems that he was pressing for a more rapid and planned development of modern industry, partly to strengthen China's defence-related industries. This policy was linked to a desire to ensure that China could give adequate economic and military support to revolutionary movements abroad. The attacks on Lin made within China itself repeatedly harp on his opposition to China's foreign policy orientation, as does the press communiqué issued by the Chinese Embassy in Algiers on 28 July 1972. This ran as follows: 'Lin Piao died on 12 September 1971. The Lin Piao affair is a reflection of the war between two lines which had been under way inside the Party for a long time. Lin Piao repeatedly committed errors and Mao Tse-tung had waged many struggles against him. Sometimes Lin Piao was obliged to quell his arrogance and thus was able to accomplish some useful work. But he was not able to give up his underhand nature and during the great cultural revolution he appeared to support the thought of Mao Tse-tung and made propaganda in favour of this thought. He was thus able to hoodwink the masses to become in their eyes the "successor" of Chairman Mao Tse-tung. But he was a two-faced man who was in reality opposed to the revolutionary line of Mao Tse-tung and to the revolutionary foreign policy worked out by him, especially after the Ninth Party Congress. . . . He fled on 12 September towards the Soviet Union in a plane which crashed in the People's Republic of Mongolia.'[29]

Although the Chinese press itself gave no straightforward report such as this there were numerous indications that foreign policy differences were an important reason for the break with Lin. It will be appropriate to examine these in detail in the context of the development of China's foreign relations as a whole. This will be done in the next chapter.

After the Purge

So far as internal affairs are concerned we have seen that the elimination of Ch'en Po-ta and Lin Piao was accompanied by an intensification of the trends that were already evident by the Ninth Congress. The influence of the political groups and mass movements which appeared during the cultural revolution had gone into a steep decline. The purge of Lin was associated with a continuing campaign against 'anarchism'. It was said that: 'While sham Marxist political swindlers promote the revisionist and opportunist line at the top level, the obnoxious tendency of anarchism is bound to run rampant at the lower levels. Although expressions of anarchism are found at the lower levels, the cause of it comes from the top level.'[30] It was also claimed that Lin's influence could be seen in resistance to the application of the new economic norms: 'For example, when the mill wanted to strengthen enterprise management further and to set up and strengthen rational regulations and systems, some said: "This is in fact like someone wearing a new pair of shoes but following the old road. Government restriction and supervision have been restored once more." When the mill unfolded labour emulation and prepared to give appropriate material rewards to those who had a good attitude to labour and had recorded outstanding achievements in accordance with socialist principles some people commented that it was championship mentality and putting bonuses in command. When the mill encouraged the workers

---

[29] *The Times* (London), 29 July 1972.

[30] *People's Daily*, 14 October 1972, article by Lung Yen. The survival of remnants of an 'ultra-left' Red Guard group at Tsinghua University, Peking, up to the summer of 1971, has also been attributed to the possible influence of Lin: see William Hinton, *The Hundred Day War*, New York 1972, p. 286.

to improve their technical knowledge for the revolution, some people still said: "This is putting technology first." All these muddle-headed ideas in the minds of the cadres and masses proved how deeply the evil influence of the counterrevolutionary revisionist line put forward by swindlers like Liu Shao-ch'i had affected them and that the evil influence was far from having been purged.'[31] Another local radio broadcast sought to link Lin with opposition to the sending of young people to the countryside: 'Swindlers like Liu Shao-ch'i viciously attacked the going to the country-side by educated young people, saying that this was disguised reform through labour, in a vain attempt to lead us educated young people astray and induce us to abandon the bright road of integrating with the workers and peasants pointed out by Chairman Mao.'[32]

Summarizing the internal trends that were associated with the removal of Ch'en Po-ta and Lin Piao we can say that it was immediately accompanied by even stronger emphasis on strengthening labour discipline and management and on combating anarchism and ultra-leftism. In agriculture private plots, side-line and subsidiary production were encouraged while egalitarian distribution and ultra-leftism were attacked. Over the economy as a whole decentralization and localized industry were encouraged; a planned concentration on the modern sector was rejected. The precise extent to which Lin or Ch'en were associated with this or that development, or with one another, it is impossible to be certain. What can be said is that certain trends established themselves across a wide front and that they constituted a defeat for – or a reversal of – the objectives proclaimed at the time of the initiation of the cultural revolution. Of course this reversal did not begin with the ousting of Ch'en or Lin but must be traced right back to the beginning of 1967.

New Alliances

There is every sign that this retreat from the proclaimed objectives of the cultural revolution was carried out under the leadership of Mao Tse-tung himself. This is not to say that everything went according to plan or that Mao did not find serious obstacles in his path in 1966–68. As we have seen, the initiatives of the centre were constantly checked or deflected, especially by local military forces. But the manner in which such resistance was tackled seems to reflect the fundamental options made by Mao. During the period following the Great Leap Forward he found himself confronted by a Party bureaucracy that was increasingly developing a life

[31] Sian radio, 6 November 1972, *Summary of World Broadcasts*, BBC, FE/4141.
[32] 7 March 1973, *Summary of World Broadcasts*, BBC, FE/4238.

of its own. The strengthening of the top Party bureaucracy represented a serious diminution of Mao's power. The cultural revolution displaced much of the 'civilian' component of this leading group. However the Red Guards and mass movements unleashed against the civilian Party bureaucracy were prevented at the crucial moment from attacking the PLA and that segment of the Party organization directly linked to the PLA. It seems possible that Ch'en Po-ta attempted to achieve by manoeuvre from the top what had not been achieved by the mass revolt from below, but without any success. The 'Three Family Village' which dominated the top Party bodies began to decompose under the pressure of the failure of the programme of the cultural revolution. Ch'en and Lin were absolutely faithful Maoists, indeed probably more faithful to what they understood as Maoism than Mao himself. In the mid-sixties they had been invaluable allies in the struggle against Liu Shao-ch'i and the civilian Party bureaucracy. Ch'en was a competent and reliable exponent of Maoist ideology and was already established in the leading bodies of the Party including the Political Bureau. Lin, as Minister of Defence and head of the Military Affairs Commission of the Party, was, of course, much more important. His institutional base in the PLA was essential to the whole strategy of the attack on Liu and his supporters. However the events of 1967–70 revealed that there were significant sectors of the PLA which were not directly answerable to Lin and his monopoly on the political influence of the PLA was completely undermined. At a certain point both Ch'en and Lin became expendable allies for Mao since they impeded the conclusion of a deal with the central administrators and the strong regional forces which asserted themselves in 1968–70. The only survivors of the original team which had led the cultural revolution were Chiang Ch'ing, K'ang Sheng and the members of the Shanghai group around Chang Ch'un-ch'iao. This inner nucleus of Mao's most faithful supporters was apparently not strong enough to impose itself on the leading organs of the party and state.

The removal of Lin's supporters seems to have made possible a return to a more effective division of functions at the local level. The extremely high participation of operative military commanders in both the Party Committees and the Revolutionary Committees must have led to an inefficient accumulation of functions in a few hands. The elimination of Lin's supporters in the provinces was accompanied by the extensive rehabilitation of Party and state officials who had been disgraced during the cultural revolution. Such men could presumably be relied upon to restore to full working order the local Party and state administration without alarming the local military commanders. According to one estimate military participation in provincial Party Committees dropped from 60% in August 1971 to 46% in the spring of 1973.[34] Though local military participation remained quite substantial it was increasingly supplemented by the resumption of administrative duties by rehabilitated cadres. The Army Day celebrations in July 1972 witnessed the reappearance in public of some thirty formerly disgraced officials. A US academic visiting China in the latter half of 1972 was able to learn of the rehabilitation of some fifty cadres who had been attacked or dismissed during the cultural revolution.[35] As we shall see, the Tenth Party Congress and the Fourth National People's Congress were to confirm these developments.

The Tenth Party Congress

On 29 August 1973 it was announced that the Tenth Congress of the Party had been held in Peking in the previous four days. Chou En-lai delivered the key-note report to this Congress, while a report on the revision of the Party Constitution was delivered by Wang Hung-wen. For the first time Lin Piao was publicly attacked by name and in much more abusive terms than had been used in the communiqué issued by the Chinese Embassy in Algiers. According to Chou: 'As we all know the political report to the Ninth Congress was drawn up under Chairman Mao's personal guidance. Prior to the Congress, Lin Piao had produced a draft political report in collaboration with Ch'en Po-ta. They were opposed to continuing the revolution under the dictatorship of the proletariat, contending that the main task after the Ninth Congress was to develop production. This was a refurbished version under new conditions of the same revisionist trash that Liu Shao-ch'i and Ch'en Po-ta had smuggled into the resolution of the Eighth Congress, which alleged that the main contradiction in our country was not the contradiction between the proletariat and the bourgeoisie, but that "between the advanced socialist system and the backward productive forces of society". Naturally, this draft by Lin Piao and Ch'en Po-ta was rejected by the Central Committee. Lin secretly supported Ch'en Po-ta in the latter's open opposition to the political report drawn up under Chairman Mao's guidance, and it was only after his attempts were frustrated that Lin Piao grudgingly accepted the political line of the Central Committee and read

[34] Editor's Introduction, *Chinese Law and Government*, Summer 1973.
[35] Parris Chang, 'Political Rehabilitation of Cadres in China: a Traveller's View', *The China Quarterly*, no. 53, March–April 1973, p. 335.

its political report to the congress. However during and after the Ninth Congress, Lin Piao continued with his conspiracy and sabotage in spite of the admonishments, rebuffs and efforts to save him by Chairman Mao and the Party's Central Committee. He went further to start a counter-revolutionary coup d'état, which was aborted at the Second Plenary Session of the Ninth Central Committee in August 1970, then in March 1971 he drew up the plan for an armed counter-revolutionary coup d'état entitled "Outline of Project 571" and on 8 September launched the coup in a wild attempt to assassinate our great leader Chairman Mao and set up a rival central committee. On 13 September, after his conspiracy had collapsed Lin Piao surreptitiously boarded a plane, fled as a defector to the Soviet revisionists in betrayal of the Party and country and died in a crash at Undar Khan in the People's Republic of Mongolia. . . . Lin Piao and his handful of sworn followers were a counter-revolutionary conspiratorial clique. . . . The essence of the counter-revolutionary revisionist line they pursued and the criminal aim of the counter-revolutionary armed coup d'état they launched were to usurp the supreme power of the Party and the state, thoroughly betray the line of the Ninth Congress, radically change the Party's basic line and policies for the entire historical period of socialism, turn the Marxist-Leninist Chinese Communist Party into a revisionist fascist Party, subvert the dictatorship of the proletariat and restore capitalism. Inside China they wanted to reinstate the landlord and bourgeois classes, which our Party, Army and People had overthrown with their own hands under the leadership of Chairman Mao, and to institute a feudal comprador fascist dictatorship. Internationally, they wanted to capitulate to Soviet revisionist social-imperialism and ally themselves with imperialism, revisionism and reaction to oppose China, communism and revolution.'[36]

These passages summarize the charges laid against Lin in the whole previous period. If the more absurd and highly coloured passages are put on one side, the account of the inner party battle does suggest some of the themes of dispute, even though in a highly tendentious form. Chou does not claim that the removal of Lin was a decision made by the Central Committee or any formal leading body. Chou's references to the Second Plenary Session and to Lin's attempt 'to set up a rival Central Committee' could suggest that Lin had sought to make a political challenge in the formal leading organ of the Party. The order grounding all aircraft throughout China in early September could well have been designed to prevent the convocation of a Central Committee meeting in which Lin

[36] *PR*, 35 and 36, 7 September 1973.

might have hoped to win a majority. Chou boasted in his Report that the whole Party, army and people had settled accounts with 'the counter-revolutionary crimes of the swindlers ideologically, politically and organizationally'. The convocation of the Tenth Congress itself was the first formal ratification of the elimination of Lin and his supporters. There is no sign that the ordinary Party member had any role whatsoever in the battle against Lin. Clearly the defeat of Lin was *organizational* rather than political or ideological.

Though the Central Committee has functioned mainly as a ceremonial rather than decision-making body, its composition does reflect underlying trends within the ruling group. Sixty-two out of one hundred and seventy-three full and alternate members of the Ninth Central Committee were not re-elected. There were fifty-five new full members and fifty-nine new alternate members. This confirms evidence from other sources that as many as a third of the Ninth Central Committee were associated with the defeat of Lin. The proportion of active military commanders fell from 46% in the Ninth Central Committee to 23% in the Tenth Central Committee.[37] This marked decline in military influence at the centre was accompanied by the rehabilitation of a large number of civilian Party officials who had been attacked or removed during the cultural revolution. Teng Hsiao-p'ing was perhaps foremost amongst these, but altogether forty of the new full members and twelve of the new alternates come into this category. At provincial level the decline of PLA influence was somewhat less marked during this time. In the Political Bureau itself the removal of the central army commanders loyal to Lin reduced the number of active officers from ten to four. However both the powerful regional military commanders who were members of the Ninth Political Bureau, Hsu Shih-yu and Ch'en Hsi-lien, were re-elected to the Tenth Political Bureau. Li Te-sheng, who combined central and regional army posts, was promoted to be a full member of the Political Bureau and also a member of the Standing Committee. Among new members of the Political Bureau were Wu Teh, Secretary of the Peking Party, and Wang Hung-wen, formerly of the Shanghai Party Committee. Wang, a young man who had risen to prominence during the cultural revolution, seems to have been promoted as spokesman for the Shanghai grouping which included Yao Wen-yuan and Chang Ch'un-ch'iao. It will be remembered that this group was responsible both for initiating the first public moves of the cultural revolution and for containing the mass resistance which emerged in Shanghai in early 1967. Neale Hunter's first-hand account of

[37] Cf. Documentation, *The China Quarterly*, no. 56, October–December 1973.

the cultural revolution in Shanghai gives an unmistakable picture of the isolation and unpopularity of Chang Ch'un-ch'iao and his associates at this time.[38]

We cannot, therefore, agree with those who regard the Shanghai Group as authentic representatives of the radical currents that emerged during the cultural revolution. Chang Ch'un-ch'iao and Yao Wen-yuan have always been closely associated with Chiang Ch'ing and seem to have followed Mao through every twist and turn since the inception of the cultural revolution. In the aftermath of the Ninth Congress they seemed to have special responsibility for directing the re-habilitation of the mass organizations – especially the trade unions and the Young Communist League. They clearly did not share Lin Piao's opposition to the economic and foreign policy that was to be adopted in the aftermath of the Ninth Congress. (It is perhaps of significance that Shanghai was a major beneficiary of the 'self-reliance' formula for economic policy.) However it does seem likely that the Shanghai leaders would be hostile to the wholesale re-habilitation of the formerly disgraced party officials promoted by Chou En-lai, and the reversal of so many of the policies with which they had been associated during the cultural revolution.

Unresolved Problems

The Tenth Congress was to prove no more definitive in its results than had the Ninth. However in December 1973 there was to be an assertion of political control over the Army, when eight out of eleven regional military commanders, including Ch'en Hsi-lien and Hsu Shih-yu, were switched to command other regions. But the latter half of 1973 and most of 1974 were dominated by a bizarre campaign to eradicate the influence of Confucius and Lin Piao.

Despite the fact that this campaign was to dominate China for months it was to produce few visible results. During the course of the campaign a large number of instances of corruption of local party and state officials were exposed, but there was no sign of a general overhaul of the administrative system. Among the examples of corruption brought to light were the buying and selling of clothes on the black market, falsification of food ration coupons, trafficking in construction materials, falsification of harvest statistics, abuses of power and extortion by functionaries – all blamed on remnants of the expropriated bourgeoisie.[39] In the absence of a genuine popular invigiliation of officials, petty corruption is bound to

[38] Cf. Hunter, op. cit., pp. 215, 228, 235, 267 etc.
[39] *FEER*, 6 September 1974.

flourish even after such a thoroughgoing campaign as the cultural revolution.

Each of the groupings in the Chinese leadership seems to have used the anti-Lin, anti-Confucius campaign for its own purposes. In Canton and Shanghai a number of thinly veiled attacks on Chou En-lai and Teng Tsiao-p'ing were published. For a brief period in mid-1974 *tatzupao* again appeared on the walls in Peking. On 13 June a wall poster appeared which accused members of the Peking Municipal Revolutionary Committee of having purged all but one of its twenty-four working-class representatives, and of having torn down eighty-nine earlier poster protests that had been posted up inside buildings. According to one foreign report most of the Peking posters that appeared during subsequent days took up the same point of the suppression and ousting of the 'working-class activists' of the cultural revolution from all posts of responsibility. Another point raised by the *tatzupao* was the increase in material privileges for leading bureaucrats; high party officials were accused of having obtained exemption for their sons and daughters from the general rule requiring young people to spend some years in the countryside.[40] There were also reports of big demonstrations and strikes – both harshly repressed by the authorities – in Kiangsi and Honan and in the cities of Wuhan and Harbin.[41] But all these signs of popular participation in the campaign ended abruptly with a stern editorial in the *People's Daily* on 1 July. This editorial insisted that all criticism should be confined to meetings organized by party committees and should remain under the control of the party. The workers were also reminded that production must not be in any way disrupted by the campaign. From its inception the anti-Lin, anti-Confucius campaign had included praise for the Legalists, opponents of Confucianism who were lauded for 'burning books and burying Confucian scholars alive' and for having consolidated, unified and strengthened the central power. The terms of this extraordinary historical analogy were eloquent enough of the extremely reactionary political message that it was seeking to convey right from the outset. Not surprisingly those who wished to revive themes from the cultural revolution had little success. Despite the strong position that the Shanghai group seemed to occupy at the Ninth Congress they proved unable to prevent their rivals from prospering. Teng Hsiao-p'ing was named a vice-premier and the rehabilitation of officials who had been disgraced and removed during the cultural revolution gathered momentum. Army

[40] *The Times*, 20 June 1974.
[41] *The Guardian*, 25 June 1974.

Day in 1974 witnessed the re-emergence in public of a further nineteen former leaders, including Yang Ch'eng-wu, who had been acting chief of staff of the PLA. In January 1975 it was announced that the Fourth National People's Congress had at last taken place between 13 and 17 January. It was announced that at the Second Plenary Session of the Tenth Central Committee, which met between 5 and 11 January, Teng Hsiao-p'ing had been appointed Vice-Chairman of the Central Committee and a member of the Standing Committee of the Political Bureau. All signs suggested that Teng Hsiao-p'ing, formerly branded as a capitalist roader and enemy agent, was being promoted to succeed the ailing Chou En-lai.

The participation of the Shanghai leaders in the Fourth National People's Congress was not very prominent and they were heavily outnumbered in the appointments announced at this time. Chang Ch'unch'iao was the only member of the group to be assigned to a government post, becoming one of twelve Vice-Premiers. However he did deliver a report to the Congress on the new constitution in the course of which he declared that: 'In some enterprises, the form is that of socialist ownership, but the reality is that leadership is not in the hands of Marxists and the masses of workers. The bourgeoisie will seize hold of many fronts if the proletariat does not occupy them. Confucius died over two thousand years ago and yet such rubbish as his does not vanish of itself.' Chang also announced that in the final draft of the constitution 'in accordance with Chairman Mao's proposal, the specification that citizens have the freedom to strike has been added . . .'.[42] Mao himself did not attend the Congress, though evidently he was not ill since he received the West German politician Franz Josef Strauss during this period. Immediately following the Congress a communiqué was issued in Mao's name to the effect that it was imperative to strengthen the proletarian dictatorship in China and to combat the dangers inherent in the eight grade system of wage differentials. Although the precise significance of this chain of events was unclear, tensions and conflicts were again growing inside the leading group of the party and state.

After nearly a decade of successive rectification campaigns, and acute internal struggles, the leadership of the Chinese party and state seemed to have moved full circle back to the problems that lay at the root of the cultural revolution: on the one hand the consolidation of a relatively

---

[42] *PR*, no. 4, 24 January 1975. See also Dave Frankel, 'Behind China's New Constitution', *Intercontinental Press*, 10 February 1975.

privileged leading stratum around Chou and Teng, on the other signs that Mao, and those closest to him, were becoming increasingly restive at the constraints imposed upon them by the functioning of the rest of the bureaucratic apparatus.

At the Fourth People's Congress Chou En-lai claimed that there had been rapid development of China's economy. Taking the relatively bad year 1964 as a base, he announced that there had been a growth of 51% in agricultural output and of 190% in industrial output. China was, in fact, continuing to industrialize but with no dramatic breakthrough in grain production which remains the vital link in the economy. The development of China's economy was continuing to score real successes, but on a scale that remained modest by comparison with the backwardness of the country and the vastness of the population.

As we have seen the recovery of the economy following the cultural revolution was accompanied by a return to many of the structures of authority and systems of payment that had been assailed by the Red Guards. The use of special campaigns and the theory of the mass line as a substitute for revolutionary democracy and workers' control of production had failed. Instead of democratic discussion and open political battles to win the majority, the institutions of the Chinese Communist Party and the People's Republic were paralysed by factional conflicts fought out in extremely mystifying terms and settled by bureaucratic manoeuvre and fiat. The following comment by a Chinese Trotskyist on the campaign against Lin and Confucius underlines one of the consequences of this degradation of political life in China:

'In present-day China all shades of popular opinion, at all levels of society, are for the most part fed up with the continuous churning out of campaign after campaign in the course of Mao's so-called "uninterrupted revolution". It is not only "bad elements" or the right wing who blanch when they hear the word "campaign" or begin to palpitate as soon as they see a "struggle" on the way. Even the toiling masses of workers and peasants, who are thoroughly dissatisfied with bureaucratic rule in all its forms, live in fear of campaigns of this sort. Twenty or more years of experience has taught them that campaigns should never be taken at face value, and that they always turn out differently in practice from what they are proclaimed to be. They might well swat dead a few house flies, or even overthrow one or two small tigers, but the end result is that the swatters end up in the same fix as the flies and sometimes in even a worse one. As for beating the small tigers, this invariably turns out to be in the interest of the biggest tigers. The campaigns are not *entirely* without advantage for the worker and peasant masses. But after it is all over nothing has really changed – they still suffer the same hardships. The "Great Proletarian Cultural Revolution" was especially disappointing. It aroused the hopes of the masses, only to dash them to the ground again. It ended up with the persecution of the true revolutionaries. From now on the masses have every reason to look upon Mao's movements and campaigns as potential man traps.'[43]

The writer concludes that launching orchestrated campaigns as a means of combating bureaucracy and corruption is 'like climbing trees to catch fish'. This comment is an apt epitaph on the decade 1965–75. Moreover it underlines the fact that although from many points of view the policy of the bureaucracy turned full circle during this decade, in the process the Chinese leadership has used up much of the enormous prestige it enjoyed consequent upon the liberation of China in 1949. (Despite the fact that China is saturated by a succession of campaigns the more astute observers detect many signs of a *de-politicization* of the mass of peasants and workers.[44]) It has also used up many of the original political and military cadres who led the Chinese Communist Party and the PLA to victory. The whole cycle of purges from the ousting of P'eng Teh-huai and P'eng Chen to the elimination of Ch'en Po-ta and Lin Piao have decimated the leading ranks of the Party without the emergence of a new generation of leaders. The cultural revolution and its aftermath produced little more than a handful of new faces in the leading organs of the Party and State. Superannuated veterans are kept on in many posts, presumably because agreement on who should replace them is difficult to reach. The deficit of new leadership cadre is made up by bringing back formerly disgraced officials. The only relatively new grouping is that around Chiang Ch'ing and Chang Ch'un-ch'iao. There is no reason to believe that the arrangements made at the Tenth Congress of the Party and the Fourth National People's Congress represent any long-run solution to the leadership crisis. But it seems likely that, given the the exhaustion of the talent and prestige available to the bureaucracy, its ability to manipulate and control future eruptions from below will be correspondingly reduced, and an explosion of the crisis in the leading organs of the party and state could well provoke just such an eruption from below.

---

[43] W.F.H., loc. cit., 'Behind the "Criticise Lin, Criticise Confucius" Campaign', op. cit.
[44] See Padoul, op. cit.

15

China's Foreign Policy

We have developed our views elsewhere on the emergence of the Sino-Soviet conflict and the attitude of the Chinese leadership at that time to the crucial problems of world politics.[1] We argued that for a variety of historical and conjunctural reasons the policies of the Chinese Communist Party were more progressive than those of the CPSU and the parties that supported it, and were capable of stimulating and polarizing left-wing Communist tendencies. As the cultural revolution drew to a close such a categorical judgement could no longer be made. In 1970–71 a sharp turn to the right coincided with the elimination of Lin Piao – though as we shall show this turn was carried out in the framework of a fundamental continuity at the level of certain important formulations about world politics and China's relation to them. These shifts reflected both the changing relationship between the masses and the leadership within China and also a transformation of the international context within which Chinese policy is formulated.

At times when the masses are aroused and exercising a pressure on policy-making there is a tendency for left themes to appear in foreign policy (e.g. the immediate post-liberation period). However this factor interacts with another, namely the pressure exerted by the external conjuncture. Thus the split with the Soviet Party reflected both the fact that imperialism was pursuing a much tougher policy towards China than towards the Soviet Union and the fact that at every level of the Chinese Party there was a revulsion against Soviet bullying tactics. Thus from the beginning we avoided explanations of the Sino-Soviet conflict which neglected these fundamental internal and external factors and dwelt instead on Mao's personality, on the relative poverty and riches of the

---

[1] *Quatrième Internationale*, October–November 1960; March 1963; November 1963. See also Ernest Mandel, *Peaceful Coexistence and World Revolution*, London and New York 1970.

Chinese and Russian bureaucracy, or on the supposedly more 'Stalinist' character of Mao in relation to the Russian leadership. We insisted that an essential feature of the differences was the fact that imperialism accepted a relationship of peaceful coexistence with the Kremlin but refused to do so with Peking.[2] The relationship of the Maoist bureaucracy to imperialism on the one hand and to the masses on the other has always been the fundamental determinant of the situation. It was obvious that during the whole of the sixties these two relationships differed only quantitatively and not qualitatively from that of the Soviet bureaucracy in its various guises of Stalin, Krushchev and Brezhnev. However in terms of this analysis it will be seen that both the cultural revolution and the inauguration of the Nixon strategy in the early seventies were bound to have important consequences. The rise of mass struggle during the cultural revolution coincided with the most overt threats to China from the imperialist aggression in Indo-China. The restabilization of the bureaucracy following the Ninth Congress coincided with the emergence of a new emphasis in imperialist strategy that combined an escalation of the war in Indo-China itself with reassurances to China that no threat would be made to her existence or territorial integrity. Before examining these developments in more detail, however, it will be convenient to examine the international policy of the Chinese leadership at the time of the cultural revolution.

If we take the period of the cultural revolution itself, we find that China supported guerrilla wars in several parts of Asia (Thailand, Burma, the Philippines, Indonesia), expressing her solidarity with parties and groups engaged in these struggles and providing aid. Apart from the particular policies put forward or supported by the Chinese leadership (we shall return to this question later), no one could under-estimate the objective importance of this support for armed struggles. Such policies generally worked to the advantage of the anti-imperialist struggle in other continents, though they also encouraged ultra-leftism and adventurism in those areas where the necessary pre-conditions for launching armed struggle did not yet exist. For revolutionary Marxists armed struggle must develop on the basis of a deeply rooted mass movement. In India the Maoists ignored this basic precept in the late sixties, leading to a

[2] This point also emerges strongly from the valuable study in the development of China's foreign policy by James Peck, 'Why China "Turned West"', *Ramparts*, May 1972. He argues that the US refusal to accompany *détente* with the Soviet Union by any concession on the question of Taiwan was a major factor in provoking the Sino–Soviet conflict, since the Soviet Union was much more concerned with a settlement in Europe and elsewhere and was not prepared to see this settlement jeopardized by Chinese intransigence on Taiwan.

wholesale sacrifice of the militants involved in the Naxalite movement. In the advanced capitalist countries, the criticism that the Chinese had been making of Communist Party opportunism helped to deepen the crisis of the Soviet-dominated bureaucratic system and encourage the spread of the new vanguard movements. All this was symbolized by the difference in the way in which China and the Soviet Union reacted to the events of May 1968 in France. Whereas the Chinese press openly sided with the revolutionary left, Moscow hurled abuse at it. Lastly, if we ignore for the moment their more than questionable analyses and motivations, China's condemnation of the Soviet invasion of Czechoslovakia encouraged the anti-bureaucratic forces not only in Czechoslovakia but in all the countries under the control of the Kremlin. Stands such as these explain why the Chinese attracted significant sections of the new vanguards, beyond the parties or groups directly linked to them.

But it is precisely because the Chinese leadership has not hesitated to define its attitude on key questions in practically every area of world politics and has managed to exercise some influence on the course of world events that any balance sheet we draw up must be based not so much on China's or the Soviet Union's declared strategic and tactical concepts as on the results they have actually achieved.

In any case, the fact that China criticizes Soviet theoretical generalizations or strategic concepts does not automatically mean that her own ideas are correct or correspond to the needs of the revolutionary struggle of the world proletariat at this stage.

We will not spend much time, as others have done, on Lin Piao's famous generalization that the 'cities of the world' (North America and Western Europe) will be encircled by the 'countryside' (the peoples of Asia, Africa and Latin America). In so far as this metaphor stated the obvious fact that for a long period, while the revolutionary movement in the developed capitalist countries was either stagnant or non-existent, the colonial peoples dealt the most devastating blows to the imperialist system, we can only agree with it. It was wrong, however, to encourage the building of theories generalizing from this fact, as Lin Piao did when he wrote: 'In the final analysis, the whole cause of world revolution hinges on the revolutionary struggles of the Asian, African and Latin American peoples who make up the overwhelming majority of the world's population.' (But note that Lin also spoke of a temporarily blocked proletarian revolutionary movement, while previous texts declared that the centre of world contradictions, of world political struggles, was not stable but changed in relation to the changes in international struggles and revolutionary situations, airing the possibility that Western Europe might again become the centre of world contradictions.[3]) The experience of the last few years has shown that to raise itself to a higher level of development, the revolution in the ex-colonial or neo-colonial countries needs the contribution of a revolutionary movement that shakes the citadels of imperialism from the inside, at the heart of the system, and that such a contribution is right now a possibility – consider the Indochinese revolution and its reciprocal relation to the anti-war movement in the United States and other advanced countries.

The Strategy of the New Democratic Revolution

But Lin Piao's strategy was still centred around the idea of a new demo-cratic or national democratic revolution led by the proletariat and a Marxist-Leninist party and aimed not against the capitalist system as such, but against 'imperialism, feudalism and bureaucrat-capitalism': it therefore involved an alliance 'not only with the workers, peasants and urban petty bourgeoisie, but also with the national bourgeoisie and other patriotic and anti-imperialist democrats'.[4]

Basically, this strategy is nothing more than a confusion of the link between the bourgeois-democratic revolution and the socialist revolu-tion, or to be more exact, of its most opportunist variant. Actually, during the very first stages of the anti-Soviet polemics Chinese theoreticians formulated ideas very close to Trotsky's permanent revolution and Lenin's ideas of 1917.[5] Lu Ting-i wrote: 'Lenin brilliantly applied and developed the Marxist idea of uninterrupted revolution, regarding it as a fundamental guiding principle of the proletarian revolution. Lenin set out the principle that the proletariat should obtain the leadership in the bourgeois democratic revolution and transform the bourgeois democratic revolution without interruption into the socialist revolution. Lenin fur-ther pointed out that the socialist revolution is not the final goal and that it is necessary to continue advancing, to accomplish the transition to the higher stage of Communism'.[6] But elsewhere and to some extent simultaneously the Chinese retained the principle of revolution in stages, which is the negation of the theory of permanent revolution in its Marxist

[3] *PR*, no. 18, 1963.

[4] *HNA*, 3 September 1965, p. 24.

[5] For the ambivalence of Lenin's ideas on this subject before 1917 see Leon Trotsky, *The Permanent Revolution*. See also Norman Geras, 'Rosa Luxemburg After 1905', *New Left Review* 89, January–February 1975.

[6] *HNA*, 23 March 1960. See also F. Charlier's article in *Quatrième Internationale*, July 1964.

and Trotskyist meaning. Lu Ting-i's article praised the Party for having succeeded in combining the revolution in stages with the uninterrupted revolution (an idea taken up again by T'ao Chu in August 1966) while the authors of one frequently quoted article wrote with much caution and little precision that 'in countries where industry is less developed, it is necessary and possible – after the proletariat leads the democratic revolution to victory – to turn the democratic revolution into the socialist revolution in good time'.[7] It is all too obvious that we are here dealing with attempts to reconcile the actual course of the revolution in China (so very unlike the course predicted) with some of the more important declarations made before the event. This must have been a most difficult task if we remember, for example, that in his report to the 1945 Congress Mao had declared: 'It is only through democracy that socialism can be attained – this is the fundamental truth of Marxism. In China the fight for democracy will be a protracted one. It would be a sheer illusion to try to build socialism on the ruins of the colonial, semi-colonial and semi-feudal order, without a united new democratic state, without the development of a new democratic state, without the development of private capitalism and cooperative enterprises, without the development of a national, scientific and popular culture that is a new democratic state, or without the liberation and development of the individual initiative of hundreds of millions of people – in short, without pushing to the end the democratic revolution which is bourgeois in character, a democratic revolution of a new type led by the Communist Party. Some people fail to understand why the Communists should advocate the development of capitalism under given conditions instead of fearing it. Our answer is simple: to replace the repression of foreign imperialism and native feudalism with capitalism developed to a certain degree is not only an advance but also an unavoidable process.'[8]

Clearly, the two variants of the Chinese interpretation of the link between the bourgeois democratic and the socialist revolution are quite different: it is one thing to speak of a democratic stage which, under the leadership of the working class, grows over 'uninterruptedly' into the socialist revolution, and another to imagine a whole 'united new democratic state' stage in which capitalism can develop. But practice tends to brush aside eclecticism and ambiguity: during the crucial years of 1946–47 the revolutionary pressure of the land-hungry peasants and the intransigence of the Kuomintang and the old ruling classes ruled out the

[7] *HNA*, 24 December 1967, p. 7.
[8] A. Fremantle (ed.), *Mao Tse-tung – An anthology of his writings*, N.Y. 1962, p. 159.

possibility of collaboration and compromise, and the Communist Party had to place itself at the head of an impetuous mass movement which was developing in an anti-capitalist and not merely in an anti-imperialist and anti-feudal direction. Its victory was not, as some apologists maintain, the result of a correct theoretical understanding of the nature of the revolution. On the contrary, it was only after the Party had abandoned its previous theory that victory became possible.

The Indonesian tragedy confirmed that the fiction of a 'new democratic' stage, with its attendant hybrid state, encouraged erroneous and ambiguous ideas that would lead to disaster. Aidit, the leader of the Indonesian Communist Party, was certainly aware that the 'main force in the Indonesian revolution was the peasantry' and always proclaimed that the anti-imperialist and anti-feudal national front should be led by the working class; he even went so far as to say that no Indian Ocean would separate the democratic revolution from the socialist one (1964). But the basic premise of his policy was the need for a national democratic stage in the revolution and hence an alliance with the national bourgeoisie, represented by Sukarno. And since, despite what was proclaimed in the documents and speeches, any alliance with the bourgeoisie in a regime that remains capitalist can only come about under the leadership of that bourgeoisie, it follows that Aidit subordinated his Party to the Indonesian national bourgeoisie, with the full support of Peking.

Sadly, the consequences of this policy (the annihilation of half a million Indonesian workers and peasants) need no comment: the catastrophic outcome was a most serious blow for the revolution, and not only in Indonesia.

We would point out in passing that the entire leadership of the Chinese Communist Party bears the responsibility for the Indonesian policy, despite subsequent attempts to make Liu Shao-ch'i the scapegoat. For example, K'ang Sheng, one of the chief promoters of the cultural revolution, said of Aidit: 'The (Indonesian Communist) Party, which has always remained (since 1951) under the correct leadership of the Central Committee led by Aidit, has set out and put into practice a Marxist-Leninist line and policy, thus ensuring the progress of the revolutionary cause of the Communist Party and the Indonesian people.' (*Pékin Information*, no. 15, 1963, p. 35 – retranslated from the French.) On 20 May 1965, Mao himself signed a message to the Indonesian Central Committee, which said among other things: 'The Central Committee of the Indonesian Communist Party, headed by Comrade D. N. Aidit, has cleverly and creatively applied and developed Marxism-Leninism, in the light of the revolutionary practice of its country: it has indonesianized Marxism-Leninism with considerable success, it has set out in total independence its own line and its own revolutionary policy in keeping with the basic interests of the Indonesian people and has led the revolutionary struggle in Indonesia from victory to victory. . . . We are profoundly convinced that the Indonesian Communist Party will continue to expand its fighting force, consolidate and extend the national united front based on the alliance between workers and peasants, and lead the national and democratic revolution of the Indonesian people to a new drive and new victories. A completely independent, democratic, prosperous and advanced Indonesia will rise up in the world.' (*Pékin Information*, no. 22, 1965 – retranslated from the French.)

In China itself the New Democracy formulas did not lead to an Indonesian type débâcle primarily because the Communist Party commanded a powerful armed force solidly entrenched in the sympathies of the peasant masses. Moreover when Mao, Chou En-lai and other Party leaders journeyed to Chungking to negotiate the construction of a New Democratic order in collaboration with Chiang Kai-shek, the latter lost little time in sabotaging the whole enterprise. Chiang launched a generalized offensive against the Liberated Areas. An eye-witness to the reaction to this offensive wrote: '. . . no matter what Mao said or did in Chungking the leaders and the troops in the Border Region were prepared to beat back any invasion of their area by Chiang Kai-shek's troops. In short they would not have surrendered the sovereignty of the Border Region to the Kuomintang even at the direction of Mao. There seems to be no doubt on this point, and everyone I talked to about this question – especially non-Communist Government officials – declared they would have fought off Chiang's troops no matter what Mao ordered.'[9]

That the policies pursued at this time caused concern in the Party and in the ranks of the Red armies was to be obliquely and dishonestly conceded in the course of the cultural revolution itself. Liu Shao-ch'i was made the scapegoat for all the equivocations and ambiguity of the Party's policy in promoting New Democracy. For example in his Report to the Ninth Congress Lin Piao declared: 'After the victory of the War of Resistance against Japan, when the US imperialists were arming Chiang Kai-shek's counter-revolutionary troops in preparation for launching an all-out offensive against the Liberated areas, Liu Shao-ch'i, catering to the needs of the US-Chiang reactionaries, dished up the capitulationist

---

[9] Jack Belden, *China Shakes the World*, London 1973, p. 106. For the general context of this crucial episode see Joyce and Gabriel Kolko, *The Limits of Power*, New York 1972.

line, alleging that "China has entered the new stage of peace and democracy". It was designed to oppose Chairman Mao's general line of "go all out to mobilize the masses, expand the people's forces and, under the leadership of our Party, defeat the aggressor and build the new China", and to oppose Chairman Mao's policy of "give tit for tat for every inch of land", which was adopted to counter the offensive of the US-Chiang reactionaries. Liu Shao-ch'i preached that "at present the main form of the struggle of the Chinese revolution has changed from armed struggle to non-armed and mass parliamentary struggle". He tried to abolish the Party's leadership over the people's armed forces and to "unify" the Eighth Route Army and the New Fourth Army, predecessors of the People's Liberation Army, into Chiang Kai-shek's "national army" and to demobilize large numbers of worker and peasant soldiers led by the Party in a vain attempt to eradicate the people's armed forces, strangle the Chinese revolution and hand over to the Kuomintang the fruits of the victory which the Chinese people had won in blood. In April 1949, on the eve of the country-wide victory of China's new-democratic revolution when the Chinese People's Liberation Army was preparing to cross the Yangtse river, Liu Shao-ch'i hurried to Tientsin and threw himself in the arms of the capitalists. . . . He clamoured that "capitalism in China is still in its youth", that it needed an unlimited "big expansion" and that "capitalist exploitation today is no crime, it is a merit". . . . In short at the many important historical junctures of the new-democratic revolution and the socialist revolution, Liu Shao-ch'i and his gang always wantonly opposed Chairman Mao's proletarian revolutionary line and engaged in counter-revolutionary conspiratorial and disruptive activities.'[10]

Although certainly exaggerated, this account points to the existence of grave suspicions about the line actually pursued by the whole Party in these years. There is overwhelming evidence that Liu's real statements and actions at this time in no way differed from those of Chou En-lai, Ch'en Po-ta or Mao himself.[11] Whatever differences of policy or emphasis there were inside the leading organs of the Party they certainly could not have taken the form which Lin claimed in his Report. In the event the intransigence of Chiang combined with the renewed wave of peasant revolt helped to simplify the problem confronting the Party. This is

[10] Lin Piao, 'Report to the Ninth National Congress of the Communist Party of China', *PR*, Special Issue, 28 April 1969, p. 14.

[11] For documentation of this point see 'Mao Versus Liu? Policy Towards Industry and Commerce: 1946–49', Kenneth Lieberthal, *The China Quarterly*, no. 47, July–September 1971, pp. 494–520.

certainly not to claim that the revolution of 1949 can be explained as a spontaneous peasant explosion triggered off by the clumsy repression of Chiang Kai-shek. In the end making a revolution must be a conscious political act. But in order to make this political choice the leadership of the CCP had to break *in practice* with the formulas of New Democracy and to acknowledge even in theory, albeit ambiguously, that there had been, to use the term employed by Lin above, a *juncture* of the democratic and socialist revolution in China.

Constant Elements in China's Foreign Policy

We saw at the beginning of this chapter how China's foreign policy was generally to the left during the period of the cultural revolution. From 1969, however, it reflected the general retreat from left positions that characterized domestic politics during this period. The first sign of this reorientation was the resumption of diplomatic links broken during the years of turmoil. This was carried to a qualitatively new stage with Nixon's visit to Peking and all that this involved. We have witnessed the gradual re-emergence in Peking of strategic concepts current during the fifties and early sixties. The turn in China's foreign policy must be seen as a response to both internal and external developments. We have surveyed in the previous chapters the rehabilitation of the bureaucratic order in the years 1968–70. On the international front there were also to be major developments encouraging the Peking bureaucracy to abandon the left positions adopted (at least at the level of rhetoric and to some extent also in practice) during the sixties. In order to see this in its true perspective it will be necessary to review the relations between the United States, the Soviet Union and China and to consider in particular the effect of the Vietnamese war on those relations.

When examining Sino-Soviet relations it is always necessary to bear in mind that they express the interaction of two partially discrepant factors. First there is a fundamental objective contradiction between imperialism and the underlying social system in both China and the Soviet Union. Secondly the bureaucracies in both Peking and Moscow, while they cannot ignore the fundamental contradiction, seek in every way to protect and promote their own special corporate interests, where necessary at the expense of the world revolutionary process. To this end they both employ the ideology of 'Socialism in One Country' developed by Stalin, together with the formulas about 'peaceful coexistence' which have always been its corollary. In general the bureaucracies alternate between adventurist policies in which they seek to weaken the capacity of im-

perialism to intervene against them and conservative policies in which
they seek to appease imperialism or a given imperialist state and form an
alliance with it. Examples in the case of the Soviet Union would be the
switch from the Comintern's Third Period to the Popular Front policy,
the switch from Yalta to a left-turn in the late forties, the switch from the
Camp David spirit to the decision to install missiles in Cuba; in the case
of China, the switch from the support for armed insurrections in '49 and
'50 to the Bandung Conference in 1955, the switch from adhesion to
the principles of *pancha sila* to the polemics against the Soviet conception
of 'peaceful coexistence', and the switch from the 'people's war' rhetoric
of the cultural revolution to the Nixon visit of 1972. These oscillations
between 'left' and 'right' policies were by no means all of equivalent
significance and they expressed differing shifts in the underlying relationship of forces both internally and externally. All the same it is striking
how the basic similarity of the bureaucracies in China and the Soviet
Union leads them to pursue fundamentally equivalent policies on all
major questions. When the approach of the Chinese and Soviet bureaucracies to the Vietnamese revolutionary struggle is studied the near-
identity of their policies at widely separate times is particularly
impressive. Thus in the late forties and early fifties both China and the
Soviet Union gave assistance to the liberation struggle since both felt it
was a necessary response to the aggressive actions of imperialism in Korea
and other regions near to their borders. At the Geneva Conference in 1954
the Peking and Moscow bureaucracies pressured the Vietnamese Communists to abandon a victorious struggle in favour of an empty diplomatic
deal with the imperialist powers. The advent of the Sino-Soviet conflict
produced polemics of hysterical virulence but led to very little differentiation in actual policy. In the sixties both the Soviet Union and China
furnished essential assistance to the renewed struggle of the Vietnamese,
with the dispute between them functioning to some extent to make them
compete for the prestige of Vietnamese support. By the early seventies
both the Soviet Union and China succumbed to the new strategy of US
imperialism and played host to President Nixon as an unprecedented
wave of US bombs rained down on Indo-China. In many other parts of
the globe there is a similar underlying homology in the foreign policy of
the two bureaucracies (e.g. Latin America) and even where their policies
appear diametrically opposed this usually involves a complementary and
politically equivalent violation of revolutionary internationalism. Thus in
Eastern Europe the Chinese leaders have sought to compete with the
Soviet Union for the allegiance of the bureaucracy rather than identified

itself with anti-bureaucratic forces. This has been part of the political meaning of their defence of Stalin. During the initial phases of the Sino-Soviet conflict China not only backed Albania but also sought to woo the bureaucracies in Poland, Hungary and the German Democratic Republic. When the Rumanian Party began to display independence of the Soviet Union, the Chinese leadership not only gave them diplomatic support but also endorsed their 'Marxist-Leninist' credentials, despite the fact that Rumania was in some respects a pioneer in the opening to the imperialist West. There is an underlying structural similarity in the policies of China and the Soviet Union towards the Indian sub-continent even though they have supported different sides. Even at the height of the cultural revolution China maintained its utterly cynical policy of support for the reactionary military dictatorship in Pakistan. Moreover it did this during the period when Marshal Ayub Khan was brutally suppressing the great wave of revolt among Pakistan's workers, peasants and students in 1968–69. Tariq Ali has commented on the Chinese reaction to the consequent overthrow of Ayub Khan in the following terms: 'Through-out the period of the upsurge the Chinese press maintained a complete silence concerning the momentous events in Pakistan. The Government changes were signalled by the barest of communiqués and it was with evident relief that the Chinese Government discovered that the new oppressors of the Pakistani people were as disposed to be friendly as those they replaced. See for example "Warm Welcome for the Pakistan Government Delegation led by Air-Marshal Nur Khan", *Peking Review*, 18 July 1969. On a visit through China earlier this year (1970) I was able to verify the highly confusing effects this had had on the political aware-ness of the Chinese masses. Thus Red Army cadres to whom I spoke at length on a train journey from Peking to Pyongyang had no inkling of the class struggles raging in Pakistan and regarded the reactionary Pakistan military clique as staunch fighters against imperialism. It may be imagined that the Chinese line has greatly contributed to the dis-orientation of the Left in Pakistan itself.'[12]

Soviet policy towards India has displayed a similar preference for short-sighted diplomatic deals running counter to the interests of the revolutionary movement – it has given full support to the bourgeois government in India even at times when it has been jailing and killing Communists in Kerala and West Bengal and it has encouraged India's manoeuvres against China. In all these cases we see Soviet and Chinese

[12] Tariq Ali, 'Class Struggles in Pakistan', *New Left Review*, no. 63, September–October 1970, p. 54.

policy governed by the same considerations: lack of confidence in the struggles of the oppressed and exploited masses, blindness towards the possibilities of the revolutionary movement combined with eagerness to flatter and influence any established Government which might toss them a diplomatic crumb. And underlying this blinkered conservatism and feeble opportunism is a certain *fear* of any untrammelled explosion of popular revolt which might ultimately undermine their own position as the patent holders of the revolutionary movement. With these considerations in mind we will now turn to the development of the Chinese leadership's international policy in the early seventies.

Indochina and the Conflict with the Soviet Union
China's relation to the liberation struggle in Indo-China must be considered the pivot of its policy and the acid test of its commitment to the revolutionary movement. With the escalation of US intervention in Vietnam both the Soviet Union and China furnished indispensable assistance both to North Vietnam and to the National Liberation Front in the South. The existence of the Democratic Republic of Vietnam and the success of the NLF in establishing themselves in the South confronted both Peking and Moscow with an established fact just as Fidel Castro and the Cuban revolution had confronted them with an established fact in 1959–61. Moreover US imperialism insisted on holding Moscow and Peking at least partially responsible for these established facts. The circumstance that the leadership of both Parties were competing for influence in the world Communist movement may also have inclined them to stand by the Vietnamese. In both cases assistance to the Vietnamese revolution was limited and cautious on both the military and the political levels. Every effort was made to limit the revolutionary struggle as far as possible to the borders of Vietnam itself. The Chinese Party did come round to advocating armed struggle in Indonesia after the coup but by this time the forces with which the PKI might have waged such a struggle (and multiplied the problems of imperialism in South East Asia) had already been wiped out. Both powers endorsed Prince Sihanouk in Cambodia and failed to support the *Khmers Rouges* who began to wage an armed struggle against him in 1967. On the military plane neither the Soviet Union nor China sought to apply any pressure on US imperialism; that is to say they were not prepared to undertake actions in solidarity with the Vietnamese which they had been quite prepared to undertake to advance their own interests (e.g. the various Berlin incidents, the shelling of Quemoy and Matsu etc.). Nor were they prepared to supply the

Vietnamese with the military material necessary to mount an offensive action against the US fleet which was bombarding Vietnam.

Of course solidarity with revolutionary movements certainly does not require a workers' state to embark on dangerous provocations or adventures. But the Indo-China policy of the two big workers' states even during the sixties was cautious and restrained. The Soviet Union furnished more notable military assistance to Egypt than it did to Vietnam, especially so far as the quality and range of equipment was concerned. China, by ostentatiously mobilizing its armed forces during the Indo-Pakistani war of 1965, applied more pressure in support of Pakistan than it did in support of the Vietnamese. However when all such reservations have been expressed it remains the case that both Soviet and Chinese support was absolutely indispensable to sustaining the struggle in Vietnam by the mid-sixties.

In *Long Live the Victory of People's War* Lin Piao made the following declaration the cornerstone of his analysis: 'At present the main battlefield of the fierce struggle between the people of the world on the one side and US imperialism and its lackeys on the other is the vast area of Asia, Africa and Latin America. . . . The contradiction between the revolutionary people of Asia, Africa and Latin America and the imperialists headed by the United States is the principal contradiction in the contemporary world.'[13] Moreover Lin stated that 'the focus of this struggle' was in Vietnam. There was, in fact, to be a certain coincidence between the area where Chinese state policy could be most effective and the area of decisive confrontation between imperialism and revolution. During the height of the cultural revolution it can be said that, within the limits specified above, China provided indispensable aid to the Vietnamese and may even have objectively restrained the Soviet Union from defaulting on its commitments.

However the cultural revolution was accompanied by a sharp deterioration in China's relations with the Soviet Union, notably expressed in the extensive border clashes in 1968 and 1969. The Soviet occupation of Czechoslovakia and Brezhnev's doctrine of 'limited sovereignty' undoubtedly gave good cause for Chinese preparedness against some Soviet aggression, perhaps a pre-emptive strike against China's nuclear establishments. However until objective evidence on the question becomes available it is impossible to ascertain which power took the initiative in these clashes – and it is likely that the bureaucracy in both

---

[13] Lin Piao, *Long Live the Victory of People's War*, Peking 1965, p. 53.

countries reacted in a clumsy and aggressive fashion, animated as they are by profound national egoism. It should be clear that any form of military conflict between China and the Soviet Union is a pure reflection of the special interests of the bureaucratic castes which dominate them. Moreover it could only do the utmost harm to the cause of the Vietnamese and world revolutionary movements. As it turned out even the accentuation of the conflict at the state level which occurred in 1968–69 was to have gravely deleterious consequences without ever reaching the stage of war.

In the mid-sixties, as we have seen, the Maoist leadership declared the Soviet Union to be a country where capitalism was being restored. This formula was to be extended and deepened during the course of 1968–69. The Soviet occupation of Czechoslovakia was to be denounced as an expression of Soviet 'social imperialism'. It was made clear that this formula applied not just to the ideology of the Soviet leadership but also to the Soviet social formation. In the scientific language of Leninism and Marxism the term imperialism is not indiscriminately applied to any and every form of oppression of one state by another, or unequal relationship between states, but refers exclusively to the particular mechanism of domination exercised by capitalist countries. This mechanism is fundamentally economic and does not necessarily entail any directly political and military accompaniment. By contrast the Soviet domination of parts of Eastern Europe *is* directly military and political and is thus structurally different from capitalist imperialism. The Chinese polemics however sought to make no such distinctions since they were aimed at establishing an equivalence between the Soviet Union and the United States. The decision to label the Soviet Union an imperialist power began the process of putting it on the same plane as the United States and before long the latter was no longer to be referred to as the number one enemy of mankind. Though the proclaimed ideology of the bureaucracy has no autonomous life of its own it would be quite wrong to deny it any significance as many Kremlinological commentators are wont to do. In addition to being a guide to the priorities of the Chinese leadership the proclaimed ideology is also taken up by Maoist groups outside China and disorients the vanguard influenced by them.

The communiqué issued on the death of Lin Piao by the Chinese Embassy in Algiers alleged that Lin first began to oppose Chairman Mao's 'revolutionary foreign policy' at the Ninth Party Congress. At the Tenth Congress Chou En-lai declared that there was conflict over the Report Lin was to deliver and that Lin was opposed to some sections of the Report eventually published. It is, of course, impossible to know whether these statements were simply part of the familiar process of projecting differences back into the past. At all events there is a certain discrepancy between the formulas employed at that time. In the new Party constitution circulated before the Congress there appeared the following formulation: 'The Communist Party of China upholds proletarian internationalism; it firmly unites with the genuine Marxist Leninist Parties and groups the world over, unites with the proletariat, the oppressed people and nations of the whole world and fights together with them to overthrow imperialism headed by the United States, modern revisionism with the Soviet revisionist renegade clique as its centre and the reactionaries of all countries, and to abolish the system of exploitation of man by man on the globe, so that all mankind will be emancipated.'[14] Lin's Report was delivered to the Congress on 1 April and Mao was said to have delivered a most important speech on the same day. In the course of the following two weeks the Report was said to be the subject of close scrutiny and debate and there were 'many good proposals for additions to and modifications of the Report'. Among those named as speaking was a soldier who had been involved in the border clash with the Soviet Union on Chenpao island. The Report was eventually adopted and published on 14 April. In contrast to the Constitution the Report consistently coupled together US imperialism and Soviet 'social imperialism'. In a key formulation it stated '. . . there are four major contradictions in the world today: the contradiction between the oppressed nations on the one hand and the imperialism and social imperialism on the other; the contradiction between the proletariat and the bourgeoisie in the capitalist and revisionist countries; the contradiction between imperialist and social imperialist countries and among the imperialist countries; and the contradiction between socialist countries on the one hand and imperialism and social imperialism on the other.'[15] The death of Ho Chi Minh later in the year and the publication of his testament calling for united action against imperialism by the Soviet Union and China led to Kosygin visiting Peking on 11 September 1969. It seems that when in Hanoi for Ho's funeral Kosygin offered to visit Peking and that his offer was taken up. Thereafter state relations between China and the Soviet Union showed some improvement. Serious clashes on the borders were avoided and

[14] *PR*, no. 18, 1969.
[15] *PR*, no. 18, 1969. The space devoted to attacking Soviet 'social imperialism' in the Report was much greater than that attacking US imperialism. However no main enemy was formally named which makes it likely that there was division on precisely this point; see James Peck, op. cit.

talks initiated on the border question with the visit of a high level Russian delegation to Peking. By the end of 1970 diplomatic relations were repaired with an exchange of Ambassadors and the first Sino-Soviet Trade Agreement since 1967 was signed on 22 November 1970. Polemical exchanges occasionally punctuated these moves in the direction of normal relations and though talks on the border dragged on they failed to reach a definitive conclusion. The polemics in question were of a very debased character consisting mostly of wild abuse and mutual slanders completely failing to engage with the vital political questions which had been at the centre of the initial debate. As for the border issue it is difficult to see how it became an issue at all since no significant revision of the frontiers is at all practical – nor indeed does either China or the Soviet Union seem to be demanding such a revision. There is perhaps something appropriately symbolic about the fact that the grossly inflated national egoism encouraged by the two bureaucracies can find nothing more substantial to take a stand upon than the shifting sand of the islets in the Ussuri River.

While the negotiations between China and the Soviet Union were dragged out month after month the policy of US imperialism began to develop a quite new course. Unable to defeat the national liberation forces on the ground in South Vietnam and faced by mounting opposition to the war domestically the strategists of US imperialism began to search for ways to attack them in their rear and deny them essential supplies. This involved a two pronged attack on the military and diplomatic fronts. Firstly it led to the invasion of Cambodia and Laos and to the resumption of massive bombing of North Vietnam. Secondly it entailed the development of a new strategy towards China and the Soviet Union. The military offensive was to have highly mixed results, producing an undeniable holocaust of death and destruction in the short-run, but a perilous complication of the essential political problem of saving Indo-China for imperialism in the longer run. The US sponsored coup in Cambodia and the subsequent invasion widened out the arena of struggle and led to the rapid growth of the Cambodian liberation forces. The attempted invasion of Laos was ignominiously repulsed. These circumstances meant that the diplomatic offensive was even more vital if the objective of a withdrawal of US ground troops in Vietnam was to be secured. The diplomatic strategy involved two aspects: firstly ensuring that neither the Soviet Union nor China would improve their support to the Vietnamese in tempo with the great intensification of aerial and naval bombardment of Vietnam. Secondly that the two big suppliers of the Vietnamese and Indo-Chinese liberation forces would begin to press for a negotiated peace with imperialism. To extract the maximum advantage from such negotiations despite its military setbacks US imperialism clearly counted upon exploiting to the full the smouldering hostility between the Peking and Moscow bureaucracies. Whereas there had been some competition to demonstrate support for Vietnam between Peking and Moscow in the sixties, they were now to be encouraged to scramble for the favour of imperialism.

At the end of December 1969 the United States announced that it was relaxing the alert status of the Seventh Fleet in the Taiwan straits. In January 1970 the Ambassadorial talks between the United States and China were resumed after a two year hiatus. However in May 1970 these talks were suspended by China following the US invasion of Cambodia though an accompanying statement added: 'As to when the meeting will be held in the future, it will be decided upon later through consultation between the liaison personnel of the two sides.'[16] Over the succeeding months public and outright opposition to US policy in Indo-China was maintained and support for Sihanouk's Government and for the liberation forces in Cambodia became a prominent feature of China's policy. In the autumn of 1970 Nixon both announced a new plan for 'peace' in Indo-China and escalated bombing raids on North Vietnam. On 7 October Nixon proposed that there should be a cease-fire *in situ* throughout Indo-China followed by an international conference. The *People's Daily* of 13 October denounced these proposals as a 'clumsy fraud', called for the complete withdrawal of US forces from the area and declared that the conference proposal was only 'a plot . . . to strangle the revolutionary struggle of the people of Indo-China through international interference'. On 21 November US forces mounted an unsuccessful raid against a supposed prisoner of war camp in North Vietnam. Chinese public statements on the war displayed a continuing or even accentuated support for the Indo-Chinese struggle. Phrases often employed at this time declared that 'China and Vietnam are neighbouring countries as closely related as the lips and the teeth' and described 'the vast expanse of China' as the 'reliable rear area' of the Indo-Chinese people. On 13 December a statement in the name of both the Government and the Central Committee called on the Chinese people and the PLA to 'give full play to proletarian internationalism and render all-out support and assistance to the Vietnamese people and the other peoples of Indo-China in their war

---

[16] *PR*, no. 22, 1970.

against US aggression and for national salvation'.[17] The association of
the Central Committee with this statement was certainly designed to give
it extra weight. This was also the time when relations with the Soviet
Union seemed to be developing on a more normal basis. The new Soviet
Ambassador had arrived in Peking on 10 October and a new Chinese
Ambassador left for Moscow on 22 November. A Soviet message was
sent on the occasion of China's National Day expressing the hope that
'normalization' of state relations and 'friendship' might be achieved:
however this message was addressed to the Chairman of the Chinese
People's Republic, a post occupied only by the ghost of Liu Shao-ch'i.
China sent a similar message on the Soviet National Day stating that
'differences or principle . . . should not hinder the two countries from
maintaining and developing normal state relations' and referring to the
Soviet people as having been educated by 'the great Lenin and Stalin'.[18]

The first half of 1971 was to witness an intensification of Nixon's
double strategy and an ambiguous response on the part of the Chinese
leadership. On 29 January 1971 the US Secretary of State, William
Rogers, announced that there would be 'no limit' on 'using air-power to
the fullest possible extent' and on 8 February the attack on Laos by the
Saigon army commenced. However at the same time as the US Government extended its 'unlimited' bombing throughout Indo-China it
announced that it intended no threat to China. On 14 February an
editorial in the *People's Daily* declared: 'While US imperialism is
"escalating" the aggressive war in a big way, the Nixon Government
deliberately spreads the word that its "action" in Laos does not "pose a
threat" to China. The Chinese people treat this "explanation" by the
Nixon Government with contempt! China and Laos are next-door
neighbours linked by the same mountains and rivers and are as close to
each other as the lips to the teeth.' What had previously been chiefly an
expression of political closeness now came to acquire a directly geo-
graphical connotation in Chinese statements. On 20 February an article
by 'Commentator' in the *People's Daily* pointed out: 'Laos is not in
North-west Europe or South America but in North Indo-China. She and
China are linked by the same mountains and rivers and have a common
boundary of several hundred kilometres. Nixon should not lose his head
and forget such common knowledge of geography! By spreading the
flames of aggressive war to the door of China, US imperialism certainly

[17] For this and other Chinese statements at this time, see *The China Quarterly*, no. 45,
January–March 1971, Documentation, p. 215.
    [18] Ibid., p. 214.

poses a grave threat to China.'[19] Far from forgetting the facts of political
geography there is every sign that Nixon was paying a very special attention to them at this time. On 15 February he devoted a lengthy passage to
'The Problem of China' in his report to the US Congress. He spoke of the
need to involve China in a 'constructive relationship with the world
community and particularly with the rest of Asia' and announced that the
United States was prepared to establish a 'dialogue' with China: 'We
cannot accept its ideological precepts, or the notion that Communist
China must exercise hegemony over Asia. But neither do we wish to
impose on China an international position that denies its legitimate
national interest.' He also referred at another point to 'The People's
Republic of China', the first time any US official, let alone a President,
had used this designation. However Nixon added that 'the evolution of
our dialogue with Peking cannot be at the expense of international order
or our own commitments. . . . We will continue to honour our treaty
commitments to the security of our Asian allies. . . . Among these allies
is the Republic of China [i.e. Taiwan].'[20] The Chinese response was to
concentrate attention on the Taiwan question: 'Nixon had the effrontery
to dwell on "the problem of China" in his report. He said: "The twenty-
two-year-old hostility between ourselves and the People's Republic of
China is another unresolved problem." Still, Nixon went on, "we will
continue to honour our treaty commitments to the security of our Asian
allies". That is to say, the United States will insist on its aggressive policy
of forcibly occupying China's territory, Taiwan province. . . . Having
completed a big circle, Nixon came back to the same old spot – still
clinging tightly to the political mummy Chiang Kai-shek and engaging
in his criminal "two Chinas" plot.'[21] There is every indication that
whereas Nixon and Kissinger were entirely aware of the connection
between the Indo-China war and their opening to the People's Republic
– the diplomatic carrot being complementary to the military big stick – the
Chinese leadership were to be increasingly disposed to treat these as
unrelated questions. In the ensuing period it was to be the heroic tenacity
of the Vietnamese on the battlefield that was more than anything else
responsible for the diplomatic satisfactions of the Chinese Government.

China's general support for the Vietnamese struggle was maintained
and increased in February and March of 1971. Chou En-lai visited North

[19] For these and a selection of other statements of Chinese policy, see *The China Quarterly*,
no. 46, April–June 1971, Documentation, pp. 396–400.
[20] Ibid., pp. 406–407.
[21] *PR*, no. 11, 1971.

Vietnam with a military and economic delegation announcing supplementary assistance and a joint communiqué was issued which stated that China would not flinch from 'even the greatest national sacrifice'.[22] Despite the implications of such a statement – though admittedly these were left imprecise – there was at the same time the first real sign that dissension within the leadership existed on China's response to a rapidly developing situation. The communiqué quoted above was published together with a statement attributed to Chairman Mao which declared: 'If anyone amongst us should say that we should not help the Vietnamese people in their struggle against US aggression and for national salvation, that would be betrayal, betrayal of the revolution.' On 15 March Nixon announced that all travel restrictions on visits to China by US citizens were lifted. Meanwhile the attempted invasion of Laos had been vigorously repulsed. This fact was greeted by a special communiqué signed by Mao, Chou and Lin Piao addressed to the Indo-Chinese liberation forces and congratulating them upon a 'most splendid battle of annihilation'.[23]

Moves Towards a Sino-American detente
In April of 1971 a US table-tennis team which had been in Japan for the World Championships was invited to visit China, and there were rumours that the US government was about to change its position on China's representation in the United Nations. A State Department spokesman said on 28 April that the status of Taiwan was 'an unsettled question subject to future international resolution'. Peking continued to concentrate attention on this point with many lengthy articles in the press about Taiwan, 'China's sacred territory', which was in no way subject to 'international resolution'.[24] It seems most unlikely that the strategists of US imperialism were unaware of the overriding significance attributed by Peking to international recognition of the People's Republic and in particular their enormous concern over the status of Taiwan. In fact it is most likely that they were precisely dangling these carrots in front of the bureaucracy in order to encourage its desire to embark on proper negotiations.

On 15 July President Nixon announced that he would be visiting

[22] *People's Daily*, 11 March 1971.
[23] *PR*, no. 14, 1971.
[24] *PR*, no. 19, 1971.

Peking in the near future. The visit had been arranged in the course of talks between Kissinger and Chou En-lai during the former's secret visit to Peking between 9 and 11 of that month. Appropriately enough arrangements for Kissinger's trip had been made through the good offices of the vicious military camarilla in Pakistan who were at that moment engaged in bloody suppression of the Bengali national movement. The Peking bureaucracy were evidently gratified that the US President had suggested the visit and was prepared to atone for past insults by journeying to the People's Republic. But there is no sign that the US was asked for any material indication of its intention to disengage and withdraw from South East Asia or even abate its escalating terrorization of the people of Indo-China. On the other hand the Peking bureaucracy was already giving a display of its preparedness to play the 'constructive' role in Asian affairs that President Nixon had asked for in his message to the US Congress. Peking's endorsement of Pakistani repression in Bengal, of Mrs Bandaranaike's slaughter of the peasant and youth revolt in Ceylon in April 1971 and of the massacre of trade unionists and Communists in the Sudan following the abortive coup there in July 1971, all displayed China's eagerness to play the part of a responsible power. In Ceylon and East Bengal, where the neo-colonial state machine was especially vulnerable, China dispatched urgent economic and military assistance as well as providing diplomatic and political cover to the forces of repression.

In the months succeeding President Nixon's announcement the establishment of good relations between the United States and the People's Republic proceeded as smoothly and methodically as the US machinery of mass murder concurrently devastating Indo-China. According to Pentagon figures from 1966 to March 1972 the United States dropped 6.2 million tons of air munitions on Indo-China, or 262 pounds of explosive for every living Indo-Chinese. Moreover the bombing conducted in 1971 and 1972 was to be the heaviest in the war up to that point. In June 1971 the US government announced the first relaxation of restrictions on trade with the People's Republic. A further relaxation in February 1972 placed the People's Republic in 'Country Group Y' which effectively put it in the same position as the Soviet Union so far as trade with the United States was concerned. And although this country group technically excludes sales of strategic goods, a special licence was issued to allow RCA Globcom to sell a $2.9 million satellite tracking station to China. A further licence in July 1972 permitted the sale of ten Boeing 707 airliners for $150 million to China. In September 1972 China purchased 400,000 tons of wheat from the United States and in

October 300,000 tons of barley.[25] However for both parties resumption of direct economic links was of less significance than developments on the diplomatic and geo-political front.

On 2 August 1971 the US Secretary of State stated that the United States would 'support action at the General Assembly this fall calling for seating of the People's Republic of China. At the same time the United States will oppose any action to expel the Republic of China or otherwise deprive it of representation in the United Nations.' Although this formulation was unacceptable to Peking it was also rejected by the Nationalist regime in Taiwan and effectively destroyed the coherence of the US bloc opposition to seating the People's Republic in all UN bodies at the legitimate government of China. After President Nixon's speech the trickle of new countries recognizing the People's Republic swelled to a flood and the line-up for the vote on China's admission to the United Nations steadily improved in favour of the People's Republic. Whether the exact course of events had been envisaged by the United States or China they cannot have come as a complete surprise to either party. On 25 October the People's Republic was duly voted into the United Nations and the Nationalist regime in Taiwan expelled against a show of US opposition – it subsequently transpired that Kissinger had been in Peking from 20 October to 26 October. That the US should still have reserved its position on Taiwan was a further indication that this would remain a crucial bargaining counter.

One of the most significant indicators of the real political meaning of the growing Sino-American *détente* was provided by the reaction of the Vietnamese. Throughout 1971 and 1972 the Chinese official press published conventional statements of solidarity with the Indo-Chinese liberation forces. However the different stages of the escalation of the US air-war were not met by massive street demonstrations, special alerts of China's armed forces or unambiguous declarations of China's intentions. Although economic and military assistance was maintained and even increased the trend of developments clearly alarmed the Vietnamese. The initial reaction in Hanoi to the announcement of Nixon's visit to Peking had been greeted by commentaries such as the following: '. . . it would be sheer stupidity and ignorance for Nixon to think that by courting and attracting one person or another and by borrowing and relying on the strength and pressure of other people, he can ease his present diffi-

---

[25] *The China Quarterly*, no. 50, April–June 1972, Documentation, p. 391; *The China Quarterly*, no. 52, October–December 1972, p. 790; *The China Quarterly*, no. 53, January–March 1973, p. 206.

culties. . . .'[26] Later in the year a leading article in *Vietnam Courier* pointed out that 'the "will" to negotiate' was 'one of the pillars of US foreign policy in the Nixon era'. Its aim was to 'lay a half-span bridge' between Washington and Moscow and Washington and Peking in order to carry out 'infiltration and sabotage' and to bring about 'a peaceful evolution – or involution – in the sense of counter-revolution'.[27] At the same time 'nationalism (and) chauvinism will be administered in large doses in an attempt to split the socialist camp, by playing off one socialist country against another'. The actual arrival of Nixon in China in February of 1972 was accompanied by further commentaries of this sort including a denunciation of the final communiqué issued by Nixon with its reference to self-determination for the Indo-Chinese nations: 'Nixon even had the cheek to say that he "thinks of all the children in the world". But the whole world has known how many Vietnamese children have been killed, wounded or maimed for life. . . .'[28] A series of major editorials in various North Vietnamese papers emphasized that in their view United States imperialism remained the number one enemy of mankind and analysed the Nixon strategy in terms such as the following: 'Genuine *détente* between nations rests on respect for the independence, sovereignty, unity and territorial integrity of all countries, big and small. But, for US imperialism, *détente* is but a perfidious policy aimed at carrying out schemes of aggression, enslavement, subversion and peaceful regression through new means, that is, the "Nixon doctrine". The imperialists pursue a policy of *détente* with some big countries in order to have a free hand to consolidate their forces, oppose the revolutionary movement in the world, repress the revolution in their own country, bully the small countries and stamp out the national-liberation movement while never giving up their preparations for a new world war. With regard to the socialist countries, the defence of peace and peaceful co-existence cannot be dissociated from the movement for independence, democracy and socialism in the world. For a country to care for its immediate and narrow interests while shirking its lofty internationalist duty is not only detrimental to the revolutionary movement in the world but will also bring unfathomable harm to itself in the end. The vitality of Marxism-Leninism and proletarian internationalism manifests itself in

[26] Liberation Radio, Hanoi, 19 July 1971, quoted in *The China Quarterly*, no. 48, October–December 1971, Documentation, p. 816.

[27] *Vietnam Courier*, 8 November 1971, quoted in *The China Quarterly*, no. 49, January–March 1972, Documentation, p. 205.

[28] *The China Quarterly*, no. 50, April–June 1972, Documentation, p. 390.

revolutionary deeds, not in empty words. In the present day world we can find many examples proving that very seldom do genuine national interests clash with the overall interest of world revolution. A principled policy of *détente* with imperialistic countries must aim at consolidating and strengthening the revolutionary forces, isolating and dividing the class enemy, and aiming the spearhead of the revolutionary forces at the leading imperialist war-mongers. To achieve *détente* in certain concrete conditions in order to push forward the offensive of the revolutionary forces is correct; but if in order to serve one's own narrow, national interests, one is to help the most reactionary forces stave off dangerous blows, one is indeed throwing a lifebuoy to a drowning pirate: this is a harmful compromise advantageous to the enemy, and dangerous to the revolution.'[29]

The whole course of the *détente* between China and the United States was shrouded in diplomatic secrecy. The communiqué issued at the end of Nixon's visit was generally uninformative and certainly gave no indication of whether China was exerting its influence to speed up a settlement in Indo-China on terms different from those publicly stated by the North Vietnamese and the Provisional Revolutionary Government of South Vietnam. The Vietnamese commentaries are therefore invaluable for assessing the subsequent development. It is clear that they did feel under strong pressure from both China and the Soviet Union even though they declared their intention of resisting that pressure. Given that the Vietnamese remained heavily dependent on Soviet and Chinese support they had every reason to maintain a diplomatic silence. The fact that they repeatedly published thinly veiled attacks on the Soviet and Chinese response to US policy is thus of the utmost significance. The commentaries that appeared in the Western press throughout this period confirmed that the US administration was gratified by the restraint exercised by both the Soviet Union and China throughout the period of the bombing escalation and the blockade of North Vietnam. The different elements present in the Chinese response were analysed in the following fashion by a Washington political scientist writing in the pages of a US government magazine: 'The North Vietnamese invasion of South Vietnam at the end of March, precipitating the American bombing of North Vietnam and the mining of Haiphong harbor inevitably complicated Sino-Soviet relations. Peking's response was essentially the same as in 1965, at the time of the earlier escalation of the war in Vietnam:

[29] 'The Revolution will Win', *Nhan Dan*, 17 August 1972; English translation from *Vietnam Courier*, September 1972.

denunciation of American actions; continued propaganda attacks on the two "superpowers" and rejection of any idea of "united action" with Soviet "revisionism"; vague promises of support for North Vietnam; additional Chinese military aid to Hanoi; rejection of Soviet requests for air and port facilities; and a willingness to collaborate within the narrow limits of Chinese capabilities in the trans-shipment of an increased flow of Soviet military aid to North Vietnam across Chinese territory.'[30]

A further indication of US estimation of the Chinese policy appeared in reports of a briefing given to Western newspapers in January 1973, following the signing of the cease-fire, by William Sullivan, Assistant Secretary of State with special responsibilities for South East Asia. *Le Monde* reported this briefing as follows: 'Questioned about the under-lying reasons for Hanoi's change in attitude in October 1972, Mr Sullivan . . . indicated that China was mainly responsible for this evolution. "It is perfectly clear," he said, "that the attitude of China was very important in the way the Vietnamese situation developed." According to Mr Sullivan China pushed Hanoi towards compromise through fear of later having a united Vietnamese state dominated by the Soviet Union. In particular he stated: "Peking prefers to have to deal with four Indo-Chinese states rather than one Indo-China dominated by Hanoi and responsive to Moscow." According to Mr Sullivan, Peking had the opportunity to exercise pressure upon Hanoi because of the mining of North Vietnamese ports ordered by Mr Nixon on 8 May 1972. This decision, declared Mr Sullivan, "created a situation in which North Vietnam became a hundred per cent dependent on China for its supplies. Everything that came from the Soviet Union had to cross Chinese terri-tory. This is when the Chinese obsession with Soviet encirclement began to play a role."'[31]

During the protracted concluding phase of the cease-fire negotiations the Chinese managed to quote every expression of Vietnamese thanks for economic and military assistance with great prominence without once mentioning the Vietnamese position on the political elements necessary for a real settlement.[32] When the cease-fire was eventually signed it was

[30] Harold C. Hinton, 'China's Current Soviet Strategy', *Current Scene*, November 1972.

[31] *Le Monde*, 30 January 1973. This report was datelined Washington and signed by Jacques Amalric.

[32] The Vietnamese, however, had not forgotten them, even if they were unable to enforce them: 'Mr Nixon wants to keep in hand that puppet army and police which will enable him to impose his will on the Vietnamese people. . . . So long as there is no political settlement, so long as Washington does not give up its will to force on the Vietnamese people a govern-ment at the Americans' beck and call, there will be no genuine peace.' *Vietnam Courier*, September 1972.

greeted with a barrage of enthusiastic speech-making in Peking and it was later declared that 'the signing of the Paris agreement has put an end to the war in Vietnam'.[33] Despite the fact that there were immediate signs that both Saigon and Washington were violating the cease-fire agreements, Peking again played host to Kissinger on 16 February. After twenty hours of discussions with Chou En-lai and a special audience in Chairman Mao's study, it was announced that Peking and Washington would be exchanging high-level delegations on a permanent basis. The following month a solemn invitation was issued to all Chinese on Taiwan to promote national unification. There would be an amnesty for all patriots 'whether they come forward early or late'. It was stated that any envoy from Taiwan would be guaranteed a safe and secret visit to the People's Republic. A former KMT General was trundled out to put the question, 'How long can Taiwan rely on the United States? Absolutely not long'.[34]

The ideological terms in which Peking prepared for and justified its international line in 1971–72 have a significance that does not seem to have been lost on US policy makers. Part of the new approach they were adopting involved taking 'Communist ideology' more seriously. There is evidence that Kissinger and others closely studied Chinese formulations about the prevailing contradictions in the world, the nature of Soviet 'social imperialism' and the like instead of dismissing it all as jargon-ridden nonsense. Another tenet of imperialist wisdom that seemed to be partly revised held that it was useless coming to agreements with the big Communist powers because they treat them as mere scraps of paper. In fact history has shown that both the Russian and Chinese bureaucracies adhere with religious scrupulousness to agreements they enter into. The new orientation in imperialist strategy was intended to take advantage of this fact. Fortunately the Vietnamese themselves had no intention of once again being sacrificed to the illusions of 'peaceful co-existence'.

The Question of United Action with the Soviet Union

The decision to label the Soviet Union an imperialist power was already an eloquent indication of the possibility and likelihood of a reorientation of China's foreign policy. Mao has often criticized the folly

---

[33] See 'Peking Celebrates Signing of Paris Agreement', *PR*, no. 6, 9 February 1973; 'Greeting the Signing of the Paris Agreement', *PR*, no. 5, 2 February 1973; 'Congratulations to the Paris International Conference on its Successful Conclusion', *PR*, no. 10, 9 March 1973.

[34] *The Economist*, 10 March 1973.

of striking out with both fists at once and of failing to take advantage of contradictions in the enemy camp. The concept that it was necessary to ally with the less dangerous against the more dangerous enemy was spelt out in long articles at the time of the ousting of Lin Piao. An article on this theme appeared simultaneously in the *Red Flag*, *People's Daily* and *Peking Review* in August 1971 which argued: 'Since the national contradiction between China and Japan during the War of Resistance heightened and became the principal contradiction, the domestic class contradictions subsided to a secondary and subordinate position and the resultant changes in international relations and domestic class relations formed a new stage in the developing situation. To isolate the die-hard forces, Chairman Mao made a profound and concrete analysis and made distinctions between the different social forces and political groupings in the enemy camp and within the middle forces. He pointed out that the pro-Japanese big landlords and big bourgeoisie who were against resistance to Japan must be distinguished from the pro-British and pro-American big landlords and big bourgeoisie who were for resistance. . . . "We deal with imperialism in the same way." The Communist Party opposes all imperialism but we distinguished between Japanese imperialism which was committing aggression against China and the imperialist powers which were not doing so, and we also made distinctions between the various imperialist countries which adopted different policies under different circumstances and at different times. The scientific distinctions made by Chairman Mao with regard to the enemy camp by using the revolutionary dialectics of one divides into two most clearly pointed out who was the principal enemy, who was the secondary enemy and who were the temporary allies or indirect allies. Such a concrete and careful differentiation isolated to the greatest extent the Chinese people's principal enemy at the time – the Japanese imperialists who were then invading China. . . .'[35]

Although Lin Piao had been prepared to denounce the Soviet Union for 'social imperialism' it seems that the implications of an analysis such as the above were unacceptable to him. Lin's only political text of substance was 'Long Live the People's War' with its fervent belief in the road of armed struggle and its burning hatred of US imperialism. Lin's past was that of a brilliant guerrilla commander engaged almost uninterruptedly in armed struggle from the late twenties until the triumph of the revolution. His most notable feat was organizing the Fourth Field

[35] *PR*, no. 35, 27 August 1971.

Army in Manchuria in 1945, building scattered and disparate guerrilla units into the decisive weapon for responding to Chiang Kai-shek's forces. While Chou entered into negotiations in Chungking Lin routed the élite troops which Chiang Kai-shek had sent to take over Manchuria after the defeat of Japan. The twists and turns of the Party's diplomacy were not his responsibility and the passage in his Report to the Ninth Congress on Liu Shao-ch'i's capitulationist role at this time may have been an oblique and dishonest expression of his distaste for these proceedings. Although he never displayed any sympathy for Soviet concepts of 'peaceful coexistence' he was in a good position to appreciate the fundamental ambiguity of the Soviet role seen in objective terms. In Manchuria the Soviet forces handed over the captured Japanese weaponry to Lin's forces even though Stalin was simultaneously pressing the Chinese Communists to do a deal with the KMT. In the fifties Lin was responsible for building up the Chinese air force along modern lines using Soviet military equipment and it seems likely that the Korean war had impressed on him, as on other Chinese army commanders, the significance of modern equipment in direct confrontations with an imperialist army. By 1971 this lesson was already very clear to the Vietnamese who needed many types of weapon for their struggle which only the Soviet Union could supply: SAM missiles, tanks, Strella heat-seeking bazookas for use against helicopters etc. Whether Lin was in favour of some agreement for united action with the Soviet Union in Indo-China is unclear but not inherently improbable. All references by Peking to Lin's disappearance mention his 'sinister links' with foreign countries and of course it was claimed in the Algiers communiqué and at the Tenth Congress that Lin died fleeing to the Soviet Union. It is a remarkable fact that all the major opponents of Mao appear to have favoured some sort of arrangement with the Soviet Union: namely P'eng Teh-huai, Liu Shao-ch'i and Lin Piao. This seems to be a reflection of the strength of the objective forces making for a Sino–Soviet rapprochement rather than an expression of ideological endorsement of Soviet positions. However 'revisionist', the Soviet Union seems a more naturally ally than the United States or any imperialist power to many Chinese Communists; with the notable exception of Mao himself. Following Lin's disappearance it was frequently suggested that he had rejected the conception of the 'new historical period' of struggle against the superpowers. There were also a number of attacks on 'Trotsky's theory of permanent revolution' with suggestions that Lin had adopted this theory. Thus the Party Committee of a PLA unit in Canton was quoted on Peking radio as stating that three questions needed to be under-stood in connection with this theory: '(1) Whether we should affirm or negate the revolutionary role of the peasants, (2) whether we should advocate the theory of revolution by stages or the transcendental theory of a single revolution, (3) whether we should uphold Lenin's brilliant theory that socialism can triumph first in one country or push the liquidationist theory of the so-called world revolution.'[36] Just as these references imply a travesty of the theory of permanent revolution – which, for example, neither negated the revolutionary role of the peasantry nor denied that the revolution will triumph first in one country – so also the attempts to link Lin Piao with it we may take to be a travesty too. But it is plausible that Lin, however commandist and authoritarian he may have been in domestic conflicts, was on the left of the bureaucracy in matters of foreign policy. With all his limitations he probably expressed a commitment to 'the so-called world revolution' which could not accept the utter cynicism and opportunism that was now to characterize Chinese foreign policy.

The Right Turn
By 1972 China's foreign policy was expressed in terms which had no connection with Marxism. Increasingly the category of 'imperialism' was replaced by that of the 'superpowers' and it became China's policy to endorse any diplomatic, economic or military arrangement that could be directed against them. The 'superpowers' in question were, of course, the United States and the Soviet Union – and very often the latter seemed more of a preoccupation than the former. Counterposed to the super-powers were the 'socialist countries' (China itself, Albania and perhaps North Vietnam and North Korea), while between these two poles stretched two 'intermediate zones'. The first 'intermediate zone' was the countries of the capitalist Third World while the second 'intermediate zone' was the advanced capitalist and imperialist countries of Western Europe and Japan. On National Day 1972 the main Peking publications carried the traditional editorial which commented in the following terms on world developments: 'It has become the common demand of the people of the various countries to oppose the power politics and hegemony of the superpowers. More and more countries in the first as well as the second intermediate zone are joining forces in different forms and on a

---

[36] Peking Radio, 5 July 1972, quoted in *The China Quarterly*, no. 62, October–December 1972, Documentation, p. 766. Also *The China Quarterly*, no. 51, July–September 1972, Documentation, p. 578.

varying scale to engage in struggles against one or two superpowers. The Third World is playing an increasingly important role in international affairs. Even some countries under fairly tight control of Soviet revisionism or US imperialism are striving to free themselves from their dictate. Egypt's announcement of the sending away of Soviet military experts and part of the Soviet officers and men, the enlargement of the Western European Common Market, the formation of the seventeen nation free trade zone, and the new diplomatic moves of Japan and some other countries – all this shows that international relations are undergoing new readjustments and changes. During the past year, China has continued to carry out Chairman Mao's revolutionary line in foreign policy in an all-round way. . . . As a result of the great achievements of Chairman Mao's line in foreign affairs, the policy of those who dreamt of isolating China has gone bankrupt and the still extant counter-revolutionary schemes to encircle China are falling apart.'[37]

In his opening speech to the United Nations General Council on 15 November 1971, Ch'iao Kuan-hua had enunciated the basic principles of China's policy and had declared: 'An increasing number of medium and small countries are united to oppose the hegemony and power politics practised by one or two superpowers and to fight for the right to settle their own affairs as independent and sovereign states and for equal status in international relations. Countries want independence, nations want liberation, people want revolution, this has become an irresistible trend in history.'[38] This dubious order of priorities was to be given the most cynical interpretation by the Peking bureaucracy. We have already seen that China's policy did not extend to giving firm support to the Indo-Chinese people's desire for revolution, liberation and independence, but rather led to diplomatic deals at their expense. Elsewhere in South East Asia the guerrilla movements which had looked to China for assistance were sharply downgraded and where support continued it was used as a lever against regimes that refused to normalize their relations with the People's Republic.[39]

A blatantly reactionary aspect of China's new course in foreign policy concerned its wooing of the countries of the two 'intermediate' zones.

[37] *PR*, no. 40, 6 October 1972.

[38] *PR*, no. 46, 1971.

[39] Thus at a time when China was hoping to improve relations with Burma and the Philippines, these two countries, where there are significant Maoist guerrilla forces, were both omitted from an 'Armed Struggle Round-up' in *PR*, 21 July 1972. Imperialist observers noted the new emphasis in Peking with evident satisfaction; see D. M. Ryan, 'The Decline of the "Armed Struggle" Tactic in Chinese Foreign Policy', *Current Scene*, December 1972.

The 'countries' which China acknowledged as wanting 'independence' were to include fully fledged imperialist states as well as some of the most repressive governments in the Third World. In a way all this can be seen as an ultra-rightist interpretation of those very formulas launched by Lin at the inception of the cultural revolution. Instead of the countryside of the world surrounding the cities of the world through successful guerrilla wars of national liberation, the strategic concept was to surround the superpowers, and in particular the Soviet Union, with a ring of diplomatic agreements and understandings with the countries of the two intermediate zones. The preparedness to make alliances with a supposedly anti-imperialist bourgeoisie was extended to include alliances with any bourgeois government, however reactionary, which was opposed to either one of the 'superpowers', again especially the Soviet Union. Although it is difficult to know how long such a dangerous and reckless policy can be pursued before encountering opposition even from within the Chinese bureaucracy it will be worth giving some examples taken from the years 1971–73.

In the year following Nixon's visit China greatly stepped up her diplomatic contacts with the imperialist and capitalist states of the 'second intermediate zone'. Diplomatic relations were resumed with such states as Japan, the Federal German Republic, Greece and Spain. Had these developments been confined to a technical diplomatic exchange this might have been a justifiable policy. But even in the most dubious cases these diplomatic contacts were embellished with the most grotesque attempts to identify common interests or traditions between the People's Republic and the state in question. Thus the *People's Daily* said on the occasion of the agreement to establish diplomatic links with the Greek military junta: 'Both our countries have ancient cultural traditions and both people have a history of long-term struggle against foreign aggression, intervention, bullying and oppression.'[40] Even Greece's NATO allies would be cautious of expressing such sentiments in a communication addressed to the Greek military regime. These new diplomatic contacts were also accompanied by numerous official visits from government representatives from these states. The new Prime Minister of Japan, Tanaka, visited China in September 1972; the Foreign Minister of France had visited Peking in July; the Foreign Minister of Britain was there in late October, shortly to be followed by the Foreign Minister of

[40] *People's Daily*, 7 June 1972. A similar statement put out at the time of the resumption of relations with Spain gave an account of the emergence of Franco which managed to omit any mention of the Civil War.

West Germany. A feature of such visits was invariably a round of public junketing and banqueting, audiences with Chairman Mao or Chou En-lai – often followed by circumstantial accounts appearing in the Western press of such matters as the causes of the downfall of Lin Piao or the Chinese view of the Japanese Communist Party. Meanwhile the Chinese official press began to take a special interest in the military posture of the countries of the second 'intermediate' zone. Thus the readers of *Peking Review* were given a detailed running commentary on NATO's attempt to increase its military preparedness in late 1972 and early 1973. An account of the Winter Session of the NATO Council was followed by an item on the successful conclusion of the extensive sea and land manoeuvres undertaken by NATO forces conducted in January 1973.[41] This was followed by comprehensive reports of the German and British military position. The British Defence White Paper was quoted to the effect that 'it emphasizes that while the Soviet Union is making strenuous efforts to expand its armaments, Britain has to strengthen its own defence further and increase defence cooperation with other Western countries within and outside the framework of NATO'.[42] An article by the West German Defence Minister was also relayed to the readers of *Peking Review* containing such reflections as the following: 'Referring to relations with the Soviet Union, the article emphasized that the West should not make unilateral concessions.'[43] Western newspaper correspondents in Peking filed reports of China's satisfaction at any strengthening of the economic or military potential of the imperialist states of the second zone. Thus *The Times* correspondent, who seemed to have access to briefing by Chinese officials at the highest level, reported China's orientation in the following terms: 'China tends to apply the terms left and right to her internal affairs rather than foreign policy. Even then she often puts the word left in quotation marks to show how it can be abused by extremists. Her present view of world affairs is based not on a left–right spectrum, but on the concept of two superpowers seeking world domination. . . . China's eagerness to see Western Europe united politically, strategically and economically is of course related to her leadership's present view of the world. . . . On the other hand China frankly recognizes that American forces in Western Europe are a lesser evil than Russian forces there would be, and she sees the alternatives just about as clearly as that.' Earlier in this report the correspondent pointed out that the

[41] *PR*, no. 51, 1972; *PR*, no. 5, 1973.
[42] *PR*, no. 9, 1973.
[43] *PR*, no. 10, 1973.

new orientation 'has led to a situation in which a China previously seen as violently left-wing is considering making itself largely dependent on a country like Britain for such a vital commodity as commercial aircraft'.[44] In seeking to convey the new atmosphere in Peking the same correspondent filed the next day a story on a recently published children's comic book: 'While the Vietnam peace talks are entering what could be their decisive phase Chinese children are reading a cartoon strip booklet which portrays the Americans in Vietnam as more pathetic than fearsome. . . . The chief villain is an American adviser called Jones, but in a sense he is a victim as well as a villain. . . . The more numerous villains are the "puppet troops" of the Saigon government whom Jones prevents from massacring the inhabitants of a village with Vietcong sympathies. "Don't shoot decent villagers. If there are some problems we should sit down and discuss them in accordance with our civilized American custom." Naturally he is shown as ridiculous but the attribution to him of such a sentiment shows a sophisticated Chinese understanding of the American dilemma in Vietnam.'[45]

In a similar spirit the Chinese press completely failed to mention the unfolding of the Watergate scandal in Washington. Indeed in an interview given to an American journalist in October 1973 Chou En-lai was reported to have said that 'he hoped President Nixon would be able to overcome his present difficulties'.[46] According to Prince Sihanouk the Chinese were failing to supply the liberation forces in Cambodia with the arms they needed to press to its conclusion their struggle against the US-sponsored Lon Nol regime.[47] The main preoccupation of Chinese policy towards the United States was the status of Taiwan: 'It was plainly indicated by Mr Chou that the basic if not the only stumbling block to full diplomacy was Taiwan.'[48]

China's policy towards the 'first intermediate zone' displayed the same cynicism as that expressed in its relation with the imperialist states themselves. And very often in this zone China's policy was to have greater scope for disorienting and disrupting the revolutionary movements which had earlier seen Maoism as a principled defender of Marxist principles. This was to be sensationally revealed by her attitude towards

[44] David Bonavia, 'Removing China's Left-wing Label', *The Times*, 15 January 1973.
[45] David Bonavia, 'Chinese Story-book on Vietnam Shows Appreciation of US Dilemma', *The Times*, 16 January 1973.
[46] *International Herald Tribune*, 29 October 1973.
[47] Sihanouk made this statement in an interview he gave in Algiers published in *The Guardian* (London), 15 October 1973.
[48] *International Herald Tribune*, 29 October 1973.

events in Ceylon, in the Sudan, in East Pakistan, and in Chile.

In Ceylon in 1971 a youth revolt flared up with deep roots in broad sections of the peasantry. A sort of holy alliance of the most disparate forces imaginable – Britain, India, Pakistan, Australia, Yugoslavia, the United States, the Soviet Union and China – came to the aid of the Bandaranaike government, in which pro-Soviet Communists and members of the Lanka Samaja Party (expelled from the Fourth International in 1964) participated. The Chinese leadership, far from expressing its solidarity with the revolutionary movement, sent the Ceylon government emergency aid in the form of Rs. 150 million and military speed-boats for anti-infiltration work along the coasts.[49] Accompanying the loan was a letter to Mrs Bandaranaike from Chou En-lai. It said in part: 'Following Chairman Mao Tse-tung's teaching the Chinese people have all along opposed ultra "left" and right opportunism in their protracted revolutionary struggles. We are glad to see that thanks to the efforts of Your Excellency and the Ceylon government, the chaotic situation created by a handful of persons who style themselves "Guevarists" and into whose ranks foreign spies have sneaked has been brought under control. We believe that as a result of Your Excellency's leadership and the cooperation and support of the Ceylonese people these acts of rebellion plotted by reactionaries at home and abroad for the purpose of undermining the interests of the Ceylonese people are bound to fail.'[50] Note that among those gaoled by the 'progressive' Bandaranaike government was Nagalingam Sanmugathasan, General Secretary of the pro-Peking Ceylon Communist Party and a bitter opponent of the uprising. Naturally, the news of his imprisonment was not reported in the Chinese press.

In the case of the Sudan, the Chinese leadership gave its unhesitating support to the Numayri dictatorship, which in July 1971 massacred hundreds of leading Communists and trade unionists after an attempted coup by pro-Communist army officers. In the United Nations Ch'iao Kuan-hua, in a reference to alleged Russian complicity in the coup, condemned the Soviet Union for its attempt 'to subvert the legal government of an African country'! On 6 August Numayri arrived in Peking to a 'grand and warm welcome' from 'several hundred thousand revolutionary people'.[51]

[49] See Fred Halliday, 'The Ceylonese Insurrection', *New Left Review*, no. 69, p. 91.
[50] For the complete text, see the issue of *New Left Review* quoted above.
[51] *PR*, 14 August 1971.

Peking gave a similarly warm welcome to Emperor Haile Selassie of Ethiopia. At the same time it reportedly cut off aid to the Eritrean liberation front which operates in the Ethiopian province of Eritrea.[52] Ethiopia is a country characterized by the most barbaric social and national oppression. It also at that time provided American imperialism with one of its main bastions in Africa.

The stand China took during the dramatic events that led up to the birth of Bangla Desh was consistent with its whole previous policy, and it is therefore absurd to say, as do some apologists, that 'the messages to Yahya Khan . . . are not easy to explain'.[53] Among these messages was one in which Chou En-lai attempted to distinguish 'the broad masses of the people from a handful of persons who want to sabotage the unification of Pakistan'. Arguments such as these totally distort the actual terms of the problem: Pakistan never had been a nation and was in fact artificially created by imperialism during the last days of colonial rule in the sub-continent. The fact that the Bengali people was aware of itself as a nation was demonstrated both by the breadth of popular support for the liberation movement and its opposition over a long period to the oppressive policies imposed by the West. By March 1971, when Yahya Khan could only maintain his hold over East Bengal by indiscriminate mass terror, to fail to recognize this was to become an accomplice in his butchery. To argue, as the Chinese do, that India is a neo-colonial state linked to imperialist interests is to ignore the fact that the same holds for Pakistan, which is even a member of a formal military treaty organization – CENTO. Nor is it a justification of China's action to argue that it is legitimate for the Chinese state – as opposed to the Chinese Communist Party – to adopt such positions. Quite apart from the fact that as a result of the close identification of state and Party in China the distinction is somewhat difficult to establish, it is one thing to carry on normal relations with a reactionary state or resort to diplomatic manoeuvres, set up trade agreements and so on, and quite another to express solidarity with a government that is engaged in merciless repression of the masses. Besides, this argument falls down for the simple fact that neither the Chinese Communist Party nor any other body came out against the repression.

---

[52] Fred Halliday in *7 Days*, 1 March 1972.
[53] Richard Hensman in *China Now*, April–May 1972, p. 7. For the text of the most significant of these messages, see *New Left Review*, no. 68.

The truth is that in Pakistan, as in Indonesia and Ceylon, the consequences of Maoist policy confirmed in no uncertain terms that the Chinese leadership subordinates the interests of the revolution in other countries to its own narrow interests and to what it considers to be the interests of the state it governs, sacrificing them completely whenever it thinks it necessary. We say 'what it considers to be its interests' because in this case support for a military dictatorship in Pakistan was actually prejudicial to the strengthening of China herself and her defences against imperialism. In the first place, China has spent valuable resources in building up an army that might at some future date be used against herself. In the second place, China's failure to support the creation of an independent Bangla Desh has seriously discredited the Communist movement in the eyes of the Bengali people, has weakened and divided the movement itself and has thus strengthened the hand of right-wing nationalism and imperialism in a key area of Asia.[54]

The final example we will give of the odious cynicism of Chinese foreign policy is the attitude of the People's Republic towards the military junta which overthrew President Allende and the Popular Unity Government in Chile in September of 1973. Whereas the Soviet Union broke off diplomatic relations with Chile following the coup the Chinese foreign ministry extended early recognition along with the imperialist states. Chile's Ambassador in Peking, who refused to support the junta, was asked to leave the Embassy and was forced to cancel a memorial meeting for Allende which was to be held there. The junta had clearly announced that they planned to extirpate all Marxist influence in their country and had already arrested and executed thousands of working-class militants in pursuit of this pledge. A motion was submitted to the leading body of UNESCO declaring its 'grave concern at the events taking place in Chile'. The only two countries not to vote for this motion were the United States and China.[55]

When Teng Hsiao-p'ing was sent to the United Nations as China's representative in April 1974 he re-stated China's view of the world in the following terms: 'As a result of the emergence of social imperialism, the socialist camp, which existed for a time after World War II, is no longer in existence. Owing to the law of uneven development of capitalism,

[54] On Chinese foreign policy towards Pakistan, see the articles by Richard Nations and Tariq Ali in *New Left Review*, no. 68. Also available in *Explosion in a Subcontinent*, edited by Robin Blackburn, Penguin 1975.

[55] *Le Monde*, 19 October 1973.

the Western imperialist bloc, too, is disintegrating. Judging by the changes in international relations the world today actually consists of three parts, or three worlds, that are interconnected and in contradiction with one another. The United States and the Soviet Union make up the first world. The developing countries in Asia, Africa and Latin America and other regions make up the third world. The developed countries between the two make up the second world.'[56] This re-classification marked a further departure from any attempt to analyse world politics in scientific terms. It reflected the fact that the Chinese leadership's obsession with the Soviet Union was the key to its reactions in every part of the globe. Thus the Chinese press was to be noticeably cool towards the developments in Portugal following the overthrow of fascism in that country in April 1974. Chinese commentators expressed the following reaction after dramatic events that led to the exile of General Spinola: 'The Soviet revisionist hand is visible in the disturbances in the . . . West Mediterranean. . . . In its fierce rivalry with that other superpower for domination over a country on the Atlantic coast which gives easy access to the Mediterranean sea, it is also plotting to seize bases in the name of "fishing" or "refuelling" ports.'[57] China was also to be distinctly restrained in its reaction to the sweeping advance of the National Liberation Front forces in South Vietnam following the Montagnard uprising in the Central Highlands in March 1975. The Vietnamese had not sought either Chinese or Soviet permission before launching their historic offensive, but from a military point of view Soviet support for the Vietnamese was necessarily very important given the scale of operations involved. This fact seemed to have moderated Chinese enthusiasm for the liberation of South Vietnam. Bizarrely enough, the most pressing Chinese pre-occupation during this period seemed to be that of securing its hold on the Spratley Islands, which it had seized from South Vietnamese puppet forces in January

[56] For a good assessment of China's foreign policy at this time see Pierre Rousset, 'The Three Worlds of Teng Hsiao-p'ing', *Inprecor*, 20 June 1974. It is interesting to note that in the same month that Teng travelled to the United Nations (April 1974) *Red Flag* published a contribution to the anti-Lin anti-Confucius campaign which attacked Minister Fan Sui of the state of Chin who had given the wrong advice to his ruler, advising him to be friendly with faraway countries and to challenge neighbouring states. The article declared that ministers of this sort should resign. This suggests the continuing presence of a faction within the Chinese leadership which doubts the wisdom of the Sino–American detente and the confrontation with the Soviet Union.

[57] *PR*, 28 March 1975. The anti-Soviet obsession of Chinese foreign policy also led to support for the CIA/Zaire-sponsored FNLA in Angola. See my article in *Inprecor*, November 1975.

1974.[58] It is not surprising that China's fanatically anti-Soviet foreign policy thoroughly disoriented the pro-Chinese parties and groups. Thus in Portugal the MRPP, one of the largest Maoist groups, saw their main task after the overthrow of Caetano as that of combating 'social fascism' (i.e. the Portuguese Communist Party) and 'social imperialism' (i.e. the Soviet Union). Similarly, when Trotskyist agitation inside the French armed forces led to widespread mutinies in the latter half of 1974, *Humanité Rouge*, a veteran Maoist newspaper, attacked them for weakening France's defences against the Soviet social imperialist threat.

One consequence of Chinese actions is that their influence in the revolutionary movement has declined at about the same rate that unprincipled dealings with the imperialist states and their clients in the Third World have expanded. Many former Maoists found themselves unable to stomach Chinese policy. Those groups that remained loyal to Peking were forced into increasingly tortuous justifications of Chinese policy and completely lost the elan and confidence that they had displayed at the time of the cultural revolution. The right turn of the Chinese leadership in 1971 was to mean that its international followers became little more than a congerie of Stalinist sects.

All this does not mean that Maoism will have no influence from now on. It carries with it the prestige of a victorious revolution, it attracts those who are disgusted with the policies of the Soviet bureaucracy and the Moscow-oriented Communist Parties, and last but not least it possesses that force of attraction that has always belonged to great states with vast material strength and resources. The Chinese revolution was born, and continues its course, under the sign of contradiction but such contradiction is not apparent to its unconditional supporters and devotees. For many people, Mao's China is the country which is building the socialism they desire, which is intransigently fighting against the symptoms of degeneration and which has overcome or is in the course of overcoming bureaucratic forms of alienation. How far this corresponds to the truth is a question they refuse to pose, or pose in such a way as to guarantee in advance a reassuring and positive answer. In reality, they see and understand what they want to see and understand.

In the thirties and the forties, the myth of the Soviet Union under

---

[58] China had seized these islands quite without any regard to such claims as the Provisional Revolutionary Government of South Vietnam might have, declaring baldly: 'The Government of the People's Republic of China hereby reiterates that Nansha, Hsisha, Chungsha and Tungsha Islands are all part of China's territory.' Statement of PRC, 11 January 1974.

Stalin had an extraordinary influence all over the world, whereas the reality was very different from the idealized picture that millions of workers and Communists had of it. With greater reason, for it is not simply a replica of the Soviet Union of thirty years ago, Mao Tse-tung's China is in a position to play a similar role. Certainly, far more explosive forces are at work today and the bureaucratic system is undergoing a serious crisis: however, the myth – which reflects a certain degree of truth and possesses a powerful material support – is capable of lasting for an indeterminable period of time.

16
The Social Nature of China

Before we embark on any critical analysis of the many contradictions that characterize Chinese society, our point of departure for any overall assessment must be that the revolution which culminated in the over-throw of Chiang Kai-shek's regime was a decisive event in the history of this century, not only for China and Asia but for the whole world. Whatever has happened since, the fact remains that the revolution, by destroying the old ruling classes and relations of production and intro-ducing collectivist relations, succeeded in unifying an immense country in which all sorts of centrifugal forces were at work, put it on the road to industrialization and enabled it, in an historically short period of time, to eliminate age-old scourges, to set up social relations which despite bureaucratic distortions represent an immeasurable advance, and to transform what was formerly the object of inter-imperialist rivalries into a protagonist of world politics.

In order that no one should be tempted to misinterpret the analyses set forth in this book, we would simply mention the parallel between the fate of China and that of India. Twenty-five years' experience has left no room for ambiguity. Whereas China has emancipated herself com-pletely from imperialist control, India is more than ever subject to imperialist penetration. Whereas China has overthrown age-old class barriers, India is still characterized by polarizations bordering on the grotesque and by the survival of a barbarous caste spirit. Whereas China has more or less succeeded in unifying the country, India is in the grip of violent centrifugal forces. Whereas China has set out on a qualitatively new path of economic development, India has witnessed the failure even of her economic plans and is unable to protect her people from the recurrent tragedy of famine. Whereas China has no foreign debts, India has indebted herself to a colossal extent. At the root of this evolution lies the qualitative difference in the mode of production and the social regime.

However, if we wish to understand the real meaning of events in China we cannot ignore the contradictions that exist within contemporary Chinese society. Foremost among these contradictions, which are proper to a society in transition from capitalism to socialism, is the one between the collective nature of the mode of production and the norms of distribution which, to quote the definition of Marx and Lenin, remain bourgeois. These contradictions, as happened in the USSR, are all the more acute because China before the revolution was an enormously backward country and was not able to insert itself into a supranational socialist economic system. Finally, they express themselves in a specific way, that is they are aggravated and magnified by the growth of a bureaucratic layer and by bureaucratic management.

The situation which we outlined in the first part of this volume and which, if our analysis is correct, remains substantially the same today, was the result of negative or contradictory aspects of the course of the revolution, both before and after the seizure of power. One first contradiction was the fact that the Party at the head of the revolutionary struggle, though non-peasant in origin, ideology and international connections, was for many years separated from its proletarian matrix, led a movement almost exclusively composed of peasants and performed the functions of a government in backward areas of the countryside. The second contradiction was that although Mao and the leading group around him on various occasions adopted positions which differed from and even conflicted with those of Stalin and the Kuomintang, attempting to exploit, under cover of formal compliance, all the margins of autonomy permitted by a special situation, they nevertheless underwent the same process of Stalinization that affected all the Communist Parties (the picture of Mao as completely immune from Stalinism is even more wrong than that of Mao as Stalin's faithful disciple). This had serious implications for the Party's political strategy, and above all it decisively influenced the methods of leadership and organization of the Party, which always remained firmly in control of the movement as a whole, and its methods of administration and government in the liberated areas.

There has been much talk about the egalitarian and democratic imprint which the experience of the liberated areas and the Yenan period was said to have left on the Party and its leadership. It is not our intention to throw doubt on facts brought to light by disinterested observers, or to ignore or underestimate their importance. In exceptional and highly transitory periods such as those passed through by a society building itself up during the course of a war, bureaucratic and authoritarian methods of leadership do not necessarily imply the short-term creation of conditions of privilege or social stratification: and a leadership conducting a struggle without quarter in a situation of extreme difficulty must constantly be on its guard lest its relations with the masses deteriorate. But that does not mean to say that a training such as the communist parties of the thirties received and the Stalinist methods in force even in the Chinese Party did not have serious and lasting consequences. There is, moreover, another aspect of the problem that deserves a fuller analysis, but which we can only briefly touch on here. The Mao Tse-tung group, during the years of the anti-Japanese war and the civil war, was not only at the head of a Party that controlled a mainly peasant army, but also acted as the government of a portion of Chinese society which began to grow considerably (in 1934, according to Snow, Mao put the population controlled by the Soviet government of that period at roughly 9 million; later, after the long march at the time of the Sian incident, the population of the liberated areas was some two million, but gradually began to grow again until it reached several tens of millions in 1943 and more than 95 million in 1945). The character and the orientations of the leadership were necessarily conditioned by this factor, by the actual – and not the theoretical – part that it played in a society in the process of being transformed but in which few collectivist structures had been introduced, a society dominated by a small and middle peasant economy and in which the political apparatus of the Party and the state was forced to use Bonapartist techniques in order to maintain the equilibrium.[1]

The failure to smash the old state machine and replace it with entirely new bodies had a particularly adverse effect on developments after the seizure of power. Instead, there developed a hybrid form, which meant that the old structure, methods and personnel continued to exercise an

[1] Very interesting information on the pre-1949 period can be found in Snow's *Red Star Over China*, London 1968, and in Belden's *China Shakes the World*, New York 1970. For the positions of Mao and the Chinese Communists we should also mention Deutscher's study, 'The Origins of Maoism', *Socialist Register 1964*. Mark Selden, *The Yenan Way in Revolutionary China*, Cambridge, Mass. 1971, documents the base areas in the anti-Japanese war. *A Documentary History of Chinese Communism*, New York 1966, edited by Brandt, Schwartz and Fairbank, presents a broad survey of documents from 1921 to 1950. Milovan Djilas and Vladimir Dedijer describe the differences between Mao and Stalin in 1945–46 in *Conversations with Stalin*, London 1962, and *Tito Speaks*, London 1953. H. R. Isaacs' book *The Tragedy of the Chinese Revolution*, New York 1966, is an important source for the events and polemics of 1925–27. For Trotsky's position, see *The Problems of the Chinese Revolution*, London 1969, as well as *The Permanent Revolution, The Third International after Lenin* and *The Chinese Revolution (Problems and Perspectives)*, New York.

important influence (this was frequently admitted in the polemics that took place during the cultural revolution). All this resulted from bureaucratic ideas in general and more particularly from the Maoist view current at that time of the nature and tempo of the revolutionary process (the aim was not the overthrow of capitalism but a so-called 'new democratic' regime of indefinite duration). In practice certain formulas broke down, but not before a number of compromises had been made: and the consequences of these compromises were not automatically eliminated. Real organs of workers' and peasants' democracy were not set up and the dominant apparatus drew away from the masses. This resulted in the formation of privileged strata, the slowing down of the rate of economic growth, the appearance of distortions and imbalances in the development of the economy and a failure to make full use of all the potential inherent in the new mode of production.

In the final analysis, the cultural revolution was determined by the developments that had gradually been taking place in Chinese society and which we briefly analysed in the first part of this volume. The leadership itself was forced to seek a way out, all the more so because of the international crisis of the bureaucratic system and its own rejection of the alternative solutions adopted in the USSR after Stalin's death and the Twentieth Congress. The various social forces in the country rushed to the apertures created by the conflicts at the top and the decision of the Maoist group to mobilize first the students and then the workers and peasants, and seized the opportunity to express their aspirations and impose solutions in keeping with their interests.

If the analysis we have made is a correct one, the cultural revolution did not involve a qualitative leap over the previous phase. Not only the basic relations of production but also the forms of organization and management of the productive apparatus in both agriculture and industry, together with social and political relations, have remained qualitatively the same, in spite of some quantitative changes that were often more talked about than put into practice. On the level of ideology, the revival of concepts formulated in other periods, in particular 1958–60, got the better of new ideas and emphases.

If there was any new element, it lay not so much in the instigation of a mass campaign – there were precedents for this too in the history of the Party and the People's Republic – as in the fact that the mobilization was conceived outside the normal channels and the normal machinery: and this aspect of the movement came more and more to the fore as it deepened and spread. But not even this factor, however important and capable of future developments it may have been, is in itself determining: the crucial question is how far it influenced the basic structures and political relations. We have already seen how the movement concluded with a partial and superficial reconstruction of the apparatus. For this reason, the cultural revolution was essentially a reformist movement in the framework of the society that had emerged from the victorious revolution and the subsequent process of bureaucratic involution. This was confirmed by the fact that the 'seizures of power' were expressly limited to the lower levels and not extended to the decisive centres of power. (In a speech in which he passed on Mao's instructions, the Shanghai leader Chang Ch'un-ch'iao, while criticizing extremist standpoints, had said quite clearly that 'the proletarian dictatorship can be improved only partially'.[2])

To characterize the cultural revolution and its aftermath in this way does not mean that we ignore its complexity. On the contrary, an understanding of the dual nature of the movement – conflicts within the bureaucracy and a mobilization of the broadest layers of society in a campaign that tended to escape control and direction from above – is indispensable for an understanding of the crisis of 1966–69. It should be clear from this study that such an interpretation is not deduced from preconceived principles or schemes, but is founded on a mass of analytical data that can be checked, directly or indirectly, in the official sources themselves.

Nor does our characterization imply that we are unaware of the shifts that took place in the relations between the different classes and social groups. After all, such shifts are typical of any real reformist movement.

The privileged stratum left over from the past, the so-called 'national bourgeoisie', saw its influence diminish, especially in economic management and administration at those levels where seizures of power took place. No decision was taken to abolish interest payments on investments taken over by the state, even though there was talk of ending the system within the near future. (Note that huge fortunes can still be inherited without death duties in China.[3]) In the countryside the top strata in the communes did not lose their position in the structure, but emerged weakened on the ideological and political plane, given the renewed emphasis on mobilizing the lower strata. The working class, which is still very differentiated from the point of view of wages and general conditions, increased its influence, though in a distorted and indirect

---

[2] *SCMP*, no. 4147, p. 2.
[3] See Wheelwright and McFarlane, op. cit., p. 138.

way, at the base of the pyramid, at the level of the production unit and, to a far lesser degree, at intermediate levels. Inside the ruling stratum it was the military bureaucracy that gained ground, especially during the decisive moments of the crisis. The purge of September 1971 removed a large part of the top PLA leadership, but, as we have already pointed out, at provincial and regional levels the army appears to have retained a strong position. More generally speaking, the cultural revolution relaunched and imposed – for how long it remains to be seen – concepts and solutions more in keeping with the inclinations and aspirations – and the interests – of the political bureaucracy and can be expected to encourage their hegemony even more.

But how did relations evolve between the masses and the bureaucracy as a whole? Whatever the more distant prospects may be, in the course of the Cultural Revolution and as a result of the movement the balance of forces tipped towards the masses. Future confrontations will therefore take place under objective conditions (given that the wear and tear suffered by the apparatus was not fully repaired during the period of reorganization) and subjective conditions (given the growth to maturity of new layers of critical young people, workers and students) more favourable to the masses than before.

As a rule, the question of the social nature of a country is not posed academically or analysed with scientific detachment; instead it is inspired by the political situation, by the forces in motion and the aspirations that animate them. Nowadays, as a result of opposing pressure from certain quarters, the tendency exists, in studying the contradictory aspects proper to a society of transition, to single out, in the case of the USSR, those elements that back up a negative characterization (i.e. as a state in which capitalism has been restored' and, in the case of China, those diametrically opposed aspects that justify holding it aloft as a model transitional society breaking with capitalism. Both these approaches are radically wrong, precisely because they assess intrinsically contradictory phenomena by abstracting one of the terms of the contradiction.

Nowadays, however, an analysis of Chinese society gives us a better understanding of the typical nature and tendencies of a society in transition. In China there are fewer of those secondary phenomena of a capitalist economy which, while not implying qualitative change, complicate the analysis and encourage mistaken or biased interpretations (for example, profit has not been introduced as a regulator, the market has more limited functions, there is less stress on material incentives and there are no relations with other collectivist countries such as those that exist between the USSR and the other Comecon countries). This is why it is easier to accept the definition of China as a transitional and not a capitalist society. It is hard to deny that, after the expropriation of the old ruling classes, non-capitalist, collectivist relations of production were introduced into the industrial economy, which constitutes the most dynamic sector and is acquiring an increasingly decisive specific weight,[4] and that a typically transitory structure, with collective forms of organization of labour and restraint on the tendencies towards a reproduction of capitalism, exists in the countryside.

More generally, the exchange economy has started to wither away, since the chief means of production no longer constitute exchange values and the law of value is contained and regulated by the Plan. Thus Kung Wen-sheng wrote in an attack on Sun Yeh-fang, former Director of the Institute of Economy at the Academy of Sciences: 'In socialist society there is still commodity production and exchange and the law of value still plays a role. But socialist commodity production differs fundamentally from capitalist commodity production. In socialist society, the law of value does not play its role spontaneously as in capitalist society. It is applied consciously by the Party and the state to serve the socialist revolution and socialist construction.'[5] (In the same article he says that profit is only one of the indices of the Plan, thereby admitting that the term profit does not automatically mean profit as it operates under capitalism.)

Finally, the monopoly of foreign trade is a solid barrier to protect China from imperialist exploitation and the free play of the world market.

(Some groups, including former Maoists such as *Progressive Labor* in the United States, maintain that China, like Cuba and North Vietnam, is a capitalist country. If these ideas were correct, capitalism, far from being in crisis, would have given proof of exceptional historical vitality, having managed to ensure the industrialization of the USSR and the incipient industrialization of China, exploit gigantic revolutionary waves for its own ends and exercise an unopposed and unceasing hegemony, either through traditional means or through the leading parties of state capitalist

[4] Chou En-lai told Edgar Snow that agricultural output in 1970 was about 25% of total combined output of industry, transportation and agriculture. According to the (reconstructed) official data, agriculture accounted for 46.1% of the net product in 1952 and 38.6% in 1957. (Ta-chung Liu, 'Economic Development of the Chinese Mainland, 1949–1965', in Ho and Tsou (ed.), *China in Crisis*, Chicago 1968, p. 627.)

[5] *HNA*, 13 August 1966, p. 33. See *HNA*, 14 November 1966, *SCMP*, no. 3844, and *SCMM*, no. 539, for other attacks on Sun.

countries or countries in which capitalism has somehow or another been restored. If this were true, we would certainly be forced to re-examine the whole of the Marxist analysis of capitalism and of the revolutionary role of the proletariat.)

On the basis of the substructures mentioned above, a political apparatus, superimposed on the masses and represented in its most concentrated form in the central leadership, wields decisive powers, taking basic policy decisions and above all deciding on what to do with the surplus product. This stratum derives its power and privileges not from direct or indirect ownership of the means of production but from the functions it performs and in exchange for which, by virtue of its political dominance, it secures a privileged share in the distribution of income. Precisely because its position, historically speaking, is very precarious and because it is aware that real democratization would mean an end to its powers and to its position as a ruling stratum, it rejects – in theory as in practice – the Leninist concept of the withering away of the state and advances instead the idea that the repressive apparatus must be strengthened.

These essential characteristics of Chinese society determine, in the final analysis, the attitude of its leading groups. But for a closer understanding we should also take into account China's more specific features deriving from her special position, special traditions and experiences, etc., which enable us to develop an adequate interpretation of episodes on the scale of the Sino–Soviet split and the cultural revolution. In this sense, we can recall her experiences in the war against Japan, the Yenan period and more particularly her special position in the international context.[6]

Mao Tse-tung's personality has synthesized and expressed the contradictions that have marked the course of the revolution, both before and after the seizure of power. After 1927 Mao criticized the policies of the Stalinist Comintern and outlined positions that pointed in a different direction to the opportunist compromise accepted at that time by the Party leadership. But for years he failed to challenge the orthodoxy of the Communist Parties and acted more or less along Stalinist lines in so far as the Party leadership and organization were concerned; he defended Stalin as a great Marxist–Leninist and continued to accept his interpretation of the events of the twenties and thirties. On occasion he expressed some of the most right-wing views in the entire world communist movement: for example, he not only supported in general the

[6] But see Gregor Benton, 'The Yenan Opposition', *New Left Review*, 93, July–August 1975.

idea of collaborating with the so-called national bourgeoisie, but even put that policy into practice with Chiang Kai-shek's Kuomintang, which after the revolution of 1925-27 had revealed its true nature for all to see. But when confronted with the need for a decisive choice during the revolutionary upsurge of 1946-47, he put himself at the head of a peasant insurrection, ignoring Stalin's 'suggestions' and wishes and leading the Red Army to conquer the country: and ten years later he once more took up the cudgels as the chief spokesman of the left wing of the Communist movement. He was at the head of the Party which played a leading role in the overthrow of capitalism, but after victory he presided over a process of bureaucratization; and then, at a certain point, he himself took alarm at the consequences of that process. He proclaimed and had it proclaimed that the masses decide everything and that it is necessary to learn from them, whereas in reality he built up a system that was extremely centralized politically and monolithic in tendency, based on an authoritarian paternalism of which the boundless cult of his person was the symbol. He maintained the need for a struggle to the death with imperialism and criticized Soviet policy in the ex-colonial countries, while at the same time inspiring a policy of collaboration and compromise with the bourgeoisie resulting in the massacre of the Indonesian Communists and the paralysis of his followers in Pakistan and East Bengal. He has posed as the standard-bearer in a battle against bureaucracy but has continued to quote Stalin, who more than any other individual symbolizes the rule and ideological hegemony of the bureaucracy. He has written poetry in the most traditional manner, and pronounced speeches of undeniable literary value, but has promoted campaigns inspired by the most brutal forms of Zhdanovism in which artistic expression is demeaned to the level of a mere instrument of propaganda. Our assessment of a personality so throughly shot through with contradictions – like the society, the political group and the social stratum of which he is an expression – can only be dialectical and dependent on the role that he has objectively fulfilled, is fulfilling or will fulfil in any given situation. Otherwise we shall either fail to understand his role or fall into the opposite trap of uncritical adulation.

But beyond Mao and Maoism, the basic problem is the fate of the revolution in China. Chinese society will only be in a position to break out of the circle of contradictions that encloses it if two basic conditions are met: firstly, the building of socialism in China must be organically linked to the building of socialism on a supranational scale, thereby smashing the barriers between nation states inherited from the old society; and secondly, it is necessary to introduce real democracy and give the workers and peasants a chance to carry out their leading role, so that they are in a position to deal with the basic issues from the angle of their own interests and aspirations, of the needs of socialist construction, freed from the distorting interference of the interests and aims of the new privileged strata. To the extent that China follows this path, she will overcome the conditions of backwardness that are at the root of, and in their turn perpetuated by, the bureaucratic involution.

The real struggle against the bureaucracy is not over, or nearly over – rather, it has not yet begun. It will have to take the form of a struggle from below for a break, for a qualitative leap, in a word, for a revolution, qualitatively different from all movements of reform or self-reform, however profound and however iconoclastic they might appear.

Appendix:
Interview with a Cantonese
Red Guard by Tariq Ali

In what circumstances did you join the Red Guards in Canton?

1966 was an important year in China. In the period preceding June 1966, the political atmosphere in the country was very tense. We felt that there would be an explosion fairly soon. In Peking High School, students had declared themselves Red Guards under the slogan: 'To Rebel Is Justified'. In our school in Canton in the same month there were only a few of us who were rebels, though we were very active. A few dozen in a school consisting of 1,400 students. We felt suppressed and uninvolved in the country's politics. Our life was dull, routinist and pedestrian. Before the cultural revolution I was very interested in reading political texts – Marx, Lenin, Mao – and was regarded as being strange since we were not supposed to show any independent interest in politics. In school, politics meant being taught what the Party line was on this or that subject.

The June Red Guards represented a trend to think independently. Our political level was very low and we put forward no demands as such. We merely made wall-posters condemning the section of the Party in the school. I'd always hated the school headmaster who was totally useless, a fact everyone in the school was aware of. He was there because he was a Party member. He was a super-bureaucrat who ate separately not only from us students, but even from the rest of the teachers. While compelling *us* to take part in physical training, he used to stand at a distance under an umbrella. He was extremely authoritarian. In June 1966 our wallposters denounced him in rather emotional terms. We also snatched some of the rifles kept in the school and hid them. There were between 20 and 30 rifles in the school, but they were under the control of the children of PLA soldiers who also studied in the High School.

In June, in almost every school the section of the Party was over-thrown by the students. For a short period the administration was elected by us. That was why Liu Shao Chi sent his work-teams to reestablish control. The work-teams claimed to support the cultural revolution, but in fact they suppressed us and warned us not to fight against the Party section. Instead, they attempted to divert our wrath towards the non-Party teachers and it was on their instructions that many ordinary teachers were insulted and humiliated. Our spontaneity was crushed.

I was personally very angry about this and put up a wall poster condemning the intervention of the work-teams and referring to both them and the Party section as gangsters. Then the work-team organized students to attack me and denounce me for being right-wing. I argued back, but during debates I was muzzled and held physically with my arms tied behind my back. From July to October I was completely isolated in my school and students kept well away from me.

By August it was obvious that Mao wanted to overthrow Liu, but the latter was very powerful within the Party apparatus and Mao was unable to deal with him via the Party constitution. So he decided to utilize the masses outside the Party to overthrow Liu. A mass movement of students was at this time being suppressed by Liu Shao Chi's work-teams. If Mao hadn't supported the struggle of the Red Guards he would have been defeated. Thus in August, Mao announced the sixteen points of the Cultural Revolution and the Red Guards were officially recognized. This action seemed to vindicate the June Red Guards as being genuine leftists and encouraged us to fight the 'capitalist roaders'.

My isolation began to decrease and students began to speak to me again, but the school was still under the control of conservative elements (sons of Red Army soldiers). From August to October the minority Red Guards began to regroup. Our main difference with the conservatives was that they supported the work-teams, but even after the teams left our school in August, the conservatives did everything possible to steer the struggle well clear of the Party bureaucracy. They did so by making scapegoats of the students who were of bourgeois origins and the latter were victimized rather brutally. Though I come from a working-class family myself, I nonetheless attacked the conservatives in very strong terms for their behaviour, which culminated in them actually killing a number of teachers and students of bourgeois origin. You must understand that this was a deliberate and conscious diversion. The period lasted from August to October 1966.

In October, I left for Peking to observe the Cultural Revolution at its base and stayed there for three days. I saw the wallposters, but not Mao, met others like myself and then returned to Canton. I travelled with hundreds of others, free of charge, in trains, ferries, trucks. It was a fantastic experience seeing the country in this manner. We really did feel liberated in this fashion without any restrictions and in the company of lots of other youths, discussing quite freely things we had not thought about in the past.

When I returned I immediately set up a Red Guard HQ in our school, and we named our group 'The East Is Red Commune'. It consisted of about forty students at the start.

What did you discuss in 'The East Is Red Commune' and what actions did you initiate?

The first action we took was to destroy the files of our school because they were used to keep the students under control. The Party section, when dissatisfied with any student, opened a file on him which could be used against him in the future. For instance, such files could be utilized to prevent dissidents from reaching university and also to harm their job prospects. The files were an important weapon against us. After we had expropriated the files, I read the dossier on myself and could hardly recognize the picture it painted. We published the files, exposed them as lies and showed the Party bureaucrats to be a bunch of liars.

As a matter of interest, what was written in your file?

I cannot remember it verbatim, but the general sense was: 'This student is unstable. He is an anti-Party, right-wing element. He ought to be carefully watched. Will be dealt with when movement subsides.'

But to continue: our second action was to release the imprisoned teachers from the cowsheds where they were being held and to put an immediate stop to the victimization of other students. We organized mass meetings and encouraged teachers to participate. We also brought the Party bureaucrats before the mass meetings. We did not attack them physically, but asked them many questions about their past. They were scared and tended to confess everything.

What did you think of Mao at that time?

We adored him, especially myself. Why? Because it was Mao's initiative which had ended my isolation and liberated me. He had given us a new lease of life and you must understand that even a break with routinism represented a big step forward for us. You can imagine the impact it had on all of us. As we saw it, Mao represented us in the top circles, where he defended our actions and encouraged us. Even though

I adored Mao, there were a few suspicions at the back of my mind. It was an instinctive suspicion. I could not rationalize it or explain it, but it was probably due to the critical spirit which I had developed and which later enabled me to criticize Mao. But this was rare, I repeat, rare amongst students in my school and was one reason for the failure of the Cultural Revolution.

Did you have any political discussion inside the 'Commune'?

Yes, we constantly analysed the revolutionary situation and our own struggle. There was no theoretical discussion – we were not educated enough. We were so obsessed with ourselves that we could even think of the Vietnamese comrades except sporadically.

How then did your struggle continue?

Our rebellion was not only confined to our school. We took it to the Canton County section of the Party. We knew that the work-teams and Party section in school had been guided by the Canton Party leadership. We joined with other local Red Guard groups to raid the Canton Party HQ. Two hundred of us carried out the action, representing all local schools. We got hold of the Party files and published what was contained in them on wall posters. The files showed us the fight taking place within the Party bureaucracy as well as the plots to suppress us, etc.

Then we went to the factories, joined the production line and ate and lived with the workers. We put up wall posters in the factory exposing the privileges of Party bureaucrats in the factories. You must know that inside the factories those small numbers of workers who had protested had been even more repressed than us. The Party section inside the factory consisted of a privileged minority compared to the rest of the workers. We linked up with the rebellious workers and called ourselves the Red Flag Faction (RFF).

Within the RFF there were many small groups – workers, students, teachers, etc. There was no centralized leadership. We used publicly to burn the official publications of the Party bureaucrats to show our complete contempt and disgust and we put out our own publications attacking the Party.

In December 1966 there was a rebellion among the peasantry and some militants set up a group called: 'The Poor and Lower-Middle Peasants' RFF'. They fought against Party members in their own communes. In December, though we were in a minority, we were in control of the situation because of our anti-bureaucratic initiatives; but we were still nowhere like as strong as the conservative Red Guards, if you compared our respective strengths on an overall basis. In the universities, it is true, there were twenty revolutionary Red Guards for each conservative. But in the schools the forces were roughly 60 : 40 in their favour; in the working class, there were only 10,000 rebels out of a workforce numbering nearly a million; and in the peasantry, there were only a few thousand rebels out of several million peasants.

But although the conservatives were very numerous, their morale was low, they had lost the will to fight and many began to move towards us.

How did the struggle develop in 1967?

January to June 1967 constitutes the middle stage of the struggle for power between the people and the bureaucrats. By the end of 1966 the Party bureaucracy was in a state of collapse. Mao's alliance with us had put him on the left and our main target had been Liu Shao Chi. But our conflict with the bureaucracy on every level had *objectively* also put us on a collision course with Mao.

A brief digression: did you really believe that Liu was a 'capitalist roader' – an agent of imperialism?

Yes, I did. But we understood capitalism in a different way from Mao. We started from the viewpoint of being oppressed and suppressed. And for us, therefore, anyone who oppressed the masses *must* be a capitalist. Mao meant it in a different way, of course. He meant it economically, politically and culturally. There were many other bureaucrats apart from Liu who were oppressors, but Mao did not denounce them. We did.

Should we return to 1967?

Yes. In 1967 the mass movement matured rather rapidly and its morale rose. And we began to understand and appreciate problems that we had not even been in a position to think about in the preceding seventeen years. Many of us reasoned that we had been suppressed because we had no power and concluded that therefore we had to have power. Thus the storm period of January began – the 'seizure of power' period. In December 1966 the bureaucrats had used a new tactic. They abandoned the administration throughout the country, hoping to create complete chaos. This forced us to begin to run affairs ourselves. In January 1967 in Shanghai, the workers and students seized power. Within a few days the same thing happened in Canton and elsewhere.

What happened in Canton? How did you 'seize power'? What changed?

We simply got the administration of the whole of Canton under our control. The bureaucrats were smashed and fled. We occupied the Party headquarters and forced the bureaucrats to hand over authority to us and to announce on the streets and in the press that we, the RFF, held power. I was responsible for the administration of some schools. In the schools the students elected their own representatives to run them.

Did the bureaucrats announce this on the radio as well?

No, the radio stations were shut down, as Mao did not want any reports of what was going on to reach the outside world.

To continue: in factories, the workers elected their own representatives to run the factories. Similar events occurred in newspaper offices. But we were very naive. In seizing power, we had no idea of what we were doing or what its implications were. The Paris Commune workers' democracy, soviets, meant nothing to us. The struggle had impelled us forward, but we had no real, politically sophisticated leadership to direct our advance. As a result, inside the RFF disputes arose solely on administrative questions related to the exercise of power. This will give you an idea of the low level of political consciousness.

How long did this situation last?

From early 1967 onwards, Mao began to separate himself from us. He wanted the struggle to end and started to move against us. When he visited Shanghai he attacked the comrades there for calling themselves a commune and told them that a commune meant a structure in which the base dominated. He said that this indicated that they did not want any leadership from the Party, told them that the Party leadership was necessary and instructed them to change their name to 'revolutionary committee'. It was here that he formulated his idea of the 'tripartite alliance': in other words that revolutionary power should be organized by revolutionary cadres (i.e. the Party), military cadres (i.e. the PLA) and mass representatives (a temporary concession). The process whereby the Maoists took power back into the hands of the Party and army was set into motion. Thus the army 'joined' the Cultural Revolution in order to stabilize the situation. By the end of February there were clashes between army units and Red Guards.

What happened in Canton and what was your own experience?

After we seized power and established the commune we discovered that the Party bureaucrats were in touch with the army. Some had fled to the army and sought its protection against us. This made us conscious that we also had to fight the army. On 8 February 1967 we invaded the military area and held demonstrations there. We captured some army propaganda cars and used them to appeal to soldiers to join us. The military bureaucrats were furious. No armed soldiers joined us, but clerks, and other army workers joined.

Meanwhile in Peking a number of Party leaders were beginning to get really alarmed and were beginning to oppose Mao because of his inability to control the situation. They (under the discreet control of Chou En-lai) began to suppress the movement in Peking by using the military. This was a tremendous boost for the bureaucracy nationally and the bureaucrats began to re-emerge, link up with the army and suppress dissident groupings all over the country. In many places they used force, but not in Canton. They arrested many people, banned the RFF, established military control and seized back power. From the information which was spread on the level of gossip and common talk, we heard that Lin Piao had been opposed to these actions, but had been over-ruled. The Party leaders who organized the repression were opponents of Lin Piao. So from February 1967 the intervention of the army started and continued till they had restabilized the situation.

Were there any doubts building up at this time in relation to the role of Mao himself?

No. Mao was reported to have been hesitant on the question of using troops till September 1967, when he threw his weight behind the suppression.

When did you realize that the Cultural Revolution was over?

In September 1967. I returned to my school and discovered that the old headmaster was back. However the atmosphere was restive and nobody really settled down. I should have mentioned that in August 1967 there were arms raids all over the country and many of us stole arms. That time there was little resistance to these raids, but in April 1968 we tried again and this time the army shot back and many comrades were killed.

What happened in China in May 1968? As you know in France there was a big upheaval led by workers and students and we even read that there had been solidarity demonstrations in Peking. Does this mean that while Mao and the bureaucracy had ordained that the Cultural Revolution be ended, it nonetheless continued?

There certainly were demonstrations in Peking and we published some publications in Canton showing our solidarity with the French comrades. Yes, in the sense you pose it the upheaval in China was not completely over. The end was uneven. After all China is not a small country and it is not easy to issue a centralized decree to end a mass movement.

In July 1968 the army marched into the schools and factories and disbanded the Red Guards. In Kwangsi they had to lay siege outside the factories for many days before the workers surrendered. After disbanding the Red Guards they set up the Tripartite Committees, but these were just rubber stamps. The situation from now on became extremely difficult.

What happened to you? When did you leave Canton?

From November 1968 to August 1971, I was sent to work on a farm. For two years I worked in Hopei and for one year in Canton. We were all extremely dissatisfied and Mao was constantly attacked in private. We felt we had been betrayed and sentenced to a grim future. But now we discussed a lot. We tried to elaborate new theories and concepts to try and analyse what had gone wrong. I joined a group of extreme-leftists in Hopei whose group was known as 'Proletarian Union of Hunan'. They had written a number of documents criticizing Mao and the bureaucracy. It was a spontaneous development. Neither they nor I had read any writings by Trotsky, but our ideas about the bureaucracy were very similar to his. We held many discussions, but by 1971 we began to get extremely demoralized, since many of us realized the enormity of the tasks which confronted us.

Is that why you decided to leave China?

Not exactly. A number of us were forced to flee for political reasons. In the first place, our groups were discovered and many comrades began to be arrested. We were all threatened. But secondly, because I wanted to read and write, which became impossible in China as the fog of Party orthodoxy descended once again and engulfed the entire country with that special kind of ignorance which is peculiar to bureaucratized states like China. Also many of my comrades, in a state of complete despair, committed suicide in prison rather than reveal the names of others. That is why a number of us decided to leave Canton. We therefore swam across to Hong Kong.

How did you discover Trotskyism?

Essentially through the *Seventies Bi-Weekly*. It was a real revelation. There was a debate being conducted in the paper between anarchism and Trotskyism. Some comrades came under the influence of anarchism, which is hardly surprising, given their experiences in China. I read articles by old Chinese Trotskyist comrades, like comrade Wang, who explained to us, for the first time, the real history of the Chinese Communist Party and the origins of Chinese Marxism.

Index

DEMCO